THE LIFE AND JOURNEY OF NEOLITHIC COPPER OBJECTS

THE LIFE AND JOURNEY OF NEOLITHIC COPPER OBJECTS

Transformations of the Neuenkirchen Hoard, North-East Germany (3800 BCE)

HENRY SKORNA

© 2022 Henry Skorna

Sidestone Press Academics

Published by Sidestone Press, Leiden
www.sidestone.com

Layout & cover design: CRC 1266/Carsten Reckweg and Sidestone Press
Cover image: Henry Skorna (©Romano-Germanic Commission of the German
Archaeological Institute)

ISBN 978-94-6427-030-3 (softcover)
ISBN 978-94-6427-031-0 (hardcover)
ISBN 978-94-6427-032-7 (PDF e-book)

The STPAS publications originate from or are involved with the Collaborative Research
Centre 1266, which is funded by the Deutsche Forschungsgemeinschaft (DFG, German
Research Foundation; Projektnummer 2901391021 – SFB 1266).

Preface of the series editors

With this book series, the Collaborative Research Centre Scales of Transformation: Human-Environmental Interaction in Prehistoric and Archaic Societies (CRC 1266) at Kiel University enables the bundled presentation of current research outcomes of the multiple aspects of socio-environmental transformations in ancient societies. As editors of this publication platform, we are pleased to be able to publish monographs with detailed basic data and comprehensive interpretations from different case studies and landscapes as well as the extensive output from numerous scientific meetings and international workshops.

The book series is dedicated to the fundamental research questions of CRC 1266, dealing with transformations on different temporal, spatial and social scales, here defined as processes leading to a substantial and enduring reorganisation of socio-environmental interaction patterns. What are the substantial transformations that describe human development from 15,000 years ago to the beginning of the Common Era? How did interactions between the natural environment and human populations change over time? What role did humans play as cognitive actors trying to deal with changing social and environmental conditions? Which factors triggered the transformations that led to substantial societal and economic inequality?

The understanding of human practices within often intertwined social and environmental contexts is one of the most fundamental aspects of archaeological research. Moreover, in current debates, the dynamics and feedback involved in human-environmental relationships have become a major issue, particularly when looking at the detectable and sometimes devastating consequences of human interference with nature. Archaeology, with its long-term perspective on human societies and landscapes, is in the unique position to trace and link comparable phenomena in the past, to study human involvement with the natural environment, to investigate the impact of humans on nature, and to outline the consequences of environmental change on human societies. Modern interdisciplinary research enables us to reach beyond simplistic monocausal lines of explanation and overcome evolutionary perspectives. Looking at the period from 15,000 to 1 BCE, the CRC 1266 takes a diachronic view in order to investigate transformations involved in the development of Late Pleistocene hunter-gatherers, horticulturalists, early agriculturalists, early metallurgists as well as early state societies, thus covering a wide array of societal formations and environmental conditions.

Henry Skorna's book presents one of the most important hoard finds in northern Germany: As early as c. 3800 BCE, various copper objects were deposited in Neuenkirchen (north-eastern Germany), documenting the rich relations with different Chalcolithic societies, especially those in eastern and south-eastern Europe. The transformation triggered by the integration of new technologies into local and regional structures describes an extremely important wider transformation of

Central European and South Scandinavian societies. As series editors, we would like to thank the author for his meticulous and at times detective-like approach to unravelling the contexts of the depot find. At the same time, we thank the State Office for Culture and Monument Preservation of Mecklenburg-Vorpommern for making the find available for analysis.

We are very thankful to graphic illustrators Carsten Reckweg and Karin Winter for their deep engagement in this publication. We also wish to thank Karsten Wentink, Corné van Woerdekom, and Eric van den Bandt from Sidestone Press for their responsive support in realising this volume and Nicole Taylor for organising the whole publication process.

Wiebke Kirleis and Johannes Müller

Foreword

The hoard find from Neuenkirchen is a key find for the archaeology of Mecklenburg Western-Pomerania. It makes it abundantly clear that the influx of copper objects in the 4th millennium BCE also reached the area along the southern Baltic coast with great impact. Behind this was not only an economic structure encompassing large parts of Europe, but also a network of cultural interaction that was at least as strong and far-reaching. In its composition and the way it was deposited, the hoard find from Neuenkirchen follows a pattern that can be traced from the Alpine region to Scandinavia. As the earliest multi-piece hoard in the midst of an artefact landscape otherwise characterised by single finds of early copper objects, it has a special potential for providing knowledge.

In his edited Master thesis, Henry Skorna not only sheds light on the far-reaching connections that can be deduced from the metal origins, the typology, and the deposition form of the Neuenkirchen assemblage, but also on the environment of the site. The results indicate that the hoard find from Neuenkirchen ended up in the ground in a thoroughly well-developed settlement landscape. Evidence of settlements is available regionally, as are further individual copper objects. However, this was a pre-megalithic landscape that had not yet undergone the transformation caused by the large, monumental structures erected in the following centuries. Obviously, therefore, the early Funnel Beaker Societies had room to manoeuvre even before that, which enabled them to break away from a purely subsistence economy.

The hoard find from Neuenkirchen also impressively underlines the role of rivers for the prehistoric communication network. The site is located on the Werder, which is surrounded by the Datze, the Tollense, and one of the latter's tributaries, the Landgraben. It stands to reason that the metal from the Northern Alpine and Eastern European regions, from which the objects in the Neuenkirchen hoard find were made, most likely travelled along the rivers for large parts of its journey. The natural transport network, along which the enormous metal demand of the Nordic Bronze Age was later satisfied, was therefore already tried and tested in the Early Neolithic. And surprisingly, even the function of the Tollense route for the connection further north, which can be observed so impressively in the Bronze Age for the Mecklenburg Group, seems to have its roots in the Early Neolithic.

With the comprehensive scientific treatment of the hoard find from Neuenkirchen and its cultural-historical environment, another decisive piece of the puzzle has been added to the large overall picture of the Early Neolithic. The knowledge gained is of great importance for further research and for the assessment of the Early Neolithic sites in Mecklenburg-Western Pomerania. Last but not least, it is also the basis for a story that can be told in the future Mecklenburg-Vorpommern State Archaeological Museum. For this, of course, we must first and foremost thank Henry Skorna, whose scientific meticulousness and wealth of ideas allowed this remarkable find speak for itself. However, those who have contributed to the success of the work in the most diverse ways should not be forgotten. Science leads to the best results when it is interdisciplinary and cultivated in an open, fair, and constructive exchange. This work is an excellent example of this.

Detlef Jantzen
Head of the Department of Archaeology of the State Office for Culture
and Monument Preservation, Mecklenburg-Western Pomerania

Acknowledgements

The hoard find of Neuenkirchen (Mecklenburg Lake Plateau district), represents one of the few large Neolithic deposits of copper objects in northern Germany and southern Scandinavia. It is matched only by the famous Danish hoard find from Bygholm, which is more extensive but probably younger. These and other copper finds are indications that people were increasingly integrated into large-scale networks in the course of Neolithic development (Müller 2017, 99 ff.). The question of to what extent the deposition of Neuenkirchen can be fitted into the horizon of early European copper finds is the main concern of this study.

I would like to thank Dr. Detlef Jantzen and Dr. Jens-Peter Schmidt from the Mecklenburg-Vorpommern State Office for Culture and the Preservation of Archaeological Monuments for the opportunity to work on this exceptional artefact ensemble and for making it available to me. I would like to thank Prof. Dr. Johannes Müller for supervising the Master's study on which this study is based, and for the instructive experiences I was able to gain during my studies and work as a student assistant with him. Furthermore, I am also grateful for the uncomplicated provision of funds for further laboratory analyses following this work. I would also like to take this opportunity to thank Dr. Christian Horn for taking on the role of second supervisor and for the intensive discussions and knowledge transfer, especially in the field of use-wear analyses, during my studies. Dr. Knut Rassmann (Romano-Germanic Commission of the German Archaeological Institute) made the trace element analysis of the objects possible at short notice by providing the infrastructure, after promised analysis results from a laboratory unexpectedly failed to materialise. A special thanks goes to Dr. med. dent. Alexander Deisler (Schwerin), who, together with his team, took X-rays of the dagger from the hoard at his premises as part of the use-wear analysis. Dr. Zofia Anna Stos-Gale (University of Gothenburg) receives many thanks for her help in interpreting the lead isotope data, as well as providing the figures and further reading material. Many thanks to Agnes Heitmann and Sara Jagiolla (both Kiel University) for taking the photographs of the find assemblage. I would also like to thank Susanne Beyer (Kiel University) for her patient instruction and help with the drawings and Karin Winter (Kiel University) for her support and work on the final versions of the figures for this publication. My colleagues and friends, Lennart Brandtstetter, Dr. Katharina Fuchs, Prof. Dr. Martin Furholt, Dr. Julian Laabs, Michael Müller, Mihalela Savu, Dr. Robert Staniuk, Dr. Sebastian Schultrich, Fynn Wilkes, and Dr. Maria Wunderlich provided intensive professional exchange and their manifold support, Anna-Lena Bock in particular with her assistance in the areas of drawing, typesetting and image editing, and Sarah Martini corrected the English summary in the initial master thesis. I would like to thank them and many others, including Igor Obzhimkin, Jürgen von Oehsen, Benjamin Kudlik, Christoph Günter and my grandmother Rosemarie Rassmann, for their motivation, encouragement and the many carefree hours spent in sport and recreation, which also contributed to the success of my studies and this study.

Finally, the greatest thanks go to my parents, Annette von Oehsen and Detlef Skorna, without whose selfless support and trust, the study of archaeology would not have been possible.

Henry Skorna

In loving memory of my grandmother

Rosemarie Rassmann

1926-2021

Contents

Preface of the series editors   **5**

Foreword   **7**

Acknowledgements   **9**

1. Introduction   **17**

    1.1 Definition of hoard finds   18

2. Topographical position of Neuenkirchen   **19**

    2.1 Landscape and waterways   22

3. State of research on the Funnel Beaker North Group in   **25**
present-day Mecklenburg-Western Pomerania

4. Chronology of the Funnel Beaker Societies   **27**

5. Anthropogenic activities in the surroundings of Neuenkirchen   **33**
at the time of the Funnel Beaker Societies

    5.1 Settlement activities   33

    5.2 The settlement sites of Warlin, Brunn, Carpin, Jatznick, Glasow   35
    and Gristow (Fig. 8)

        5.2.1 The settlement site of Warlin   35

        5.2.2 The settlement site of Brunn   35

        5.2.3 The settlement site of Carpin   37

        5.2.4 The settlement site of Jatznick   37

        5.2.5 The settlement site of Glasow   38

        5.2.6 The settlement site of Gristow   38

    5.3 Funnel Beaker period hoards and megalithic graves in the vicinity   42
    of Neuenkirchen

        5.3.1 Deposits (Fig. 11)   42

        5.3.2 Megalithic graves   43

    5.4 Summary of anthropogenic activities in the vicinity of Neuenkirchen   44

6. Finds and features of the hoard find from Neuenkirchen   **47**

    6.1 Feature and artefact descriptions   47

        6.1.1 Dagger (Plate 1)   48

        6.1.2 Flat axe (Plates 2a and 4c)   50

        6.1.3 Spiral arm ring (Plates 2b, d and 4a)   50

        6.1.4 Band spiral (Plates 2c and 4b)   50

        6.1.5 Sheet metal fragment (Plates 2e and 4d)   51

        6.1.6 Ceramic Vessel   51

7. Analysis of traces of manufacture and use   **53**

   7.1. Damage   53

      7.1.1 Fracture   54

      7.1.2 Cracks   54

      7.1.3 Notches   54

      7.1.4 Dents   54

      7.1.5 Impact marks   54

      7.1.6 Bending   54

      7.1.7 Twisting   55

   7.2 Reworking   55

      7.2.1 Hammering, peening (*Dengeln*)   55

      7.2.2 Grinding, polishing, filing, whetting   55

   7.3 Addressing possible signs of use and manufacture on the Neuenkirchen hoard inventory   56

      7.3.1 Dagger   56

      7.3.2 Flat axe   60

      7.3.3 Spiral arm ring   66

8. X-ray fluorescence and lead isotope analyses   **67**

   8.1 History of research on chemical metallurgical analyses in archaeology   67

   8.2 Functionality of X-ray fluorescence analysis   68

   8.3 Limits and difficulties   69

   8.4 Information depths and patina   69

   8.5 Procedure for the author's pXRF analyses   72

   8.6 Results   73

      8.6.1 Greifswald (Inv.-No. ALM 99/1139)   73

      8.6.2 Weltzin (Inv.-No. ALM 2010/1853, 8)   73

      8.6.3 Altwigshagen (Inv.-No. ALM 2009/1015)   75

      8.6.4 Neuenkirchen   75

      8.6.5 Notes on the differences between the pXRF and laboratory ED-XRFA measurements   76

      8.6.6 Discussion of the results   77

      8.6.7 Lead isotope analyses   80

9. Early Copper in Mecklenburg-Western Pomerania   **83**

   9.1 Overview of the copper finds   83

   9.2 Chronological position of the copper finds   84

10. Typo-chronological analyses of the Neuenkirchen artefacts   **91**

   10.1 Dagger   91

   10.2 Dagger typology   93

      10.2.1 Lancet and flange hilted daggers *(Lanzett- und Griffzungendolch)*   93

      10.2.2 Type Frumusica   96

      10.2.3 Notched Daggers of the Late Copper to Early Bronze Age   98

      10.2.4 Rivet daggers of the Cucuteni type   99

      10.2.5 Type Balkány   105

      10.2.6 Type Dolné Semerovce/Malé Leváre   105

      10.2.7 Type Usatovo   108

10.2.8 Special forms similar to the Dolné Semerovce/Malé Levăre daggers   109

10.2.9 Italic daggers   110

10.2.10 Greek daggers   114

10.2.11 Daggers with tang hilt   116

10.2.12 Summary of the dagger typochronology   118

10.2.13 Typo-chronological classification of the dagger from Neuenkirchen   119

10.3 The flat axe from Neuenkirchen   120

10.4 The arm spiral from Neuenkirchen   124

10.5 The band spiral from Neuenkirchen   128

10.6 The sheet metal fragment from Neuenkirchen   129

10.7 Excursus: *Pars pro toto* of a necklace of band spirals and pendants?   130

10.8 Overall chronological assessment of the hoard from Neuenkirchen   135

10.8 1 Selected hoard finds of the 4th millennium   136

10.8 2 Neuenkirchen between Bygholm and Stollhof   142

11. Neuenkirchen in light of the Development of Early Metallurgy in Southeast Europe   **145**

12. Neuenkirchen – profane, ritual, and/or social practice?   **151**

13. Summary   **157**

14. References   **159**

Plates   **191**

1. Introduction

At the end of the fifth millennium in northern Germany began the slow transition from the mobile or seasonally-sedentary lifestyle of Mesolithic hunter-gatherers to the subsistence economy of Neolithic societies, characterised by agriculture and animal husbandry. This was accompanied by major anthropogenic interventions in nature to create arable and agricultural land and settlements. In northern Germany, this is associated with the appearance of the Funnel Beaker Societies from 4100 BCE. The first phase of the Early Neolithic, which lasted until 3800 BCE, is initially characterised by only limited, local human activity. The introduction of new technologies, such as the ard, enabled an intensification of land use and contributed to a much greater opening up of the landscape (Müller 2011, 19 ff.). The expansion of settlement activity and a significant increase in population numbers were accompanied by the construction of countless monumental burial sites and ditch works, some of which still characterise the landscape today. An estimate of 5537 megalithic graves in Mecklenburg-Vorpommern alone (Rassmann /Schafferer 2012, 110) shows how strongly the image of this first cultural landscape must have been determined by megalithic graves, in addition to the pre-existing non-megalithic long mounds, which were erected from 3800 or from 3600 BCE. At the same time, deposits with amber beads and raw amber, axe blades, ceramic vessels, but also human bones were also placed. This practice reached the north-eastern German area around 3400 BCE at the latest (Müller 2011, 19 f.). The deposition of axes with pointed butts at Viervitz on the island of Ruegen (Kibbert 1980, 62) and Baalberg amphorae at Nustrow (Rostock district) (Staude 2013, 145 ff.), among others, speak for a beginning of a Neolithic deposition practice as early as Early Neolithic I.

At about the same time as the neolithisation process, the first metal also appeared in the western Baltic region. While the oldest pieces from this early copper horizon still represent imports from the early metallurgical centres of the fifth millennium in the Balkan-Carpathian area, an extensive inventory of local forms develops with increasing metal quantities between 3800 and 3300 BCE (Klassen 2000, 235 ff.). The unusual material also finds its way into the depositional practice of the Early and Middle Neolithic in southern Scandinavia and northern Germany. The depot find from Neuenkirchen seems to be the first of its kind in Mecklenburg-Western Pomerania; it is the first known multi-piece deposition from the Funnel Beaker Period. In an article by Lüth (2005), the finds complex was already briefly presented and assigned to the Funnel Beaker Societies (TRB[1]).

To verify this assumption, the analyses of the finds ensemble rest on several factors. The focus is on the typological, geochemical examination and use-wear

---

1   For the "Trichterbecher" (Funnel Beakers) societies the abbreviation TRB is used.

analyses of the Neuenkirchen finds. In addition to the typochronological classification of the objects in the early copper horizon of southern Scandinavia and northern Germany, the aim is to narrow down the period in which the deposition of the copper artefacts could have taken place in Neuenkirchen. For this purpose, information on the natural environment, the chronology of the Funnel Beaker Culture, as well as their settlement activities and deposition practices in the vicinity of Neuenkirchen, are included.

The first step is to determine the landscape in which the hoard of Neuenkirchen was deposited; the scene is set in the post glacial landscape of modern Mecklenburg-Western Pomerania, where the site was most likely interconnected with the rest of the Neolithic world through the network of waterways. The research discourse surrounding the chronology of the northern group of the TRB is summarised and then combined with an overview of settlement, burial, and deposition activities in the vicinity of Neuenkirchen. Taking available radiocarbon dates connected to these activities into account helps to narrow down possible time frames in which the deposition of the hoard could have taken place.

The heart of this work is the analysis of the hoard itself. A brief description of the single objects is followed by thorough use-wear analysis which gives insights into the biography and possible manipulation of the objects before their deposition. To gain a better understanding of the composition and provenance of the metal used for the objects different geochemical analyses were performed. Special emphasis was given to the method of the energy dispersive X-ray fluorescence analysis under consideration of corrosion processes as in a first step own analysis where performed with a portable device on the surface of the objects. The additional data which were obtained through later laboratory-based X-ray fluorescence and lead isotopes analyses were incorporated, complemented the already gathered information

An overview of the available Neolithic copper finds in Mecklenburg-Western-Pomerania sets the stage for the following typo-chronological analysis of the objects from Neuenkirchen. It focuses in particular on the dagger from the deposit, since the other objects—such as the arm and band spirals—are chronologically unspecific or—like the axe fragment or the other fragment—were not sufficiently preserved for a precise typological approach. In addition, the opportunity was taken to supplement and update the overview of the south-eastern European and northern alpine daggers. These results are then put into the context of comparative hoard finds from the 5th/4th millennium and the development of early metallurgy in Southeast Europe. The final chapter is devoted to the question of the context in which the hoard find from Neuenkirchen was deposited.

1.1 Definition of hoard finds

One of the three major pillars of the archaeological source corpus are the so-called hoard finds, for which the term 'depot finds' is used synonymously, as in the following explanations (Neumann 2015, 5). A hoard is generally understood to be two or more objects that are found within one archaeological feature and that do not show any signs of being related to a grave context. The definition of hoards and their significance have been the subject of intense research discussions since the 19th century. I will refrain from a new compilation of definitions here and refer to the relevant literature (*e.g.* Eggert 2001, 78 ff.). As one example of the numerous definitions, the definition by H. Vankilde (1996, 33) is listed here: "A hoard is defined as an assemblage containing more than one object which did not accompany a burial". Klassen (2000) and Vankilde (1996), among others, additionally note that individual finds can also be regarded as depots.

2. Topographical position of Neuenkirchen

The area of present-day Mecklenburg-Vorpommern has been strongly influenced by the last ice ages. Based on the multiple alternation of unstratified and stratified gravels, sands, and clay marls, three glaciations can be traced; Elster, Saale-Warthe and Vistula Ice Ages (Hurtig *et al.* 1957). They left behind a broad spectrum of glacial terrain forms (Fig. 1). Thus, in addition to the most diverse forms of ground moraine types (slightly undulating to almost flat ground moraine surfaces; dome-shaped ground moraine landscapes, kettles, osses, kames, and drumlins), end moraines, outwash plains, old moraines, glacial valleys and various periglacial forms can also be found. Hurtig *et al.* (1957) divide Mecklenburg into six major landscapes:

1. the coastal area
2. the gently undulating to flat north-eastern lowlands
3. the hinterland of the lake district
4. the Mecklenburg Lake Plateau
5. the foreland of the Mecklenburg Lake Plateau
6. the Mecklenburg lowlands of the Elbe.

The major landscape No. 3 is further subdivided into four sub-regions:

1. central Warnow land, including the Bützow and Güstrow basins
2. hilly upper Peene area, including Malchin basin
3. hilly Tollense area, including Tollense basin
4. hilly Uckermark clay area, including large valleys.

The village of Neuenkirchen is located in sub-region 4, where it belongs to a small region known as Werder (Fig. 2). Originally, 'Werder' referred to enclosed and protected land; the meaning changed over time to river island and land between standing water (Schneeweiß 2000, 1). In today's usage, these meanings have been displaced by the term 'island' (*e.g.* Kaninchenwerder or Ziegelwerder in Lake Schwerin). Nevertheless, it has survived in numerous place names and district names (*e.g.* the city district Schelfwerder of Schwerin).

The Werder itself lives up to its original literal meaning and denotes a Pleistocene island bounded to the west and northwest by the Tollense and Kleiner Langraben valleys, to the south and east by the Datze valley, and to the north by the Großer Landgraben, Ramelower-Dishleyer and Dishley-Schwanbeck valleys. Two larger, morphologically-distinct units can be noted: A smaller north-eastern part, whose flat knolls reach between 30 m and just under 50 m a.s.l. (= above sea level), and a

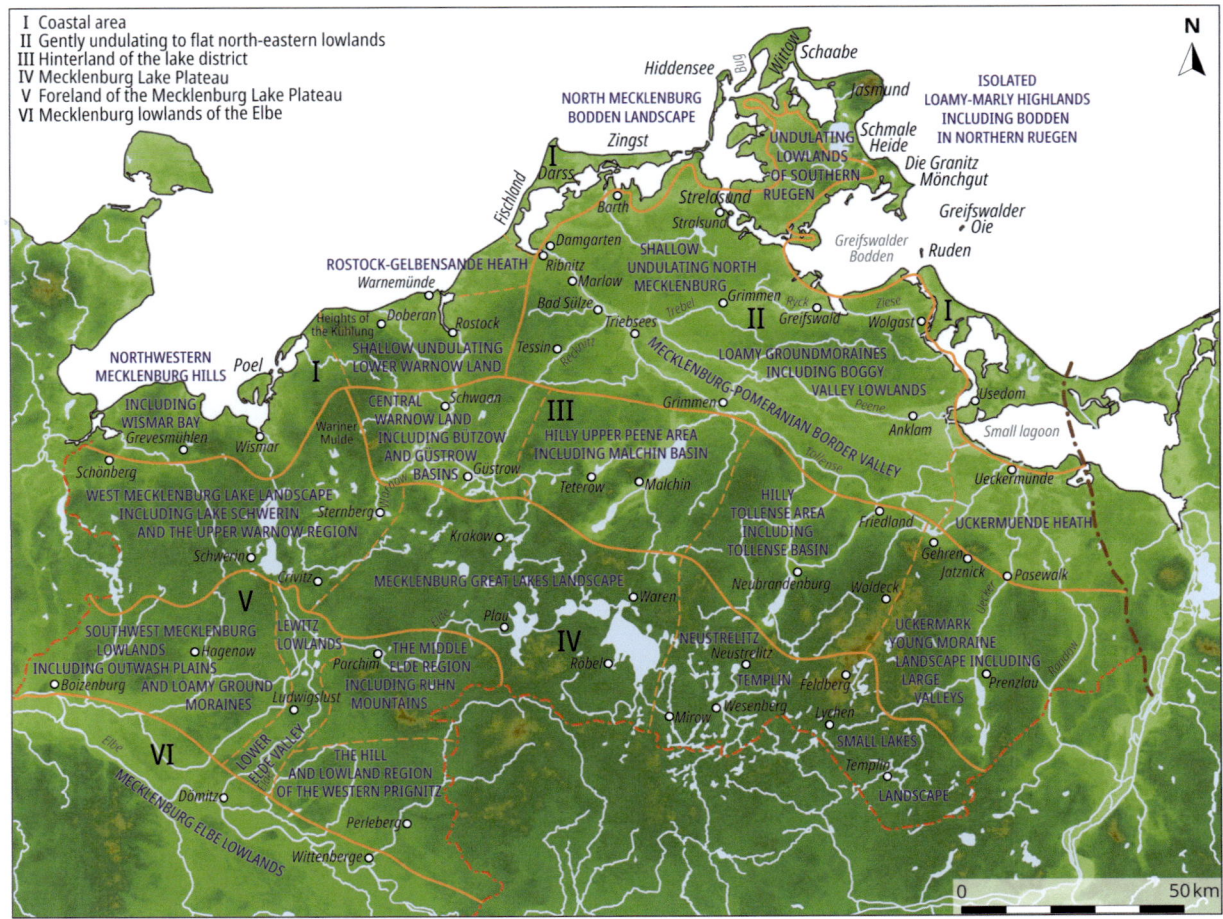

Fig. 1. Major landscapes in Mecklenburg-Western Pomerania (after Hurtig et al. 1957, Map 1).

larger south-eastern part, in which Neuenkirchen is also located, which is characterised by steeply rising hills (up to 83 m a.s.l.) and numerous meltwater courses (*ibid.*, 4).

The formation of the landscape is closely linked to the genesis of the Tollense basin, regarding which there are different opinions. The glacial tongue model and the tunnel valley model are opposed to each other. (Buddenbohm 2010, 72). In a comparative analysis of both models, Kanter (2000) concludes that the Tollense basin, based on the geomorphological and geological features, must be a tunnel valley of the Weichselian-Pomeranian stage. The preference for this model also reflects current research opinions (Buddenbohm 2010, 79).

The tunnel valley, also called glacial channel, is a glacial manifestation that occurs when the glacier begins to melt in an ice-marginal position. The water seeps through pore spaces and crevasses to the base of the glacier and accumulates, together with subglacial meltwaters, under the glacier. From there, it flows along the hydrostatic gradient to the glacier margin. Due to the pressure of the overlying ice masses, the water is literally pressed towards the edge of the ice and washes out the subsoil (Buddenbohm 2010, 73). The resulting meltwater tunnels can be several dozen metres wide. Erosion and sedimentation processes take place within the tunnel, which can lead to multiple displacements of the tunnel. This can create valleys 2 to 3 km wide (Kanter 2000, 11). An important argument in favour of a tunnel valley is the absence of Weichselian sediments in the bedrock of the Tollense valley, which would be typical for a tongue basin. Furthermore, the genesis of a basin is opposed by glacial dynamics outside of valleys (Kanter 2000, 12 ff.). The model, however does not explain how the glacier tongue advances against a rising

Fig. 2. Werder with the site of Neuenkirchen in the Mecklenburg Lake Plateau district; LIDAR image provided by the State Office for Culture and Monument Preservation, Mecklenburg-Pomerania (Dr. Detlef Jantzen) (adapted by the author).

Fig. 3. Water network system in eastern Mecklenburg-Vorpommern and the location of the site Neuenkirchen).

relief. Similar geomorphologies are found in other valleys and basins formed in the northern Mecklenburg lowlands, for example the Warnow valley or the Malchin basin, which underline the interpretation as a subglacial tunnel valley (*ibid.*, 22 f., in more detail). The Datze valley in the immediate vicinity of Neuenkirchen must also be addressed as such. The complete melting of the ice of the so-called Pomeranian phase made the Tollense basin and valley visible. The resulting channel was also utilised by the meltwater produced during the thawing of the last ice advance during the 'Mecklenburg Phase'. The meltwater sands thereby sedimented in the Tollense and Dasse valleys up to the level of the northern shore of Lake Tollensee (*ibid.*, 19).

2.1 Landscape and waterways

The landscape around the Neuenkirchen site is characterised by a comparably high relief energy. Thus, in the direction of the Datze valley, the terrain drops from 75 m above sea level to approximately 10 m above sea level within approximately 1.2 km. The drop towards the Tollense basin, which is about 12 km away, is even more pronounced, with the bottom of the basin lying 20 m below sea level. Thus, the site of Neuenkirchen lies on a comparatively dry moraine surface, even though there is a larger kettle lake about 240 m to the southwest. At the same time, the site is very well connected to the regional and supra-regional water network (Fig. 3). It lies between two small valleys where two streams drain into the Datze. The water system in eastern part of Mecklenburg-Western Pomerania is mainly characterised by river valleys lying just below the level of the Baltic Sea. The main axes (northeast-southwest: Peene and Tollense; northwest-southeast: Recknitz, Trebel, Peene lower reaches) reflect the movement and subglacial drainage of the former inland glaciers

(Lorenzen 2014, 15 ff.). The Datze River, which flows in the immediate vicinity of the site, connects the Tollense and Landgraben valleys. The Landgraben in turn drains east into the Zarow and is connected to the Oderhaff via the latter. In addition, the Großer Landgraben flows into the Tollense, which in turn flows into the Peene near Demmin. From there, the western and north-western Mecklenburg-Western Pomerania and the Baltic Sea coast can be reached via the river system Ibitzgraben-Trebel-Recknitz-Warnow. The Peene itself flows into the Peene strait in the east, which is one of the three estuaries of the Oder. The Werder and thus the Neuenkirchen site are therefore located at a geographical transport node.

3. State of research on the Funnel Beaker North Group in present-day Mecklenburg-Western Pomerania

The first significant work on prehistory took place in Mecklenburg as early as the 19th century. Closely connected with this first research are the names Friedrich Lisch and Robert Beltz. Beltz's work (1910), in which he published a complete overview of the finds kept in the Grand Ducal Museum in two volumes, deserves special mention. He also pointed out that Mecklenburg belonged to the 'Nordic Stone Age province' (Beltz 1910, 20; Vogt 2009, 143). The prehistory of Pomerania was described in detail by Kunkel (1931) with a large illustrated catalogue. In his field of work, he was one of the first to describe the funnel beakers and collared flasks (*Kragenhalsflaschen*) as proper forms of the 'megalithic culture'. Extensive basic research was carried out by Sprockhoff (1930, 1938), who was primarily concerned with megalithic graves, and Schuldt (1966, 1970, 1972a, 1972b), who examined a total of 106 megalithic graves (75 of which were excavated) in the area of the Recknitz and Schwinge rivers and evaluated their inventories. At the same time, Nilius (1971) compiled the material published up to 1964 on the Funnel Beaker Societies as part of her dissertation. Nagel (1985, 1991) compiled another overview—on part of the inventories of megalithic graves—in her work on Globular Amphora ceramics. The works published until then concentrated mainly on megalithic graves, while there was a complete lack of overview results on the settlement landscape. Thus, publications were mostly limited to individual sites or small regions. These include the settlement of Gristow, district of Vorpommern-Greifswald, presented by Nilius (1973, 1975) and Nagel and Wechler (1992); the dune dwelling site of Lanz, presented by Wetzel (1969); the island settlement in Lake Malchin near Basedow, published by Schuldt (1974); or the site of Zislow, investigated by Schoknecht (1991). A first overview of all finds of the Funnel Beaker Societies in the area of the former GDR district of Neubrandenburg was compiled by Wolff (1991, 17 ff.). Regarding the immediate Neuenkirchen area, the settlement site Brunn 17 was presented by Vogt (2009, 136 ff.).

The archaeological monitoring of the construction of the Baltic Sea motorway (from 1994) and, above all, the DFG Priority Programme 1400 'Early monumentality and social differentiation - on the emergence and development of Neolithic large buildings and first complex societies in northern Central Europe', ensured intensive research in the field of the Funnel Beaker Societies. As Staude (2013) and especially Lorenz (2018) noted, the previous chronological classification of the TRB in Mecklenburg-Vorpommern could not be regarded as secure. The stage classification created by Nilius (1971) was based primarily on the Scandinavian model, while Nagel's (1985) classification is merely a summary of it (Staude 2013, 1 f.). Lorenz (2018) criticises the analytical comprehensibility of bothworks; inadequate presentation of the data basis as well as the method, and lack of detailed presentation of the results. As early as the 1990s, Terberger and Piek (1998) attempted to create a revised chronological scheme for the Early and Middle Neolithic by means of the radiocarbon dates available at that time. However, since most of the data came from collective graves that were used several times, and thus lacked clearly assignable burial ensembles, the results remained blurred (Staude 2013). At least for the area of the Mecklenburg Bay, Hartz and Lübke (2005, 119 f.) were able to define the early phase of the TRB (Wangels/Flintbek,) as well as the following Siggeneben phase for the first time by means of fine-stratigraphic and absolute dated settlement inventories. In the recent past, Müller and Staude (2012) and Lorenz (2012; 2018) made important contributions to the classification of the Funnel Beaker Societies in the Mecklenburg region (cf. chapter 4). Rassmann and Schafferer (2012, 107 ff.) made a significant contribution to the analysis of the settlement landscape and population density, using GIS-based calculations to identify four large settlement areas for Mecklenburg-Western Pomerania (cf. chapter 5). On this basis, considering the megalithic graves, they also calculated the estimated population figures for the individual regions.

4. Chronology of the Funnel Beaker Societies

A clear chronological division of the different regional groups of the Funnel Beaker Societies, as well as the synchronisation of the different chronological systems, is a prerequisite for dealing with the cultural and social processes of these societies (Müller *et al.* 2012, 29). The seminal work for the so-called Northern Group of the Funnel Beaker Societies was presented by Madsen and Petersen (1984). With the help of similarity analyses of the find inventories, they developed the classification of the Early Neolithic which is still used today, and which in the following years could also be chronologically anchored to real dates using absolute dating. Chronological studies of the Early Neolithic in the areas of present-day Schleswig-Holstein and north-eastern Germany, based on purely typological investigations, were carried out by Schwabedissen (1979) and Hoika (1987). In the recent past, these have been significantly revised by several studies using absolute dating methods. These include the various works and regional studies by Hartz and Lübke (2005, 119 f.) in the area of the southern Mecklenburg Bay, Dibbern (2016) on West Holstein, Brozio (2016) on East Holstein, and Hage (2016) on the Eider Valley in central Schleswig-Holstein. The Early Neolithic (EN Ia) begins in northern Germany around 4100 BCE (Fig. 4). The pottery is characterised by, among other things, the occurrence of wide-mouthed funnel beakers. The range of shapes in the phase known as Wangels also includes funnel bowls, round-bottom jars, and flasks, as well as loop vessels and clay discs. The decoration of the vessels is limited to the rim area and consists of incisions and arcaded rims (*ibid.*; Bock 2016, 19). In the neighbouring southern Scandinavian area, EN Ia is, according to the current state of research, placed 100-200 years later, with the local groups Volling and Svalekint, which are mostly contemporary. The ceramic inventory of these groups also includes beaker with eyelets (*Ösenbecher*), the entire surface of which is decorated with furrowed incisions (*Furchenstichtechnik*). In addition, thin-butted flint axe blades are found in the material for the first time (Madsen 1998, 428 f.). The following EN Ib phase starts c. 3800 BCE and is called Siggeneben-Süd in Mecklenburg-Vorpommern and the southern Jutland area, after the Siggeneben-Süd site in Schleswig-Holstein. In western Holstein, Dibbern (2016, 143 ff.) first records Funnel Beaker period pottery around 3750 BCE with his phase Westholstein I (WH I: 3750-3550 BCE). As in EN Ia, funnel beakers are rare in the area of western Mecklenburg and then only sparsely decorated in the rim area with indentations, small, circular incisions, fingernail impressions, incised lines or cord impressions (Hartz/Lübke 2005, 124 f.). Funnel beakers and clay discs are found in western Holstein. The main decorations consist of fringes, fingerprints and simple zigzag lines (Dibbern 2016, 145 ff.). Undecorated funnel beakers dominate the range of finds in East Holstein, and there are other forms such as beakers and flasks with eyelets, as well as clay discs and lamps (Brozio 2016, 188). Here, too, only a few vessels are decorated, but the decorations in the form of finger nail indentations, stamps, incised lines, cord and twisted cord impressions (*Wickelschnureindrücke*), among others, are clearly more complex than in the preceding Wangels phase of EN Ia (*ibid.*). Eponymous for the contemporary stage in southern Scandinavia is the Oxie site, whose ceramic material, however, largely corresponds to the Siggeneben stage. In addition, the Volling Group continues to exist. From c. 3500 BCE onwards, the EN II begins—represented in the southern Jutland region and Mecklenburg-Vorpommern by the Wolkenwehe 1 stage—which finds its equivalent in southern Scandinavia in the Fuchsberg or Virum stage. For western Holstein at this time, Dibbern (2016, 145 ff.) defines his phase WH II (3550-3350 BCE). While the range of vessel forms hardly changes in comparison to the previous phases, there are now more decorations in the belly area of the funnel beakers. Typical for this phase is an ornamental element formed by angular bands (Hoika 1994, 92; Madsen 1998, 428 f.). This is also largely true for Westholstein, where the old forms are largely retained, but the shouldered cup (*Schultertasse*) enriches the inventory. The WH II phase is also associated with the appearance of zigzag patterns and rim decorations made of vertical rows of incisions (Dibbern 2016, 145 f.).

The stage classification of the Funnel Beaker North Group in the subsequent Middle Neolithic, which still largely holds today, was established by Becker (1954, 1957). While this work was based on the evaluation of settlement sites, Ebbesen (1975, 1978) was able to fit most of the funerary pottery into this system. The relevance of this chronological division was confirmed by absolute dating (Koch 1998; Madsen 1998). These first stages of the Middle Neolithic are called 'Troldebjerg' (MN Ia) or 'Klintebakke' (MN Ib) in southern Scandinavia, corresponding to the seminal sites, and 'Wolkenwehe' (MN Ia and Ib) in the southern Jutland region. In the more recent work by Dibbern (2016) and Brozio (2016), the phases are named after the respective working areas of Westholstein (WH) and Northeast Holstein. According to Dibbern (*ibid.*), the phases WH III (a/b) comprise the end of the Early Neolithic and the Middle Neolithic I (WH IIIa: 3350-3250 cal BC; WH IIIb: 3250-3100 BCE). The phase Northeast Holstein 1, according to Brozio (2016), comprises the entire Early Neolithic II and the Middle Neolithic I. Characteristic for the MN I is the appearance of new vessel forms such as clay spoons, fruit bowls, foot bowls, and numerous new forms of decoration. While the older form of the funnel beaker, which continues to exist, is characterised by the older style of decoration with vertical lines, the cups with eyelets are characterised by the new style of decoration (Madsen 1998, 428). For western Holstein, Dibbern (2016, 149) can also trace this increase of forms and ornamentation in his phase WH III (a/b). The existing inventory is enlarged through, among other things, foot bowls, three-part conical vessels, and funnel rim bowls. New decoration forms like hanging triangles, ladder bands, and multiple stacked angular engravings are introduced. In the late phase Northeast Holstein Phase 1, a similar trend emerges (Brozio 2016, 184), but this development can only be seen more clearly in the further course of the Middle Neolithic.

The subsequent stages or phases of the Middle Neolithic were named Wolkenwehe 2, Nordostholstein 2, as well as Oldenburg (both MN II) and Bostholm (MN III-IV), in the southern Jutland area. In southern Scandinavia it was divided into the stages 'Blandebjerg' (MN II), 'Bundsø' (MN III), and 'Lindø' (MN IV) (Madsen 1998, 428). The ceramic forms, such as funnel beaker, bowls with banded decoration, footed bowls (*Fußschalen*) and shouldered vessels remain in use and are supplemented by the biconical vessels that now appear. Differences in the regions can be seen above all in the design of the decoration. The ornamentation is only slightly altered from that of MN I. The thin-butted flint axes are now replaced by thick-butted types (*ibid.*, 429). Before the Single Grave Phenomenon begins in southern Scandinavia, a last phase of MN V can be identified with the Store-Valby

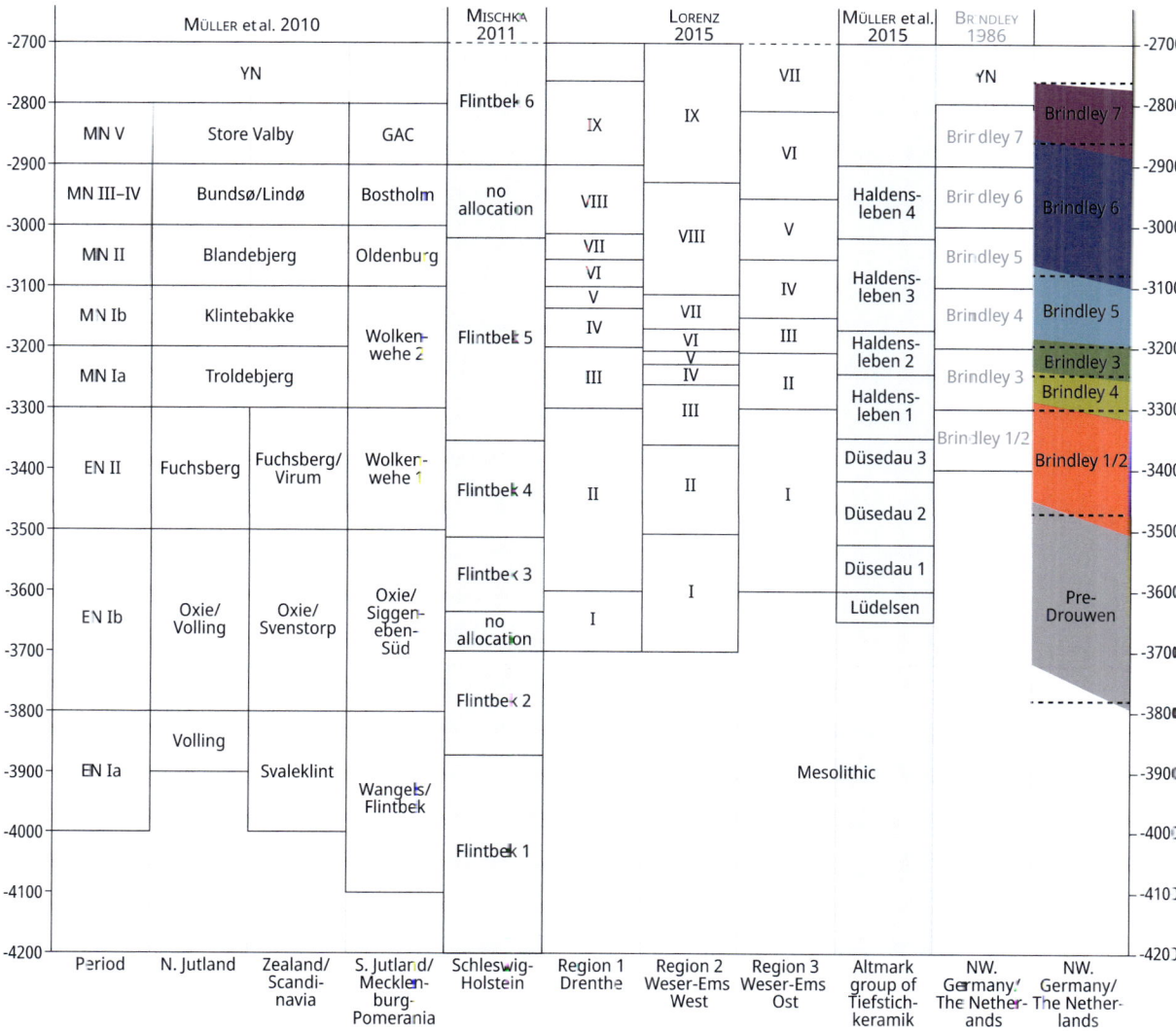

Fig. 4 Chronological scheme of the regional groups of the Funnel Beaker Societies (EN = Early Neolithic, MN = Middle Neolithic, YN = Young Neolithic, GAC= Globular Amphora Phenomenon) (after Menrenga 2017, 94, fig. 49).

stage, which lasted from 2950 to 2790 BCE. For the North German area, a slow transition to the Late Neolithic Globular Amphora Phenomenon is postulated for this period. The decoration of the pottery clearly decreases and coarse, bucket-shaped vessels dominate (*ibid.*, 428 f.).

The chronologies presented here are mainly based on the southern Scandinavian and southern Jutland material; only the work of Hartz and Lübke (2005, 119 f.) refers to the northwesternmost Mecklenburg. Comprehensible typological studies that are validated via absolute dating methods are, with the exception of Müller and Staude (2012) (cf. below), missing for the rest of Mecklenburg-Vorpommern (Lorenz 2018). However, the work of Klatt (2009) and Vogt (2009) suggests that synchronisation with the stages of the southern Jutland region is relevant (Müller *et al.* 2012, 31 f.).

With the evaluation of the finds and features of the Funnel Beaker site at Triwalk in Mecklenburg Western Pomerania, Müller and Staude (2012) and Staude (2013) presented one of the few sites where a systematic, chronological differentiation of the material has been carried out. By means of typological investigations, pit stratigraphies, and ¹⁴C data, they determined several phases of the settlement and postulated a transferability of the results to the rest of north-eastern Germany. This could be confirmed by Lorenz (2012) on the basis of investigations of the duration of ceramic styles and the period of use of the north-east German megalithic graves.

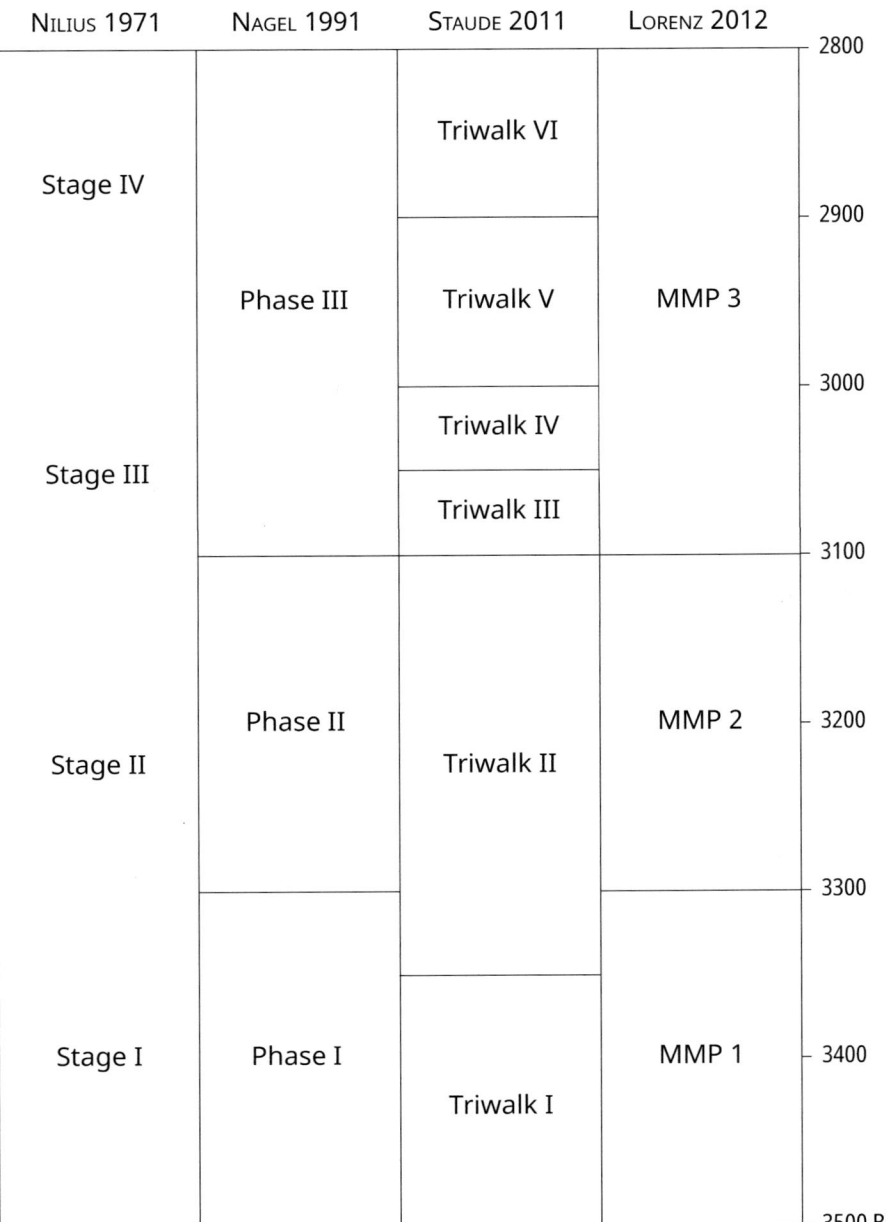

Fig. 5. Chronological scheme of the Funnel Beaker Period settlement of Triwalk and stages of Mecklenburg Megalithic pottery (Lorenz 2012, 72, fig. 9).

On the basis of typological investigations of the vessel inventories from megalithic graves, in which she also considered pottery finds from settlements and flat graves, she created a typo-chronological model and supported it with the radiocarbon dates from Triwalk. Her investigations resulted in a tripartite subdivision into the groups of Mecklenburg Megalithic Pottery MMP 1 (3500-3300 BCE), MMP 2 (3300-3100 BCE), and MMP 3 (3100/3050-2800 BCE) (see Fig. 5).

This model was significantly expanded and refined by her dissertation (Lorenz 2018). For ten sub-regions of her area of research, which comprised the southern Funnel Beaker North Group and the Funnel Beaker West Group, she was able to work out the pottery sequences and occupation duration of the megalithic graves, as well as large-scale communication structures (*ibid.*, 154 ff.). For each of these sub-regions, she delineated stages characterised by different forms and patterns of decoration. Thus, a differentiation according to ceramic groups is now also available for north-eastern Germany, for the period from c. 3300 BCE

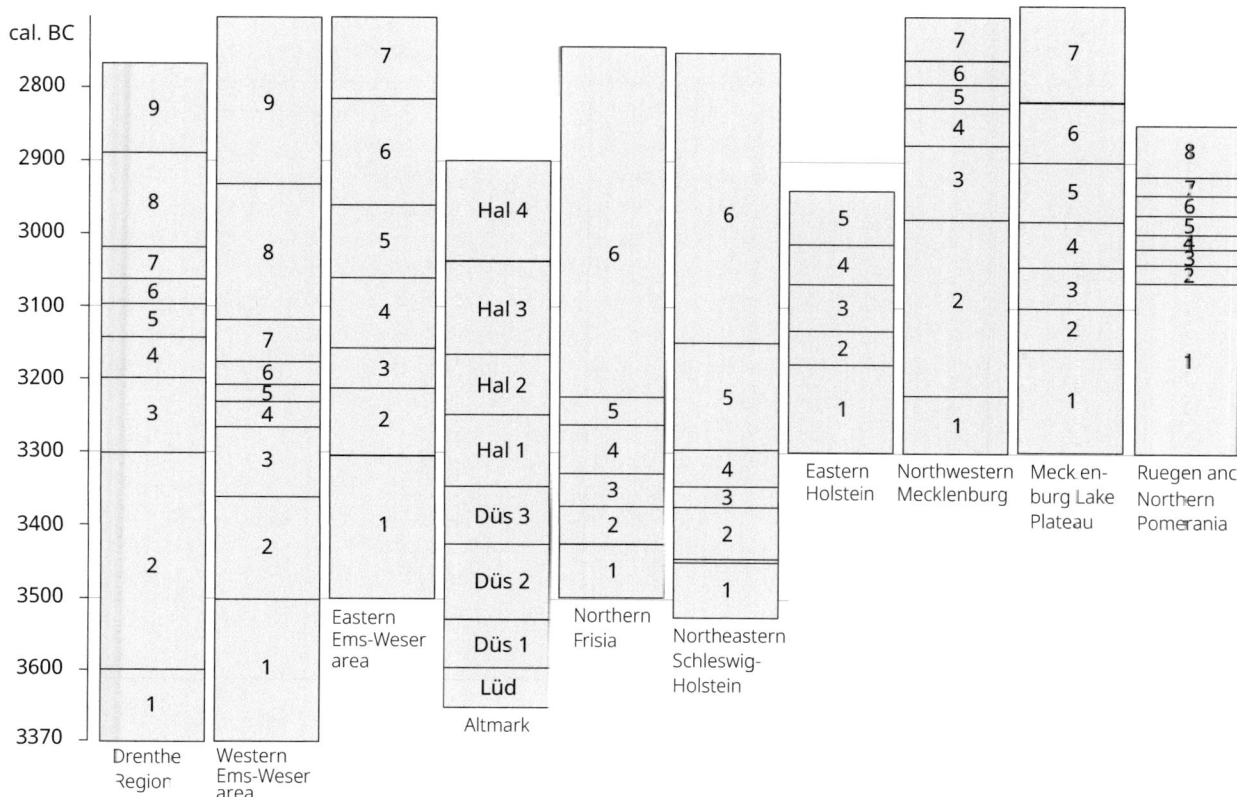

Fig. 6 Overview of typo-chronological models of megalithic pottery (adapted from Lorenz 2018, fig. 7.79).

onwards, which was created on the basis of correspondence analyses and bound to the absolute chronology by means of natural scientific data. Three of the ten study areas in the north-central European lowlands first identified by Lorenz are in present-day Mecklenburg-Western Pomerania (north-western Mecklenburg, Mecklenburg Lake Plateau, and the island Ruegen plus the adjacent mainland). For a detailed description of the individual stages in north-eastern Germany see Lorenz (2018). For the region 'Ruegen and the adjacent mainland', in which the Neuenkirchen site is located, Lorenz (*ibid.*) proposes a division into eight chronological stages (1. c. 3300-3070 BCE; 2. 3070-3030 BCE; 3. 3030-3015 BCE; 4. 3015-3005 BCE; 5. 3005-2995 BCE; 6. 2995-2988 BCE; 7. 2988-2975 BCE; 8. 2975-2675 BCE) (Fig. 6). It should be considered that only very few radiocarbon dates were available and that these stages are also only visible to a very limited extent in the correspondence analysis (*ibid.*, 165). Whether the results achieved under these conditions justify such a fine-resolution stage classification as Lorenz (*ibid.*) undertakes cannot be determined here due to the limited scope of this work. However, the short stage durations of only 7, 10 or 15 years which she calculated seem ambitious due to the few absolute dates. Furthermore, this stage classification only refers to pottery from megalithic graves, so that differences are to be expected for settlements and burials.

In summary, for north-western Mecklenburg, the beginning of the Early Neolithic has been well captured by the work of Hartz and Lübke (2005). For the eastern parts of Mecklenburg, the research discussion is still in flux. Early dated sites, such as the settlement site of Carpin (Mecklenburg Lake Plateau district), points to a possible earlier beginning of Funnel Beaker related activity around 4000 BC (cf. settlement environment of Neuenkirchen). The earliest absolute-dated site in the immediate vicinity of Neuenkirchen, Warlin, can be dated to 3709 BCE (BLN 3984, 4790 ± 80 BP, 3709-3370 BCE). The influence of Baalberg and Michelsberg on the genesis of the Funnel Beaker Societies is still under discussion. Numerous sites in eastern Mecklenburg, for example, have typical Baalberg amphorae (including Neuenkirchen, site No. 1). Although Vogt (2009) does not want to place the pointed-bottomed vessel from the site Brunn 17 in a Michelsberg context, the boundary of the occurrence of Michelsberg pottery has clearly shifted northwards in recent years, as sites in the Havelland show. The transition from Early to Middle Neolithic is represented by the site Brunn (site No. 17). The funnel beakers of the Uckermark group found here can be assigned to the transitional horizon postulated by Kirsch (1993) (Vogt 2009, 160). From 3500 BCE (at the latest from 3300 BCE) onwards the use of the megalithic graves in Mecklenburg-Vorpommern can be identified (Lorenz 2012, 73 ff.). The occupation of said graves continues throughout the MN in eastern Mecklenburg. Lorenz (2018) even postulates a continued use beyond MN V until 2675 BCE, but would like her chronological analysis of the megalithic pottery to be understood merely as a tendency (*ibid.*, 309).

5. Anthropogenic activities in the surroundings of Neuenkirchen at the time of the Funnel Beaker Societies

5.1 Settlement activities

As already described in the history of research, work on TRB settlements in Mecklenburg-Vorpommern was initially limited mainly to the publication of material from a few single sites. Although the increasing consideration of settlement sites in research led to a noticeable improvement in the understanding of settlement structures, house finds from this period are rare or even non-existent. This leaves only the archaeological features like pits and settlement layers, as well as surface finds, for the identification of settlements. In the case of the latter indicator, it is often unclear whether this is sufficient for a settlement to be identified. Rassmann and Schafferer (2012, 108) used an alternative approach for the identification of settlement areas. On the basis of 3,606 sites with flint axes, they calculate an island-like Neolithic settlement structure for Mecklenburg-Vorpommern, with a size of 6,126 km². According to the aforementioned calculations, the Neuenkirchen site is located in a rather sparsely settled area but not far from a smaller settlement chamber at the northern end of Lake Tollense (Fig. 7). In the mid-1980s, Mende (1985) listed a total of 28 sites of various dates in the Neuenkirchen district, of which only three were considered Neolithic. While all three can be assigned to the Funnel Beaker Societies, only site 21 with two pits shows clearer evidence of a settlement. In his compilation of Early and Older Middle Neolithic sites in the district of the former GDR Neubrandenburg, Wolff (1991) mentions another settlement site, which, however, has no archaeological features. Although the number of sites had increased to 49 by the 2000s, these did not provide any evidence of a further settlement of the Funnel Beaker societies. Outside the Neuenkirchen district, however, about 4 km north of the present village, pits are known from sites 31 and 42 in the Neverin district; these can be assigned to the Funnel Beaker Societies and also contained daub. In addition, several sites were discovered during the large-scale linear excavations carried out as part of the projects to accompany the construction of the A20 motorway and the OPAL and NEL gas routes, which contributed to the understanding of the Funnel Beaker period settlement landscape around Neuenkirchen.

Further evidence of settlement activities can be obtained from the waterlogged sediments of lakes and bogs, in which the pollen and seeds of plants have become embedded and preserved. These archives, accessed by core drilling, allow conclusions to be drawn about the settlement and vegetation history of the

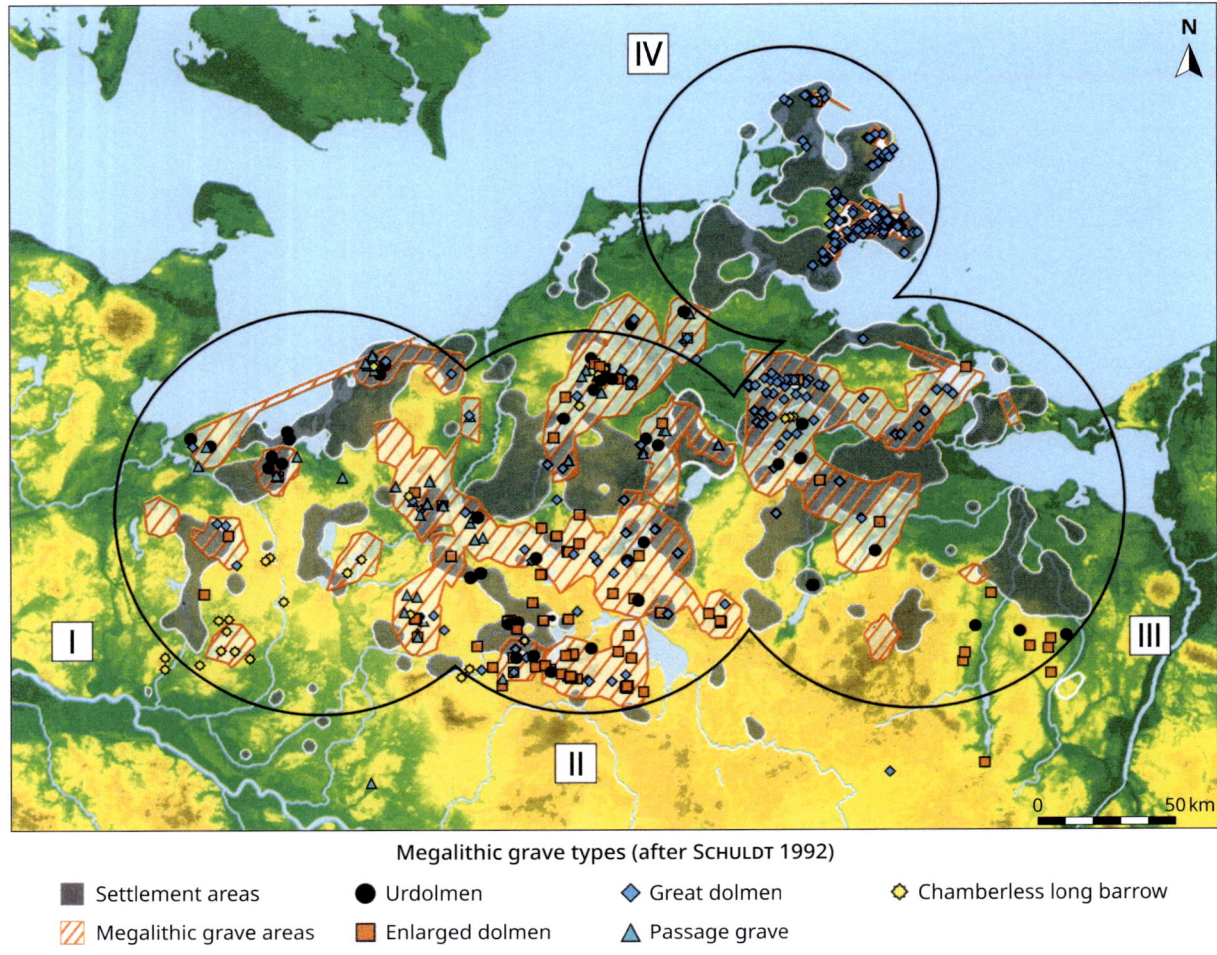

Megalithic grave types (after SCHULDT 1992)

- Settlement areas
- Megalithic grave areas
- ● Urdolmen
- ■ Enlarged dolmen
- ◆ Great dolmen
- △ Passage grave
- ◇ Chamberless long barrow

Fig. 7. Reconstructed settlement chambers of the Funnel Beaker Societies (grey) after Rassmann/ Schafferer 2012, 109, fig. 1).

surrounding area. The size of the lake or bog determines, among other things, the extent to which local, extra-local, and regional developments are reflected in a pollen profile (see Jacobson/Bradshaw 1981, 80). The smaller the waterbody or bog, the more the local development is reflected. For today's eastern or southeastern part of West Pomerania, there is currently only one palynological study by Endtmann (2004), but only two of the archives she evaluated are located in the eastern part of Western-Pomerania, while the majority come from the island of Ruegen. The only other radiocarbon-dated pollen profiles from the region around Neuenkirchen come from the work of Müller and Kohl from 1966, which deals with the area around Thurow (district of Mecklenburg Lake Plateau), about 30 km away. However, the oldest radiocarbon date of the study falls in the late Middle Neolithic around 2800 BCE (*ibid.*), so that this contribution can only be considered to a limited extent. The investigations carried out by Jahns (2001) at Lake Unterucker in northeastern Brandenburg near Prenzlau (district of Uckermark), which would be a good candidate for statements on the landscape reconstruction around Neuenkirchen due to the spatial proximity, unfortunately show a hiatus in the sedimentation between c. 7000 and 2900/2800 BCE. Further palynological studies are available for western Mecklenburg (summarised by Feeser/Dörfler 2015, 291 ff. and Feeser *et al.* 2016, 1ff.) as well as for the area of the lower Oder in north-eastern Brandenburg and north-western Poland (Endtmann 1998 and 2004; Jahns 2000).

The beginning of the Early Neolithic in northern Germany is roughly associated, in terms of pollen stratigraphically, with a strong decline of the elm population (Feeser *et al.* 2016, 3). This event, also referred to as elm decline, can extend over several centuries. For the northern German region, it falls within the period 4100-3800 BC (*ibid.*). For eastern Mecklenburg-Western Pomerania, Endtmann (2004, 37 and 151 ff.) places it around 3750 BCE. During investigations in the Lower Oder valley, Jahns (2001) was able to show, on the basis of radiometric data, that the elm decline in this region began 150 years earlier. The pollen profile from Lake Felchow (Uckermark district), which is most suitable for establishing the time of the elm decline in the region around Neuenkirchen due to its spatial proximity (approx. 75 km) and the radiocarbon dating, shows the decline of the elms around 3890 BCE. In about the same period, the first anthropogenic activities can be detected in the pollen spectra in eastern (Müller/Kohl 1966; Endtmann 2004) and central Mecklenburg (Schoknecht 1996, 24 ff.). They are evident through secondary settlement indicators, such as ribwort plantain (*Plantago lancelota*) in particular, which indicates an opening of the landscape associated with agricultural activities such as pastoralism and cereal cultivation (Feeser *et al.* 2016, 11). Direct evidence of cereal pollen is found in only a few pollen profiles during this period, such as from Serrahn (Mecklenburg Lake Plateau district) (Müller/Kohl 1966, 412) and Anklam/ Hoher Stein (Endtmann 2004, 110 f.). This is in line with the development in western Mecklenburg. As Feeser *et al.* (2016) were able to demonstrate, human influence there is rather weak in the beginning of the Early Neolithic and is mainly evident in changes in forest composition. The cultivation of cereals seems to have taken place only locally and on a small scale. A major part in the opening up of the forest landscape was probably played by livestock farming, based on leaf fodder and forest grazing, the adoption of which represented the main change in subsistence strategy in the early phase of Neolithization (*ibid.*, 12). In western Mecklenburg, Feeser *et al.* (*ibid.*) were able to show different phases of human activity in varying strengths for the advancing Neolithic. Such fine-resolution pollen profiles and interdisciplinary research projects are not yet available for central and eastern Mecklenburg-Western Pomerania, but Endtmann (2004, 154) states a closed pollen curve for secondary settlement indicators for the period from 3800 BC onwards. Overall, only weak settlement activities are evident in the pollen profiles during the Neolithic. The resumption of sedimentation in the profiles of Lakes Oberucker and Unterucker (see above) from only 2900/2800 BC onwards shows settlement activities that are manifested in relatively high pollen values of sweet grasses (Poaceae), consistent evidence of cereal pollen, and secondary settlement indicators.

5.2 The settlement sites of Warlin, Brunn, Carpin, Jatznick, Glasow and Gristow (Fig. 8)

5.2.1 The settlement site of Warlin

The discovery of the settlement sites Warlin (site No. 2) and Brunn (site No. 17) (both in the district of the Mecklenburg Lake Plateau) led to a substantial expansion of the knowledge about the Funnel Beaker period settlement in the surroundings of Neuenkirchen. About 2.5 km away from the site, and already south of the river Datze, a Funnel Beaker period settlement layer and two pits, as well as two stone packings, were documented under a Bronze Age burial mound in Warlin. A total of 1900 pottery remains came from the features, which can be assigned to sherds of funnel-rim vessels, funnel beakers, funnel-rim bowls, two- and four-handled amphorae, and spoons, among other forms. In addition to vessel types and decoration patterns which are known from the late EN, the ceramic inventory also points to the early phase of MN I (Mende 2001, 21 ff.). The charcoal sample recovered

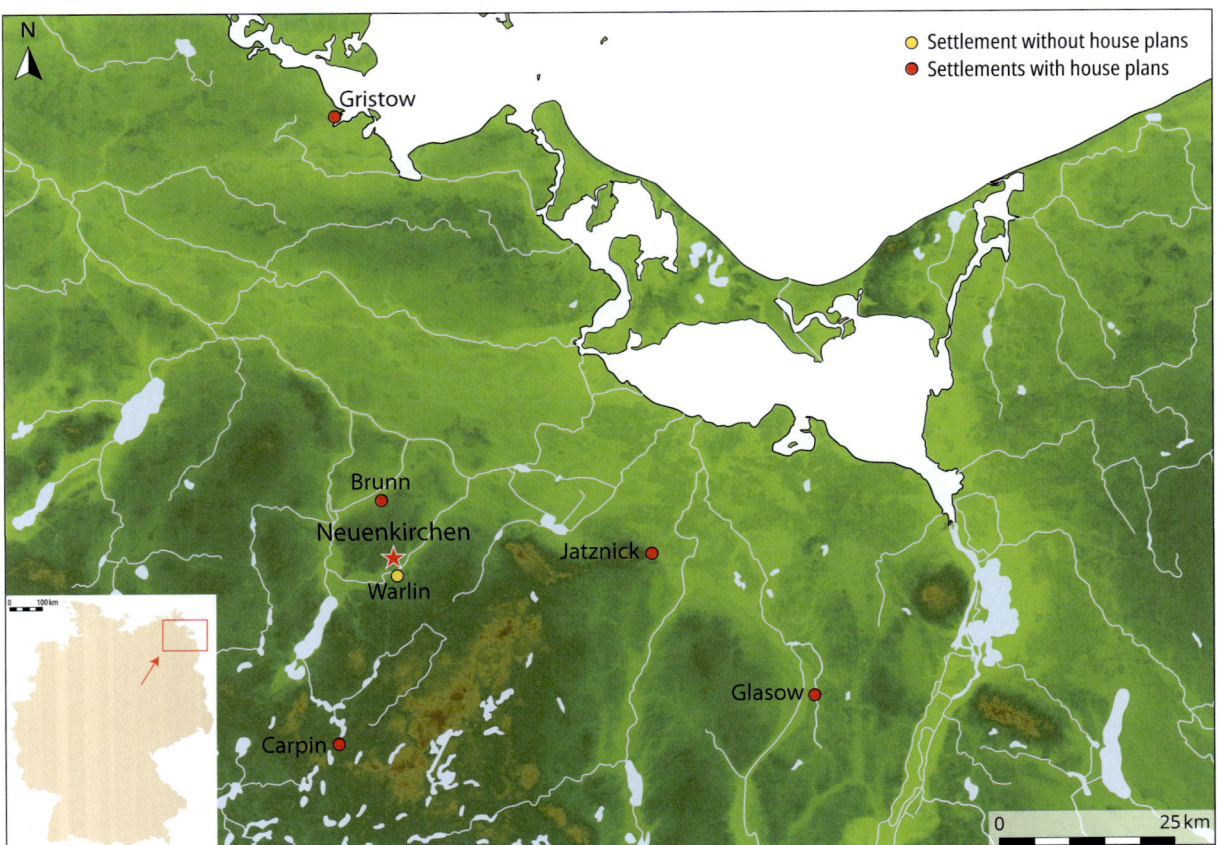

Fig. 8. Mapping of the Funnel Beaker period settlement sites in Mecklenburg-Western Pomerania within the vicinity of Neuenkirchen.

from pit 4 only yielded a very broad dating between 3709 and 3370 BCE (BLN 3984, 4790 ± 80). However, there are indications of an earlier, EN Ib, occupation of the site. Numerous Funnel Beaker period ceramics from the mound fill, as well as surface finds from the surrounding area, also suggest a larger settlement area.

5.2.2 The settlement site of Brunn

Another settlement was excavated in the course of the archaeological supervision of the construction of the A20 motorway, about 8 km north of Neuenkirchen. Within an area of about 8,000 m², 83 features were documented at Brunn (site No. 17). These were mainly fire pits and rubbish pits, most of which were devoid of finds. Two large settlement pits, however, were filled with a large amount of Funnel Beaker period pottery. Of particular importance are the 14 securely-identified post pits, which represent the remains of a two-aisled post-built house that was still preserved to a length of 12 m. The total width is 5.8 m, the width of the naves is 2.8 and 3.0 m respectively (see Fig. 9b). Unfortunately, the house area is free of finds, except for an indeterminate sherd. Vogt (2009, 171) would like to place the house in the Bronze Age and relies mainly on architectural features. In her opinion, the absence of wall ditches and the lack of internal division do not support an assignment to the Funnel Beaker Societies. The rounded corners she identifies are associated with findings from Late Bronze Age houses. However, it should be noted that houses without wall ditches and internal divisions are known from the Northern Group of the TRB (Steffens 2009, Fig. 20). Furthermore, the rounded house corners postulated by Vogt (2009, 174) cannot be reconstructed from her published drawing of the feature. Moreover, it seems that the features she refers to as late Bronze Age-early Iron Age intersect the house features and are thus at least younger than these.

Unfortunately, this fact cannot be clearly deduced from the drawings. Likewise, the possible overlaying of a Funnel Beaker period feature by the house ground plan, as mentioned by her, is not recognisable. A clear classification as a Funnel Beaker period house cannot be made, but all the architectural reasons put forward by Vogt (*ibid.*) for excluding a date earlier than Late Bronze Age are inconceivable. It is quite true that the house plan has similarities with a Late Bronze Age find from Gützkow (East-Western Pomerania district), but an assignment to the Funnel Beaker Period house type Dagstorp II (Artursson *et al.* 2003, 118; Steffens 2009, fig. 20, b) is also reasonable. In addition, there is a very similar house find from Glasow (Mecklenburg Lake Plateau district), which certainly dates to the first half of the fourth millennium (cf. 5.1.5). The Neolithic pottery assemblage comprised only a few decorated funnel beakers, funnel bowls, funnel neck vessels, a collared flask fragment, an amphora fragment, a pointed-base vessel, as well as fragments of indeterminate vessels. On the basis of the forms and decoration of the pottery, as well as the lithic finds material (including pointed-butt stone axes and thin-butted flint axes), Vogt (2009, 166 ff.) places the transition from the Early Neolithic to the Middle Neolithic. A dating of the site by means of radiometric analyses has not yet been carried out, despite numerous animal bones found in the material.

5.2.3 The settlement site of Carpin

Apart from Brunn, another site has a Funnel Beaker period house that can be identified by post pits: The site of Carpin (Mecklenburg Lake Plateau district) is located about 30 km south-southwest of Neuenkirchen at the southern end of Lake Rödlin. At the multi-period site, the remains of three houses, as well as a ditch with two larger posts at the inner side, could be documented. While the 20 m long 'House II' (Fig. 9e) was only barely recognisable and 'House III' was only partially excavated, 'House I' (Fig. 9d) was distinguished by clearly recognisable features. It is a two-aisled long house (18 × 5 m) with central posts and wall ditches in which split planks and post holes are recognisable (Brauer 1995, 61 ff.; Terberger and Piek 1998, 21 ff.). The houses can be attributed to the Mossby/Wittenwater type because of their two naves, the rounded ends, and the hints of internal division (cf. Artursson *et al.* 2003 and Steffens 2009). A special feature are wall ditches, which are otherwise not common with this type. A ^{14}C-analysis can be used for the dating of House I. Unfortunately, the charcoal samples used for dating were taken from several different features of House I. This circumstance, and the possible old wood effect of charcoal, must be considered when assessing the result. The analysis yielded an age of 3937-3642 BCE (Bln 4625, 4957±51 BP). Apart from a presumably Early Funnel Beaker amphora sherd, the site yielded no other finds that could have provided further clues for dating (*ibid.*). Two more radiocarbon dates exist from the site: A pit is dated to the Late Mesolithic (Bln-4626, 6467 ±56 BP, 5522-5322 BCE) and a post hole, which belongs to the aforementioned ditch near House I, to the late Mesolithic (Bln-4667, 5550 ±51 BP, 4492-4328 BCE). In the case of the latter date, the extraction of samples from different features (postholes) is also problematic, so that a mixture of younger and older material is possible (*ibid.*). A dating of the house plan to the Early Neolithic cannot be assumed with definite certainty. In the light of the likewise early settlement of the Warlin site (cf. above) and the house plan from Glasow (cf. 5.2.5), however, such a dating seems likely.

5.2.4 The settlement site of Jatznick

In the course of the archaeological monitoring of the construction of the 'OPAL' gas route, numerous settlement and post pits, as well as an 850 m² cultural layer with a thickness of between 0.3 and 0.7 m, were uncovered at Jatznick (district of

Western Pomerania-Greifswald), which is located about 36 km east of Neuenkirchen (Selent 2014, 71 f.). The quantities of pottery encountered within this layer indicate intensive settlement activity. The range of sherds encountered includes parts of undecorated cylindrical and funnel-neck vessels, decorated sherds of funnel beakers, and collar bottles, the latter often with handles. The ceramic material allows an attribution to the Middle Funnel Beaker Societies (MN I) (*ibid.*, 73). Of particular importance, however, are the 15 post holes found below the cultural layer, 9 of which can be combined to form the floor plan of a small building (Fig. 9a). The building, which was at least 8.5 m long and 3.5 m wide, was oriented east-west. The overall length remains unclear, as a post hole which was to be expected in the eastern area was missing, suggesting a continuation beyond the excavation limits. An assignment to one of the types of Funnel Beaker period houses is difficult due to the incomplete nature of the house plan. There is no finds material from the features. However, since the ground plan of the building was overlaid by the Middle Neolithic cultural layer, the building was erected in the Middle Neolithic at the latest (*ibid.*).

5.2.5 The settlement site of Glasow

In the course of the archaeological monitoring of the 'NEL' gas route, a Funnel Beaker period house floor plan was uncovered near Glasow (Mecklenburg Lake Plateau district) in 2011. Although Glasow is a little further away than the aforementioned settlement sites, with a distance of approx. 64 km from Neuenkirchen, this site has the only house floor plan that can really be dated with certainty to the Funnel Beaker period, and should therefore be listed here. The northnorthwest-southsoutheast oriented, two-aisled building has a width of 6 m and a length of at least 13.7 m (Fig. 9c), whereby the southeast end is not clearly defined and a continuation to the south is suggested (Weiss 2014, 67 f.). In the northern area of the house, the remains of a hearth were found. The house may be of the Dagstorp II type (cf. Artursson et. al. 2003, 40 ff., cf. also Müller 2017, 22 f.). As there was no material from the house interior itself that could be dated with certainty, two charcoal samples were analysed radiometrically. One sample was obtained from the post pit of a ridge post and the other from the post pit of a corner post of the house. They date the house to the first half of the fourth millennium (Erl-17625, 4716 ± 54 BP, 3635-3372 BCE; Erl-17164, 5040 ± 59 BP, 3962-3707 BCE (*ibid.*). The finds material (including fragments of a beaker with eyelets with slightly flared rim and handle loop) from a pit encountered directly west of the house wall confirmed the chronological position of the house floor plan in the time horizon of the Funnel Beaker Societies (*ibid.*).

5.2.6 The settlement site of Gristow

The multi-period settlement site of Gristow (district of Greifswald-Western Pomerania), presented by I. Nilius as early as 1973, has not been considered in the more recent work on Funnel Beaker Societies house floor plans in Mecklenburg-Western Pomerania, but it is certainly of interest. The site, located about 10 km from Greifswald, was excavated in two campaigns in 1961 and 1962. Like the site of Glasow described above, it is somewhat further away from Neuenkirchen, but with the two further house floor plans from this site, all known house floor plans of the TRB from today's Mecklenburg-Western Pomerania can be summarised for the first time, and should therefore also be mentioned here. The settlement, probably originally 250 m x 150 m in size, was extensively damaged and partly destroyed by sand mining. Nevertheless, numerous features were documented. Despite the several rows of posts holes that were encountered, Nilius (1973) did not want to 'forcibly' reconstruct them as houses because of the incompleteness and the multitude of possible interpretations. In light of the newly-discovered Funnel Beaker period house plans, however, a reconsideration seems appropriate. At this point, the suggested interpretation of the post pits is as a house with rounded corners (Fig. 9f), as known from Carpin (cf. Fig. 9). A further similarity is the apparent subdivision of individual house sections in the interior. These features are known from the Mossby type (according to Artursson 2003 *et al.*) or the Mossby/Wittenwater type (cf. Müller 2017, 19 f.; cf. settlement site Carpin), to which this house can also be counted.

Only a few metres north of the eastern end of the house postulated above, a c. 6 m long, on average 2 m wide oval pit was encountered during the excavations, which is interpreted by Nilius (*ibid.*) as a house floor (Fig. 9g). This was shallow, trough-shaped and cut to a maximum of 0.30 m into a clay lens. Along the long sides ran a whitish silt layer, which was anthropogenically-applied to the clay layer. In the western area there was a stone packing (1.20 by 1 m), which is interpreted as a destroyed hearth. Between the often worked stones, which had a crumbly structure due to fire exposure, were found numerous vessel sherds and a large number of animal bones (*ibid.*, 250). The stones found at the ends of the pits (cf. Fig. 9) can be related to post settings. A special feature is the deposition of a two-handled amphora at the eastern end of the house floor.

Since only a single radiometric dating is known from the site, which yielded an Iron Age date for the hearth, the ceramic finds material must be used to date the Neolithic house floor plans. A total of over 15,000 sherds were recovered from the site. The inventory is dominated by funnel beakers, but there are also beakers with eyelets, two-handled amphorae, small funnel bowls, bowls, and clay spoons. The finds material can mainly be assigned to the Middle Neolithic (MN I) (*ibid.*, 260 ff.). However, older forms are also represented among the funnel beakers and beakers with eyelets, as well as amphorae, so that a dating of the settlement to the transition from the Early Neolithic to the Late Neolithic seems reasonable.

0 ___ 5 m

a

0 ___ 5 m

b

0 ___ 5 m

c

0 ___ 5 m

d

Fig. 9. House plans from Funnel Beaker period settlements in Mecklenburg-Western Pomerania: a) Jatznick (district Western Pomerania -Greifswald), b) Brunn, c) Glasow d) Carpin house 1 e) Carpin, house 2 (b-e district Mecklenburg Lake Plateau district), f) Gristow, post house g) Gristow, deepened house floor without post holes (f-g district Western Pomerania -Greifswald) (basis of illustration for a) Selent 2014, 71; for b) Vogt 2009, 171, fig. 10; for c) Weiss 2014, 68, fig. 3; for g) u. g) Nilius 1973, 249 ff, figs. 10 and 12; all illustrations digitised and modified by the author).

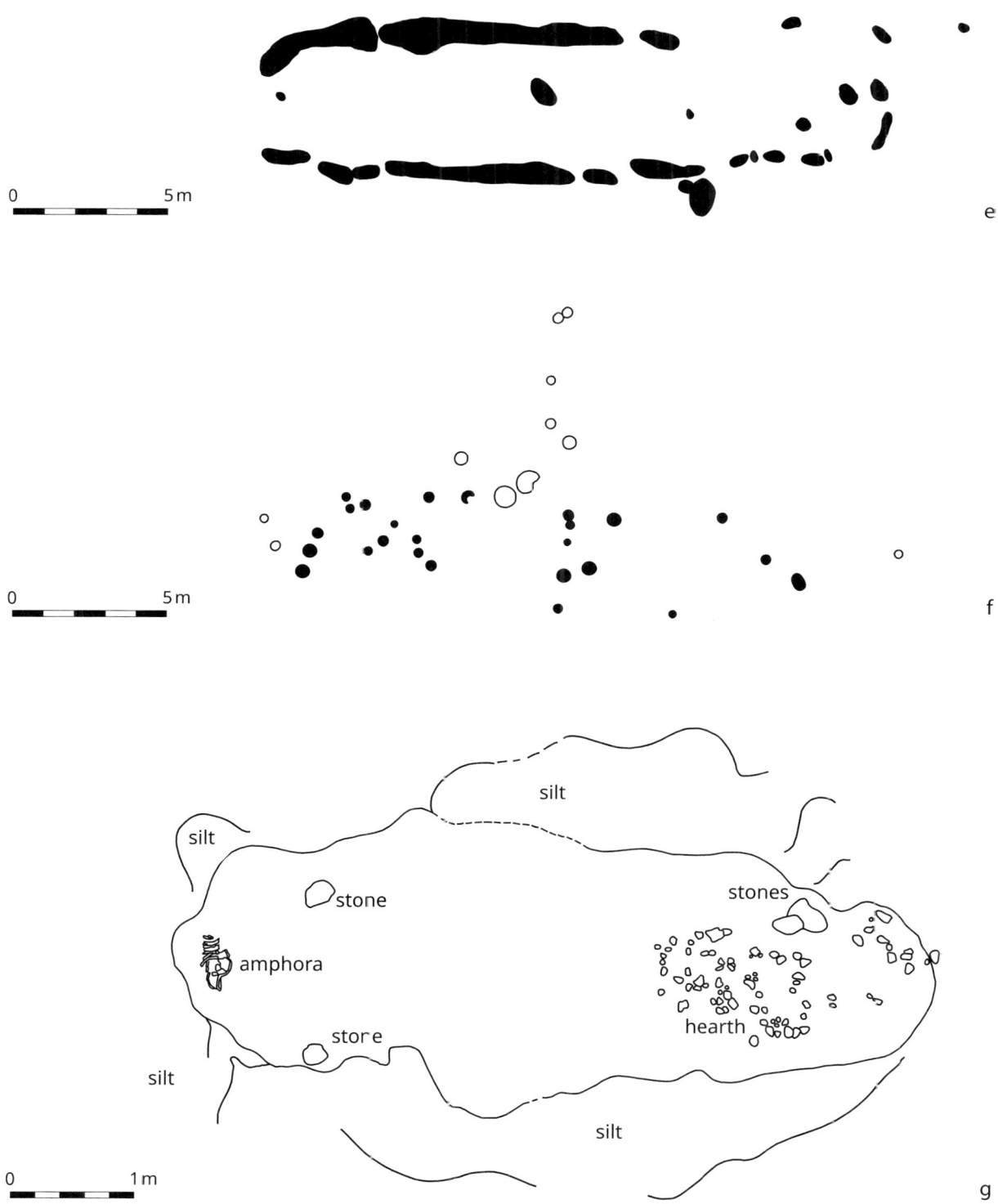

0   5 m

e

0   5 m

f

silt

silt

stone

stones

amphora

store

hearth

silt

silt

0   1 m

g

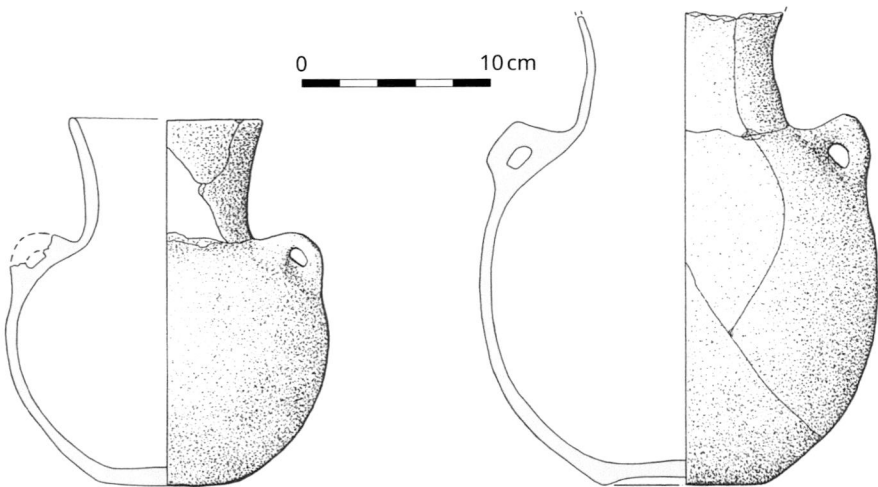

0   10 cm

Fig. 10. The vessel deposit of Nustrow (Schirren 2004, 622, fig. 17).

5.3 Funnel Beaker period hoards and megalithic graves in the vicinity of Neuenkirchen

5.3.1 Deposits (Fig. 11)

From the immediate vicinity of Neuenkirchen, c. 800 m to the east, at the former dairy Louisenhof, comes one of the rare vessel hoards from northern Germany. In 1885, while excavating a '*Moderbruch*' (probably a swampy depression or bog hole), a small funnel beaker with rim decoration, three amphorae, a sherd of an amphora, and a fragment of the cutting edge of a stone axe were found. Another bowl-like vessel and a flint blade are now lost (Hollnagel 1962, 61). Unfortunately, no further details are known. Two other deposits of such amphorae are known from northern Western Pomerania (Schirren 2004, 622). In Nustrow (district of Bad Doberan), two amphorae standing on their bases were found at the bottom of a former stream (Fig. 10).

More sherds from the excavated soil point to possible further vessels. An absolute date is available for each of the two amphorae: KIA-26410, 5040 ±30 BP, 3951-3764 BCE (94.5%), 3723-3716 BCE (0.9%), and KIA-26411, 5075 ±25 BP, 3956-3892 BCE (34.6%), 3884-3798 BCE (60.8%)[2] (Staude 2013, 145 f.). In the neighbouring Böhlendorf (Bad Doberan district), comparable amphorae were recovered from a bog hole (Schirren 2004, 622.). Both aforementioned deposits were found in a waterlogged environment or small streams, which indicates that the find at Louisenhof is also to be regarded as a vessel deposit. The amphorae indicate influences from Baalberg. The funnel beaker, which is only decorated at the rim, also does not contradict a dating to Early Neolithic I. Another pottery deposit with two vessels, including a funnel beaker, comes from Pasewalk (district of Western Pomerania-Greifswald) (Hellmundt 1964, 55). No other depot finds clearly belonging to the TRB are known from the immediate vicinity of Neuenkirchen. Although there is a deposit of five rectangular flint axes of unknown type from near Altentreptow (Mecklenburg Lake Plateau district), 13 km away (Walter 1901, 247), as well as a depot find of an indeterminate flint axe blade, two stone axe blades, and three grinding stones from Gültz (Mecklenburg Lake Plateau district) (Stubenrauch 1904, 106; Walter 1904,

---

2   Data recalibrated with OxCal v.4.2.4 using dataset INTCAL13 (Reimer *et al.* 2013).

Fig. 11. Neolithic hoard finds mentioned in the text.

154-155), these can only be generally assigned to the Neolithic. This is also the case for the hoards known in the wider area (30-40 km) (all Western Pomerania-Greifswald district) from Eichhof (three thick-butted flint axes and one thin-butted flint chisel), Waldeshöhe (two pointed-butt flint axes), Stolzenburg (seven flint axes of unknown type), Heydenhof (two flint axes of unknown type), and Tutow (five rectangular flint axes of unknown type) (Berliner Katalog Voss 1880, 819; Walter 1901, 247; Walter 1910, 182; Kunkel 1926, pl. 3.1; Kunkel 1939, 277; Rech 1979, 103, No. 103). Only the aforementioned hoard find from Eichhof can possibly be considered as dating to the Funnel Beaker period. A dissertation on the deposits of the Northern Group of the Funnel Beaker Societies is currently pending at the Free University of Berlin: First results indicate that Funnel Beaker period settlements, megalithic graves, and hoards have different distribution centres, and that hoards are always found at the edge of settlement areas (including megalithic graves)[3].

5.3.2 Megalithic graves

The megalithic graves of the Funnel Beaker societies line up like beads along the rivers Tollense and Großer Landgraben (Fig. 12). Interestingly, there are comparatively few megalithic graves on the Werder, with the exception of the area around the stream Großer Landgraben. There are two concentrations of megalithic graves near Neuenkirchen. About 3.6 km to the northeast, between Bassow and

---

3   Personal communication with Michael Müller, M.A. (FU Berlin), who is thanked at this point for the uncomplicated provision of the compilation of finds from the wider Neuenkirchen area.

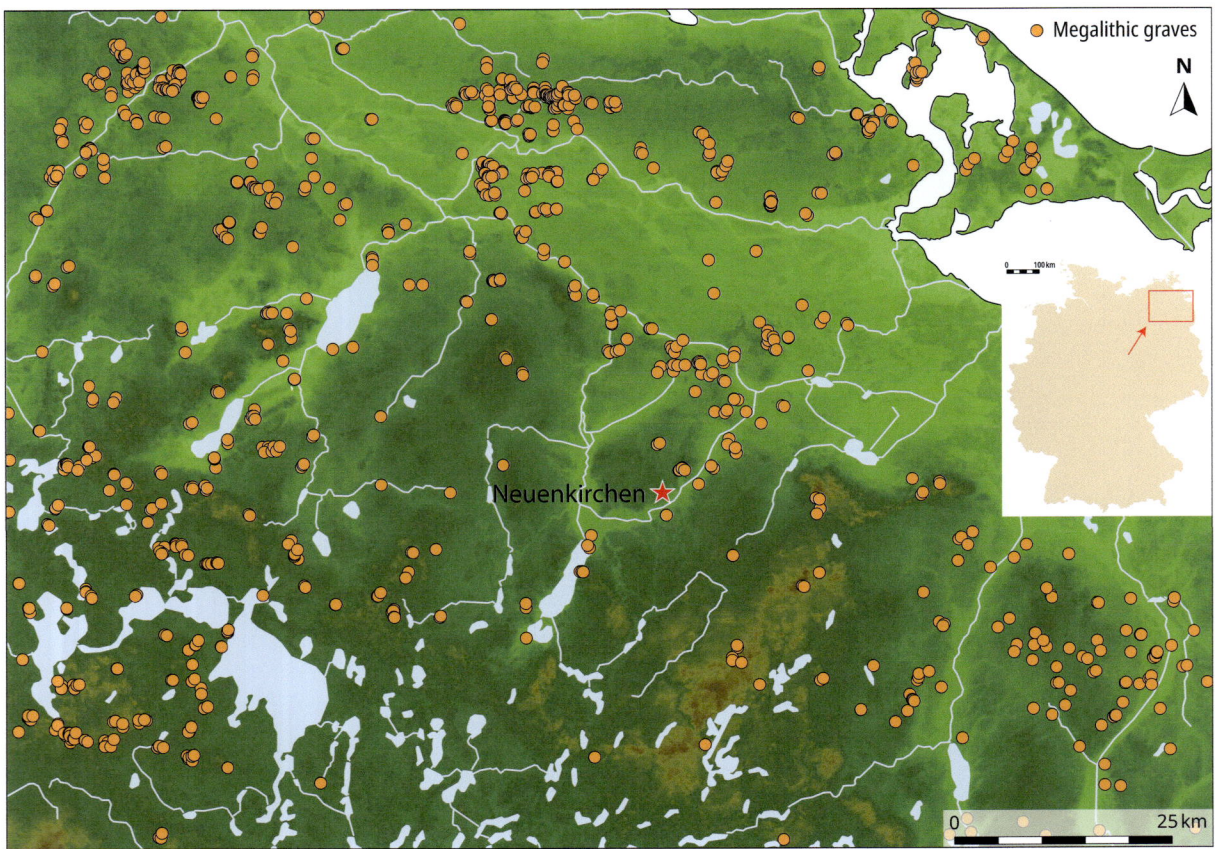

Fig. 12. Map of megalithic graves in the vicinity of Neuenkirchen (data basis G. Schafferer).

Stavenhagen, there is a group of five graves, and about 6 km to the north, between Rossow and Roggenhagen, there is a group of three megalithic graves. Both groups of graves are located on the highest point of the terrain. While on the Werder the graves are rather grouped and elevated, on the other side of the Datze valley, at the transition between the river valley and the rising terrain, they are again lined up along the river.

5.4 Summary of anthropogenic activities in the vicinity of Neuenkirchen

So far, a Funnel Beaker period occupation from the first half of the fourth millennium onwards (from c. 3800/3700 BCE) can be proven for the area around Neuenkirchen. The settlements of Warlin and Glasow, which were reliably dated by radiocarbon dates, indicate that settlement activities already took place at the beginning of the fourth millennium. The radiometric date from the settlement site of Carpin, which has so far been regarded with some scepticism by researchers due to the sample collection, fits seamlessly into these dates (cf. 5.2.3). The similarity of the house ground plan from Brunn with that from Glasow suggests a similar early date for the latter. Strikingly, the two larger settlement sites are located at the edge of the Werder (Brunn) and in the immediately adjacent area (Warlin), at the transition to the riverine fens of the Datze and the Großer Landgraben stream, respectively, while the majority of the higher moraine area, with a few exceptions, apparently remains settlement-free (cf. Fig. 8). It is remarkable that all known Funnel Beaker period house floor plans or post-built buildings from Mecklenburg-Western Pomerania are located within a radius of about 65 km around Neuenkirchen (Brunn c. 8 km;

Carpin c. 28 km; Jatznick c. 36 km; Gristow c. 64 km, Glasow c. 65 km). This radius also includes 14 of the 28 sites with copper artefacts dated to the Neolithic from Mecklenburg-Vorpommern. The archaeological evidence of the Funnel Beaker period settlement around Neuenkirchen is also reflected in the results of the palynological studies. They show a clearing of the forest across the early Neolithic landscape at the beginning of the fourth millennium BCE. The human activity detected in the pollen profiles points to small-scale cultivation, which fits well with the picture drawn by Müller (2017, 36 ff.) of a settlement structure characterised by individual farmsteads or small hamlets during the early phase of the development of North German settlement in the Neolithic. Thus, livestock farming with forest pasture and small-scale cereal cultivation can also be expected in the vicinity of Neuenkirchen from c. 3800 BCE onwards. Although there is currently still a lack of high-resolution pollen profiles in the study area, comparable to those available for Schleswig-Holstein and western Mecklenburg, the further development of the settlement landscape in eastern Mecklenburg-Western Pomerania presented by Müller (2017, 48 ff.) can be assumed. The human activities of the Early and Middle Neolithic can also be grasped, albeit sparsely, through the deposits from Neuenkirchen and Louisenhof. The numerous megalithic graves along the Tollense, Datze, and Großer Landgraben also indicate continued settlement in the younger Funnel Beaker period.

6. Finds and features of the hoard find from Neuenkirchen

6.1 Feature and artefact descriptions

In 1998, as part of the preliminary investigations for the construction of the A20 Baltic Sea motorway, evaluation trenches were dug using an excavator at the already-known site of Neuenkirchen No. 45. Following the planned route of the A20 motorway, the topsoil was removed and eight archaeologically-relevant features were uncovered. The site was heavily disturbed in parts by intensive agricultural use. The use of a subsoiler was partially visible down to a depth of 50 cm. The features were documented in drawings and their locations were measured. In the period from 3rd to 12th of May 1999, follow-up investigations were carried out to examine the recorded features in more detail.

A total of eight features were found during the excavation. These were three postholes and five pits. The postholes (features 1, 3, and 6) were free of finds with the exception of a few charcoal remains (features 1 and 3). The pits (features 4, 5, 7, and 8) were also free of finds except for a few charcoals remains (features 5 and 8) and a prehistoric pottery sherd (feature 8).

Feature No. 2 was an exception. The oval pit with grey-black, loamy backfill had a diameter of 60 cm and a preserved depth of 24 cm. The pit surface encountered in the planum was 61 cm below the excavation surface. The deposit of several copper objects was encountered directly below the planum; a spiral arm ring, two fragments of a band spiral, a dagger, a fragment of sheet metal, and a fragment of a flat axe. The objects were deposited in such a way that the spiral arm ring was aligned north-south and the remaining pieces were placed inside the spiral arm ring (Fig. 13-17).

About 50 cm north of the edge of the pit, the remains of a vessel were found in the trench profile. The vessel had already been half-destroyed by the mechanical excavator. The still-preserved upper edge of the vessel was 29 cm below the surface. Since the depth of the trench was 61 cm and no information about the original dimensions of the pit is available, it remains unclear to what extent there was a connection between the vessel and the hoard find. There is no photographic documentation available, therefore no conclusions can be drawn (Figs. 13 and 15).

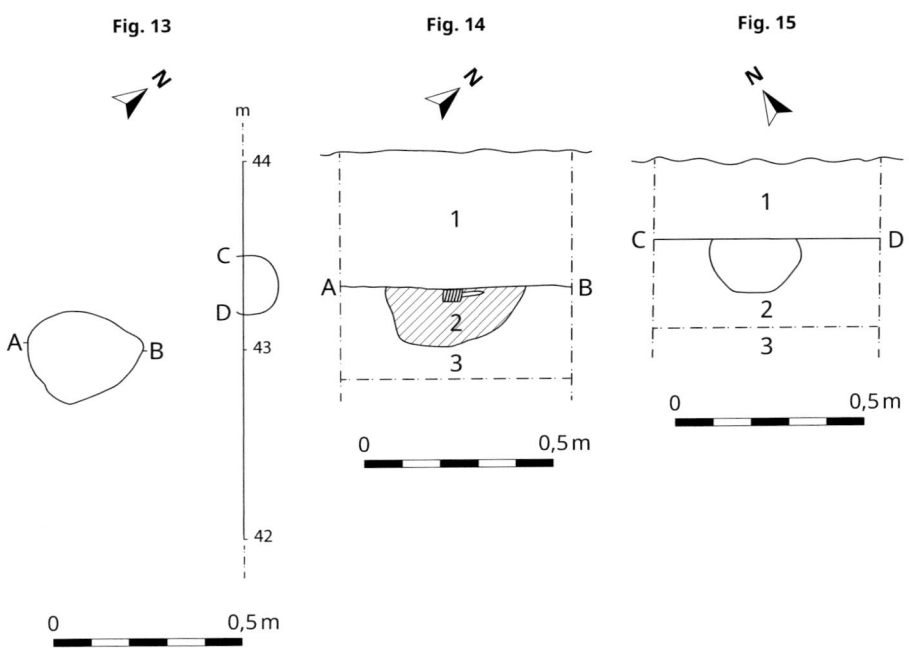

Fig. 13. Neuenkirchen, site No. 45: Feature No. 2, planum (drawing by V. Schmidt, digitised by H. Skorna).

Fig. 14. Neuenkirchen, site No. 45: Feature No. 2, pit profile A-B, 1. plough horizon; 2. pit fill; 3. the natural soil (drawing by V. Schmidt, digitised and modified by H. Skorna).

Fig. 15. Neuenkirchen, site No. 45: Feature No. 2, pit profile C-D: 1. plough horizon; 2. soil already excavated during the preliminary investigation; 3. the natural soil (drawing by V. Schmidt, digitised and altered by H. Skorna).

Fig. 16. Reconstructed arrangement of the Neuenkirchen hoard (Photo A. Heitmann, Kiel University).

6.1.1 Dagger (Plate 1)

The blade of the dagger, which can be regarded as a hilted dagger, is elongated and slightly triangular and has a weakly-pronounced but clearly visible midrib on one of the flat sides. On the other flat side a minimal bulge is visible only in the central area, which can be interpreted as a midrib. The slightly pronounced, yet clearly visible, midrib runs almost the entire length of the blade. At the distal end it is more difficult to recognise due to corrosion. At the lateral end, the midrib flattens somewhat and then merges into the midrib-less hilt area. The cross-section is semi-rhombic, with a

Fig. 17. Inventory of the Neuenkirchen hoard (Photo A. Heitmann, Kiel University).

hint of a slightly rhombic shape in the aforementioned middle section of the blade. The state of preservation of the cutting edges of the dagger varies greatly. What both have in common, however, is that where the original surface is preserved, the cutting edges are relatively thick and strongly rounded, resulting in a blunt blade. On the side which is less affected by corrosion, the preserved cutting edge is still about 10.5 cm long. The cutting edge runs nearly straight until almost the lateral end of the piece before it tapers strongly in the hilt area, and again where it transitions into the tang. The transition area from cutting edge to hilt to tang is also heavily affected by corrosion. The other side of the blade is in somewhat worse condition. It is only preserved to a length of about 6.3 cm. Towards the lateral end, at about the level where the midrib begins to flatten, the cutting edge is damaged or corroded and curves in a slight arc towards the tang. Towards the distal end, about 3 cm before more severe corrosion also begins on the opposing side, the cutting edge is badly damaged and curves in an almost crescent shape over a length of 2.2 cm. After that, the edge is heavily corroded on both sides. The grip tang of the dagger is broken off shortly after the transition to the blade. The hilt area, as well as the remaining tang with a rectangular cross-section, is bent over towards one of the flat sides. The overall length is still 16.6 cm; the dagger blade length is 16.2 cm and the remaining tang is thus 0.4 cm. The midrib-less hilt section still measures about 1 cm in length to the base of the tang. The greatest width measures 2.4 cm and the weight is 69g.

The dagger blade shows a smooth, dark green and brownish patina in the well-preserved half. The greenish patina layer lies above the brown one. In some places there are isolated, more corroded areas that are distinguished by light green patination. From about the halfway point, however, the piece is more corroded, so that on one side the material is strongly reduced. In the distal area, the surface is very uneven due to the heavy corrosion and only isolated small patches of the original smooth surface have survived

6.1.2 Flat axe (Plates 2a and 4c)

The flat axe, which was also deposited as a fragment in the form of a butt remnant, has a rectangular cross-section at the break edge and the butt. The narrow sides of the thick, straight butt are slightly rounded. In the cross-section, it can also be seen that the sides are slightly convex. Only under magnification does a very weakly pronounced ridge formation become apparent, which is almost invisible to the naked eye. According to the geometry of the axe fragment (L. 3.4 cm, max. W. 3.1 cm), it was originally a trapezoidal piece. The butt width is 2.4 cm, the neck thickness 0.6 cm, and the greatest thickness 1.5 cm. The weight is still 84g. The patina of the axe is mainly smooth and dark green. Some smaller areas show heavier corrosion, which is then light green in colour. This is often associated with smaller, round holes (pitting) in the surface.

6.1.3 Spiral arm ring (Plates 2b, d and 4a)

The spiral arm ring, which was still preserved in two fragments when the piece was recovered, is now present in three larger and five smaller pieces. The three larger fragments, consisting of three quarters of a turn, two turns and six turns, can be put together to form a larger piece on the basis of the partially fresh fractures. The five smaller fragments together represent one turn, although only two pieces can be fitted together to form about half of a turn on the basis of their fresh breaks. The remaining three fragments show only older breaks. It is no longer possible to determine whether the pieces belong together. The total number of turns can only be given as at least 9¾, as no clear end of the piece is recognisable due to the corrosion. The diameter is 5.3 to 5.6 cm, and the the copper band from which the arm ring was made is 0.5 cm in width with a flattened lenticular cross-section. The total weight is still 122g.

The patina is of dark and light green colour. In places, the surface of the coils has been so badly corroded that only 1 mm of the actual copper has survived. The surface of the inner sides is less affected by corrosion and mostly dark green and smooth. The outer surfaces in particular are sometimes heavily affected by corrosion. In these areas the patina is light green and very rough.

6.1.4 Band spiral (Plates 2c and 4b)

The band spiral was found in two fragments, each with nine turns and a length of 6.2 cm and 6.4 cm respectively. One piece already had 1½ turns broken off. It is unclear whether this was already the case in situ or if only happened during its recovery. Due to the partially very strong corrosion, the spiral has again broken several times, so that it is now fragmented into five pieces:

- 1. 6⅔ turns, L. 4.8 cm
- 2. 7 turns, L. 5.1 cm
- 3. 3 turns, L. 2.3 cm
- 4. approx. ⅔ of a turn
- 5. approx. ⅓ of a turn.

Fragments (1) and (2) each have a fresh broken edge that can be fitted together exactly, resulting in a spiral with 13⅔ turns and a length of 9.4 cm. At the same time, traces of glue from a restoration can be seen on fragment (2), on the coil after the modern break, suggesting that it was possible to assign the two fragments found in situ to a single band spiral.

The fragments (2) and (3) can no longer be easily put together, as the fragment (2) is only a few tenths of a millimetre thick in this area due to corrosion, and both fragments were probably only connected to each other by a narrow bar. However, that they do belong together can be determined by the fresh breakage edges, which suggest that the fragment broke off from one of the two originally found, larger pieces mentioned above. Fragments (4) and (5) together represent a turn, but without showing any connection to each other or to the other fragments. Altogether, it can be assumed that there was a single copper band spiral with at least 18 turns, but it had already been deposited in two pieces.

The total length of the piece is still preserved to 12 cm, the outer diameter is 0.8 cm, band thickness is 0.1-0.15 cm and the band width is 0.5-0.6 cm. The total weight is still 14g. The band cross-section is rectangular. The band is coiled into a spiral in such a way that a clear gap is visible between the individual turns (up to one millimetre). The gaps are partially filled by corrosion products and the turns are cemented together. As described above, the corrosion of the piece is very severe in some areas. In these sections the patina is light green in colour and very rough. The areas less affected by corrosion have a smooth, dark green patina.

6.1.5 Sheet metal fragment (Plates 2e and 4d)

The shape of the sheet metal fragment can be roughly described as triangular, but the tip is strongly rounded and the base slightly concave. The original, slightly bulging edge has been preserved at the base. The piece of sheet metal is somewhat convex overall. The width at the base is 1.3 cm, the height 1.3 cm, and the thickness between 0.15 and 0.2 cm. The weight is 1g. This fragment is not found in the original excavation documentation. It can be assumed that it came from the soil sample taken from the inside of the spiral ring. Numerous small copper particles and corrosion products can still be seen in this sample today.

6.1.6 Ceramic Vessel

The sherds found belong to a vessel with a flared rim (rim diameter 22 cm, base diameter about 10 cm). The ceramics have a very roughened surface and a coarse grain. At the time of writing, access to the vessel or its remains was not possible due to a relocation of the archive, so that the vessel is only roughly documented in a sketch (cf. Fig. 15).

7. Analysis of traces of manufacture and use

The analysis of traces stemming from manufacture and use on prehistoric copper-based metalwork is a rather young field within archaeology. While pioneering case studies like Kristiansen (1978) and Schauer (1979) paved the way for further research, early studies were, according to Dolfini and Crellin (2016, 79), characterised by non-specialist scholars, a lack of methodological sophistication (e.g. lack of experimental trials with replica objects) and eclectic approaches. A strict methodology was introduced by Kienlin and Ottaway (1998), who used a three-step approach in their work on flanged axes of the north-alpine region (field tests on replicas, dental casts of cutting edges, use of low power stereo-microscopes). Since then, a wide array of studies used this approach (with adaptations), studying use-wear on copper-based metalwork, especially weapons; advancing our knowledge and correcting old but firmly-believed interpretations. Chalcolithic and Early Bronze Age halberds, for example, were interpreted as ceremonial implements that had no practical application in fighting due to their supposed weak hafting and clumsiness (Ó Ríordáin 1937, 241; O'Kelly 1989, 164f.; Dolfini/Crellin 2016, 80). O'Flaherty (2007), for example, showed the usability of Early Bronze Age halberds by conducting experimental trials with replicas. Amongst others, Horn (2014) showed that the prehistoric halberds indeed show signs of extensive combat use. Using a similar approach, Molloy (2007; 2008; 2010; 2011) disproved the alleged division between Middle and Late Bronze Age swords, which were believed to be used in different fighting styles. Instead, the comparison of field-tested replicas and their prehistoric equivalents showed similar combat wear for both styles (cut/slash and thrust) in both time periods (Dolfini/Crellin 2016, 79). Further research from Horn and von Holstein (2017, 90 ff.) emphasised that the general properties of the material in combination with corrosion (especially within burial contexts), as well as the aftermath of plastic deformations and repairs, greatly diminish the observability of use-wear traces. This probably led to an under-identification of use-wear on prehistoric copper/copper alloy objects and has to be considered in this and future studies.

A comprehensive and more detailed overview of the research history, current problems, and a manifesto towards a more structured and formalised approach to metalwork wear analysis can be found in Dolfini and Crellin (2016).

7.1. Damage

Basically, a distinction can be made between damage and reworking (Horn 2014, 182 ff.). The classification is based on the cause of the trace left behind. Sáez and Lerma (2015) use a different classification based on the type of trace. They distinguish between the three groups 'plastic deformation', 'physical and chemical deformation', and 'added elements'. Most damage and reworking marks fall into the category of 'plastic deformation'. Both possibilities are understandable, but for the sake of clarity, the classification by Horn (2014) will be followed here. The following descriptions are each based on the work of Horn (2013, 3 ff.; 2014, 184, ff. and 209 ff.) and Sáez and Lerma (2015, 176 ff.), so that repeated references are dispensed with for the sake of readability.

7.1.1 Fracture

Two types of breakage can be distinguished: Force fracture is the result of a singular load. The type known as vibration fracture is brought about by multiple stresses where material fatigue occurs. Fractures may also result in plastic deformation of the piece.

7.1.2 Cracks

Like fractures, both repeated and sudden stress can lead to the formation of cracks, which are addressed as a precursor to fractures. However, cracks can also be triggered by the stress created in the material by corrosion.

7.1.3 Notches

Notches are v-shaped damage to the cutting edge or blade of an object caused by a brief application of force (single and powerful). The object must meet a similarly shaped counterpart of approximately the same hardness. Notches are usually associated with the visible displacement of material.

7.1.4 Dents

Dents are described as shallow, often arc-shaped, depressions in the material caused by a single sudden impact of force. However, high pressure exerted over a certain period of time is also possible.

7.1.5 Impact marks

Impact marks or traces are small, long oval to oval or round impressions. In the type of damage, they resemble notches, but are not located in the cutting area, rather on wider surfaces of the objects. The smaller dimensions of impact marks, compared to those of notches, are explained by the fact that a force is weakened more when it hits a wider surface.

7.1.6 Bending

Bending describes the deformation of an object or its parts. Depending on the strength, a distinction is made between 'bent over', 'deviated', or 'bent'. A section is described as bent over if it is at an angle of at least 90° from its original position. If the angle is less than 90°, the object is called bent. Only weak deformations, on the other hand, are called deviated. In the case of the strongest form of deformation, a constant application of force can be assumed, while the weakest variant is more likely to be due to short, possibly repetitive, impulses of force. Bending can be accompanied by dents, notches, and unfolding of the material.

7.1.7 Twisting

Twisting is described as deformation along the longitudinal axis of the artefact for which a high force is required. It is accompanied by the formation of cracks. This rare type of damage is often associated with intentional destruction, but can also be the result (in the case of a blade) of forcible removal of an object from a fixed position by means of a twisting movement (here specifically: Horn 2013, 13).

7.2 Reworking

7.2.1 Hammering, peening (*Dengeln*)

Hammering leaves marks that are mostly visible as shallow and wide dents in the material. They are sometimes found on the entire surface, individually or in groups, and can have different appearances. However, these traces can be of different origin, so that exact identification is often difficult. In some cases, it can also be proven that during repairs, already repaired imperfections were polished again. However, evidence of clear hammer marks also exists (Horn 2014, 195) (Fig. 18.3-4). As traces of peening, *i.e.* the sharpening of the cutting edge by driving it out with hammers, can only be identified with the naked eye on the basis of hammer marks in the cutting-edge area. Another possibility is to take X-ray images to visualise the thinning of the material that occurs during the peening process. Horn (2014, 196) shows the thinning of the material on a halberd blade where a haft plate was secondarily hammered out (Fig. 20.2).

7.2.2 Grinding, polishing, filing, whetting

Prehistoric grinding marks manifest themselves as patinated scratches, some of which are visible to the naked eye and distinguishable from scratches of other kinds. After casting, the objects had to be ground and sometimes polished. Traces of this treatment are unevenly distributed over the entire surface of the object. Traces of polishing are difficult to detect because they are often hidden by patina and are only detectable in corrosion-free areas (Sáez and Lerma 2015, 183). Scratch marks in the cutting area that are particularly close together and in the same direction indicate the sharpening or re-sharpening of an object. Horn (2014, Fig. 124) was able to demonstrate such machining marks on a number of halberds. Individual scratches that run irregularly over the surface, on the other hand, are probably the result of use, as Sáez and Lerma (2015, 176) were able to show with their experiments on Pamela points (*Pamela-Spitzen*). Careful repair of damage to halberd blades, such as notches, can be seen in arch-shaped, evenly-spaced flaws (Horn 2014, 196). Other traces of repair are secondary rivets as well as singular anomalies noted by Horn (*ibid.*, 194), which are interpreted as intentional nipping/chiselling of the material. Because of their irrelevance to the hoard find from Neuenkirchen, they will not be described here (for more details, see *ibid.*). Indirect indications of possible damage or reworking can be provided by the corrosion of the object. Areas where the material is weakened are penetrated by corrosion much more quickly and strongly. Such weakening' is caused, for example, by the aforementioned notches or cracks. Repair or re-sharpening work that leads to thinning of the material also makes it more susceptible to corrosion.

7.3 Addressing possible signs of use and manufacture on the Neuenkirchen hoard inventory

Several conspicuous features were noted on the dagger and the axe fragment respectively, which may provide clues as to the method of manufacture and the use of the objects.

7.3.1 Dagger

As already listed in the artefact description above, the grip tang is broken off just after the hilt. Evidence in the metal that would indicate a faulty casting, such as blowholes, is not evident. In addition, a part of the hilt has been bent along with the tang. Immediately below the tang, a compression of the material is visible in the hilt area (Fig. 18.1). Below this, a semi-circular anomaly is visible, which is characterised on the one hand by a differently coloured patina, and on the other hand partly by a depression of the material, which extends to the edge on the better-preserved side (Fig. 18.2). This conspicuous feature possibly represents an imprint of the hilt.

On this side of the blade, there are also traces of working, which manifest themselves as elongated and partly right-angled depressions in the material and are interpreted as hammer marks (Figs. 18.3 and 18.4). In addition, there are numerous patinated, shallow scratches on both sides of the blade, some of which are aligned and lying flat. In the cutting-edge area, such scratches are visible both longitudinally and transversely to the course of the cutting edge, where they partly overlap (Fig. 19.3). Both sides of the cutting edge show a partly wavy course (Fig. 19.2). Such deformations of the cutting edge indicate repaired defects or repaired damage (see above), but may also only represent irregular material removal through use.

Thanks to the kind support of Dr. med. Alexander Deisler (Schwerin), it was possible to carry out an X-ray examination of the Neuenkirchen dagger in his practice. While a first X-ray image failed because the sensitivity of the device was too high, it was possible to capture the dagger in a series of five images using an older model (Fig. 20.1). It can be seen that the object has a flawless cast throughout without blowholes or inclusions. Thinning of the material can be seen in the edge area, particularly at the distal end. In this section the blade is particularly affected by corrosion resulting in a loss of material. At the lateral end, the damage or stronger corrosion of the cutting-edge area is also visible in the X-ray image. Interestingly, in the area of the crescent-shaped indentation in the cutting-edge area, no thinning of the material is visible, as is the case in the more corroded areas. This section appears to be literally broken off.

Fig. 18. 1.-2. Detailed photographs of the hilt section of the dagger with displaced material and hilt imprint; 3.-4. Hammer marks on the dagger; 5. Hammer marks on halberd blade (1.-4. author's photographs with 50x magnification; 5. Horn 2014, 194, fig. 123a).

Fig. 19. 1. Ground dents and notches on a halberd blade; 2. Comparable dent on the dagger from Neuenkirchen; 3. Possible grinding marks on the dagger from Neuenkirchen (1 Horn 2014, 199, fig. 128c1; 2-3 author's photographs with 60x magnification).

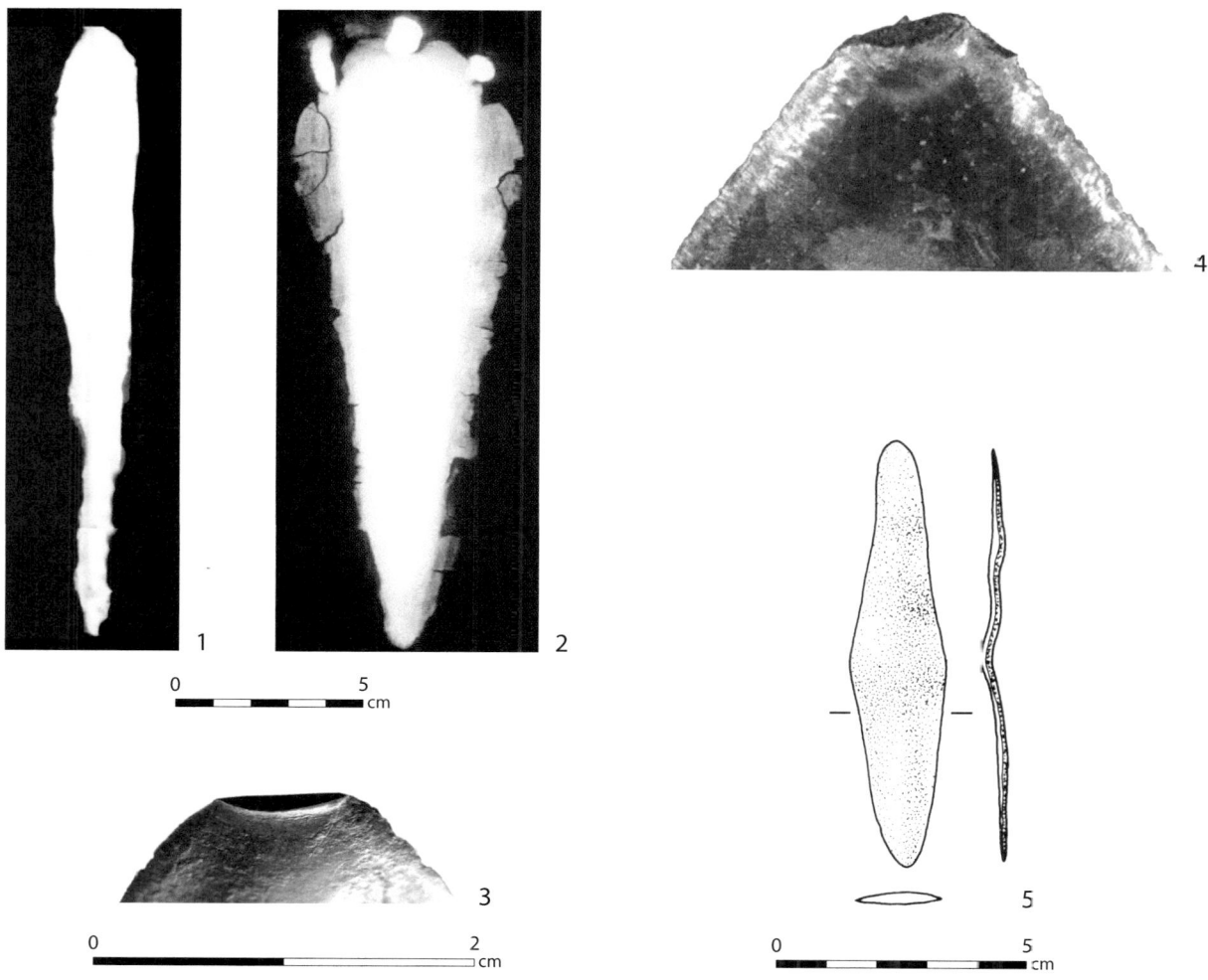

Fig. 20. 1. Radiographic image of the dagger from Neuenkirchen; 2. Radiograph of a halberd blade with thinned cutting edge; 3. Damaged tip of a halberd from Scotland; 4. Experimentally-induced damage to a dagger tip; 5. Damaged dagger from Pecica (1. author's image; 2. Horn 2014, 194, Fig 123c; 3. Horn 2014, 192, Fig 119a; 4. Sáez/Lerma 2015, Fig 9.2-5 a-b); 5. Vajsov 1993, 123, Fig 19.1).

7.3.1.1 Interpretation of the anomalies found

For the production of the dagger, a casting in either an open mould or in a closed mould is possible. If the latter were the case, however, the recess for the central rib in the mould would have been very small. The hammer marks on parts of the blade would then be interpreted as the middle rib having been hammered flat in this area. It seems much more plausible, however, that it was cast in a single-shell, open mould. With the dagger blade thus produced, an attempt was then made to work out a middle rib on the flat side by means of hammering. Obviously, this was only partially successful or not completed. The scratches on the surface can be interpreted as traces of grinding after the cast. The mutually-overlapping transverse and longitudinal scratches and grinding marks indicate that the cutting edge was worked. One possible interpretation is the sharpening or re-sharpening of the cutting edge, another is processing after casting or intentional blunting/rounding. All the aforementioned grinding marks are patinated, so that they must be traces of processing from prehistoric times (Horn 2014, 193). The same applies to the breakage at the hilt area, so that it can be assumed that damage to the handle must also have taken place before the dagger was deposited. The fact that part of the hilt is also bent indicates that the former grip was still attached to the tang. Such plastic deformations of an object indicate a prolonged application of force (see above). Since the hilt is much wider than the tang, it can be assumed that a considerable amount of force was applied. This is also indicated by the discolouration and the displaced material in the hilt area. In the author's opinion, this damage created a negative impression of the handle on the hilt (Fig. 18.2). In addition, the force has weakened the material in the hilt area and made it more susceptible to corrosion. This can be seen in the greenish patina and pitting in this area. The stabilising effect of the midrib is also clearly visible; only in the area where it is no longer visible is the dagger blade also bent.

The heavily-corroded area at the distal end, the crescent-shaped loss of material at the bottom, and the damage at the lateral end of the blade can only be interpreted to a limited extent. The severe corrosion may indicate increased stress in the material in these areas. As mentioned several times, heavily-stressed areas are much more susceptible due to cracks in the material and general material fatigue. Thus, the corrosion of the artefact provides only limited and indirect evidence of use.

The traces found paint the picture of a dagger that may have been heavily used before it was deposited, as evidenced by possible worn notches, traces of grinding, and corrosion induced by stress. While the aforementioned marks can plausibly be explained by use, this is not readily possible for the broken grip tang and the bent hilt area. Such a damage pattern would be expected if the dagger hit a harder surface during a thrusting or stabbing movement. In this case, however, a compression of the dagger tip would also have to be recognisable. Since the original tip of the dagger has not survived, it remains unclear to what extent this was the case. In addition to the compression, a deformation of the entire distal area would be expected from such a violent impact (Fig. 20.3-5). Another damage pattern that such a scenario may entail is an undulating bending of the dagger blade along its longitudinal axis. A Copper Age dagger with such a deformation, but without a stabilising midrib, is known from Pecica, Romania (Vajsov 1993, 123) (Fig. 20.5). The dagger from Neuenkirchen shows none of the damage patterns that would result in the scenario described above. Even if the original tip of the dagger is not preserved and a stabilising midrib is present, such a fracture with bending would at least have to show some deformation of the blade in the distal area. Despite the visible traces of the application of a strong force at the lateral end, such a deformation of the blade is not visible, and therefore it must be assumed that the tang was intentionally broken off.

7.3.2 Flat axe

It was only during the analysis of the use marks that a shallow, very faint flange formation was noticed on the piece (Fig. 21.1-2). Due to this minimal formation, it cannot be ruled out that it was caused by the pressure and movement of the axe blade in the haft or that it was an unintentional product of the casting process. A conspicuous feature of the axe is a line on the fracture surface, which consists of displaced material. It runs parallel to the fracture edges and is particularly visible in the central area (Fig. 21.3-4). Two further peculiarities are the two indentations in the butt area. A long oval indentation of the material can be seen on one side of the blade (Fig. 21.5). The dimensions are approx. 1.2 cm x 0.7 cm. On the opposing side, directly opposite, there is a slight indentation in the butt, which extends superficially about 0.5 cm onto the axe body (Fig. 22.1). In this area, numerous smaller irregular depressions or damage are noticeable. On the same side of the axe blade, another drop-shaped indentation is visible. It is located at approximately the same height as its counterpart, but in an inverted position. The dent is much flatter and smaller (approx. 0.5 cm x 0.2 cm) and can only be seen clearly in changing light conditions (Fig. 21.6). Both sides of the axe partly show clearly visible scratches running parallel to, as well as along, the edges of the blade. However, isolated scratches also

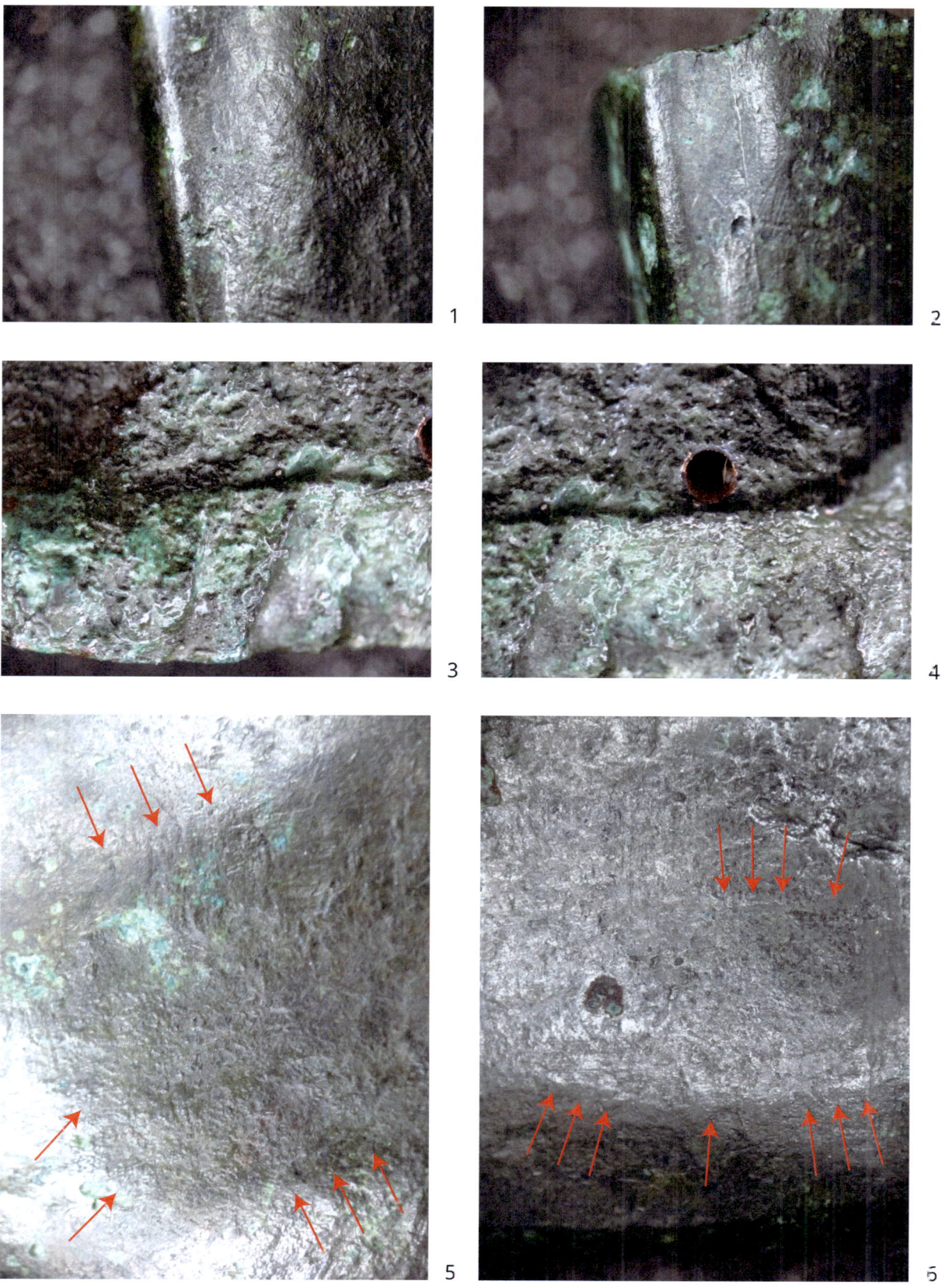

Fig. 21. Detailed images of the flat axe from Neuenkirchen: 1.-2. Indicated marginal ridges; 3.-4. Raised material on the fracture surface; 5.-6. Dents on the sides of the blade (1.-5. author's images, 60x magnification).

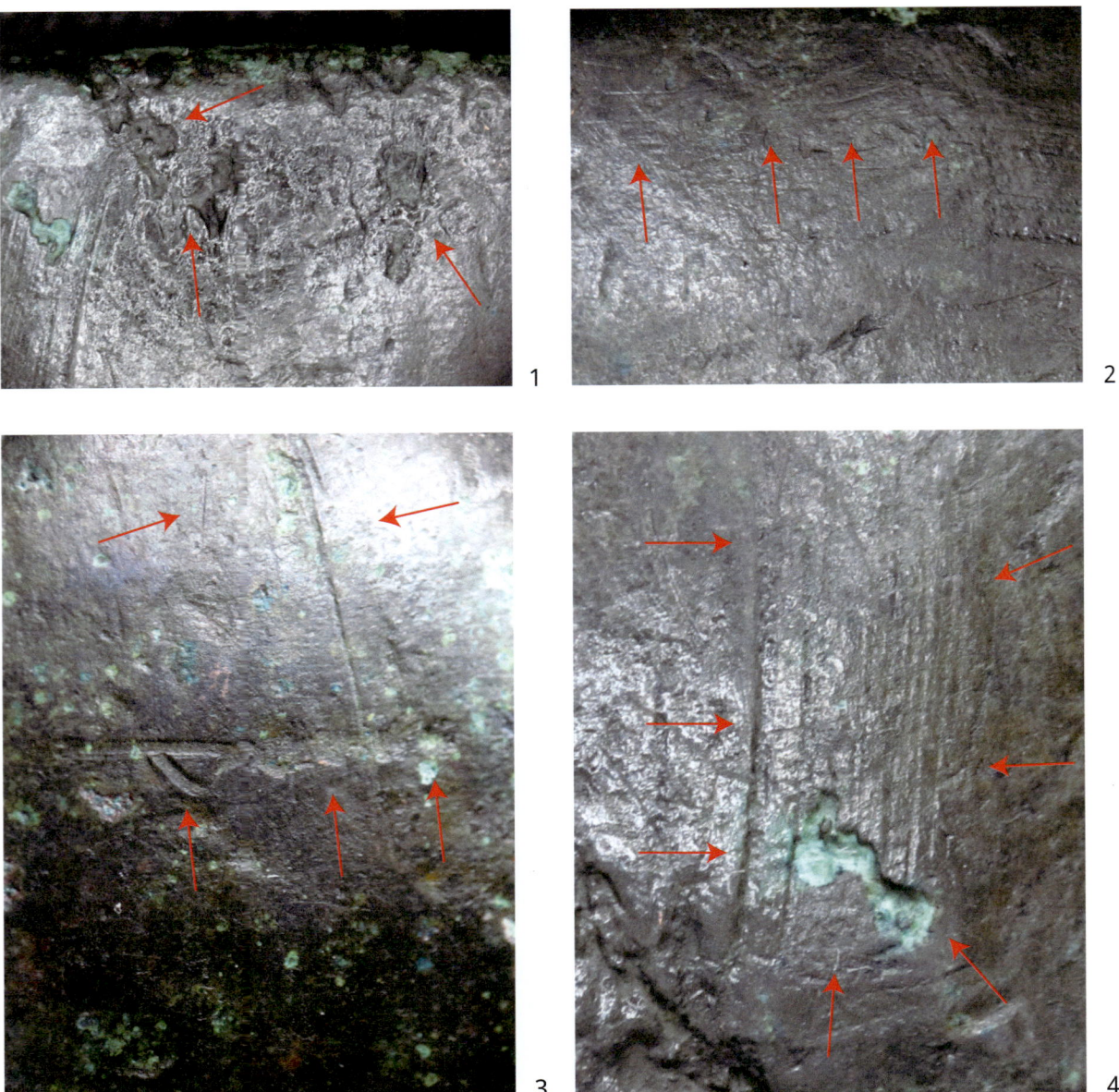

Fig. 22. Detailed images of the flat axe from Neuenkirchen: 1. Damage to the butt area; 2.-3. Scratch and grind marks; 4. Ground casting defect (1.-4. author's images, 60x magnification).

run diagonally across the axe body (Fig. 22.2-3). Directly on the surface of the butt, two long oval, grain-like indentations are visible (L. 3 mm, W. 1 mm, and L. 2 mm, W. 0.5 mm, respectively) (Fig. 23.1) In addition, the entire surface shows minor damage as well as larger and smaller scratches. This is accompanied by light green patina formation which is otherwise dark green, especially at the edges.

Fig. 23. 1. Impact marks on the neck area of the flat axe from Neuenkirchen; 2. Comparable damage on a halberd blade (1. author's image; 2. Horn 2014, 186, fig. 116b).

7.3.2.1 Interpretation of the anomalies found

The line in the flat axe cross-section described above indicates a violent fracture of the object. The lack of signs of compression, as well as the aforementioned line, indicate a very sudden and strong force of impact (personal communication with Dipl. Ing (FH) Kay Rath, Institute for Material Science, Kiel University). According to Horn (2014, 189), dents such as those found on both sides of the axe are often the result of pulse-like forces, but they can also be the result of pressure maintained over a longer period of time. The grain-like small dents located directly on the neck surface look very similar to the marks on Early Bronze Age halberds, which Horn (*ibid.*) refers to as impact marks. The numerous scratches on the sides of the axe blade and directly on the butt can be of various origins. The smaller, closely spaced scratches, which also run parallel to each other, are probably — as in the case of the dagger — traces of grinding, which originate from processing after casting or from grinding carried out at a later time. The somewhat coarser and deeper scratches, which run parallel to the edges of the track, could possibly be caused by the movement of the axe blade in the hilt. In this case, either the material of the haft itself or sand and/or small stones that got between the axe and the haft during manufacture are responsible. The same could be true for the two small impact marks directly on the neck mentioned above. However, the author is not aware of a detailed study that deals with signs of use caused by the haft; as such, no adequate comparisons can be made. The scratches could also be rough grinding marks. One section of the neck area in particular has partially coarser scratches above a spot of minor material loss, which is marked by a light green patina. It is possible that there was an unevenness in the casting here which was repaired in this way (Fig. 22.4).

In the author's opinion, the traces encountered indicate that the breakage of the axe did not occur during a normal process of use. Arguments for this assumption are, on the one hand, the absence of recognisable casting defects in the fracture. On the other hand, the dents on the flat sides of the axe are either an indication that the axe was fixed at these points, possibly by wedging it into a gap of some kind, or are signs of impact. In the former case, the massive impact of force, as evidenced by the fracture line described above, would have had to have occurred on the cutting-edge area and caused the axe to break apart. In the second case, the axe would have to have been fixed in the missing area and broken by powerful blows against the neck. However, if the axe body had been directly impacted, much more pronounced dents would be expected. A possible explanation would be that the axe body had been indirectly impacted, for example by a piece of wood being placed on it and force being applied to it. The further damage in the butt area also indicates the application of force, which in the author's opinion would not be expected if the axe had broken during use. This is supported by the only find of a shafted copper flat axe, which was found with the glacier mummy from Hauslabjoch (Klassen 2000, 278). The flanged axe is only half visible and is so deeply embedded in the shaft that such a breakage during use is highly unlikely.

In the meantime, after the initial version of this study, new crucial research regarding metalwork and the deliberate destruction of copper (alloy) objects was published (in particular, Knight 2017, Kuijpers 2019, Knight 2021 & 2022). These studies, among others, describe the phenomomen of 'hot-short' visible in the archaeological record. Hot-short means that the metal is under under great thermal stress and little force needs to be applied to cause the metal to snap (Kuijpers 2019, 127). This can, for example, happen accidentally during the production process when the temperature is too high during annealing the metal, but can also be done on purpose. The temperature of copper alloys during the annealing process can be determined by the colour of the metal and the furnace (*ibid.*, 122). The risk for hot shorts rises as the metal (tin bronze) changes from cherry, red to yellowish in colour.This translates to high temperatures (600–1000°C) (*ibid.*). At higher temperatures (yellowish colour of the heated tin-bronze), a slight touch to the material is enough to cause a fracture (*ibid.*). Important for the interpretation for the flat axe of Neuenkirchen is the fact that hot short results in a sharp and clean fracture. Together with the indentation (Fig. 21.5), which can be interpreted as hammer blow, a deliberate fracturing using hot-shorting (i.e., heating and striking as in Knight 2022, 158) is the most likely scenario for the flat axe from Neuenkirchen. Knight (*ibid.*) rightfully points out that this suggests the presence of a metalworker with sound knowledge about the properties of the material, as well as the necessary understanding about heating and striking of (in his case) bronze objects. If one follows the proposed dating of the Neuenkirchen hoard (cf. 10.8) this knowledge might have been present far earlier than previously expected.

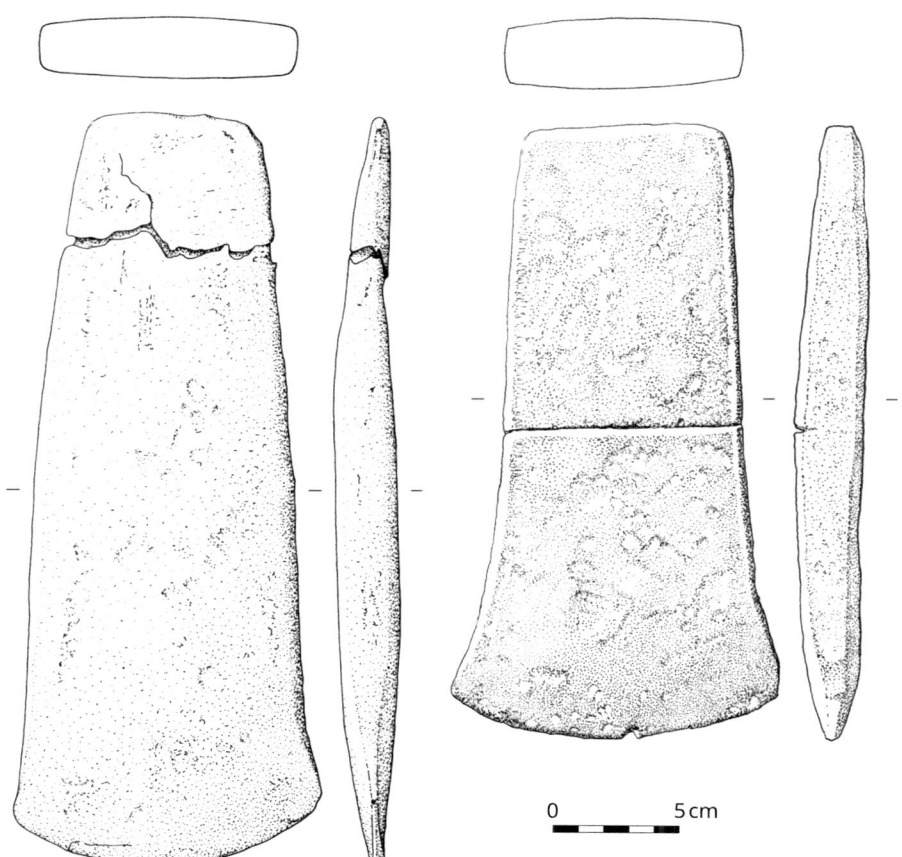

0   5 cm

Fig. 24. Damaged axes from the Funnel Beaker North Group: South Funen (left); Denmark, no specific site (right) (Klassen 2000, pl. 4.19; pl. 7.28).

From the flat axe inventory of the early copper finds in the area of the Funnel Beaker Societies, several examples of broken or partially broken axes are known. The piece from South Funen (Fig. 24) and a piece from an unknown site in Denmark are representative examples, as they show different traces of destruction. The axe from South Funen is broken at the butt and shows a bend along the longitudinal axis on both fragments. In addition, a bulging of the material on the side to which the neck is bent can be observed at the edge of the break. Such a bulge is to be expected with prolonged pressure (Horn 2012, 189). With repeated application of pressure in combination with a change of direction, such a bulge is to be expected on both sides of the fracture (personal communication, Dipl. Ing (FH) Kay Rath, Institute for Material Science, Kiel University). This kind of breakage is also, to a lesser extent, recogniseable on the flat axe from Ettrup (Denmark) (Klassen 2000, pl. 3.12).

The axe from an unknown site in Denmark, on the other hand, has an indentation across the entire body of the axe, which occurred during the prehistoric period (Fig. 24). In Klassen's catalogue (2000, No. 28) the damage is cited as 'sawn'. It is possible, however, that the furrow, several millimetres deep, was also caused by the use of a chisel. In addition, the axe is slightly bent lengthwise. In cross-section, the indentation is very clearly visible. The traces can be interpreted as an attempt to weaken the material at one point and then to break at this point by bending or hammering. Such an attempt should, therefore, also be possible to detect on other objects by means of a corresponding notch and the bent fragments.

The flat axe from Neuenkirchen has neither the characteristics of the flat axe from South Funen nor those of the flat axe found at the unknown site in Denmark. Thus, one of the hypotheses described above can be assumed for the origin of the fracture with hot-shorting being the most likely scenario. Klassen (2000, 278) agrees with the assessment that the axes must have been in an unhafted condition at the time of the

Fig. 25. Enlarged view of one turn of the spiral arm ring (author's photograph, 60x magnification).

damage. Similar signs of breakage are visible on two flat axes from the largest hoard find of the northern TRB group in Bygholm (Denmark). Two of the four flat axes show a circumferential crack roughly at middle, but are not completely broken. On one of the flat axes (Fig. 72, middle) this crack is more pronounced than on the other (Fig. 72, right corner). Both specimens show no signs of bending. The same is true for the depot from Lackalända (Sweden), where both flat axes were completely broken in two pieces but without showing any signs of bending (Klassen 2000, pl. 27.100 A+B). Therefore, attempts and successful attempts at breaking flat axes, possibly using hot-shorting as a method, are only known from multi-piece depositions, and only in the case of the hoard from Neuenkirchen was just one fragment deposisted. Interesting to note is that most damaged or broken flat axes are known from the rare multi-piece depositions (5) while from single piece depositions, which represent the majority of all copper finds, only four cases are known.

7.3.3 Spiral arm ring

The wire of the spiral ring has a flattened lenticular or D-shaped cross-section, with the flattened side on the inside. However, on some turns an edge is visible on the inner surface (Fig. 25). In addition, the inner surfaces of the turns appear very smooth in places.

According to Lorenzen (1967), the cross-section is transferred to the wire by means of a template; a die (bead or a profiled channel made of wood or another material). It seems unlikely that different profiles were used on the same piece. Especially since pieces with changing profiles do not appear in the literature known to the author. The aforementioned edges could therefore be the result of material abrasion caused by continuous wear.

8. X-ray fluorescence and lead isotope analyses

Copper was, and is, an attractive material for prehistoric and modern people. It is characterised by high electrical and thermal conductivity and has good mechanical properties at low, normal, and slightly elevated temperatures (Tuck et. al., 2010, 1938 ff.). Due to their good resistance to corrosion, prehistoric copper artefacts have been preserved in various environments over the millennia, in some cases excellently.

In the course of processing the hoard find, Dr. Robert Lehmann, formerly at the Institute for Inorganic Chemistry at the University of Hannover, was to carry out extensive geochemical investigations on the metal of the artefacts from Neuenkirchen. The results obtained by means of X-ray fluorescence analyses and the investigation of the lead isotope ratios were intended to enable, among other things, a discussion on the origin of the objects. At the same time, the State Office for Culture and Monument Preservation of Mecklenburg-Western Pomerania, the Brandenburg State Office for Monument Preservation, and the Stralsund Museum provided a large part of the Neolithic copper objects from Mecklenburg-Western Pomerania, as well as some objects from Brandenburg, for the determination of the lead isotope ratios. Unfortunately, access to these data and results was not possible in the course of the original thesis, nor prior to the publication of this study. However, in order to at least gain an insight into the trace element composition of the individual copper objects of the hoard find, it was possible to carry out initial X-ray fluorescence analyses with a portable ED-XRFA device thanks to the support of the Romano-Germanic Commission of the German Archaeological Institute. Following the submission of the master's thesis, lead isotope and X-ray fluorescence analyses were financed by the Institute of Pre- and Protohistory at Kiel University and carried out by the Curt-Engelhorn-Zentrum Archäometrie gGmbH. In the following, the focus is initially on the methodology and results of the analyses carried out by the author. The laboratory results of the X-ray fluorescence analysis, which are only now available, will be integrated in the presentation of results and finally discussed in consideration of the results of the lead isotope analysis.

8.1 History of research on chemical metallurgical analyses in archaeology

Chemical analyses of metal objects played a role early on in archaeological research. The first quantitative analyses on archaeological artefacts were already carried out by the Berlin chemist M. H. Klaproth (1763-1817) (Pernicka 1990, 64). As early as the last third of the 19th century, attempts were made to use metal analyses not only to get closer to the dating of objects, but also to determine their origin. For this purpose, ore analyses from the deposits were compared with those of the objects (Klassen 2000, 58). The first comprehensive and systematic works in this field were done by H. Otto and W. Witter (1952), as well as R. Pittoni (1957), who placed special emphasis on the mineralogical and geochemical aspects of determining the origin (Pernicka 1990, 66). From 1954 onwards, the publication of the more than 22,000 analyses obtained within the framework of the Stuttgart Metal Analysis Project 'Studies on the Beginnings of Metallurgy' (SAM for short) began. Optical emission spectrometry (OES) was used for these investigations, which today has been largely replaced by mass spectrometry with inductively coupled plasma (ICP-MS) as excitation (Pernicka 1990, 1979). Neutron activation analysis (NAA) and wavelength dispersive X-ray fluorescence analysis (WD-XRFA) became available as further analytical methods from the 1950s, and energy dispersive X-ray fluorescence analysis (ED-XRFA) from the 1970s. As the miniaturisation of the X-ray tube progressed, portable versions for ED-XRFA were developed, enabling flexible use (Helfert/Böhme 2010, 12 f.). Primarily intended for material control in industry, these devices increasingly found their way into archaeometry from the 2000s onwards. For some years now, the possible uses and applicability of this mobile variant have been intensively discussed, especially in German research (Helfert 2013, 15 ff.). The focus here is on the quality and reliability compared to conventional, laboratory-based methods such as NAA and ICP-MS. However, numerous case studies on test series of ceramic and metal artefacts, as well as soil samples, certainly indicate the usability (*ibid.*, Gauss *et al.* 2013, 2942, Orfanou and Rehren 2015, 387 ff.).

8.2 Functionality of X-ray fluorescence analysis

The P-ED-XRFA (Hereinafter referred to as pXRF) used for our own measurements is a non-destructive measurement method that offers several advantages for archaeological work. On the one hand, the investigations can be carried out independently of location and laboratory (Helfert/Böhme 2010, 13), so that the objects do not necessarily have to be borrowed. On the other hand, the non-destructive nature of the examinations is more attractive for, among others, museums that are concerned about the integrity of their holdings. In addition, the elimination of extensive sample preparation, which is not necessarily required, makes it possible to carry out a large number of relatively inexpensive analyses in a short amount of time. The comparatively short duration of an analysis also puts the scientist in a position to decide quickly whether an object is at all suitable for possible further sampling and more detailed investigation. For example, simply speaking, the measurement result 'tin bronze' would disqualify an object for a study on Neolithic copper artefacts.

The basic operating principle of the method is based on using an X-ray photon of sufficient energy to release an electron from the inner shell of the electron shell of an atom of the material. In an effort to achieve as stable a state as possible, an electron from the next higher shell jumps onto this, now free, shell. The energy emitted during this change is called fluorescence radiation or primary radiation, which is specific for each element and thus an X-ray fluorescence spectrum of all elements of the object is generated (Helfert/Böhme 2010, 13). In principle, the radiation generated by the X-ray tube must be more highly energised than the fluorescence radiation of an element to be produced, otherwise the electron transitions will not be excited. Similarly, if the excitation energy is greatly excessive, no electron transitions will be excited if the energy level of the element is significantly lower (Hahn-Weinheimer *et al.* 1995, 11). To determine the different energy levels, the analyser uses the filters Main Range (M), Low Range (L), High Range (H), Light Range (Li).

In an energy-dispersive XRF device, the X-ray fluorescence radiation emitted by the sample is detected by a detector. The Niton XL3T 900 used for the analysis uses a silicon drift detector (Geometrically Optimised Large Area Drift Detector, GOLDD for short), which is distinguished from conventional Si-PIN diodes by, among other things, significantly shorter measurement times and improved light element detection (Helfert/Böhme 2010, 15). The incoming fluorescence radiation triggers the formation of electron-hole pairs in the aforementioned detector, the number of which is proportional to the energy of an X-ray quantum (*ibid.*). The device simultaneously measures the energy of the individual X-ray quantum as well as the number of the same. Thus, the chemical elements (qualitative analysis) and their concentration in the sample (quantitative analysis) are determined.

8.3 Limits and difficulties

With an excitation voltage of up to 50 kV, which corresponds to the voltage of stationary instruments, as well as the primary beam filters mentioned above, the modern handheld instruments are able to detect elements from magnesium (Z = 12) to uranium (Z = 92). In principle, however, light elements are more difficult to detect. As the atomic number decreases, so does the emitted fluorescence radiation and thus its energy, which in turn is absorbed more strongly in the air and in the windows of both the entrance and the detector. These effects are counteracted, among other things, by rinsing the measuring head (see Helfert/Böhme 2010, 14 f.).

The sensitivity of the devices used must also be considered. A distinction is made between the 'Limit of Detection' (LOD) and the 'Limit of Quantification' (LOQ). The detection limit indicates the concentrations up to which an element can be detected in a sample. Peak overlaps, especially in complex samples, can worsen the detection limit. For the elements Mg, Al, Si, and P, the sample geometry and the handling of the instrument also have a significant influence. The analytical determination limit indicates the concentration above which the quantitative determination of an element can be considered reliable. In the case of the instrument used here, it is approximately 3.3 times the detection limit (*ibid.*, 15 f., Tab. 1).

8.4 Information depths and patina

A very important role for the evaluation of XRF data of metal objects is played by the depth of information and the closely-related influence of patina on the measurement results. The depth of the element information does not correspond to the penetration depth of the X-ray radiation. Thus, the assumption that the higher the power of the X-ray tube, the higher the penetration depth, and the higher the depth of information is not correct (Helfert/Böhme 2010, 16 ff.). The decisive factor is that the emitted energy reaches the detector. Since the radiation is subject to absorption on the way to the detector, and this in turn depends on the strength of the energy, each element has a specific information depth. Light elements have only a low information depth due to their low emitted fluorescence radiation when excited. With increasing atomic number, the information depth also increases. (For absorption see Hahn-Weinheimer *et al.* (1995, 15 ff.), for a table on the information depth of elements see Helfert/Böhme (2010, 17, Tab. 2).

When evaluating the results obtained by P-ED-XRF, an understanding of the influence of corrosion on copper artefacts is particularly necessary. The term patina is generally used to refer to the corrosion layer(s) that, if still present, surround the actual metal core of the object. Corrosion (from the Latin corrodere: to decompose, to eat away) is the localised reaction of a material with the substances of the media surrounding it (Tostmann 2001, 10). In the course of this reaction, a material transport occurs, which results in a material removal at the original surface. In the most common type of corrosion, external corrosion, the material oxidises and the corrosion product is deposited on the surface or dissolves in the form of ions in the medium (*ibid.* 10 ff.; for further information on corrosion processes in general, see *ibid.*; Kunze 2001, 77 ff. and Richardson et. al. 2010). In contact with air, copper initially forms a thin layer that can consist of copper oxides (I + II) as well as the oxides of alloying or trace elements and copper sulphide (Cronyn 1990, 216 ff.). If the object reaches the ground, this type of patina initially slows down the corrosion, which, however, progresses in a moist and oxygen-rich environment and forms a compact layer consisting mainly of red/brown copper(I) oxide ($Cu2O$). The corrosion penetrates the surface along the boundaries of the metal crystals (intergranular corrosion) (Fig. 26). In the further course, the dissolved copper migrates through the aforementioned layer and forms an additional, secondary layer of $Cu2O$ above it. This reacts with other elements in the surrounding soil to form a third, irregular crust consisting of copper carbonates (malachites: $CuCO3$ $Cu(OH)2$ or azurites: 2 $CuCO3$ $Cu(OH)2$) (*ibid.*). In addition, elements of the corrosive environment (mainly O, Si, P, Al, Fe, Ca, and Cl) also settle in it (Robbiola *et al.* 1998, 2091). If the corrosion continues, the dissolved copper either accumulates in the inner copper oxide layer or migrates further into the outer crust to form more copper carbonates there. This process is accelerated by chloride ions that penetrate the protective copper oxide layer and stimulate corrosion there. Nantokite (copper(I) chloride ($CuCl$)) is formed, which reacts with water to form further $Cu2O$ (Cronyn 1990, 216 ff.). If the chloride content in the surrounding soil is high, the corrosion can progress so quickly that the growing corrosion layer is so porous that water and oxygen can penetrate and react with the nantokite to form paratacamite. The reaction is so fast that no compact crystalline structure is formed, but a non-adherent, powder-like paratacamite. The cohesive patina layers that form in less chloride-containing environments and slow down corrosion cannot be formed and the artefact fades much faster (*ibid.*). In addition to the formation of the patina layers, corrosion phenomena such as pitting (Tostmann 2001, 7) and corrosion pustules with copper chlorides underneath can still occur (Scott 2002, 8). Pitting may also be caused by microorganisms that live in the soil and use copper as a nutrient, among other things (Tostmann 2001, 104).

The formation of natural patina layers on archaeological bronzes has been dealt with in detail by Robbiola *et al.* (1998) and Robbiola and Portier (2006). The three-layered patina structure described above corresponds with the patina type II postulated there for copper-tin alloys (Figs. 26-27). In contrast to type II, type I is only characterised by a two-layer structure. The outer layer contains comparatively little copper, but significantly higher proportions of tin, as well as chemical compounds from the surrounding soil, such as silicates, carbonates, and sulphides. Crucial for the analyses carried out in this work is the finding that, in addition to tin, trace elements such as arsenic and nickel also accumulate in the patina layers (Robbiola 1998, 2096). For arsenic bronzes, Constantinides *et al.* (2002, 93 ff.) were able to prove that arsenic accumulates in the inner layer of the patina (type II according to Robbiola). The values in the middle and the outer layer are also higher than in the actual alloy. Likewise, antimony and lead (Orfanu/Rehren 2015, 392 ff.), as well as silver (Rehren and Prange 1998, 193 ff.), seem to accumulate in the patina. The study by Mödlinger and Piccardo (2013) also concludes that the trace elements contained in the metal (Ag, As, Ni, Pb) accumulate in the patina. The presence of the elements in the corrosion layers is a sure indicator of their presence in the original metal (*ibid.* 1078 f.). In their investigations, the tin content in the patina was up to ten times higher than in the actual object (*ibid.*).

The problem that trace elements can accumulate in the patina, making it difficult to draw conclusions about the original alloy or composition of the metal by means of XRF analyses of the surface, has long been the subject of research discussion (*e.g.*

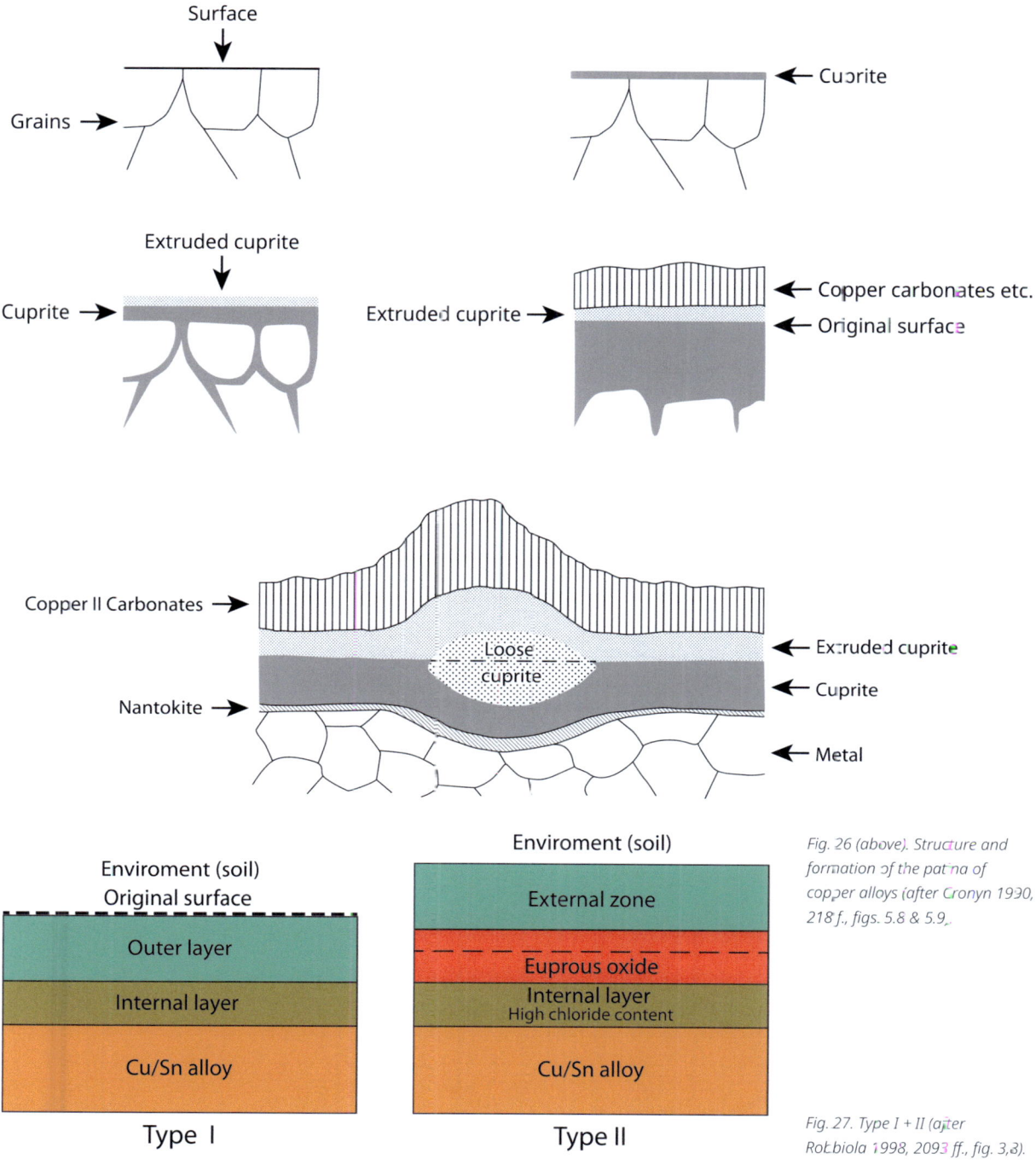

Surface

Grains →

Cuprite →

← Cuprite

Extruded cuprite

Extruded cuprite →

← Copper carbonates etc.
← Original surface

Copper II Carbonates →

Loose cuprite

← Extruded cuprite

Nantokite →

← Cuprite

← Metal

Fig. 26 (above). Structure and formation of the patina of copper alloys (after Cronyn 1990, 218 f., figs. 5.8 & 5.9).

Enviroment (soil)
Original surface

Outer layer

Internal layer

Cu/Sn alloy

Type I

Enviroment (soil)

External zone

Euprous oxide

Internal layer
High chloride content

Cu/Sn alloy

Type II

Fig. 27. Type I + II (after Robbiola 1998, 2093 ff., fig. 3,8).

Hall 1961 and Zwicker *et al.* 1979). In a case study by Busch (1996, 2 ff.), for example, the objects sometimes show striking differences between the measured values of the trace element concentrations in the patina and the actual metal. However, in interpreting his results he does not consider the different behaviour of the individual elements during the corrosion process and paints a rather pessimistic picture of the knowledge gained from surface analyses. So far, there is a lack of comparative studies based on a larger number of investigated artefacts. As a representative example of the current state of research, reference should be made here to the analyses by Orfanou and Rehren (2015, 387), who have published one of the most recent and comprehensive analyses on this topic with 41 objects. They compare the results from the electron beam microanalysis of the metal core with those obtained from the surface using pXRF. In each case, a measurement was carried out on the patina as well as on a spot freed of the patina. The results obtained in this way underline previous research and show significantly increased values for tin and lead on the surface. Like Robbiola (1998, 2006 ff.) and Constantinides *et al.* (2002, 93 ff.), they were also able to prove the enrichment of antimony and arsenic in the patina, although the values for antimony appear to be more reliable (Orfanou and Rehren, 395 f.). In recent research, attempts are being made to make the removal of patina or sampling obsolete by combining (p)XRF and stochastic methods (including Monte Carlo simulations) (on the method, cf. *e.g.* Manso *et al.* 2015, 93 ff. and Bottaini *et al.* 2015, 9 ff.). The calculations consider the structure of the patina as well as the irregularities of the surface. The first results of the pilot studies show the potential of this method (cf. *ibid.*). Another archaeologically-focused and extensive case study comes from Nørgaard (2017); using pXRF analyses as well as scanning electron microscopy (SEM), she investigated the possibilities and limitations of pXRF measurement on patinated Bronze Age objects from Mecklenburg-Vorpommern and Lower Saxony. The results support the studies presented so far and also show higher values of the alloying metal tin in the patina compared to the actual tin content in the source material. In addition, the values fluctuated in the different layers of the patina. The example of the Gielow bracelet, which was measured once on the patinated area and once on a polished, patina-free area using pXRF, shows once again that all trace elements accumulate in the patina (Nørgaard 2017, 112). However, most of the previous research on this topic has focused mostly on copper alloys such as tin bronzes or brass, so that the other trace elements — arsenic, silver and antimony *etc.*, which are important for the assessment of early copper objects — are less in focus. With regard to non-alloyed copper, there is still a considerable need for research.

The described structure and genesis of patina thus have a very significant influence on the evaluation of the pXRF measurement results from patinated surfaces. Depending on how thick the patina is and what type it is, different results can be obtained. This does not only differ from object to object; several stages of corrosion and patina types can also occur simultaneously on one artefact (Robbiola/Portier 2006). This also means different element concentrations at the different locations. Furthermore, the reliability of the measurement results must be checked individually for each element (Orfanou and Rehren 2015, 395 f.). Given the uncertainties of the method described above, the measurement results obtained can therefore only be seen as an approximation to the actual values.

8.5 Procedure for the author's pXRF analyses

The measurements were carried out with the pXRF instrument already described in more detail above, which was combined with a lead-insulated measurement chamber and controlled via a connected computer. The fixed instrument and chamber allowed for a reproducible measurement environment. To ensure proper functioning of the instrument, a system check of the instrument was carried out and a certified standard sample was measured several times before the actual measurements were performed. In the further course, the artefacts were placed on the measuring table above the detector window in such a way that there was as little distance as possible between the measured object and the detector. This was to minimise the absorption and geometry effects. This was sometimes difficult due to the shape of the objects, so that special consideration must be given to this when looking at the results. In some cases, a support had to be used to stabilise the individual objects, which was made of plastic and always placed outside the measurement area. To account for the different energy levels of the elements, the measurement routine included four measurement filters (Main, Low, High, Light) of 30 seconds each. The spectra of the elements were quantified using a basic algorithm that is stored in the device as a special measurement mode (Cu/Zn mode) (Gauss *et al.* 2013, 2947). While in larger measurement series a decision has to be made between effectiveness and measurement accuracy when deciding on the number of measurements per object, the low number of artefacts and sufficient time meant that as many measurements could be carried out as the author of this work considered useful. Decisive factors were the size and shape of the object, as well as the condition of the patina. A measurement strategy with multiple measurements at different points of the object and averaging when using pXRF devices is regularly used in research (*e.g.* Stapfer *et al.* 2018). With the exception of one object, at least four measurements were carried out per artefact (Cu/Zn mode). After carrying out a series of measurements on an object, but at the latest after ten measurements, a control measurement of the standard sample was carried out and this was compared with the corresponding values.

8.6 Results

According to Pernicka (1999, Tab. 1), indicators for the origin of the metal can be the elements As, Cd, Co, In, Hg, Re, Sb, Se, Te, Tl, Au, Ag, Bi, Ir, Ni, Os, Pd, Pt, Rh, Ru, Zn, Sn, and Pb. The elements As, Au, Sb, Ag, Bi, Ni, Pb, Pt, Sn, and Zn were measured. Cd, Co, Hg, and Se remained below the detection limit. As fluctuating measurements were to be expected due to the patina, the median was calculated as it is particularly robust against outliers. The measurement results of the pXRF mentioned below in the text are the rounded median values in mass percent. In the case of the objects from Neuenkirchen, the results of the ED-XRFA analyses, which were carried out by Curt-Engelhorn-Zentrum Archäometrie gGmbH (Mannheim), are also added to the results of the self-performed pXRF analyses. The sample material was copper chips without corrosion material, obtained through drillings. The exception is the sample of the indeterminate fragment from which a piece of non-corroded material was obtained.

8.6.1 Greifswald (Inv.-No. ALM 99/1139)

A total of eight measurements were carried out on the flat axe from Greifswald. The thick type II patina according to Robbiola (1998) is reflected in the comparatively high values for the elements associated with the corrosion process (Fe: 8.244 %, Al: 8.921 %, Si: 3.098 %, P: 0.442 %). Among the archaeologically-relevant trace elements, arsenic and antimony dominate in roughly equal proportions, followed by smaller proportions of silver and nickel. Only traces of lead, zinc, and tin were found (cf. Fig. 28). Overall, the nickel values were much more scattered than those of the other elements. One measurement showed a content of 9.5 %, which can certainly be linked to corrosion.

8.6.2 Weltzin (Inv.-No. ALM 2010/1853, 8)

The axe from Weltzin is very well preserved and shows only a little patina of type I, and isolated, small spots of type II according to Robbiola (*ibid.*). There are some adhesions in the cutting-edge area, which were avoided during the nine measurements carried out on the object. Due to the very good state of preservation and the low patina formation, elements related to the corrosion process are represented only very little or not at all (Fe: 0.051 %, Al: - %, Si: 0.442 %, P: 0.042 %).

Site	Object	Inventory No.	Sample No.	Method	Cu %	Mn %	Fe %	Co %	Ni %	Zn %	As %	Se %	Ag %	Cd %	Sn %	Sb %	Te %	Pb %	Bi %
Altwigshagen	flat axe	ALM 2009/1015	own meas.	pXRF	89.894	<LOD	<LOD	<LOD	<LOD	<LOD	1.528	<LOD	<LOD	<LOD	<LOD	1.213	-	<LOD	<LOD
Greifswald	flat axe	ALM 1999/1139	own meas.	pXRF	69.343	<LOD	8.244	<LOD	0.262	0.026	1.652	<LOD	0.732	-	0.034	1.605	-	0.007	<LOD
Weltzin	flat axe	ALM 2010/1853, 8	own meas.	pXRF	94.071	<LOD	0.051	<LOD	0.315	<LOD	0.034	<LOD	0.922	-	<LOD	<LOD	-	<LOD	<LOD
Neuenkirchen	flat axe	ALM 1999/1039, 2	own meas.	pXRF	89.126	<LOD	0.347	<LOD	<LOD	<LOD	1.582	<LOD	0.025	-	<LOD	0.016	-	0.024	<LOD
Neuenkirchen	flat axe	ALM 1999/1039, 2	MA-191691	EDRFA	97	<0.005	<0.05	<0.01	0.050	<0.100	2.480	0.005	0.011	<0.002	<0.002	0.013	<0.005	0.020	0.005
Neuenkirchen	dagger	ALM 1999/1039, 1	own meas.	pXRF	93.565	<LOD	0.387	<LOD	<LOD	<LOD	<LOD	<LOD	0.257	-	<LOD	0.176	-	<LOD	0.008
Neuenkirchen	dagger	ALM 1999/1039, 1	MA-191692	EDRFA	100	<0.005	<0.05	<0.01	<0.010	<0.100	0.007	<0.005	0.220	<0.002	<0.002	0.184	<0.005	<0.005	0.011
Neuenkirchen	arm spiral	ALM 1999/1039, 4	own meas.	pXRF	85.020	<LOD	0.598	<LOD	<LOD	<LOD	0.005	<LOD	0.727	-	<LOD	0.307	-	<LOD	0.051
Neuenkirchen	arm spiral	ALM 1999/1039, 4	MA-191689	EDRFA	100	<0.005	<0.05	<0.01	0.010	<0.100	0.005	<0.005	0.210	<0.002	<0.002	0.186	<0.005	<0.005	0.013
Neuenkirchen	band spiral	ALM 1999/1039, 3	own meas.	pXRF	89.482	<LOD	0.968	<LOD	<LOD	<LOD	0.070	<LOD	0.168	-	<LOD	0.087	-	0.006	<LOD
Neuenkirchen	band spiral	ALM 1999/1039, 3	MA-191688	EDRFA	100	<0.005	<0.05	<0.01	<0.010	<0.100	0.018	<0.005	0.224	<0.002	<0.002	0.107	<0.005	<0.005	0.008
Neuenkirchen	fragment	ALM 1999/1039, 5	own meas.	pXRF	81.132	<LOD	0.654	<LOD	<LOD	<LOD	0.012	<LOD	0.520	-	<LOD	0.176	-	0.009	0.014
Neuenkirchen	fragment	ALM 1999/1039, 5	MA-191690	EDRFA	100	<0.005	<0.05	<0.01	<0.010	<0.100	<0.005	<0.005	0.187	<0.002	0.017	0.174	<0.005	0.019	0.011

Fig. 28. Results of the pXRF-Analysis and the XRFA carried out by Curt-Engelhorn-Zentrum Archäometrie gGmbH. For reasons of space, not all elements of the pXRF measurements are shown here. <LOD = under detection limit, - = Element not measured.

Among the archaeologically-relevant trace elements, antimony dominates, closely followed by silver and significantly less nickel and a small proportion of arsenic (cf. Fig. 28). Lead (median: 0.012 %) was detected in only three measurements, six measurements remained below the detection limit.

8.6.3 Altwigshagen (Inv.-No. ALM 2009/1015)

The series of measurements (six measurements) on the axe from Altwigshagen is the only one that was carried out on a patina-free sample. For the examinations, two chips were obtained from the axe by means of a drill. However, these were originally intended for mass spectrometric analysis in the laboratory and not for examination with a pXRF device. Helfert and Böhme (2010, 18) specify 35 mm as the minimum thickness of a sample, which was not achieved in this case. The small sample size is also reflected in the irregular measurement results. For example, two measurements show no arsenic, while in the other measurements the proportion varies between one and four per cent. The median for arsenic is 1.52 %. Similar measurement results were found for lead and silver, which are, however, no longer represented due to the application of the median (cf. Fig. 28). Applying the arithmetic mean results in a trace element combination (As 1.79 %, Pb 0.055 % and Ag 0.023 %).

8.6.4 Neuenkirchen

8.6.4.1 Flat axe (Inv.-No. ALM 1999/1039, 2)

The axe fragment is well-preserved and shows mainly a type I patina, as well as smaller spots of type II according to Robbiola (1998). A total of ten measurements were taken. Due to the good state of preservation and the low patina formation, elements related to the corrosion process are represented to a lesser extent compared to the Greifswald axe (Fe: 0.347%, Al: 2.142%, Si: 1.913%, P: 1.279%). Arsenic clearly dominates the archaeologically-relevant trace elements. Antimony, silver and lead are only present to a small extent.

Surprisingly, the laboratory analysis (MA-19691) shows almost one percent more arsenic than the pXRF result (cf. Fig. 28). The studies described in 8.4. actually led us to expect the opposite. Similarly, unexpected were the almost identical measurements for antimony and lead. Only in the case of silver was it shown that the actual content in the metal was about half that of the pXRF measurement on the patina. In addition, nickel and small traces of bismuth were detected, which remained below the detection limit in the pXRF measurement.

8.6.4.2 Dagger (Inv.-No. ALM 1999/1039, 1)

The dagger shows mainly the type I patina, but in the distal area more severe type II corrosion is visible according to Robbiola (*ibid.*), which was avoided in the six measurements. The elements related to the corrosion process are represented to a similar degree as in the axe fragment (Fe: 0.387 %, Al: 2.654 %, Si: 3.292 %, P: 1.144 %). The measurement pattern of the archaeologically-relevant elements is determined by silver and, to a somewhat lesser extent, antimony. Traces of bismuth were also detected.

The laboratory analysis (MA-191692) again shows very similar results for antimony, but also for silver and bismuth. The laboratory analysis shows slightly more antimony and bismuth and slightly less silver. In addition, traces of arsenic were detected, which remained below the detection limit in the pXRF measurement (cf. Fig. 28).

8.6.4.3 Band spiral (Inv.-No. ALM 1999/1039, 3)

Both patina type I and II according to Robbiola (1998) are present on the band spiral. In places it shows severe corrosion, so that only a little of the original copper was preserved. However, the four measurements were carried out on the well-preserved areas with patina type I. The elements associated with the corrosion process are represented to a similar degree as in the axe fragment and dagger (Fe: 0.968 %, Al: 1.662 %, Si: 2.036 %, P: 1.405 %). Silver dominates the archaeologically-relevant trace elements. The elements antimony and arsenic are represented to a low degree and lead to a very low degree.

Contrary to expectations, the laboratory analysis (MA-191688) shows higher values for silver and antimony than the pXRF measurement on the patina. In contrast, the elements arsenic and lead show lower concentrations. However, the ratios of the element composition remain similar. Silver dominates, followed by antimony and arsenic. In addition, small traces of bismuth were detected, which remained below the detection limit in the pXRF measurement (cf. Fig. 28).

8.6.4.4 Spiral arm ring (Inv.-No. ALM 1999/1039, 4).

The spiral arm ring exhibits both patina type I and II according to Robbiola (*ibid.*). In places it shows severe corrosion, so that only a little of the original copper was preserved. However, the four measurements were carried out on the well-preserved areas with patina type I. The elements associated with the corrosion process are represented to a similar extent as in the flat axe fragment, dagger, and band spiral from Neuenkirchen (Fe: 0.598 %, Al: 3.648 %, Si: 3.103 %, P: 1.346 %). Again, silver represents the largest share among the trace elements, followed by antimony and small traces of arsenic.

The laboratory analysis (MA-191689) shows significantly lower values for the elements silver and antimony than in the pXRF measurements, which, however, remain the dominant elements. While the element concentration is also significantly lower for bismuth, the result is the same for arsenic. In addition, nickel could be detected that remained below the detection limit in the pXRF measurement (cf. Fig. 28).

8.6.4.5 Fragment

The fragment shows mainly type I patina and smaller spots of type II according to Robbiola (*ibid.*). Due to the small size of the object, only two measurements were taken. The elements related to the corrosion process are represented in a slightly higher degree than in the other Neuenkirchen objects (Fe: 0.654 %, Al: 7.837 %, Si: 5.679 %, P: 1.542 %). Silver is also the dominant element here, followed by antimony and lower element concentrations of bismuth, arsenic, and lead.

The laboratory analysis (MA-191690) shows a significantly lower value for silver than in the pXRF measurements, but it remains the dominant element. In contrast to the spiral arm ring, the element concentration of antimony is almost the same in the laboratory measurement. While the value for lead is somewhat higher, the result for bismuth is somewhat lower. In addition, tin could be detected, which remained below the detection limit in the pXRF measurement (cf. Fig. 28).

8.6.5 Notes on the differences between the pXRF and laboratory ED-XRFA measurements

Overall, it can be stated for the pXRF measurements that the trace element ratios found are very similar to the laboratory measurements, even though the actual values measured naturally differ. Contrary to the assumption that higher element concentrations would be measured in the pXRF measurements due to

Analysegruppe	As	Sb	Ag	Ni
I	0.0090	0.1800	0.2235	0.0013
II	0.1670	0.0358	0.2460	0.0013
III	0.0300	0.0200	0.2600	0
IV	0.0004	0.0004	0.0011	0.0117
V	Sp	Sp	0.0200	0.0012
VI	Sp	<0.0050	0.2600	0.0400
VII	0.6600	0.0100	0.0100	<0.0100
VIII	0.4100	0.0400	<0.0100	Sp

1

Analysegruppe	As	Sb	Ag	Ni
I	0.0040–0.0012	0.0100–0.5500	0.1000–0.2600	0–0.0057
II	0.1140–0.2200	0.0316–0.0400	0.1400–0.3520	0–<0.0030
III	0.0300	0.0200	0.2600	0
IV	0.0004	0.0004	0.0110	0.0117
V	<0.0003–Sp	0.0001–Sp	0.0100–0.0371	0–0.0012
VI	Sp	<0.0050	0.2600	0.0400
VII	0.0380–1.9100	0–0.0800	0–0.1000	0–0.0600
VIII	0.1500–1.3500	0.0200–0.1200	Sp–<0.0100	0–0.0100

2

Fig. 29. Analysis groups (1.) and the spreads of the element concentrations (2.) of the eight groups by Klassen (2000, fig. 101 and 102, altered).

the enrichment in the patina, the opposite was sometimes the case (*e.g.* with the axe fragment). A uniform trend that an element showed fundamentally higher or lower values compared to the laboratory measurements could not be proven (cf. Fig. 28). The relatively similar measurement results are probably related to the good preservation of the objects and the predominance of type I patina (after Robbiola 1998). In addition, Constantinides *et al.* (2002) were able to show that significant dissolution of copper occurs in almost all copper alloys except for copper alloyed with arsenic. Nørgaard (2017, 120) sees this as an opportunity to provide detailed information on the original material composition through XRF analyses. This may also be the case for objects made of pure copper with only few other trace element contents. This is at least indicated by the comparison of the analysis results available for Neuenkirchen. Due to the small number of analyses and the lack of a more detailed examination of the corrosion (*e.g.* with SEM), the results can at best be classified as anecdotal evidence.

8.6.6 Discussion of the results

Originally, the discussion of the results and the assignment to the respective copper variety was based on the pXRF measurements carried out by the author himself. In the case of the Neuenkirchen hoard, the results of the current ED-XRF measurement have been considered. Here, however, the assignment only changes in the case of the band spiral and the fragment (see below). For the interpretation, the elements Ag, As, Sb, and Ni are used, which Klassen (2000, 60 ff.) used for the formation of his material groups by means of cluster analyses (cf. Fig. 29). An attempt will be made to classify all measured objects into the aforementioned analysis groups according to Klassen (2000). In addition, the material groups defined by the Stuttgart Metal Analysis Project (SAM), which also took bismuth into account in the formation, are given. The author is aware of the imprecision of the measurement on patinated surfaces as well as the difference in quality of the applied measuring methods (cf. 8.4): Nevertheless, in the case of the flat axes (Altwigshagen, Greifswald, and Weltzin), which were only measured by means of pXRF, an allocation shall be made on the basis of the ratio of the trace element contents.

The axe from Altwigshagen (Inv.-No. ALM 2009/1015) can clearly be classified in the analysis group VII according to Klassen (2000) or in the material group E01 of the Stuttgart Metal Analysis Project (SAM) due to its arsenic content and only low silver content (Sangmeister *et al.* 1968). It would then be of the so-called Mondsee copper variety (cf. below). The strongly-fluctuating measured values, however, make the result appear questionable.

The results of the axe from Greifswald (Inv.-No.1999/1139) show how much the measurement results depend on the state of preservation of the object. Of all the objects measured, this one shows the strongest corrosion. Underneath the outer brown patina, another green patina consisting most likely of malachite is visible. It can therefore be assumed to be a strongly pronounced patina type II according to Robbiola *et al.* (1998). The strong corrosion is also reflected in the measurement results. High values of iron and aluminium (up to 10% and 11 % respectively) show how the elements of the corrosive environment have been deposited in the patina. It cannot be fitted into any of the groups formed by Klassen (2000, 221 ff.). The combination of roughly equal arsenic and antimony values with not insignificant silver and somewhat low nickel contents is not found there. In the SAM nomenclature, it would correspond to material group FB 1. However, it can be assumed that the actual material composition is strongly distorted by the considerable patina, so that no further reference is made to it here.

The axe from Weltzin (Inv.-No. ALM 2010/1853, 8) cannot be fitted into one of the analysis groups according to Klassen (2000). The measured values allow an assignment to the SAM material group B2. Due to the trace element combination, a Late Neolithic or Early Bronze Age dating of the objects is often assumed. However, within this material group there is also an axe of the Bygholm type (cf. Schmitz 2004, 335), which thus can be dated at least typologically to the Funnel Beaker Period.

The heterogeneity of the deposit find must be emphasised as a central result of the metal analyses. This can be seen in the visualisation of the principal component analyses carried out (Fig. 30 and 31) as well as in the ternary plot of the measurement results (Fig. 32). It becomes clear that the copper used for the production of the objects comes from at least two different regions. The high arsenic content of the flat axe fragment, with only small traces of other elements, is characteristic for the copper objects from the environment of the so-called Mondsee Group, which is absolutely dated between c. 3800 and 3200 BCE on the basis of ^{14}C data (Klassen 2000, 221 ff.). The lake gives its name to both the group and the copper variety. The source is intensively discussed in research. Klassen and Stürup (2001, 57 ff.) assume an eastern Alpine origin, while Frank and Pernicka (2012, 124 ff.) want to exclude this region for the time being on the basis of lead isotope and chemical analyses for the deposits they studied. Striking similarities to the Serbian Majdanpek deposit are evident, but cannot be matched beyond doubt. The clear origin of the copper remains unclear for them (*ibid.*), but a centre for the processing of this variety in the Alpine region is attested by finds of casting spoons (*Gusslöffel*) and copper artefacts (*e.g.* Maurer 2014, 174 f.). In the latest research, Nørgaard *et al.* (2021, 9 f.) rule out that the Mondsee copper is of Eastern Alpine origin, rather it most likely originates from deposits in Serbia and Bulgaria. The comparatively high proportion of arsenic in the flat axe fragment from Neuenkirchen can possibly be attributed to an intentional addition of arsenic in the form of iron arsenide (*ibid.*, 10). This innovation is only attested with certainty in Iran at the end of the fourth millennium (Rehren *et al.* 2012; Thornton 2009), but possibly also took place earlier in south-eastern Europe (Nørgaard *et al.* 2021, 9 f.). This explains the dominance of arsenical copper in the fourth millennium in south-eastern Europe and also the flat axes made of such copper in the area of the Funnel Beaker Societies, whose lead isotope signature corresponds to deposits in Bulgaria and Serbia (*ibid.*, 10). This copper may have reached northern Germany and southern Scandinavia from or via the Mondsee

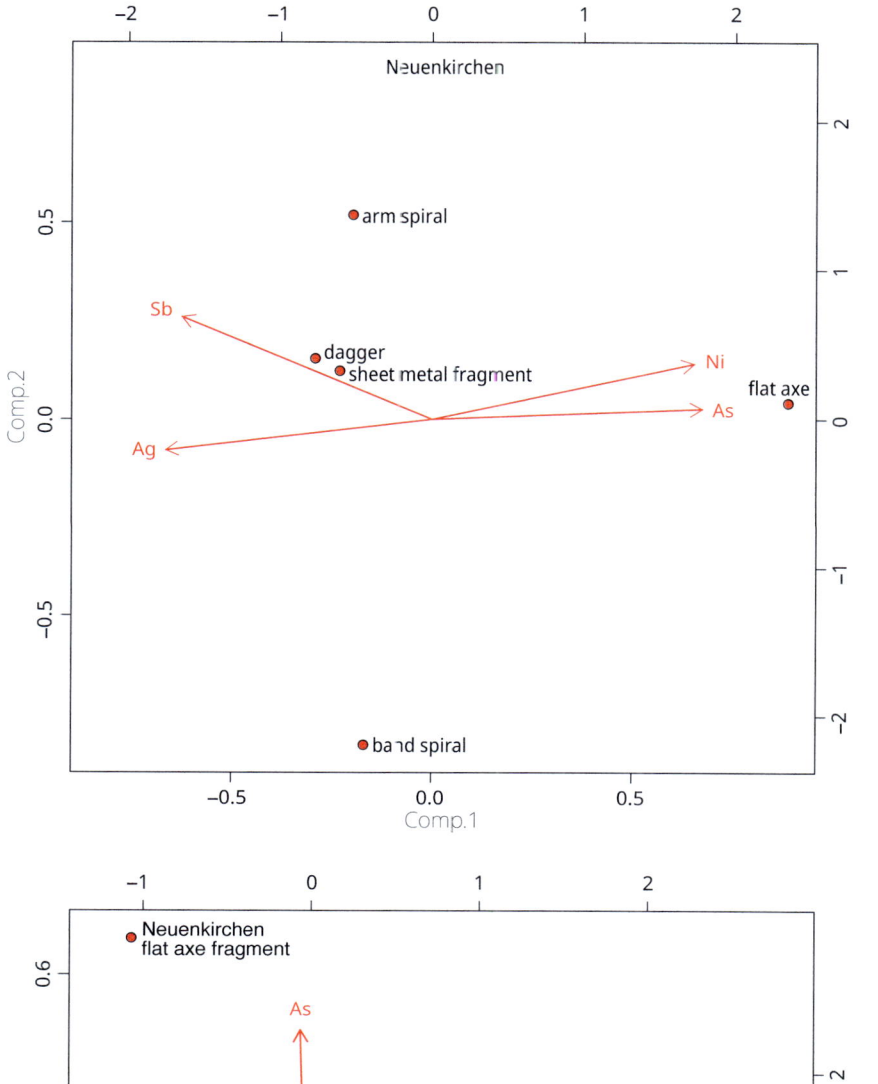

Fig. 30. Visualisation of the principal component analysis of the ED-XRFA measurements of objects from the hoard of Neuenkirchen. Elements: arsenic, antimony, nickel, and silver. Carried out with R, command pca (R Core Team 2016).

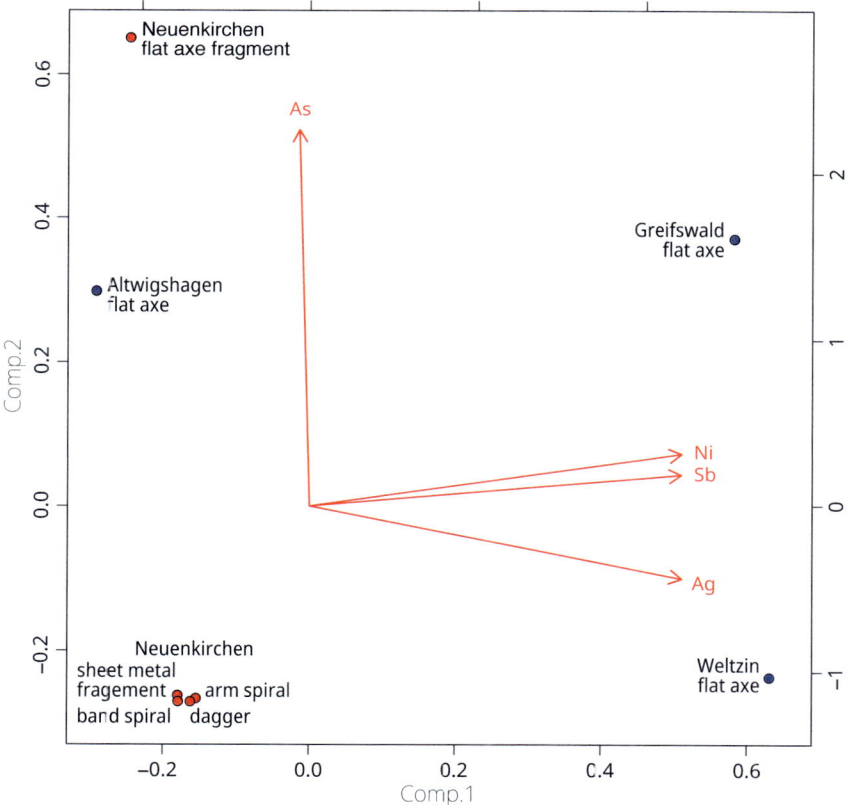

Fig. 31. Visualisation of the principal component analysis including the ED-XRFA measurements of objects from the hoard of Neuenkirchen, as well as the results of the pXRF measurements of the flat axes from Weltzin, Greifswald, and Altwigshagen. Elements: arsenic, antimony, nickel, and silver. Carried out with R, command pca (R Core Team 2016).

Fig. 32. Visualisation of the results of ED-XRFA measurements of the objects from the hoard of Neuenkirchen (ternary plot carried out with R, command pca (R Core Team 2016).

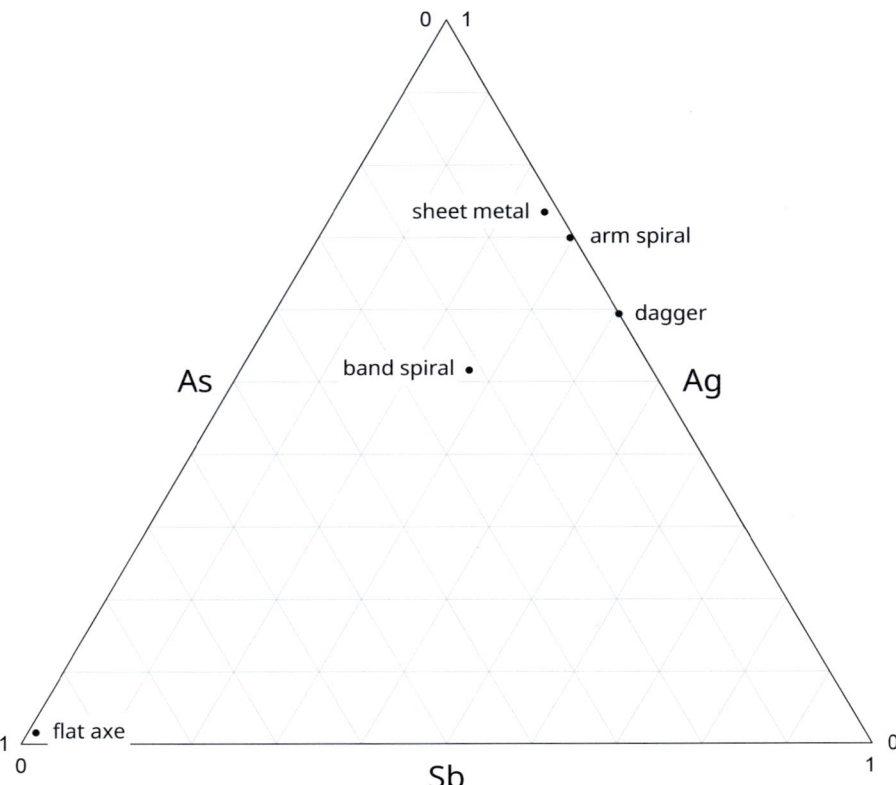

Sample No.	MA-191691
Object	flat axe
Inventory No.	99/1039.2
^{208}Pb/^{206}Pb	2.0786
^{208}Pb/^{206}Pb 2σ	0.0001
^{207}Pb/^{206}Pb	0.8439
^{207}Pb/^{206}Pb 2σ	0.00003
^{206}Pb/^{204}Pb	18.471
^{206}Pb/^{204}Pb 2σ	0.001
^{208}Pb/^{204}Pb	38.393
^{208}Pb/^{204}Pb 2σ	0.007
^{207}Pb/^{204}Pb	15.588
^{207}Pb/^{204}Pb 2σ	0.001

Fig 33.1. Results of the lead isotope analysis (MA-191691) of the flat axe fragment from Neuenkirchen.

Fig 33. 2 (right). ^{207}Pb/^{204}Pb and ^{206}Pb/^{204}Pb isotope plot of the flat axe of Neuenkirchen and copper deposits from South-Eastern Europe; 2. ^{208}Pb/^{204}Pb and ^{206}Pb/^{204}Pb isotope plot of the flat axe of Neuenkirchen and copper deposits from South-Eastern Europe. Figure by Dr. Z. Stos-Gale. Ore data from: Baron et al. 2011, Gale et al. 2003, Kuzmanov et al. 2005, Marcoux et al. 2002, Pernicka et al. 1993, Radivojević et al. 2010, Schreiner 2007, and Stos-Gale/ Bajenaru 2020.

Group at an early date. Based on the results of the lead isotope analysis and the arsenic content, which are now available, the flat axe fragment from Neuenkirchen fits in well with this assumption (cf. 8.6.7).

The trace element composition of the other components of the hoard from Neuenkirchen, on the other hand, points to the Carpathian environment. The copper of the dagger, arm spiral, band spiral, and the fragment can be assigned to the copper variety Nógrádmarcal or the SAM group C1B. While the dagger and the arm spiral could already be assigned to this copper variety by the pXRF measurements, this was not the case for the band spiral and the fragment. The band spiral and the fragment were assigned to the copper variety Handlova, which, however, is close to the Nógrádmarcal copper (Schmitz 2004, 532 ff.), considering the scatter of the element concentrations of the analysis groups by Klassen (2000, 222). The results of the laboratory analyses have now made it possible to specify that it is also the Nógrádmarcal copper variety or C1B copper according to SAM. The origin of Nógrádmarcal and Handlova copper, which is expected to have been used around 4000 BC[4], is presumed to be north-west Slovakia or the Carpathian region (Klassen 2000, 221 f.).

8.6.7 Lead isotope analyses

In addition to the trace element analyses, lead isotope analyses were also carried out on the Neuenkirchen samples. However, due to the low lead content in the objects, only the analysis of the sample of the flat axe fragment was successful (Fig. 33.1). By comparing the lead isotope ratios (204, 206, 207, 208) of archaeological objects and

---

4   Artefacts with the copper type Nógrádmarcal and Handlova are known from contexts of younger Bodrogkeresztúr, which according to current research ends around 4000 cal. BCE. The use of copper therefore begins somewhat earlier, but in principle the figure of 4000 BCE is not incorrect.

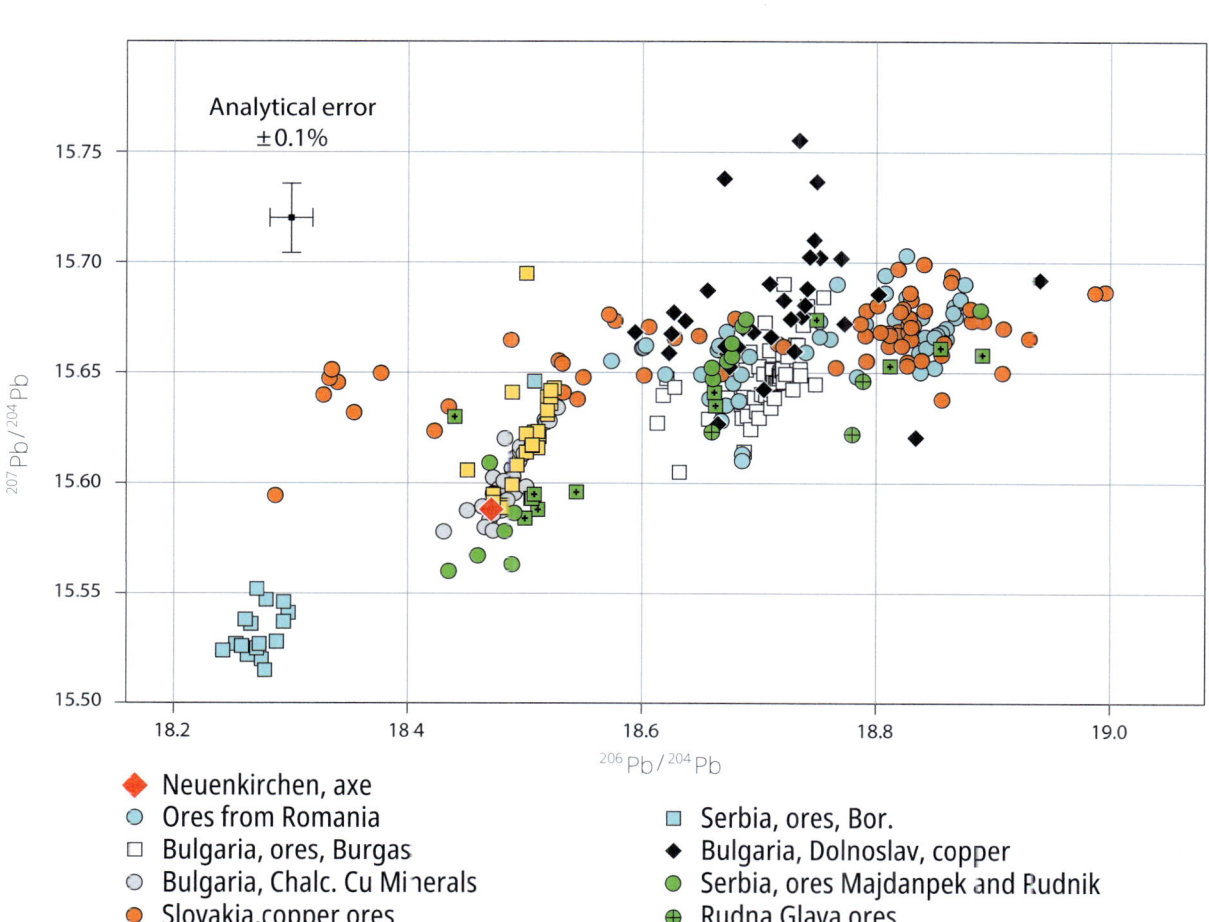

- ◆ Neuenkirchen, axe
- ● Ores from Romania
- □ Bulgaria, ores, Burgas
- ● Bulgaria, Chalc. Cu Minerals
- ● Slovakia, copper ores
- ⊞ Serbia, Belovode and Plocnik

- ■ Serbia, ores, Bor.
- ◆ Bulgaria, Dolnoslav, copper
- ● Serbia, ores Majdanpek and Rudnik
- ⊕ Rudna Glava ores
- ▢ Ai Bunar

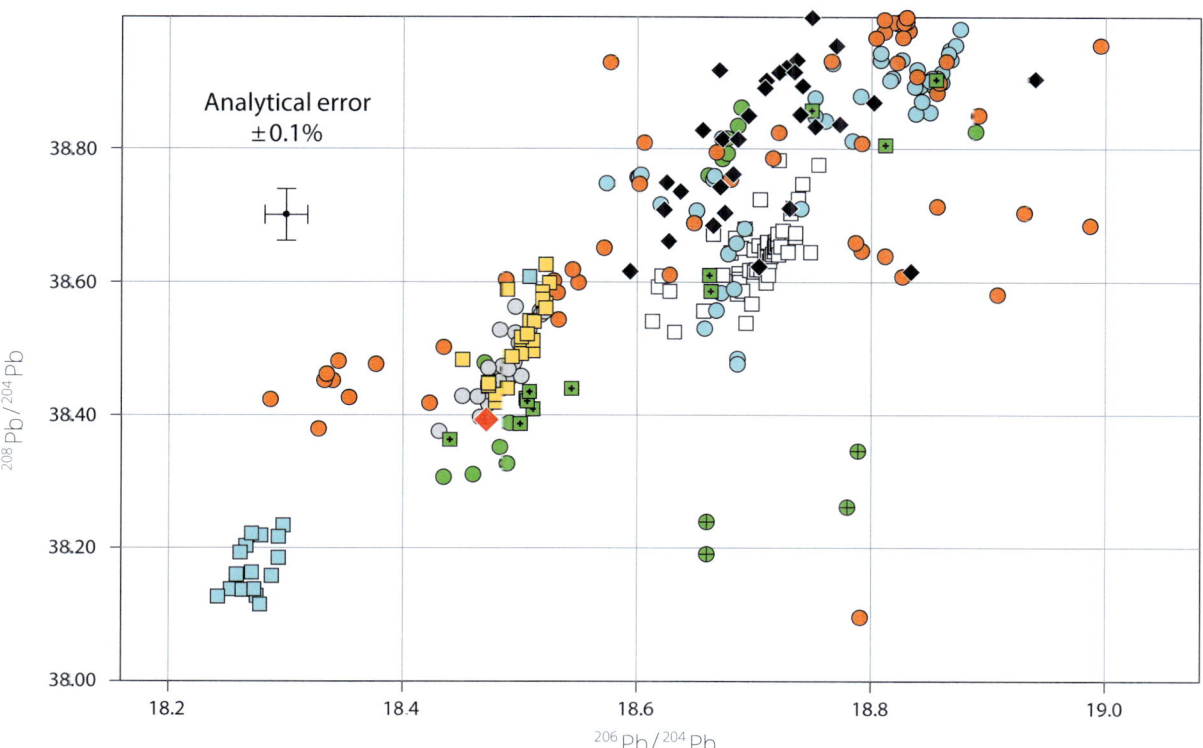

deposits, an attempt is made to determine the provenance of the related material. For a detailed overview of the method and research history, compare Stos-Gale and Gale (2009).

As shown in Fig. 33.2.[5], the lead isotope ratios of the flat axe fragment from Neuenkirchen are consistent with the data published for the copper mines in Majdanpek, Serbia (Pernicka *et al.* 1993; Radivojević *et al.* 2010). However, they are also on the margin of the data from Ai Bunar (Bulgaria). So far, only a use as pigments was known for these ores (Gale *et al.* 2000 and 2003), but Nørgaard *et al.* (2021, 9 f.) classify the flat axes from Slusegård and Viborg as comparable to the data for mines in the Bulgarian Ai Bunar (Stara Zagora, Burgas). In the case of the flat axe from Slusegård, however, the measurement also lies in the area of eastern Serbian mines such as Madjanpek or Rudna Glava (*ibid.*, 10). Even if the use of copper from Ai Bunar seems possible, at least for a flat axe, the lead isotope ratios of the Neuenkirchen axe suggest an origin from the Serbian mine of Majdanpek, even if deposits in the Bulgarian Ai Bunar cannot be completely ruled out.

---

5   Gratefully provided by Dr. Z. A. Stos-Gale (University of Gothenburg), who is expressly thanked here for her help in interpreting the data.

9. Early Copper in Mecklenburg-Western Pomerania

9.1 Overview of the copper finds

The copper finds of Mecklenburg-Western Pomerania were summarised for the first time by Jacobs (1986) in the context of his diploma thesis on the Neolithic metal finds in the territory of the former German Democratic Republic (GDR; East Germany). The copper objects were supplemented by new finds and placed in the context of the early metal horizon in the so-called Nordic circle by Klassen (2000), who lists 15 copper objects for Mecklenburg-Western Pomerania in his work about early metal finds and early metallurgy southern Scandinavia and northern Germany.

Since then, the number of finds has increased again. As of January 2017, a total of 32 artefacts or their remains are known from 28 sites (Fig. 34). The inventory of Neolithic copper was supplemented by several flat axes and a needle. The largest addition in terms of quality and quantity is the hoard find from Neuenkirchen. The presentation of the aforementioned assemblage should be used to briefly summarise the current inventory of Neolithic copper in the area of Mecklenburg-Vorpommern. At this point it should be noted that the inventory of copper artefacts has not doubled within only 17 years, but that old finds are also considered here, which Klassen (2000) probably does not list in his catalogue due to their uncertain circumstances of discovery and unknown whereabouts. In addition, this count also includes axes with indications of ridges (flanged axes) which, according to recent research (Klimscha 2010), can already date from the second half of the 4th millennium. The old finds are not illustrated here, unless they are used for comparison purposes. The new finds, if available, are included as plates.

The largest group of objects, 23 pieces, are flat axes or flanged axes with only indicated ridges. The previously known old finds (n=13) were supplemented by the new finds from Altwigshagen and Nadrensee. The axes with indicated ridges from Tilzow and Eggesin are joined by the new finds from Weltzin (Plate 3), Greifswald (Plate 3), Niepars, and the flat axe fragment from the Neuenkirchen depot. With the exception of the two depot finds from Neuenkirchen and Pantelitz, all axe finds are to be regarded as single finds without a context.

All other object groups are represented only once. A fragment of a tube made from sheet metal from Liepen and a ring fragment from Wüstenfelde, both from a megalithic grave, and copper remains from a burial that could not be identified further, which are connected to the earthwork at Plate (site 14) (Behrens et. al. 2013), represent the few reliable copper finds from grave contexts in Mecklenburg-

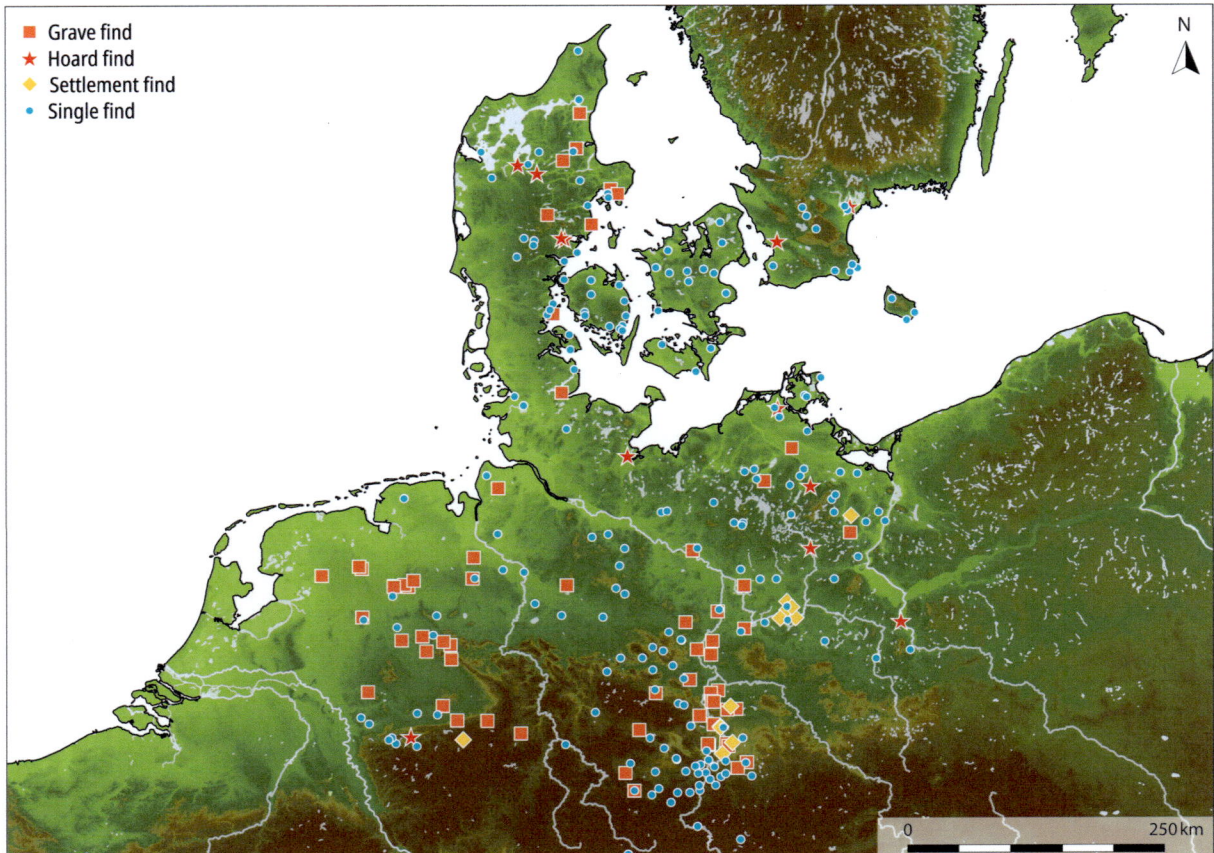

- ■ Grave find
- ★ Hoard find
- ◆ Settlement find
- • Single find

Fig. 34. Overview of all copper finds in the Northern German Plain, Southern Scandinavia, and the finds from the Dutch megalithic graves between 4200 and c. 2800 BCE (map basis NaturalEarthData).

Western Pomerania. The aforementioned copper remains from Plate are traces of arsenic copper that have been deposited like a film on several human teeth (*ibid.*). A similar find is known from Melzow in Brandenburg, where a necklace consisting of band spirals and a pendant lay under the greenish discoloured jaw including teeth (for details cf. 10.7), so that in Plate it could possibly also be the remains of such a necklace. A dagger, a bracelet, and a band spiral are part of the hoard from Neuenkirchen. A copper chisel (Kersten 1958, 38, no. 371), probably from the Tollense stream near Altentreptow, did not find its way into the compilations by Jacobs (1986) and Klassen (2000), probably due to the lack of metal analysis.

9.2 Chronological position of the copper finds

The oldest copper object from Mecklenburg-Western Pomerania is probably the axe from Bülow, Rostock district, which is characterised by its sturdy body and can be clearly assigned to the Pločnik type. A possibly cast example comes from the eponymous depot find in Serbia and dates there to the Vinca D2 phase between 4600-4300 BCE (Klassen 2000, 121). The axe arrived in the area of present-day Mecklenburg-Vorpommern during the Late Mesolithic. Settlement by the Lietzow group of Ertebølle has been proven for this area (Lutz *et al.* 1998, 47). Chronologically, the flat axes from Raden and Kirch Jesar, as well as the axe-adze (kreuzschneidige *Axthacke*) from Steinhagen, follow this piece. Klassen (2000, 98 f.) assigns the specimen from Kirch Jesar to the type Kaka defined by him, which dates between 4100-3900 BCE (*ibid.*; Klassen *et al.* 2011, 19 ff.). The pieces from Raden and Mescherin made of the same type of copper (Nógrádmarcal) also date to around 4000 BCE. A typologically-similar specimen is associated with pointed-butted flint axes typical of Michelsberg in a hoard from Großheubach in Bavaria (Klassen 2000, 104 f.). The axe-adze of the Jászládany type from Steinhagen represents the northernmost example of this form, which is mainly distributed in the Carpathian Basin. Chronologically, Klassen (*ibid.*, 166 ff.) places this Jászládany type in the period around 3800 BCE. Klimscha (2016, 159 ff.) notes that these axe-adzes fall mainly into the Hungarian High Copper Age, but can also date earlier (c. 4700-4200 BCE) and much later (3700-3200 BCE). Klassen (2000, 169 ff.) also dates the flat axe from Ruegen to around 3800 BCE, which — with its elevated arsenic values — can be assigned to the Mondsee copper variety. With some caution, he postulates a northern Alpine origin for the piece. However, as there was no evidence for such an early occurrence of this copper variety in the area of the northern group of the TRB, he understood this classification as a working hypothesis. This assumption is now supported by a burial with copper jewellery made of copper of the Mondsee variety in northern Brandenburg, which could be dated absolutely by means of ^{14}C analyses to around the year 3700 BCE. The artefacts named so far all fall into Phase I (c. 4500-3750 BCE) postulated by Klassen (*ibid.*, 236), which is characterised by the import of flat axes with stocky bodies, early trapezoidal flat axes, and axe-adzes. From the second phase (3750-3500 BCE), in which the range of shapes is characterised by trapezoidal flat axes and local sheet metal ornaments, only one object is represented in Mecklenburg-Vorpommern; the flat axe from Pantelitz, which is also the only copper artefact from a deposition context from this import phase. Klassen (*ibid.*, 42 and 156) assigns the slender, almost rectangular axe to Viby and refers to the object, also made of Mondsee copper, as a northern Alpine import piece, which finds its counterparts in finds from Bottighofen (Switzerland) and Abtsdorfer See (Bavaria). The former of these comparative finds comes from a lakeside settlement of the Late Pfyn, which would probably place the Pantelitz axe in the Late Early Neolithic (*ibid.*). In his phase 3 (3500-3300 BC) — which is characterised by an extensive inventory of local forms of tongue-shaped, as well as trapezoidal flat axes, and various forms of jewellery — he classifies a flat axe from Mecklenburg, the exact site of which is unknown (*ibid.*, 169). Several comparative finds from the area of the northern group of the TRB, which he combines into the Avnslev type, find no equivalents in the northern Alpine region, so that, according to Klassen (*ibid.*), a local form must be assumed, which was produced by re-melting copper objects from the eastern Alpine region (*ibid.*). The new find of the axe from Altwigshagen probably also belongs to this phase. This is indicated by its tongue-like shape and the copper composition, which suggests that it belongs to the Mondsee copper variety. As mentioned previously (see 8.6.6) this could be an earlier import of arsenic copper from south-eastern Europe. The fragment of the sheet metal tube from near Liepen and the fragment of a ring (or a needle) from Wüstenfelde, both objects from a megalithic grave, can be placed in the period between 3400 and 2800/2700 BCE (Lutz *et al.* 1998, 48). According to Schmitz (2004, 311), the chisel from Altentreptow has similarities to the Tiszanagyfalu type and dates to the Middle Copper Age at the earliest. According to his terminology, this begins in central Germany with Salzmünde, and in southern Scandinavia with the younger TRB (MN I) (*ibid.*, 117 and 554).

Difficult to place is a group of axes that are unusual either because of their metal composition and/or shape. These include the flat axe from Hornshagen, which, according to its shape, can certainly be placed in an Early Funnel Beaker context, but whose complex trace element composition, in the view of Lutz *et al.* (1998) and Klassen (2000), speaks more for a post-Funnel Beaker dating. The same applies to the axe from Jasmund, which Klassen (*ibid.*, 42) refers to as a singular piece and Schmitz (2004, 192) places in his cluster 8 with small, trapezoidal flat axes, which he assigns to the older Funnel Beaker Societies. A clear contradiction between typological features and metal composition is shown by a flat axe from Hagenow, whose shape indicates a Late Funnel Beaker context, but which has a tin content of over nine per cent (Lutz *et al.* 1998, 49). Due to a lack of metal analyses and/or insufficient illustrations, the flat axes from Jaebetz, Lindenbeck, Meyenburg, Strasburg, as well as one from near Neustrelitz, and a newer find from Nadrensee cannot be assessed.

From a chronological point of view, it is also difficult to address the group of (flanged) axes that are characterised by only slightly elevated ridges. Since the discussion on early flanged axes is relevant for the discussion of the new finds from Mecklenburg and the depot find from Neuenkirchen investigated here, the following is a summary of the detailed work by Klimscha (2010), which deals with this topic in detail. Traditionally located at the transition to the Bronze Age at the earliest, the discovery of the Ötz valley ice mummy in the Alps made it necessary to reconsider the chronological position of the flanged axes. The remains of the deceased, who was carrying a flanged axe (see Dolfini 2013, 43, fig. 7), were examined by means of radiocarbon dating and yielded a date of around 3400 BCE. Klimscha (2010) took the presentation of some axes from Aqaba in Jordan, which can be dated before 3500 BCE, as an opportunity to discuss the early flanged axes diachronically. In this context, he understands 'flanged axe' to mean pieces that are accompanied on the edges of the broad sides by ridges that stand out clearly from the rest of the axe body. Together with the axe from the Ötz valley, the finds of chisels and axes from the Jordanian Tall Hujayrāt al-Ghuzlān near Aqaba represent the oldest known pieces with such elevated ridges. They come from a settlement stratum dating between c. 3650/3600 and c. 3550 BCE (*ibid.*, 103). Other such early pieces are missing in the Near East, however, except for a chisel dating between 3800-3400 BCE from Arslantepe in eastern Anatolia. It is only from the third millennium onwards that there are several records of such chisels in western Anatolia, such as from Troy. The same applies to the Balkans and the Carpathian Basin. The earliest securely dated find of a flanged axe from Southeast Europe comes from Tell Ezero in Bulgaria and can be dated to around 3000 BCE (*ibid.* 113). For the Alpine region and Upper Italy, the axe from the Ötz valley in the Alps is the pivotal point of the chronological discussion. On the basis of absolute dating, the typologically-similar pieces from the hoard in Remedello-Sotto, Lombardy, as well as from tomb 102 from the same site, can be dated to around 3400 BCE. Other flanged axes are known from hoards and grave contexts from Upper and Central Italy and are typologically connected to the axes from Remedello (*ibid.*, 117). For the wider Alpine region, southern Germany, and the Czech Republic, Klimscha (*ibid.*, 119) discusses flanged axes whose form corresponds to or is close to the Neyruz type (after Kibbert). For some specimens made of pure copper, for which there is a typological proximity to the Remedello type, a much earlier dating than in the older Early Bronze Age is suggested. A dating from the turn of the 4th/3rd to the first half of the third millennium seems possible (*ibid.*).

North of the Alps, some axes with elevated ridges on the broad sides are known from the second half of the fourth millennium. In some cases, the ridges are irregular; for example, only on one side of the axe (*ibid.*, 127). One of these is an axe from Groß-Gerau (Hessen), in which the edge of one side is slightly raised. The piece is assigned to the Bygholm type according to Kibbert (1980), who also places it in the time horizon of the eponymous hoard. In connection with the hoard of Bygholm (Denmark), which according to Klassen (2000) dates between 3500-3000 BCE, the fact that the smallest axe of the deposit also had a raised ridge is of particular interest. Klimscha (2010, 125) interprets these pieces as possible precursors of flanged axes. A number of axes made of copper with slightly elevated ridges are also known from the areas north of the Alps, without, however, being able to be located more precisely. The axes with hammered ridges from Mecklenburg (Eggesin and Tilzow) are assumed to belong to the Single Grave Phenomenon. This classification is based on the metal composition, in which all relevant trace elements are elevated (Lutz *et al.* 1998, 49). Such trace element combinations are known from stratified copper

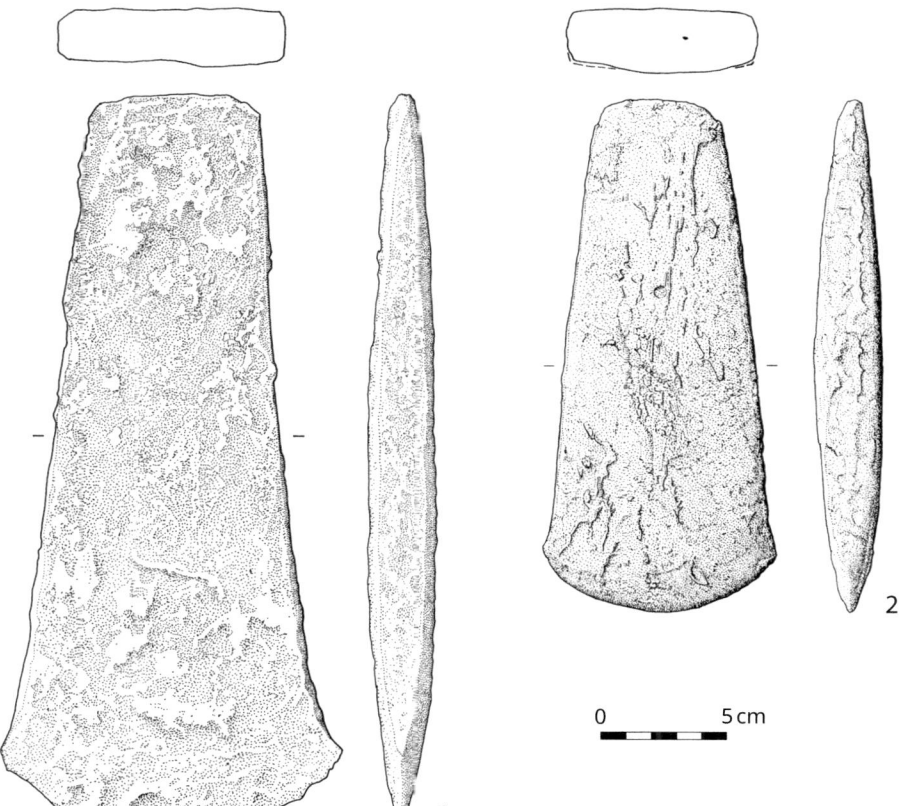

0 ____ 5 cm

Fig. 35. Flat axe finds from Ågård (left) and Sønder Kollemorten (right) (Klassen 2000, pl. 7.29 u. 5.22)

finds of the Corded Ware Phenomenon from the Elbe-Saale area. Another possible interpretation is offered by Klimscha (2010, 131), who points out that the pieces may also represent imitations of contemporaneous flanged axes. Since there are connections with the Bygholm hoard via the Mondsee copper to the Alpine region, where the first flanged axes exist at the same time, this seems quite plausible (*ibid.*).

The new Mecklenburg find from Weltzin, which has ridges of different heights (Plate 3a), can possibly be connected to this. The piece is also difficult to locate typologically apart from the indicated ridges. Although there are a number of large, slender axes with trapezoidal axe bodies and flared cutting edge corners in the northern group of the TRB, these axes generally have a straight butts and not a rounded one like the Weltzin piece. Moreover, most of them are thick-butte and none of them has such a thin butt, which can almost be described as sharp. The best example, with the aforementioned limitations, is the Kerteminde type axe from Ågård (Denmark) (Fig. 35). Klassen (2000) assigns axes of this type to its phase 3 (3500-3300 BC). An axe with indicated ridges and rounded butt end is found in Vietznitz (Brandenburg) in the Havelland, but the cutting corners 'flare out' much more, with trapezoidal broad sides. In contrast to the axe from Weltzin, the indicated ridges are regular on both sides. The investigation of the metal composition showed increased values for all relevant trace elements, as Lutz *et al.* (1998, 45) also show for the axes with slightly elevated ridges from Mecklenburg and Brandenburg. A direct comparison of the results is not possible here, since the Weltzin axe was measured on the patinated surface (cf. Chapter 8). In addition, SAM group B2, in which the Weltzin axe could be classified, unites Late Neolithic, Early Bronze Age but also Funnel Beaker Period objects, so that a later dating also seems possible.

The same applies to the new find from Greifswald (Plate 3b), which is also heavily corroded and for which an increase in all relevant trace elements is also evident. It is not possible to assign this piece to one of the types created by Klassen

Fig. 36. Hoard find from Kałdus (Adamczak et al. 2015, fig. 15).

(2000). On the one hand, the piece is damaged in the cutting edge and neck area, so that it is not entirely clear whether it had a rounded neck. On the other hand, the axe appears slightly asymmetrical, especially in the cutting-edge area, as one side of the cutting edge is clearly more flared than the other. Due to the more corroded surface, it is also difficult to recognise and judge the slightly elevated ridges. The piece most closely parallels the axe from Sønder Kollemorten (Denmark). The new find of axe from Niepars has so far only been published with a photo that is difficult to assess, so that an assignment to a specific type must still remain elusive. The trace element analysis carried out revealed a copper content of 97 % (Schirren 2013, 243).

Detailed results of the analysis have not yet been published. The assignment to the Mecklenburg Late Neolithic (*ibid.*), which was made on the basis of the metal composition (and probably also on the basis of the slightly elevated ridges), cannot be reconstructed due to the lack of detailed information. Artefacts with trace element contents of more than 3 % are also known from older objects (cf. Vajsov 1998,

235 ff.). It can be stated at this point that flanged axes appear in Europe from the middle of the fourth millennium onwards. For the northern group of the Funnel Beaker Societies, however, there is no evidence of 'real' flanged axes. In Europe, axes with slight, hammered ridges in the period between c. 3500 and 2750 BCE are only reliably attested for Italy, the Alpine region, the Balkans, and the Carpathian Basin (Klimscha 2010, 130). The axes with indicated ridges from Mecklenburg have so far been dated to Single Grave periods due to a lack of evidence and typological parallels, mainly because of their metal composition (Lutz *et al.* 1998). This is based on the assumption that the copper ore used for the production of the objects was extracted from deposits, or areas of deposits, that were only mined after the Funnel Beaker Period. Arsenic, antimony, and silver, for example, only coexist in ores containing sulphur and arsenic (Adamczak *et al.* 2015, 211), so that objects whose metal composition is characterised by the common occurrence of the aforementioned elements must have been made of copper extracted from such sulphurous ores (Lutz *et al.* 1998, 49). The artefacts of the hoard find from Kałdus, województwo kujawsko-pomorskie (Kujawsko-Pomorskie Voivodeship), Poland, show such a constellation of trace elements and can be dated between 3500 and 3100 BCE due to inclusion of a Usatovo-type dagger, among others (Vajsov 1993, 253, Adamczak *et al.* 2015, 211) (Fig. 36). The find from a settlement of the classical and late Wiórek phase shows that, in the temporal horizon of the Funnel Beaker Societies, copper objects do occur that have such a metal composition. In the light of this new find, the dating of the flanged axes from Mecklenburg-Western Pomerania to the Single Grave Phenomenon, based on the metal composition, should be viewed critically. An earlier dating of some specimens seems possible. For the pieces from Weltzin and Greifswald especially, which show only very minimal and irregular ridges, an affiliation to an experimental stage of the fourth millennium, as suggested by Klimscha (2010, 131), is quite conceivable. It cannot be ruled out that the ridges were created accidentally (*ibid.*, 130). Nevertheless, the specimens from Tilzow and Eggesin, which have regular, indicated ridges, can also be dated after 2800 BCE.

10. Typo-chronological analyses of the Neuenkirchen artefacts

10.1 Dagger

Since the first typological investigations of Copper Age daggers and their linkage with metallurgical analyses by I. Vajsov (1993) and I. Matuschik (1998), their number has continued to increase. Typo-chronological dating, however, remains problematic because, as Müller (2012) notes, quantitative feature comparisons are still almost completely lacking. The creation of types and attribution of the known specimens is difficult, above all, because their appearance may have been altered by re-sharpening during their phase of use. In addition, artefacts of value seem to have circulated in Neolithic societies over a longer period of time, so that they may have been deposited only after a long time (*ibid.*, 48).

The classification of Matuschik (1998), who took up the work of Vajsov (1993) and reappraised the south-eastern European and northern Alpine daggers, still holds today. During the research for the classification of the Neuenkirchen dagger, a number of new finds were recorded, which were taken as an opportunity to create an updated distribution map of the early daggers up to 2800 BCE (Fig. 37). Also included in the mapping is a considerable number of early copper daggers from the Italic region, which are still missing from Matuschik (1998). However, since the chronological framework established for this work only includes the first two centuries of the 3rd millennium, a general inclusion of the Copper Age daggers of Italy was not possible. The Chalcolithic groups Remedello, Rinaldone, and Gaudo originate in the second half of the 4th millennium or at the turn of the millennium, and extend beyond the first half of the 3rd millennium (*e.g.* Dolfini 2010, Fig. 6; Passariello *et al.* 2010, 25 ff.). The original assumption that Remedello-type daggers date exclusively to the third millennium has since been refuted. Moreover, since some dagger types, such as Remedello, represent very long-lived forms (Dolfini 2010, 707 ff.), which were also produced with only a few formal variations, their more precise chronological determination on the basis of typological characteristics is not possible with any certainty. Generally, therefore, only the Guardistillo dagger type was considered, which, with the radiocarbon-dated grave finds from Ponte San Pietro (graves 21 and 23), has already been reliably proven to date to the beginning/middle of the fourth millennium until the beginning of the third millennium. Although Dolfini (*ibid.*, 716) suggests the possibility of an even longer duration of this type, the most recently discovered pieces have absolute dates between 3331-2900 BCE (Casanuova, LTL-1783A, 4396 ±60 BP) and 2909-2704 BCE (Garavicchio, Tomb 3,

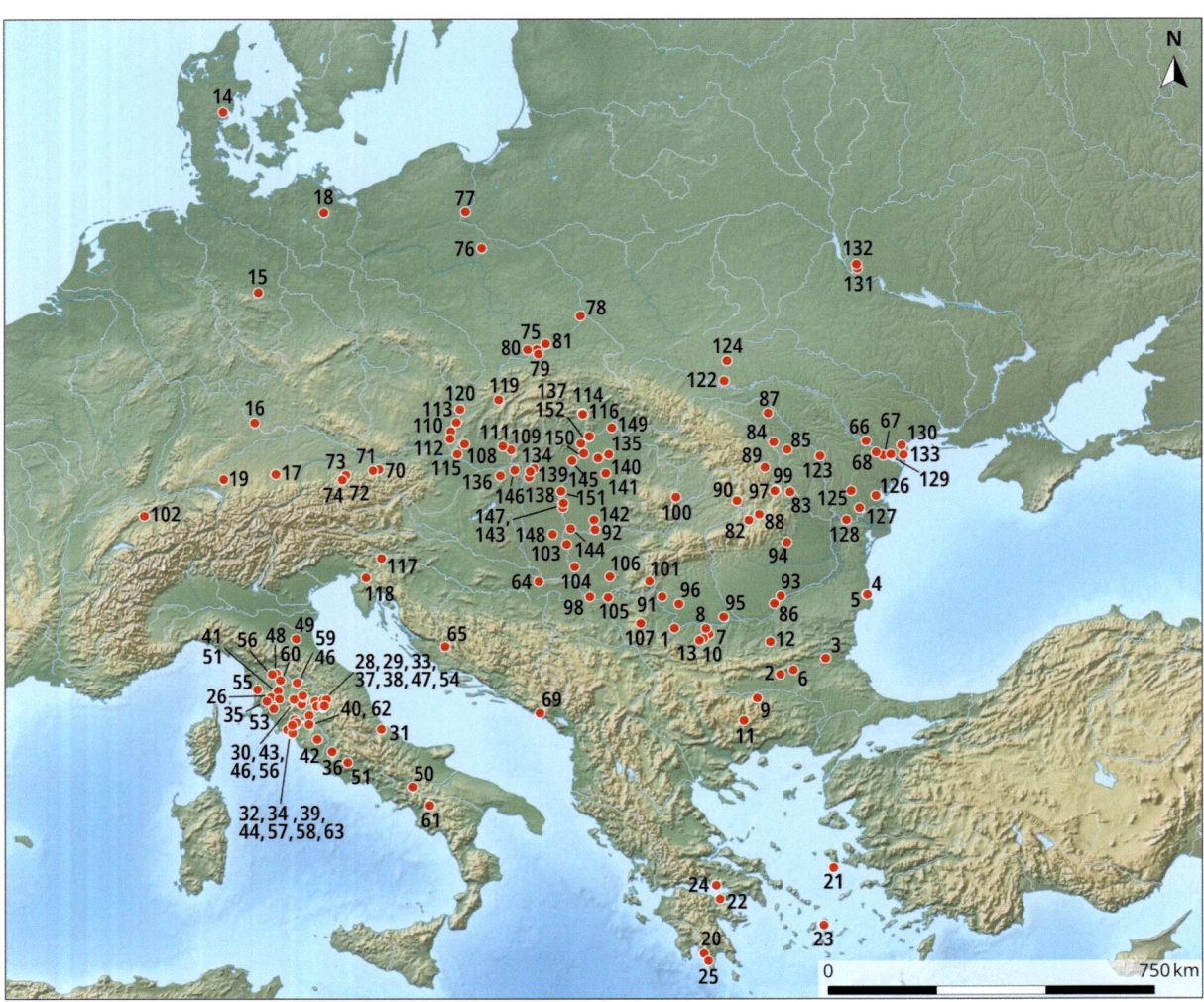

Fig. 37. Distribution map of Chalcolithic daggers. **Bulgaria:** *1. Arcar, 2. Bereketska, 3. Dragantsi, 4. Durankulak, 5. Durankulak, Big Island, 6. Ezero, 7. Galice, 8. Glozhene, 9. Kulceto, 10. Malorad, 11. Haramijskata Dupka, 12. Hotnica-Vodopada, 13. Lesura,* **Germany:** *15. Aspenstedt, 16. Gunzenhausen, 17. Kempfenhausen, 18. Neuenkirchen, 19. Reute,* **Greece:** *20. Aghios Dimitrios, 21. Emporios, 22. Korinth, 23. Zeushöhle (Zas), 24. Agia Marina, 25. Alepotrypa,* **Italy:** *26. Maremma, 27. Battifolle, 28. Canalicchio, 29. Casanuova di San Biagio, 30. Cetona, 31. Chieti, 32. Chiusa Ermini, 33. Costano, 34. Garavicchio, Grave 3, 35. Grotta della Spinosa, 36. Lunghezzina, 37. Marcellano, 38. Marsciano, 39. Monalto di Castro, 40. Orvieto, 41. Partena, 42. Pianetti-Ortaccia, 43. Pienza, 44. Pitigliano, 45. Pozzo di Gualdo Cattaneo, 46. Pozzuolo, 47. Rivototro, 48. San Casciano in Val di Pesa, 49. San Francesco, 50. San Martino, 51. Sgurgola, 52. Solaia, 53. Grotta del Fontino, 54. Gualdo Cattaneo, 55. Guardistillo, 56. Montespertoli, 57. Naviglione, near Farnese, 58. Palombaro, 59. Petrignano di Pozzuolo, 60. Querceto, 61. Buccino, 62. Rinaldone, 63. Ponte San Pietro,* **Croatia:** *64. Lovas, 65. Topolje, near Knin, 66. Sukleja, 67. Tudora (Tudorovo), 68. Purkary,* **Montenegro:** *69. Velika Gruda,* **Austria:** *70. Ertl, 71. Laussa 'Langensteiner Wand', 72. Unterach a. Attersee 'Misling II', 73. Weyeregg am Attersee, 74. Unterach a. Attersee 'See am Mondsee',* **Poland:** *75. Goszyce, 76. Janiszewko, 77. Kałdus, 78. Kichary Nowe, 79. Kraków-Nowa Huta (Wyciaze), 80. Ojców 'jaskinia ciemna', 81. Słonowicach,* **Romania:** *82. Ariușd, 83. Contesti, 84. Cucuteni, 85. Frumusica, 86. Ghizdaru, 87. Hanesti, 88. Leț (Varhegiu/Léczfalva/Várhegy), 89. Mastacăn, 90. Merești, 91. Ostrovu-Corbului, 92. Pecica, 93. Pietrele, 94. Sărata-Monteoru, 95. Vadastra II, 96. Verbița, 97. Viisoara, 98. Vinca, 99. Tîrgu Ocna (Podei), 100. Cheile Turzii (Pestera Ungureasca), 101. Baile Herculane - Peştera Hotilor,* **Switzerland:** *102. Sutz-Lattrigen,* **Serbia:** *103. Čoka, 104. Elemir, 105. Petka, 106. Vršac, 107. Zlot (Zlotska Pecina),* **Slovakia:** *108. Budmerice, 109. Dolné Semerovce, 110. Kúty, 111. Levice-Umgebung, 112. Malé Leváre, 113. Skalica, 114. Barca Baloty, 115. Bratislava, 116. Šebastovce,* **Slovenia:** *117. Ljubljana, 118. St. Kanzian – Tominzgrotte,* **Czech Republic:** *119. Ovčiarsko, 120. Velehrad Rákoš,* **Ukraine:** *121. Alexandrovka (Oleksandrivka), 122. Bil'che-Zolote am Seret, 123. Danku, 124. Horodnica, 125. Horodnje (Ogorodnoje), 126. Nerušaj (Nerushai), 127. Utkonosovka, 128. Karltal (Orlovka), 129. Majaki, 130. Usatovo, settlement, 131. Krasny Chutor (Cervonij Chutir), 132. Sofievka, 133. Usatovo,* **Hungary:** *134. Aszód, 135. Balkány-Abapuszta, 136. Bánhida-Szelim, 137. Bodrogkeresztúr, 138. Budapest-Rákoscsaba, 139. Gödöllo, 140. Hajduböszörmény, 141. Konyár, 142. Magyar Dombegyháza, 143. Magyartés, 144. Maroslele, 145. Négyes-'Nyárádka', 146. Pilisszántó, 147. Pusztaistvánháza, 148. Szeged-Bilisics, 149. Fényeslitke, 150. Tiszapolgár-Basatanya, 151. Rákóczifalva, 152. Tiszalúc (Map basis NaturalEarthData).*

OxA-8231, 4236 ±29 BP). Therefore, only pieces that have been absolutely dated on the basis of radiocarbon analyses, or that can be reliably placed in the period before 2800 BCE on the basis of the finds associated with them, have found their way into the recording and mapping presented here. This suggests a paucity of finds in northern Italy that most probably does not exist.

In the two overview studies (Matuschik 1998 and Vajsov 1993), Greece has so far been left out, which is most probably due to the difficult access to Greek literature because of the language barrier. Fortunately, finds of copper daggers are now also published in English. A total of six daggers — mostly cave finds — are known from Chalcolithic sites and have also been included in the maps. Other Copper Age daggers are known from the Iberian Peninsula and from France. As with the specimens from Italy, they originate from contexts connected with Chalcolithic societies, the duration of which extends beyond the period covered by this work. Due to the lack of daggers that can be clearly dated before 2800 BCE, they had to be left out of the maps.

10.2 Dagger typology

The decisive typological features that are used to identify daggers are the form and type of hafting, and the presence or absence of middle ribs or ridges[6]. In the typological subdivision of Copper Age daggers, a distinction has so far been made between the 'lancet and hilt daggers' and the 'rivet and notched daggers'. As will be shown in the following, these must be supplemented by the group of 'tanged daggers'. In his study of Chalcolithic daggers, Matuschik (1998) divides the collection into a total of nine types, some of which are further subdivided into variants and sub-variants. In terms of relative chronology, with the exception of the northern Alpine daggers, he refers to the chronological system of the Hungarian Copper Age according to Kalicz (1982).

10.2.1 Lancet and flange hilted daggers *(Lanzett- und Griffzungendolch)*

The first large group are the lancet and flange hilted daggers (Matuschik 1998) (Figs. 38 and 39). These include, on the one hand, the lancet and flange hilted daggers of the early High Copper Age of the Pusztaistvánháza or Bodrogkeresztúr type and, on the other hand, the daggers of the same forms of the late High Copper Age, whose range of shapes is far less uniform than that of the earlier phase. These include smaller lancet-shaped daggers, among others from Slovakia, some of which have middle ridges on one side and are referred to by Slovakian researchers as the Šebastovce type (*ibid.*, 214). Comparable daggers are found during the late High Copper Age period in the entire eastern Carpathian Basin up to the south-eastern Carpathians (*ibid.*, 214). Other lancet daggers come from the Sofievskaya local group of Trypillia in present-day Ukraine.

A series of new radiometric dates proves that some daggers from this group of lancet-shaped daggers must be considered older than previously assumed. Raczky and Siklosi (2013) suggest, on the basis of AMS dates from the Tiszapolgár-Basatanya cemetery, that Tiszapolgár, which began in 4500/4400 BCE, largely overlaps with Bodrogkeresztúr. Brummack and Diaconescu (2014) argue against this and attribute this greater overlap to a plateau in the calibration curve. Using a Bayesian calibration model, considering results from correspondence analyses, they show a sequence of

---

6   Whereas middle ridges result from a rhombic cross-section of the dagger body (Matuschik 1998, 217), middle ribs are differently shaped thickenings in the middle area of an otherwise flat dagger, clearly offset from the blade.

Tiszapolgár-Bodrogkeresztúr-Lažňany/Hunyadihalom (*ibid.*, 245 ff.). For Tiszapolgár, a high probability density of dates between 4400 and 4290/4240 BCE is shown, whereas for Bodrogkeresztúr (A) this occurs between 4300 and 4200 BCE. Thus, only a short phase of simultaneity, if any, seems possible (*ibid.*, 252). The previously assumed beginning of Bodrogkeresztúr is thus shifted forward by 200 years to c. 4300 BC and ends already at the turn of the 4th millennium (Rosenstock *et al.* 2016, 79 f.). Accordingly, the lancet-shaped daggers of the Pusztaistvánháza/Bodrogkeresztúr type, whose occurrence was traditionally only placed from 4000 BCE onwards, are earlier. The daggers of the Šebastovce type mentioned above, which are known from the cemeteries of the Lažňany group from Šebastovce and Barca, are also considerably older than assumed by Vajsov (1993), for example. Two graves with daggers from the cemetery in Barca were dated by means of radiometric analyses. Both human and animal bone material were analysed, with the dates of the human remains ~100 and ~200 years older, respectively, than the date of the pig bone. Burial 18 from the cemetery in Barca, Slovakia, yielded the following dates (*ibid.*, 7 ff.):

- MAMS-14242, 5002 ±29 BP, 3938-3871 BCE (24.1%) 3812-3703 BCE (71.3%), pig bone; MAMS-14243, 5208 BP ±27, 4047-3966 BCE (95.4%), human bone;
- MAMS-14244, 5102 ±24 BP, 3966-3911 BCE (35.6%), 3879-3803 (59.8%) human bone.

Two dates of human bone come from tomb 21, which contained a dagger of the same type:

- MAMS-14250, 5074 ± 24 BP, 3956-3891 BCE (34, 6 %), 3885-3798 BCE (60.8 %);
- MAMS-14253, 5102 ±26 BP, 3969-3907 BCE (36.3 %), 3880-3801 BCE (59, 1 %)[7].

The possibility of the 'reservoir effect', caused among other things by nutrition, must therefore be considered. A similar discrepancy in the dating of human and animal bones from the same burial contexts is already known from the cemetery in Varna (Bulgaria) (Brummack 2012, 9).

Further absolute dates from contexts of the settlement of Tiszalúc (Hungary) (*ibid.*), confirm the occurrence of lancet and flange hilted daggers in the Lažňany-Hunyadihalom cultural group in the period between c. 4000/3950 and 3800/3750 BCE. Brummack (*ibid.*, 13), however, does not want the dates to be understood as an absolute time span and duration of this cultural group, as they are only based on a total of seven dates from two sites. The occurrence of vessels with typological features of the Lažňany-Hunyadihalom group in cemeteries of Bodrogkeresztúr (Zalai-Gaál 2016, 400) indicates a somewhat earlier onset before 4000 BCE. For the daggers of the Sofievskaya group of the late Trypillia (stage CII), a date from c. 3300 BCE can be assumed (Diachenko/Harper 2016, 84 ff.).

---

7   Data recalibrated with OxCal v.4.2.4 using dataset INTCAL13 (Reimer *et al.* 2013).

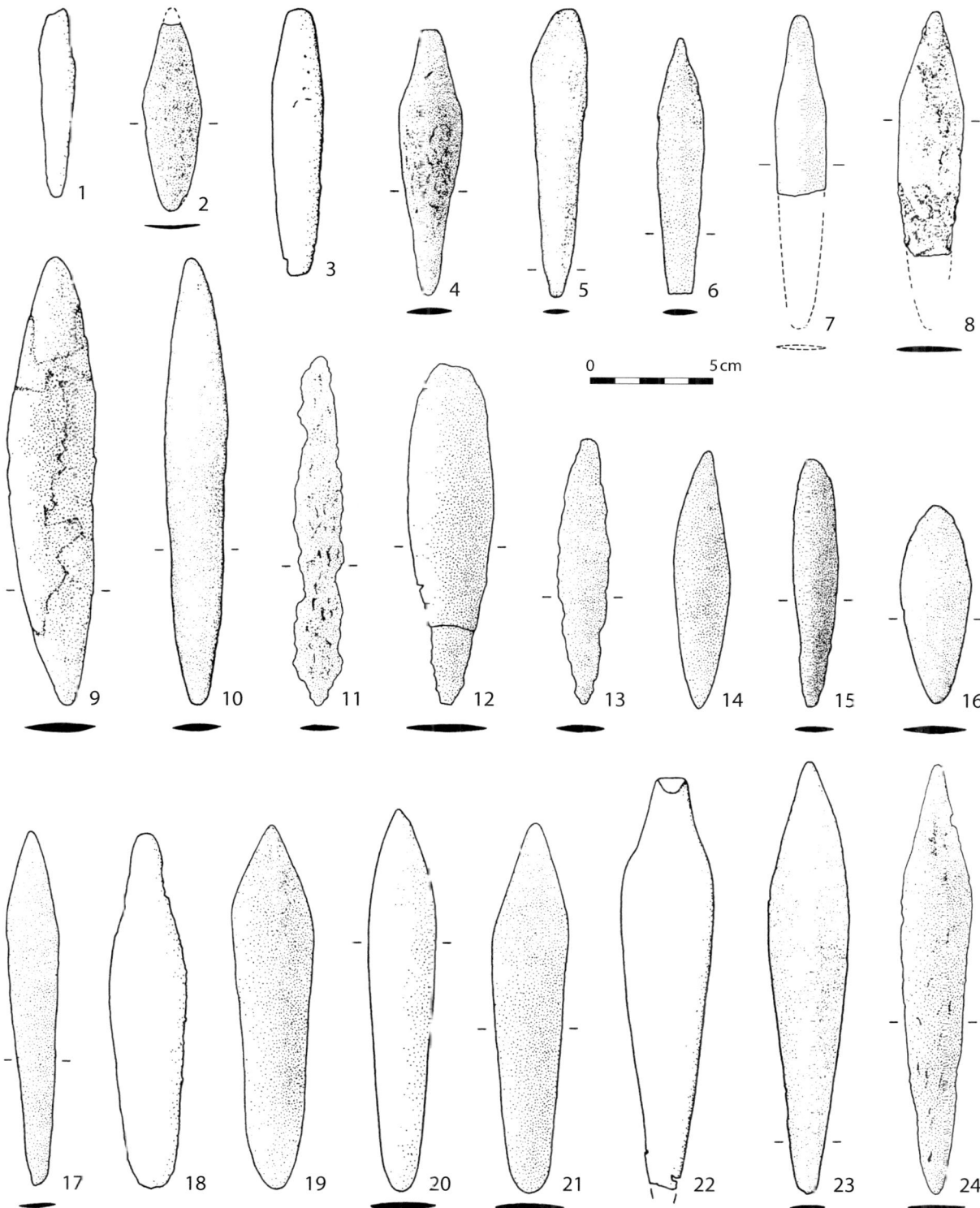

Fig. 38. Lancet and flange hilted daggers (Pusztaistvánháza/ Bodrogkeresztúr type): 1. Coka; 2. Baile Herculane; 3. Hungary, exact location unknown; 4. Horodnica; 5. Gödöllo; 6. Bodrogkeresztúr; 7. Tiszapolgár-Basatanya; 8. Baile Herculane; 9. Ariusd; 10. Konyar; 11. Fényeslitke; 12. Magyartes; 13. Fényeslitke; 14. Piliszántó H; 15. Mastacan; 16. Vinca; 17. Budapest-Rákoscsaba; 18. Szeged-Bilisics; 19. Tiszapolgár-Basatanya; 20. Ostrovu-Corbului; 21. Meresti; 22. Aszód; 23. Magyar Dombegyháza; 24. Pusztaistvánháza (Matuschik 1998, 216, fig. 217).

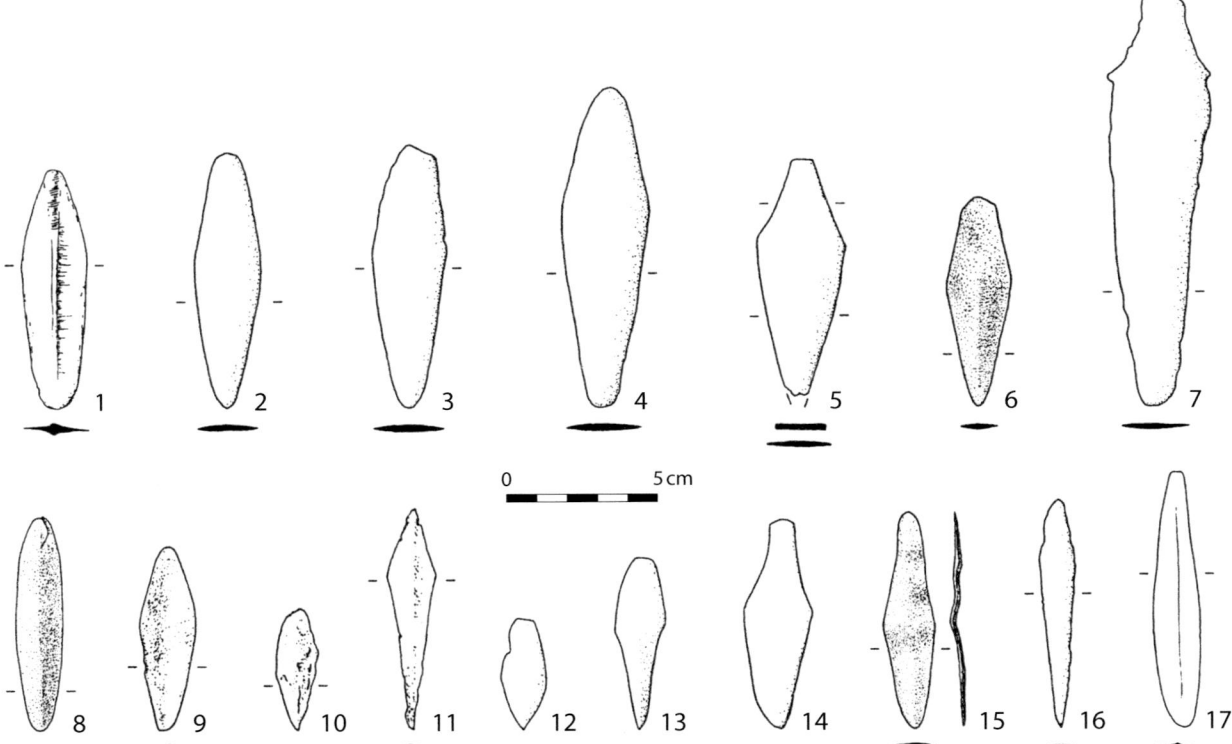

Fig. 39. Lancet and flange hilted daggers of the late High Copper Age (No. 1-10) and Late Copper to Early Bronze Age (No. 11-17): 1. Ljubljana; 2-4. Sofievka; 5. Kulceto; 6. Haramijskata Dupka; 7. Bereketska; 8. Barca (Grab 18); 9. Barca (Grab 21); 10. Šebastovce (Grab 24); 11. Šebastovce (Grab 35); 12-14. Tiszaluc; 15. Pecica; 16. Verbita; 17. Viisoara (Matuschik 1998, 218, fig. 218).

10.2.2 Type Frumusica

Matuschik (1998) considers a group of three lancet-shaped daggers without midribs and with double rivets as a typological link, which he calls type Frumusica (Fig. 40). In his opinion, this type mediates between the lancet and the riveted daggers in general. He agrees with Novotná's (1982) dating to the Cucuteni B stage. Vajsov (1993) argued for a slightly older dating into the AB 2 stage. In general, however, the absolute chronology of the Trypillia/Cucuteni complex is not very secure and the internal relative division of Cucuteni can only be roughly reproduced on the basis of the ^{14}C data obtained so far (Rosenstock *et al.* 2016, 82) (cf. Fig. 41). It is also possible that the Cucuteni AB stage is merely a local expression that does not justify a chronological stage. The pottery typical for this assumed stage comes from only a few settlement sites with existing stratigraphic information, which, however, do not show any pottery of the preceding Stage A or the following Stage B[8]. If the previously postulated Stage AB does not exist and belongs to Stage B, this would mean a longer Stage B, with a duration between 4200-3600 BCE. This contrasts with the previous dating of Stage B from c. 3800 to 3500 BC (Govedarica/ Hauptmann 2004, 227; Govedarica and Manzura 2015). If one follows Matuschik's (1998) and Novotna's (1982) dating to the 'traditional' stage B, the Frumuscia type is located in the early fourth millennium from c. 3800 BCE. Vajsov's (1993, 122 ff.) classification in level AB 2 would currently imply a marginally older dating between c. 3900 and 3800 BCE. The dagger from the Serbian cave Pecina supports such a placement of the type around the turn of the millennium or

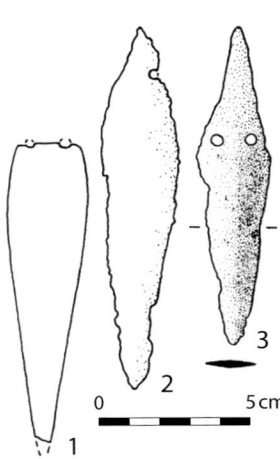

Fig. 40. Frumusica-type rivet daggers: 1. Hajdúböszörmény; 2. Zlotska Pecina; 3. Frumusica (Matuschik 1998, 221, fig. 222).

8   Friendly personal communication from Alexandr Diachenko, 14.02.2017.

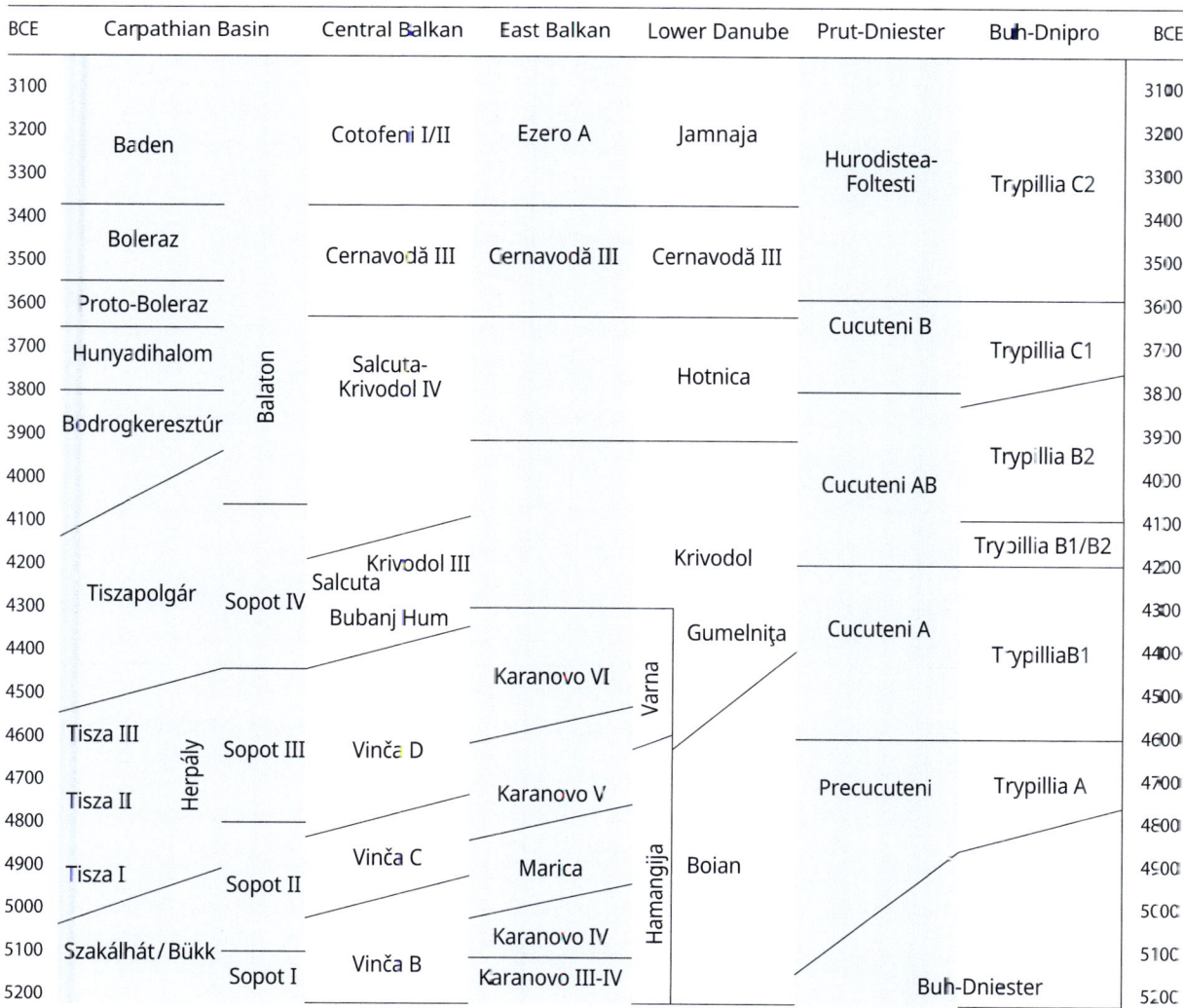

BCE	Carpathian Basin		Central Balkan	East Balkan	Lower Danube	Prut-Dniester	Buh-Dnipro	BCE
3100								3100
3200	Baden		Cotofeni I/II	Ezero A	Jamnaja	Hurodistea-Foltesti	Trypillia C2	3200
3300								3300
3400	Boleraz		Cernavodă III	Cernavodă III	Cernavodă III			3400
3500								3500
3600	Proto-Boleraz					Cucuteni B		3600
3700	Hunyadihalom		Salcuta-Krivodol IV		Hotnica		Trypillia C1	3700
3800								3800
3900	Bodrogkeresztúr	Balaton				Cucuteni AB	Trypillia B2	3900
4000								4000
4100							Trypillia B1/B2	4100
4200	Tiszapolgár	Sopot IV	Krivodol III / Salcuta		Krivodol	Cucuteni A		4200
4300			Bubanj Hum		Gumelnița		TypilliaB1	4300
4400				Karanovo VI	Varna			4400
4500								4500
4600	Tisza III	Herpály / Sopot III	Vinča D					4600
4700	Tisza II			Karanovo V		Precucuteni	Trypillia A	4700
4800								4800
4900	Tisza I	Sopot II	Vinča C	Marica	Boian			4900
5000					Hamangija			5000
5100	Szakálhát / Bükk	Sopot I	Vinča B	Karanovo IV				5100
5200				Karanovo III-IV		Buh-Dniester		5200

Fig. 41. Overview of the Chalcolithic groups of eastern and south-eastern Europe (Müller/Rassmann 2016, 2, fig. 2).

first centuries of the fourth millennium. The piece was found in a layer that can be assigned to stage IV of Salcuta, which is considered contemporaneous with Hunyadihalom (*e.g.* Patay 2005, 121; Govedarica/Hauptmann 2004, 227). The absolute dates discussed above for the Lažňany-Hunyadihalom group, to the period between 4000/3950 and 3800/3750 BCE, strengthens the case for a Frumuscia-type chronology to that date.

10.2.2.1 Excursus on further typological links

Three new dagger finds can possibly be addressed as typological links (between lancet and riveted daggers) which do not belong to the aforementioned Frumuscia type. These come from the burial ground of Bodrogkeresztúr from Rákóczifalva, Hungary, dating between 4334-4075 BCE (Csányi *et al.* 2010, 263 f.). The dagger from grave 140 (Fig. 42.1) can easily be assigned to the Pusztaistvánháza/Bodrogkeresztúr type according to its external shape. Its best analogy is the slender dagger from Konyar (Hungary) (Fig 38.10). However, two semi-circular, opposing indentations in the upper third are conspicuous. Such notches are typical for the so-called notched daggers, which are only known from Late Copper Age and Early Bronze Age contexts in the Ukraine, Bulgaria, and Serbia (Matuschik 1998, 215). None of the pieces of the Pusztaistvánháza/Bodrogkeresztúr type known so far have such notches.

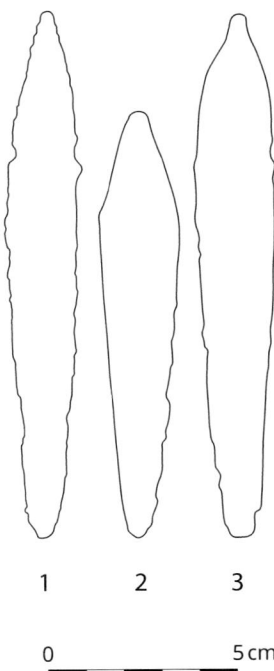

Fig. 42. The daggers from the Rákóczifalva cemetery (1. grave 140, L. 14.2 cm; 2. grave 141, L. 11.5 cm; 3. grave 145, L. 14.1 cm (after Csányi et al. 2010, 23, fig. 9).

For the dagger from grave 141, Csányi *et al.* (2010, 267) see an exact parallel in a piece from the Pusztaistvánháza cemetery. In principle, the assignment to this type can be agreed with, but the piece has two special features. On the one hand, the lower third of the blade shows a middle rib or ridge, and on the other hand, the shape of the haft area is more likely to be trapezoidal, with shoulders offset towards the blade. The Pusztaistvánháza/Bodrogkeresztúr type, on the other hand, does not have a central rib or ridge. If this assumption is confirmed, this would be a transitional type to the later midrib daggers or daggers with a rhombic cross-section. The same applies to the trapezoidal hilt area, which only appears in the younger Cucuteni type (after Matuschik 1998, 221 ff.). Up to now, there has been a controversial discussion about the functional interpretation of the Pusztaistvánháza/Bodrogkeresztúr type as a dagger or possible knife, since daggers without a central rib have a lower resistance to buckling (Matuschik 1998, 213). That the pieces were certainly used as thrusting weapons is shown by the damage to some specimens (*e.g.* cf. Fig. 20.5). The middle rib thus represents a technological innovation that improved the use of daggers as thrusting weapons. Since it can be assumed that, as Matuschik (*ibid.*) writes "[...]the idea of the dagger as a thrusting weapon did not 'fall ready-made from the sky', but developed only gradually", an experimental phase is quite conceivable, which manifests itself in the possible early central rib and the slightly different hilt shape of the dagger from grave 141. The third dagger from the Rákóczifalva cemetery, from grave 145, can also be assigned to the Pusztaistvánháza/Bodrogkeresztúr and this piece also has a special feature. In contrast to the other representatives of the type, the end of the haft is more strongly cinched and then ends in a thorn-like extension (cf. Fig. 42 .3). This typological feature will be taken up again in the following discussion to the dagger from Neuenkirchen.

The daggers discussed so far have only been published as photographs, so that the postulated midrib of the dagger from grave 140 is only a conjecture for the time being, since the piece has been described as 'flat' (Csányi *et al.* 2010, 267). The notches of the dagger from grave 141, on the other hand, have found their way into the description, as has the thorn-like hilt end of the dagger from grave 145 (*ibid.*).

10.2.3 Notched Daggers of the Late Copper to Early Bronze Age

As mentioned above, Matuschik (1998, 215) groups a number of daggers with notches, some of which also have a middle rib, into the group of notched daggers (see Fig. 43). In research, these daggers were mostly referred to as riveted daggers (*Nietdolche*), as riveting could be detected in many daggers (*ibid.*). However, the rivets used to fix the handle are not located over the dagger body as a whole, but only in the edge areas, so that the characteristic notches are created. Daggers of this type occur in Ukraine, Bulgaria, and Serbia during the Late Copper to Early Bronze Age. New absolute dates allow the chronological position to be can be specified with greater precision (on this see Diachenko/Harper 2016, 84 ff.). Thus, the Ukrainian specimens can be dated to 3550-3100 BCE (Usatovo) and 3300-3000 BCE (Sofievka Group of the Late Trypillia). The Bulgarian specimens probably date to the middle of the fourth millennium, as Vajsov (2002, 161 ff.) points out for the dagger from grave 982 of the Copper Age cemetery Durankulak. Daggers from Ezero of the Bulgarian Early Bronze Age are found from 3200/3100 BCE onwards (*ibid.*, 163).

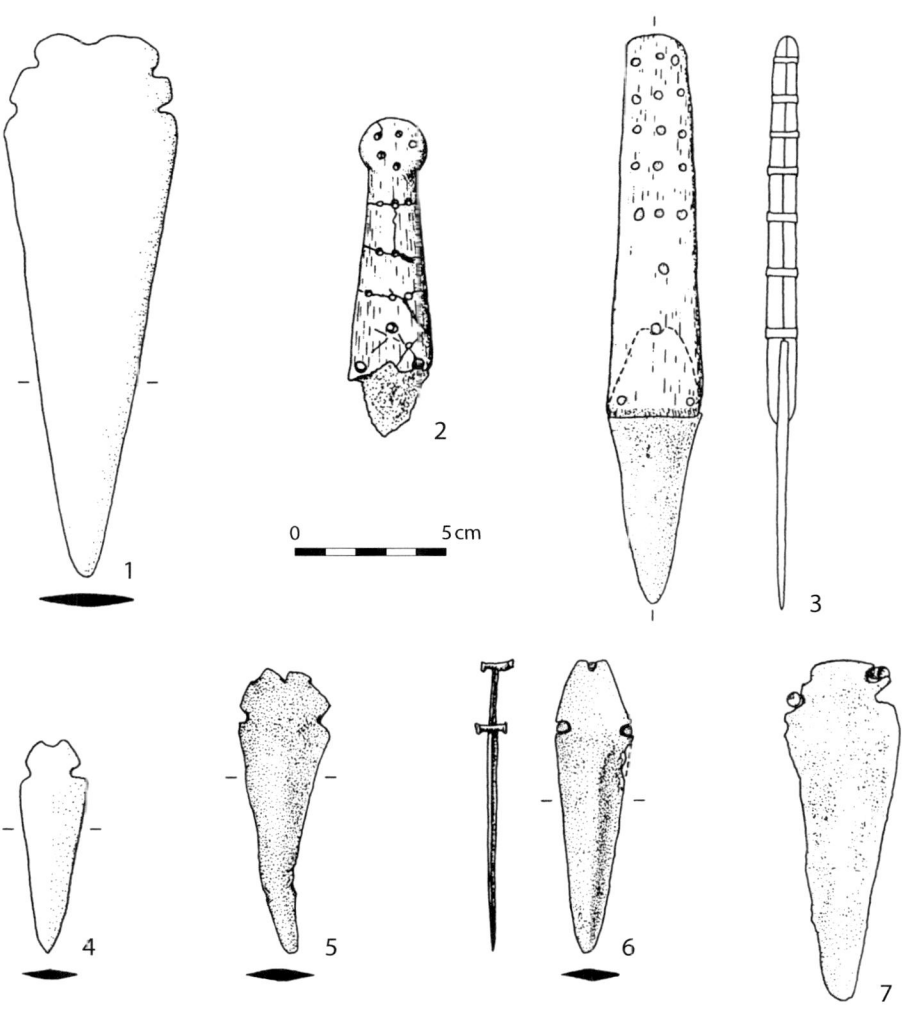

Fig. 43. Notched daggers of the Late Copper Age to Early Bronze Age: 1. Cervonij Chutir; 2. Nerušaj; 3. Ogorodnoje; 4. Elemir; 5. Danku; 6. Durankulak, grave 982; 7. Usatovo, Nekr. I, Kurgan 4 (Matuschik 1998, 220, fig. 221).

10.2.4 Rivet daggers of the Cucuteni type

Matuschik (1998, 221) combines a large group of midribless rivet daggers with three to five rivet holes, as well as with trapezoidal, ogival, and partly flange hilt plates, into his type Cucuteni, which is further subdivided into the variants Vădastra, Lovas A and B, as well as Mondsee A and B.

10.2.4.1 Variant Vădastra

The Vădastra variant includes relatively large and stocky daggers characterised by a basically flat-rhombic cross-section (Fig. 44). The trapezoidal to ogival/triangular hilt ends usually have three rivet holes, in a few cases four. The distribution area of the dagger type extends from the lower Danube, through the Eastern Carpathian, to the North Pre-carpathian and Northwestern Pre-carpathian regions (*ibid.*, 222 ff.). According to Vajsov (1993) and Matuschik (1998), the daggers generally date to the end of the High Copper Age but also to the Late Copper Age. There are no known pieces with absolute dates, but some stratified finds can be indirectly dated. For example, one dagger comes from the settlement Vădastra II, which is assigned to the Salcuta IV stage, which, as already mentioned above, is contemporaneous with the Lažřany-Hunyadihalom cultural group. The available radiometric dates range between 4000/3950 and 3800/3750 BCE and confirm a dating to the late Middle

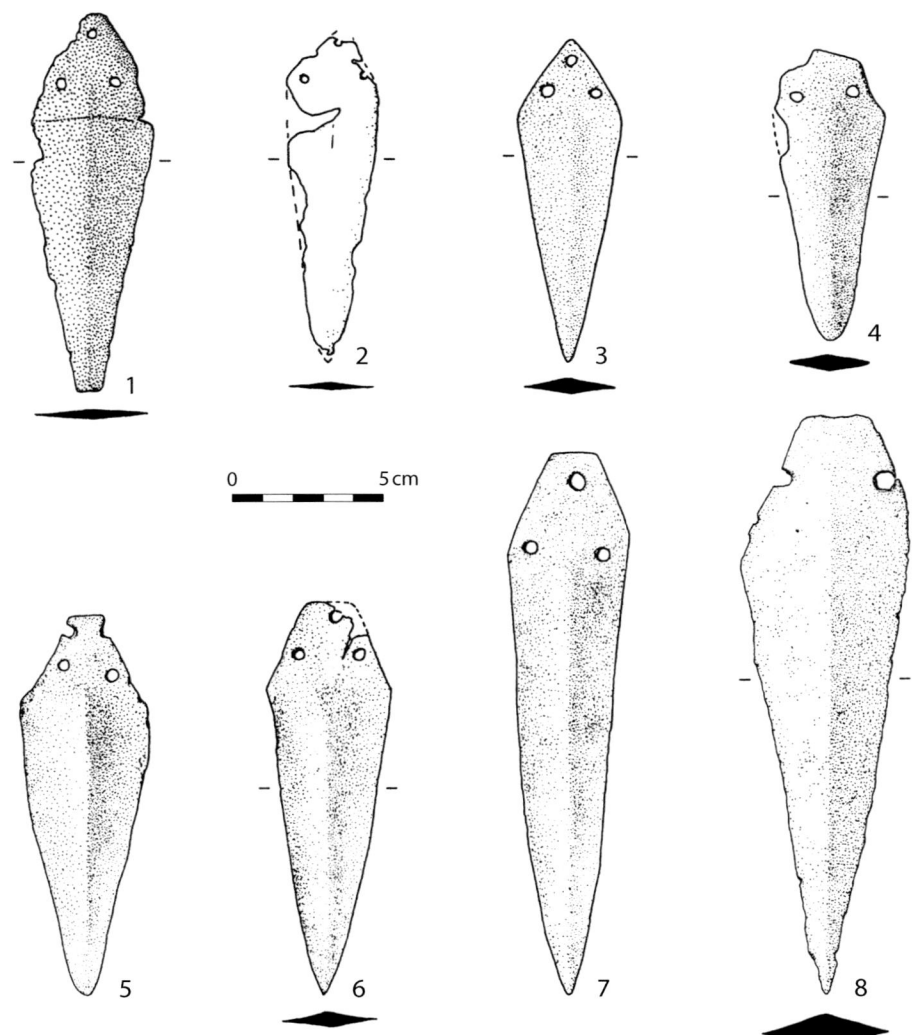

Fig. 44. Rivet daggers of the Cucuteni type, variant Vădastra: 1. Nowa Huta-Wyciaze; 2. Baile Herculane, layer e5; 3. Vădastra; 4. Sarata Monteoru; 5. Cucuteni; 6. Galice; 7. Hanesti; 8. Levice (Matuschik 1998, 222, fig. 223).

Copper Age. The specimens from layers e5 and f of the Baile Herculane cave[9], which are assigned to Coțofeni (Mareş 2002, 188 f., Nos. 75 and 76), confirm the postulated dating to the late Copper Age. Except for one representative from the Romanian Conțeşti[10], which is made of Nógrádmarcal type copper enriched with antimony, silver, and bismuth of the, the daggers of this variant are made of arsenical copper[11] (Matuschik 1998, 222 f.).

10.2.4.2 Variants Lovas A-C

The daggers of the Lovas A variant, which vary in size, are characterised above all by a long, narrow shape (Fig. 45). The trapezoidal to tongue-shaped hilt always has three rivets. The cross-section varies in equal proportions; half of the examples are flat and the other half flat-rhombic. Variant B is only distinguished by facets on the cutting edges (Fig. 47).

9   The layers of the Coțofeni group (from e5) are above those of the Hunyadihalom group (e2), which is also represented (Mareş 2002, 188 f.; Patay 2005, 121).

10   Classification as a Vădastra variant is uncertain.

11   There are contradictory analyses for a dagger from Nowa Huta-Wyciaze in Poland. One analysis shows pure copper and another shows copper containing antimony, arsenic, silver, and bismuth (Matuschik 1998, 221).

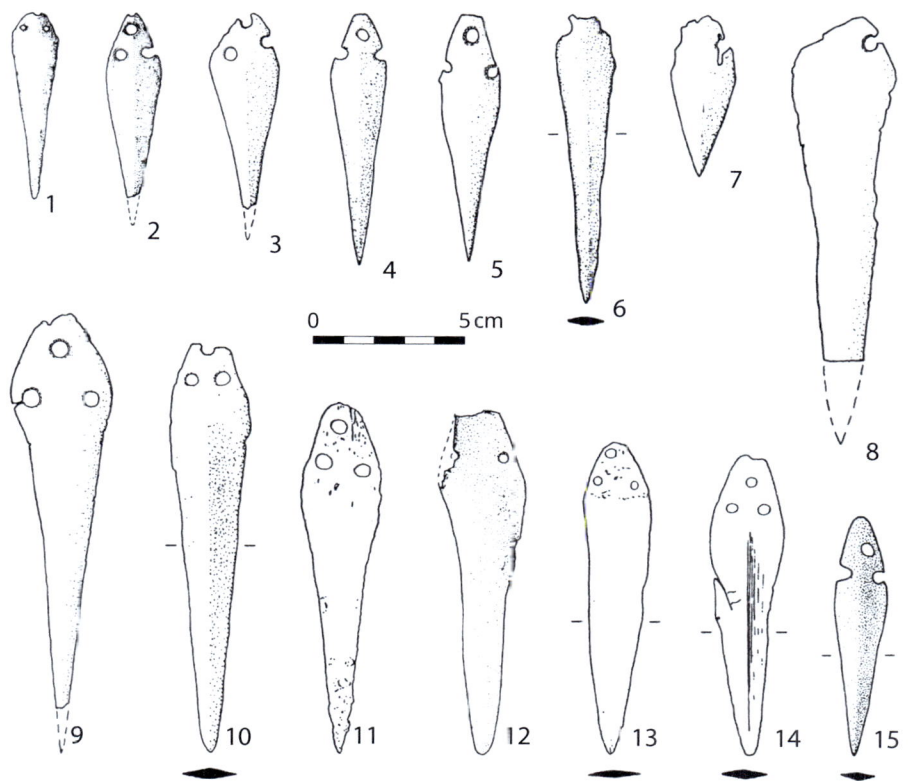

Fig. 45. Rivet daggers of the type Cucuteni, variant Lovas A:
1. St. Kanzian, 2. Lovas; 3., 5., 7.-9. Unterach-See a. Mondsee; 4. Topolje; 6. Unterach-Misling II; 10. Arcar; 11. Museum Pecs, site unknown, 12. Tirgu Ocna; 13. Negyes; 14. Ghizdaru, 15. Hotnica-Vodopada (Matuschik 1998, 223, fig. 224).

A piece from Kempfenhausen was provisionally assigned to variant A by Matuschik (1998). After publication of the piece by Pflederer *et al.* (2009), this classification could be verified on the basis of the shape. However, the dagger has an asymmetrical blade cross-section caused by a middle-rib-like thickening on one side of the blade (Fig. 46.5). Matuschik (*ibid.*) assigns only daggers without midribs to the Cucuteni type, so that strictly speaking, the specimen should not be assigned to this type. However, since there are other pieces with such peculiarities, the author is of the opinion that the introduction of a separate variant is justified, whose decisive typological feature is the formation of a unilateral middle rib or a unilateral middle rib imitation, while in its other typological features it is close to the Lovas A variant. Following Matuschik's nomenclature (*ibid.*), the variant is to be called Lovas C. This variant includes the daggers from Kempfenhausen, Bratislava, and Weyregg, as well as a dagger from Italy, the exact location of which is unknown (Fig. 46.4). Matuschik (*ibid.*, 232) has already assessed the specimens from the latter two sites as being close to the Lovas variant, but has set them apart as special forms due to the formation of the middle ribs, which he interprets as an influence of the Malé Leváre/Dolné Semerovce dagger type. With the new find from Kempfenhausen, which, minus the one-sided middle rib formation, so clearly corresponds to the Lovas A variant of the Cucuteni type, the affiliation of the pieces to the Lovas C variant becomes clear.

The daggers of this variant are distributed from the northern Alpine region, to the area of the northern Adriatic region, to the surroundings of the Dinaric mountains, and from the Carpathian basin to the lower Danube (*ibid.*, 227). The majority of the finds are unstratified single finds, so that an exact dating is difficult. However, for some settlements of the Late Neolithic Mondsee and Altheim groups, from which unstratified daggers originate, absolute dates are available. From the lakeside settlement of Kempfenhausen, where the dagger described in more detail above was found, dendrochronological data indicate a single-phase construction activity around 3720 BCE. The annual felling dates of the ash and oak trees were between 3723 and 3719 BC (Pflederer *et al.* 2009, 127). For two other daggers from

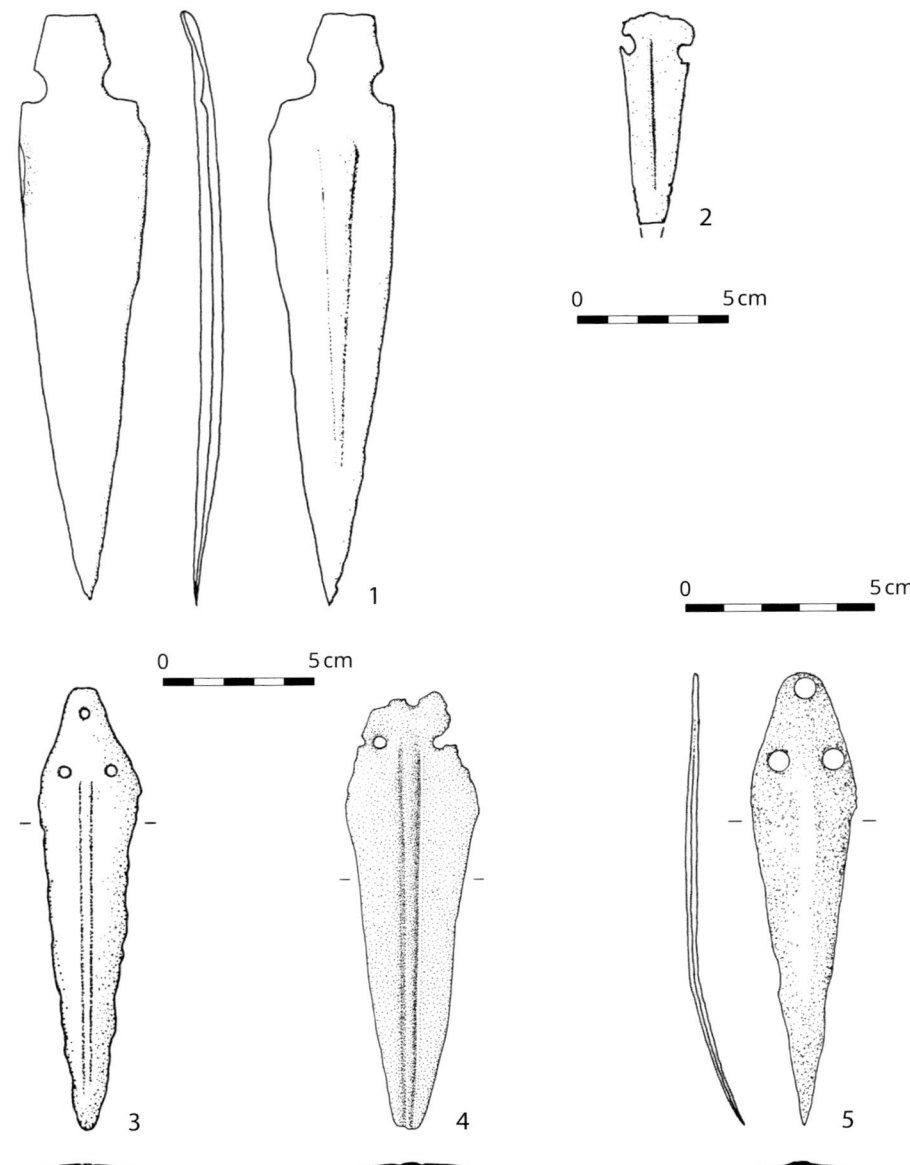

Fig. 46. Cucuteni-type rivet daggers, newly formed variant Lovas C: 1. Bratislava; 2.-3. Weyeregg; 4. Italy, site unknown; 5. Kempfenhausen. (1.-3., Matuschik 1998, figs. 228-4; 4., 6. & 7., Bianco Peroni 1994, pl. 9.11; 5., Pflederer et al. 2009, 130, fig. 7.3).

the lakeshore settlement of Weyregg, two radiometric dates are available, which, however, show a wide range (Stadler 1995, 218):

- VRI 732, 4640 BP ± 110, 3645-3031 BCE (95.4 %);
- VRI 733, 4660 ± 100 BP, 3645-3623 BCE (81.7 %),3245-3101 BCE (13.7 %).

The same applies to the three radiocarbon dates from the lakeshore settlement Misling II at Lake Attern, which also yielded a dagger, but which appear somewhat younger overall (*ibid.*): VRI 355, 4390 ±90 BP, 3346-2888 BCE (95.4 %);

- VRI 4710 ±90 BP, 3695-3678 BCE (0.6 %),3671-3331 BCE (92.6 %), 3214-3186 BCE (1.1 %), 3156-3217 BCE (1.1 %);
- VRI 357, 4610 ± 90 BP, 3634-3552 BCE (8.2 %), 3541-3089 BCE (86.7 %), 3047-3037 BCE (0.5 %).

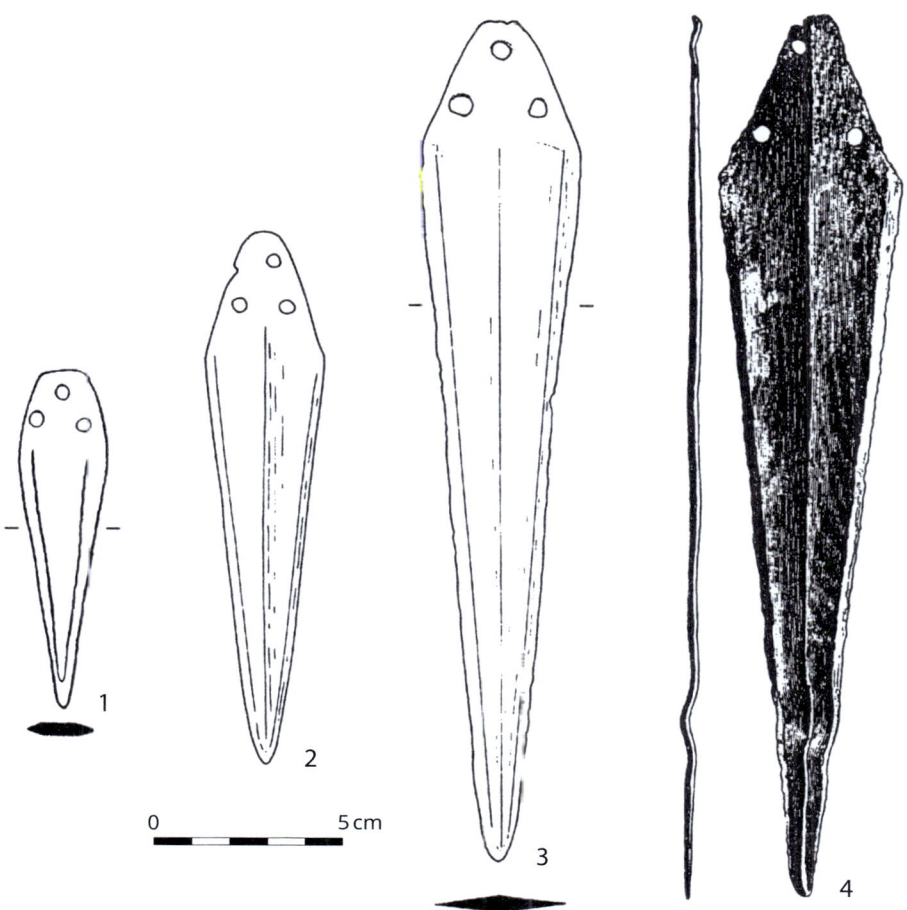

Fig. 47. Rivet daggers of the Cucuteni type, Lovas variant B: 1. Lesura; 2. Museum Timisoara, exact location unknown; 3. Let; 4. Hungary, exactly location unknown (Matuschik 1998, 224, fig. 225).

Matuschik (1998, 224) places a dagger from the Slovenian Tominz cave near St. Kanzian (San Canzian) roughly in the horizon of the Late High Copper Age. The reason for his assessment is a flat axe found in the same stratum, which is typologically close to the axes of the Kornwestheim type, which date to the early horizon of the Pfyn-Altheim-Cortaillod. From the absolutely-dated settlement Hotnica-Vopoda, of the Pevec group in Bulgaria, come two daggers of this variant (both from Horizon I). In total, five radiometric dates are available from both settlement layers (I+II), but the dates from the stratigraphically-younger layer provide older dates[12] (Horizon I: BLN 3680, 4830 ± 60 BP, 3760-3742 BCE (1.2%), 3715-3505 BCE (89.6%), 3428-3381 (4.6%); Horizon II: BLN 3681, 4830 ± 60 BP, 3760-3742 BCE (1.2%), 3715-3505 BCE (89.6%), 3428-3381 (4.6%); BLN 3682, 5110 ± 50 BP, 4036-4023 BCE (1.4%), 3994-3785 BCE (94%); BLN 3683, 4950 ± 60 BP, 3941-3858 BCE (13.5%), 3816-3638 BCE (81.9%); BLN 3684, 4950 ± 60 BP, 3941-3858 BCE (13.5%), 3816-3638 BCE (81.9%); BLN 3685, BP 4890 ± 60 BP, 3893-3883 BCE (0.6%), 3799-3626 BCE (84.7%), 3597-3526 BCE (10.0%) (Vajsov 1993, 117)[13].

The cutting facets characteristic of the Lovas B variant are reliably attested in south-eastern Europe from the Boleráz horizon at the earliest, so that Matuschik (1998, 227 ff.) places this variant in the early Late Copper Age. A cumulative calibration of the 26 radiometric dates for the Boleráz horizon recorded in the Kiel ^{14}C database 'RADON' (Hinz *et al.* 2012) shows a peak between 3694-3354 BCE.

---

12   The sample material is unknown, so possible old wood and reservoir effects could be responsible for this.

13   Data recalibrated with OxCal v.4.2.4 using dataset INTCAL13 (Reimer *et al.* 2013).

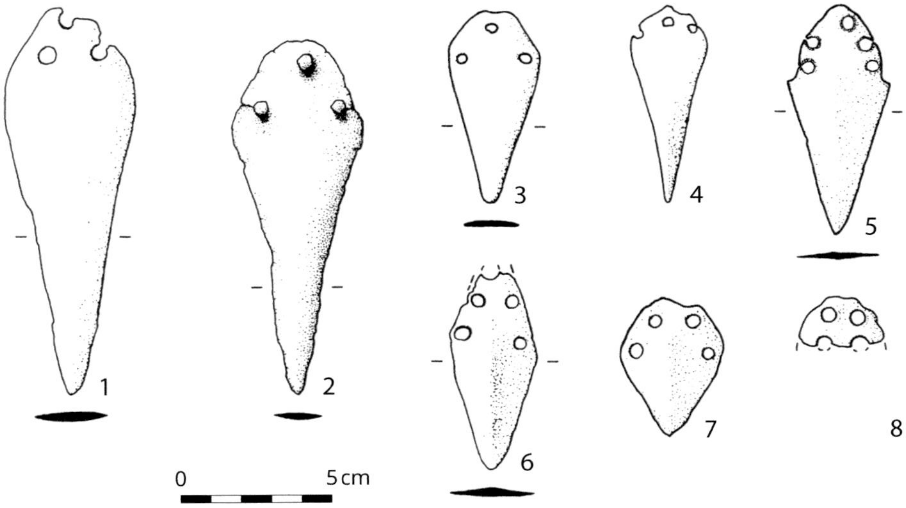

Fig. 48. Rivet daggers of the Cucuteni type, Mondsee variant: 1. Moravia/Upper Hungary (=Slovakia), site unknown; 2. Reute; 3. Bratislava vicinity; 4. Laussa; 5. Ertl; 6. Sutz-Lattrigen; 7. Museum Gunzenhausen, site unknown; 8. Unterach-See (Matuschik 1998, 225, fig. 226).

Of the pieces examined, all the daggers are made of a copper with elevated arsenic content except for the piece from Négyes in northern Hungary, which is made of Nógrádmarcal copper.

10.2.4.3 Variant Mondsee

In this variant, Matuschik (*ibid.*, 227 f.) groups together a number of smaller and squat daggers with ogival and trapezoidal hilts (Fig. 48). He again divides the variant into two groups on the basis of the number of rivet holes: Group A with three and Group B with four to five rivet holes. The spectrum of cross-sections ranges from flat to flat-rhombic pieces. A dagger from Sutz-Lattringen in Switzerland (Fig. 52.6) has an asymmetrical blade cross-section. In contrast to Matuschik (*ibid.*), however, the author does not consider this to be a middle ridge, but rather a slight middle rib formation, because the cross-section is not flat-rhombic or semi-flat-rhombic, but rather comparable to the dagger from Kempfenhausen discussed above with a unilateral midrib. As already discussed for the Lovas variant, the presence of a middle rib contradicts Matuschik's typological dogma for the Cucuteni type (*ibid.*, 221). However, as has already been shown for the newly-introduced Lovas C variant, in some cases this must be abandoned. The daggers from Reute, Bratislava, and another dagger from Slovakia, are very close to the Vădastra variant and differ only in their flat cross-section (*ibid.*, 228).

Daggers of the Mondsee variety are known mainly from the northern Alps, from the Swiss midlands, and from the area between Moravia and Slovakia. Only the dagger from the Late Neolithic settlement of Reute, which is dated to c. 3740 BCE on the basis of dendrochronological analyses, comes from a securely-documented context (*ibid.*, 209 ff.). Some other pieces are old finds from sites for which a Late Neolithic settlement is also known. For the lakeshore settlement of Sutz-Lattringen (Hauptstation), a settlement period between 3825-3013 BCE in eight settlement phases has been proven by a large number of dendrochronological analyses (Hafner 2005, 41 ff., Hafner 2010, 132 ff.). Reference can be made to the aforementioned absolute dates for the settlements of the Mondsee group, Ertl and Unterach/Attersee. Ceramic material from the settlement in Ertl also shows influences from the Boleráz Group (Maurer 2014, 145 ff.) and thus indicates occupation in the second half of the 4th millennium. As far as trace element analyses are available, the daggers consist of Mondsee copper, which contains arsenic (Matuschik 1998, 229).

10.2.5 Type Balkány

Two rivet daggers with central ribs and cutting-edge facets are grouped together by Matuschik (1998) to form the Balkány type (Fig. 49). Due to the typological similarity, he sees the older variant Lovas B of the Cucuteni type as a possible typological link to the Balkány type. On the basis of the shaft-necked axes of the Kozarac type associated with the dagger, which are attributed to Vučedol, he dates this type of dagger to the end of the Late Copper Age (Matuschik 1998, 225). For the find of the golden(!) dagger from Velika Gruda, radiometric data are available that place the grave at the turn of the 3rd millennium (directly from the grave: ETH 7613, 4335 ±80 BP, 3336-3211 BCE (10.6%), 3193-3151 BCE (2.5%), 3138-2859 BCE (77.9%), 2809-2753 BCE (3.6%), 2721-2702 (0.9%); from the tumulus: ETH 7685, 4355 ±65 BP, 3327-3219 BCE (9.2%), 3176-3160 BCE (1.1%), 3121-2879 BCE (85.2%)[14].

10.2.6 Type Dolné Semerovce/Malé Leváre

Matuschik (*ibid.*, 229 ff.) assigns a group of daggers with a pronounced midrib on both sides and four to five rivets to his Dolné Semerovce/Malé Leváre type spectrum (Fig. 51). The distribution of this type, which appears standardised due to its external form, is limited to a small area in Slovakia and Moravia. The only exception is a fragment from San Francesco (Italy), which also comes from an Iron Age(!) hoard. Its typological homogeneity is also reflected in the trace element composition, as all pieces consist of Nógrádmarcal copper[15]. The basis for the chronological positioning of the daggers of this type is mainly based on the finds from two hoards associated with them. One specimen was found together with two massive, flat-rectangular chisels in Velehrad-Rákoš in the Czech Republic. Typologically-similar, but much smaller, chisels are known from graves of Tiszapolgár (most recently Zimmermann 2007, 53; Horn 2014, 73). Horn (2014, 73) places the comparative pieces from graves and hoards in the Bodrogkeresztúr phase. The hoard from Malé Leváre in Slovakia contains, in addition to the dagger, a flat axe, a fragmentary spectacle spiral and an axe-adze (Fig. 50). The axe is assigned to the Nógrádmarcal type, which is close to the Jászládany and Tîrgu-Ocna types (Vulpe 1975, fig. 1 and Zimmermann 2007, 52). Both Zimmermann (*ibid.*) and Horn (2014, 73) refer in their relative chronological positioning to the character of the axe-adze as a diagnostic form for High Copper Age Bodrogkeresztúr and classify the hoard accordingly. Matuschik (1998, 230) also assumes that the hoard belongs to the High Copper Age and, on the basis of the associated flat axe, which he places in the vicinity of the Kornwestheim-type axes (cf. the discussion of the dagger from St. Kanzian), further delimits it to the Late High Copper Age. Němejcová-Pavúková (1970) places the hoard in the Cucuteni B phase (Klimscha 2016, 155). In terms of absolute chronology, Horn (2014)[16], among others, still assumes an end of Bodrogkeresztúr around c. 3400 BCE. According to the most recent research discussion, however, this end is to be assumed as early as around 4000 BCE. Klimscha (2016, 155) has recently shown that axe-adzes are closely linked to Bodrogkeresztúr, but also occur in earlier, as well as later, chronological contexts. The axe-adzes of the Tîrgu-Ocna type originate in Bulgaria from secure Cucuteni and Usatovo contexts (*ibid.*). As mentioned above in the discussion of the chronology of the Frumusica type and the notched daggers, the beginning of the Cucuteni B phase is traditionally dated around 3800 BCE and Usatovo around 3550 BCE. The long duration of the axe daggers, and the fact that all types are already represented at the time of Bodrogkeresztúr, make it difficult

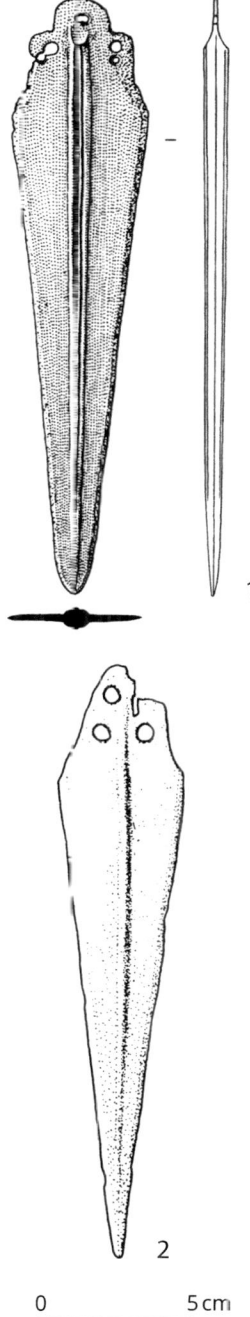

Fig. 49. Balkány type: 1. Balkány-Abapuszta 2. Velika Gruda (Matuschik 1998, 230, fig. 231).

---

14   Data recalibrated with OxCal v.4.2.4 using dataset INTCAL13 (Reimer *et al.* 2013).
15   No trace element analysis is available for the piece from Italy.
16   Horn (2014, 73 ff.) refers to these daggers as halberds.

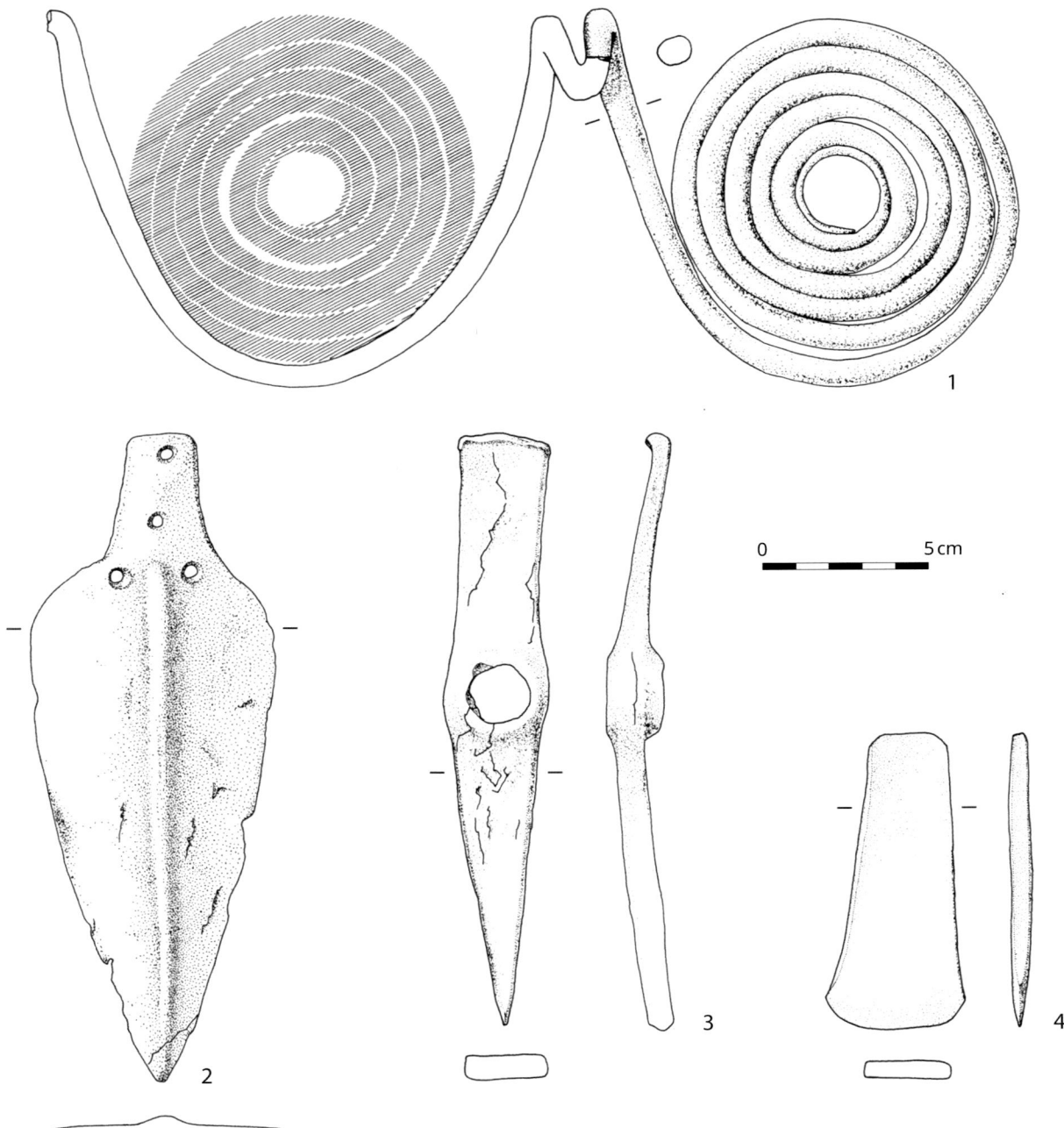

Fig. 50. Hoard find from Malé Leváre (after Vajsov 1993, 131, fig. 3.5-7).

to date them precisely on the basis of this object type. In addition, a hoard find from Kałdus, Poland, shows that heavy tools were still found together with daggers in the second half of the 4th millennium (see dagger type Usatovo). The related Nógrádmarcal copper speaks in favour of dating the manufacture of axe daggers to around 4000 BCE. If one accepts Matuschik's (1998, 230) postulated similiarity of the flat axe to the Kornwestheim type axes, which date to the early horizon of Altheim-Pfyn-Cortaillod, then one must reckon with deposition of the hoard and the emergence of the Malé Leváre/Dolné Semerovce dagger type from 3800 BCE onwards. However, a date as early as around 4000 BCE also seems possible.

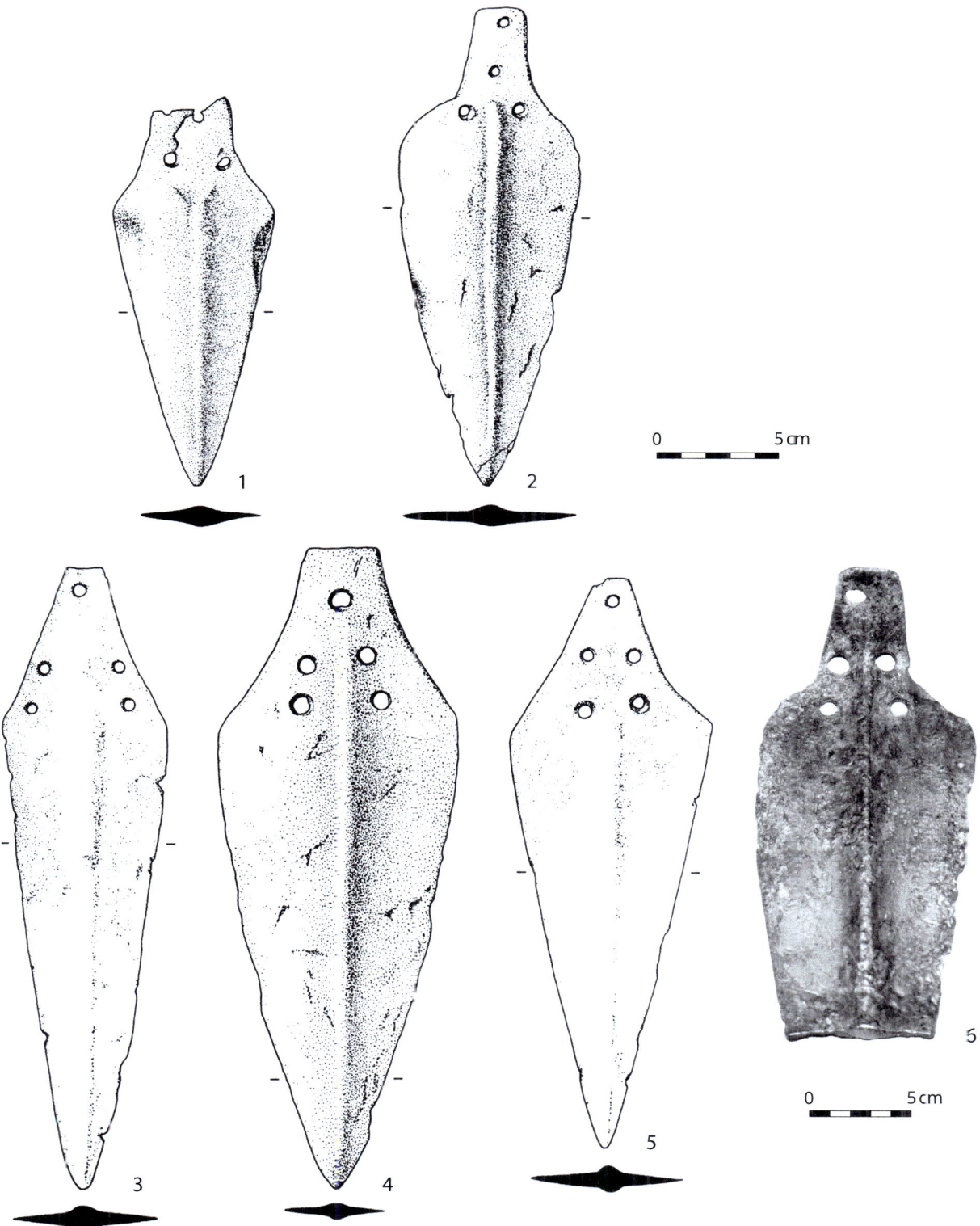

Fig. 51. Rivet daggers with middle rib of Malé Leváre/Dolné Semerovce type: 1. Kuty; 2. Malé Leváre; 3. Skalica; 4. Velehrad-Rákos; 5. Dolné Semerovce; 6. San Francesco (1.-5., Matuschik 1998, 226, fig. 227; 6. L. 10.6 cm, Zimmermann 2007, 51, fig. 1).

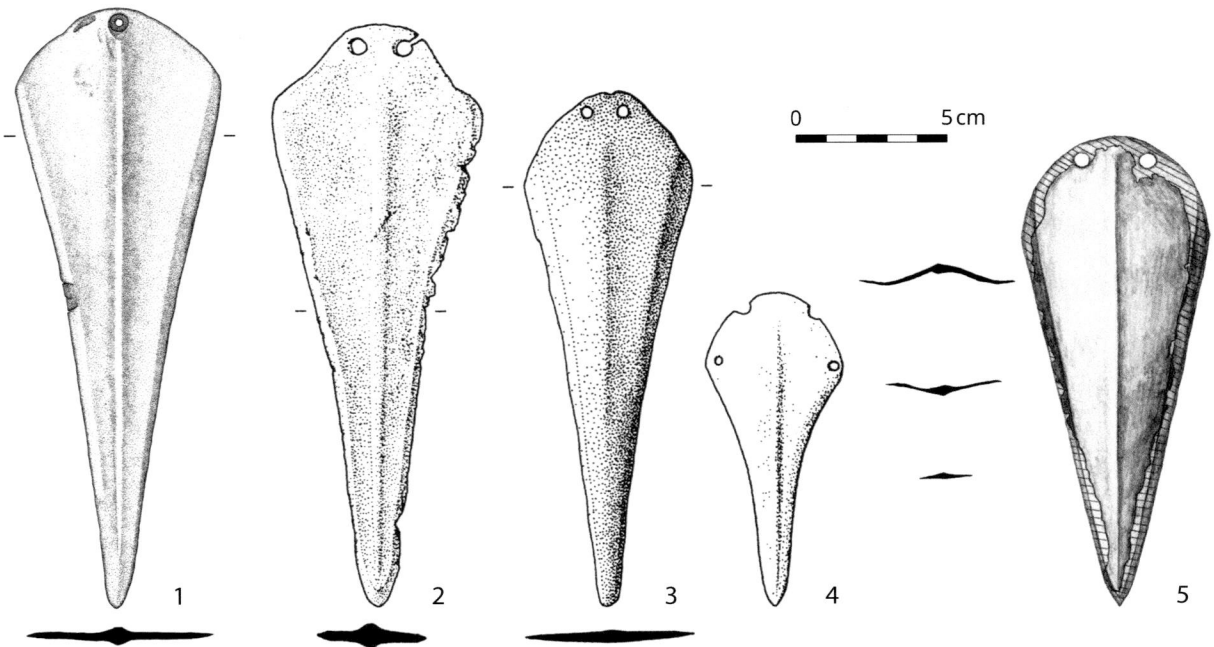

Fig. 52. Usatovo-type rivet daggers with middle ribs:
1. Kałdus; 2. Usatovo; 3. Goszyce;
4. Petka; 5. Słonowice
(1. Adamczak et al. 2015, 207,
fig. 9; 2.-4., Matuschik 1998, 231,
fig. 232; Przybyla/Tunia 2013,
146, fig. 7/2b).

10.2.7 Type Usatovo

Matuschik (1998) names a group of large triangular daggers with oval, in part with somewhat offset hilt ends, after the Ukrainian site where two of these almost standardised-looking daggers were found. The pieces have one or two rivets and a clearly pronounced midrib on both sides (Fig. 52). An exception is a dagger from Goszyce, Poland, which only has a slight middle rib on one side of the blade. At the time of publication of the compilation by Matuschik (1998), a total of four specimens were known. In addition to the two pieces from the eponymous site, another came from Petka in Serbia and from the aforementioned Gosycze. According to current data, a further distribution centre is evident in the area of present-day Poland, in addition to today's Ukraine. The new Polish finds include the 1 piece from Kałdus and the 2 from Słonowice[17] (Adamczak et al. 2015 and Przybyla/Tunia 2013). All daggers, except for the piece from the hoard find in Kałdus, come from graves. The single find from Petka comes from a burial mound, so that a burial context can be assumed. The chronological position is comparatively clear due to the well-documented finds from Ukraine and Poland.

The Ukrainian pieces come from burial mounds of the Usatovo group, which dates between 3550 and 3100 BCE (Diachenko/Harper 2016, 84 ff.). The Polish daggers can be regarded as roughly contemporary. The Kałdus hoard was encountered in a stratigraphic context with a pit containing numerous ceramic materials assigned to the Classic and Late Wiórek phase of the Funnel Beaker Societies and thus dated between 3600/3500 and 3200/3100 BCE (Adamczak et al. 2015, 203). The dagger from Gosycze comes from a shallow grave of the Funnel Beaker Societies, which has not been further classified (Przybyla/Tunia 2013, 157). Three radiometric dates are available from the grave complex with non-megalithic long mounds from Słonowice, which do not come directly from the central grave with the dagger from long mound VIII, but from graves accompanying this long mound. Tomb 55 dates

---

17   A total of three daggers are known from the site (personal communication from Dr. Krzysztof Tunia). The author of this work reliably assigns one specimen to the Usatovo type, the assignment of another is still uncertain. No further information is available on the third piece beyond its mere existence.

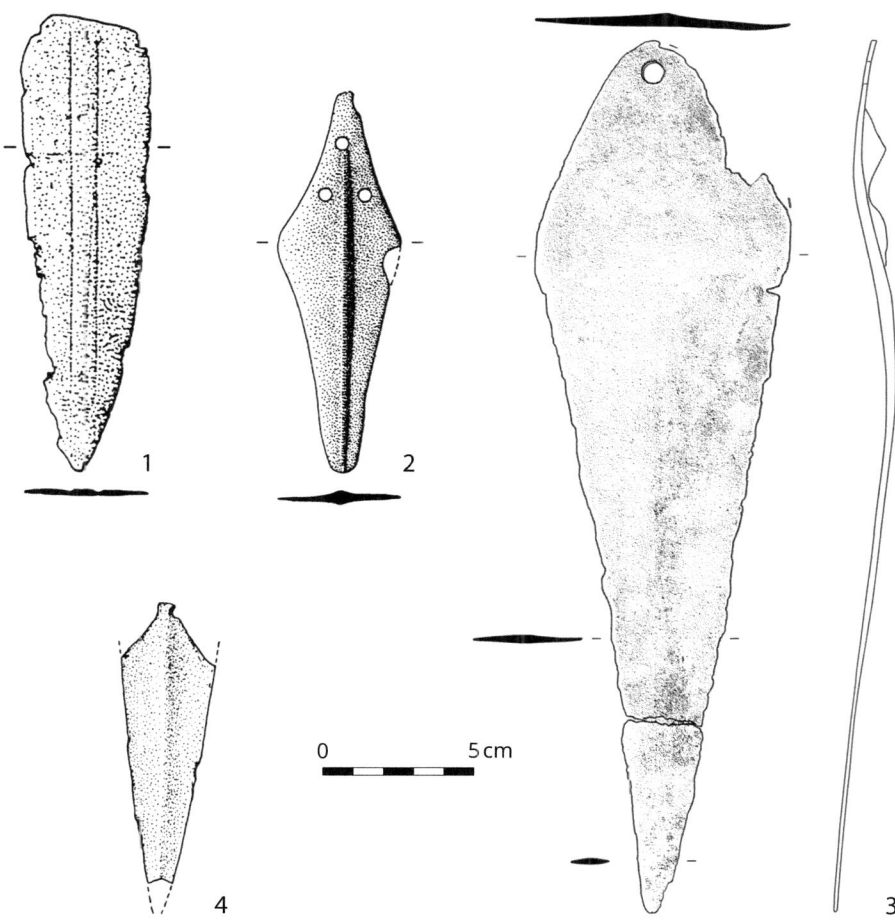

Fig. 53. Special forms: 1. Bygholm; 2. Ojców; 3. Aspenstedt; 4. Bilcze Zlote (1., 2. & 4., Matuschik 1998, 227, fig. 228.1 3 and. 5; 3., Müller 2012 47, fig. 3).

to 3516-3128 BCE (Poz-53329, 4605 ± 35 BP), tomb 111 to 3621-3364 BCE (Poz-53330, BP 4665 ±35) and tomb 131 to 3632-3372 BCE (Poz-53331, 4705 ± 35 BP) (*ibid.*). Apart from the great similarity in shape and chronology, the daggers are linked by a special feature in their trace element composition. As far as they have been analysed, the objects have an unusually high arsenic content of between 5 and 10 %(!). The high arsenic content causes some pieces from Usatovo to have a silvery-looking surface (Vajsov 1993, 113)[18].

10.2.8 Special forms similar to the Dolné Semerovce/ Malé Leváre daggers

Matuschik (1998) summarises under this term a group of daggers whose middle rib formation or imitation is the connecting typological element with the daggers of the Dolné Semerovce/Malé Leváre type, but which cannot be assigned to this type due to formal deviations (Fig. 53). As has been shown, due to typological similarities, a group with an imitated or one-sided middle rib can be separated into the Lovas C variant newly formed by the author. After deduction of these specimens, the group of special forms includes daggers with a clear, double-sided middle rib (Ojców, Poland and Bilcze Zlote, Ukraine), as well as the dagger from the hoard of Bygholm (Denmark) with an imitated, single-sided middle rib. Matuschik (1998, 232) sees in the long, narrow form and the absence of cutting edge facets an approximation of

---

18   The high arsenic content applies not only to daggers of the Usatovo type but also to at least one other notched dagger from the eponymous cemetery (Vajsov 1993, 111, no. 11.5).

the Bygholm dagger to his variant Lovas (A) of the Cucuteni type. If this were true, the piece would have to be sorted into the newly-created variant Lovas C because of the imitation of a middle rib.

In the opinion of the author of this work, however, the indications are too vague, so that this must remain in the group of special forms. The dagger, which is geographically closest to the Neuenkirchen hoard, is also a special form. It was found in Aspenstedt (Saxony-Anhalt), about 245 km away as the crow flies. From there, a long narrow rivet dagger with a triangular grip plate, a singular rivet and a weakly-pronounced central rib on both sides was found in a grave (Fig. 53.3). In terms of its external form, the dagger best corresponds to the Vădastra variant of the Cucuteni type, in which the triangular hilt plate is also found. The decisive factor for the dagger's categorisation as a special form with similarities to the Dolné Semerovce/Malé Leváre daggers — how Müller (2012) also categorises the piece —, is the element of the central rib that connects them. The author is only familiar with the single rivet from the Chalcolithic dagger spectrum from the new find of the dagger from Kałdus (cf. above), which, however, has a completely different shape.

A radiometric date is available from the grave which yielded the aforementioned piece from Aspenstedt, which shows that the dagger cannot have been made later than c. 3400/3300-3100 BCE (KIA 3800, 4540 ± 50 BP, 3491-3470 BCE (2.1 %), 3374-3090 BCE (93.3 %)[19]. Further absolute dating is not available for the remaining daggers. The dagger from Bygholm, or the depot, can be dated to EN II/MN Ia, c. 3500-3300 BCE, on the basis of the decorated funnel beaker contained in the hoard (Klassen 2000, 351 ff. u. Müller 2012, 49). The cave from which the dagger from Ojców came, yielded finds from Lengyel and Baden. Without further details on the stratigraphy, the piece dates to Baden at the latest (from c. 3500 BCE). However, an earlier dating is quite possible, also in view of the trace element composition (cf. below). The dagger, which also came from a cave, was accompanied by finds of 'Tripolje C1 materials' (Matuschik 1998, 248, No. 23). According to the current state of research, Stage C1 of Trypillia dates between c. 3850 and 3600 BCE (Müller and Rassmann 2016, 165, fig. 4). The metal analyses carried out on the daggers from Aspenstedt and Bygholm revealed an arsenical copper corresponding to the 'Mondsee' copper variety (Klassen 2000, 351, no. 94; Müller 2012, 56). The dagger from Ojców consists of the Nógrádmarcal copper variety (Matuschik 1998, 236, fig. 233 no. 75), which would also support a pre-Baden period dating.

10.2.9 Italic daggers

As already described in the introduction, a number of Italic daggers have to be included in the horizon of early daggers due to new absolute dates. For example, specimens attributed to the types Remedello, Gaudo, Pianetti, Buccino, and Guardistallo according to Bianco Peroni (1994) can, in part, already be dated to the end of the first half of the 4th millennium (inter alia Dofini 2010). The daggers of Italy were compiled and typologically addressed by Bianco Peroni (1994). In the more recent research on the Chalcolithic by Dolfini (2010) and Manfredini (2009), among others, the focus has been placed on the development of metallurgy in Italy and the updating of the chronology, taking radiometric data into account. To the author's knowledge, the inclusion of the Italian daggers in the early dagger horizon of Europe has not been done so far, as the daggers have traditionally been dated much younger. While the Remedello type has a very distinctive form that has no equivalent in the rest of Europe, the Guardistallo type does have formal similarities with other contemporary dagger types. In addition to a brief description of the individual types, these parallels will be considered without claiming to be a typological analysis.

---

19   Data recalibrated with OxCal v.4.2.4 using dataset INTCAL13 (Reimer *et al.* 2013).

10.2.9.1 Type Remedello

The Remedello type, which has a strongly standardised appearance, is characterised by a fundamentally, strictly triangular blade, at the end of which is a clearly stepped, narrow flange hilt, which usually has one rivet hole, and more rarely two rivet holes (Fig. 54). Exceptions are two specimens that are riveted at the base of the blade instead of the flange hilt. The specimens with a middle rib form variant A, the small group without central ribs variant B (Bianco Peroni 1994, 1 ff.). The main areas of distribution are Tuscany and Emilia-Romagna, but finds from both more northerly and more southerly areas indicate that this type of dagger was widespread throughout Italy (*ibid.*, 5).

Traditionally, the Remedello type has been dated to the third millennium at the earliest (Dolfini 2010). A series of radiometric dates from a cave in Tuscany that was used as a burial ground paints a somewhat different picture. In the Grotta della Spinosa, several Chalcolithic layers were encountered, interspersed with disarticulated and fragmented human remains, and terminated by a layer of stones. A dagger of the Remedello type is present from the uppermost layer, but it could not be assigned to any burial. A human bone from near the dagger gave a date between 3485 and 3103 BCE (OxA-18391, 4555 ± 34 BP) (Dolfini 2010, 717, Tab. 2, No. 21). Further absolute dates from the strata of the cave between c. 3600 and 2900 BCE support Dolfini's (*ibid.*) postulate that the Remedello type can also be dated as early as the fourth millennium. The use of arsenical copper is attested for this type (de Marinis 2006, 218).

10.2.9.2 Type Gaudo

The Gaudo type is also characterised by a triangular shape (Fig. 55). Unlike the Remedello type, however, it has no flange hilt (*Griffzunge*) and a narrower blade. The three to four-fold riveting is usually found at the end of the base. The pieces are characterised by pronounced midribs as well as flat cross-sections. The type is widespread mainly in central and southern Italy, but is also scattered beyond, like the Remedello type (Bianco Peroni 1994, 6). An absolute date is available for a cave find from the Grotta del Fontino (Tuscany): 4500 ±50 BP, 3362-3082 BCE (89.5%), 3068-3027 BCE (5.9%)[20] (de Marinis 2006, 218). The results indicate that representatives of this dagger type can already date to the last third of the 4th millennium. The use of arsenical copper is also attested for this type (de Marinis 2006, 218).

10.2.9.3 Type Buccino

In its long, narrow triangular form and single to double riveted flange hilt, Type Buccino resembles both Type Gaudo and Type Remedello (Fig. 56). The distribution of the type is restricted to southernmost Italy (Bianco Peroni 1994, 11 f.). An absolute date is available for a grave with a dagger from Buccino (Campania), which indicates that the type is also to be expected as early as the last third of the fourth millennium (4350 BP ±100, 3516-3397 BCE (11.5%), 3385-2925 BCE (83.9%)[21] (de Marinis 2006, 218).

10.2.9.4 Type Guardistillo

A series of daggers characterised by a great diversity of typological features is grouped by Bianco Peroni (1994) under the type Guardistillo. The unifying element of this group is the hilt shape, which is either ogival or rounded. In particular, the pointed-arched shape is accompanied by a slight shoulder formation. The daggers

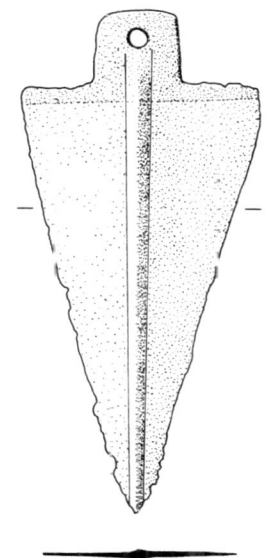

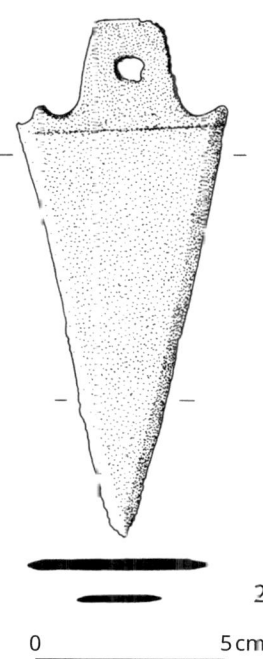

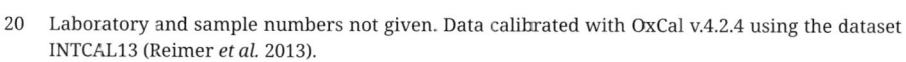

1

2

0   5 cm

Fig. 54. Remedello type daggers variants A (left) and B (right) (Bianco Peroni 1994, pl. 1.1 & pl. 2.16).

---

20   Laboratory and sample numbers not given. Data calibrated with OxCal v.4.2.4 using the dataset INTCAL13 (Reimer *et al.* 2013).

21   See No. 20

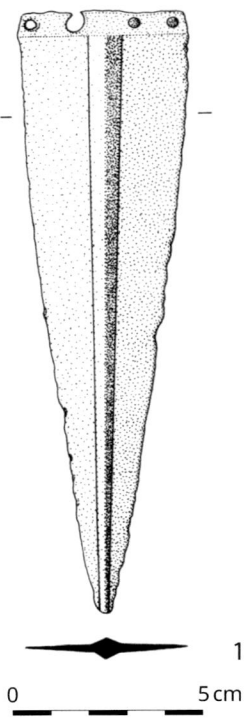

Fig. 55. Type Gaudo (Bianco Peroni 1994, pl. 3.23).

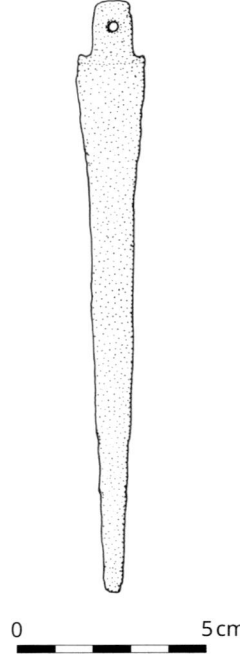

Fig. 56. Type Buccino (Bianco Peroni 1994, pl. 5.55).

mainly have a flat cross-section, but there are pieces with middle ribs as well as with middle ridges (Fig. 57). Two specimens with imitation middle ribs in the form of furrows deepened into the blade are conspicuous. Also represented are daggers with cutting edge facets and one specimen that imitates them by means of furrows. A large number of the daggers show hafting traces, which manifest themselves in various forms. The spectrum of shapes ranges from simple lines running across the blade path to semi-circular and horseshoe-shaped impressions. One to five rivet holes are typical, according to which Bianco Peroni (*ibid.*) also divides the type into five sub-variants. In the specimens with three rivet holes, these are usually arranged triangularly. The main area of distribution is central Italy (Tuscany, Umbria, and Latium), with one specimen from Abruzzo (*ibid.*, 19).

In recent research, a relatively long period is assumed for the Guardistallo type, from the early/middle 4th millennium to the beginning of the 3rd millennium (Dolfini 2010, 716), which can also be reconstructed on the basis of absolute dating. Radiometric examination of the remains of a burial with double daggers from Ponte San Pietro (Lombardy) gave a date at the transition between the Late Neolithic and Early Copper Age[22]: OxA-18217, 4872 ±35 BP, 3748-3745 (0.2%), 3713-3632 (91.3%), 3560-3537 (3.9%). Two further dates of graves with daggers from Casanuova (Umbria) and Garavicchio (Grosseto), gave a date in the Early and Late Middle Copper Age. Garavicchio: OxA-18281, 4236 ±29 BP, 2909-2860 BCE, 2809-2756 BCE (27.0%), 2720-2705 BCE (3.6%); Casanuova: LTL-1783A, 4396 ±60 BP, 3331-3214 BCE (17.6%), 3186-3156 BCE (3.3%), 3128-2900 BCE (74.5%). For the Guardistallo type, copper with elevated arsenic content, as well as copper with elevated arsenic and antimony content, is documented (de Marinis 2006, 211 u. Dolfini 2010, 718.). The elevated arsenic and antimony contents are already documented in the daggers from San Pietro (see above), which date to the early Copper Age, so that it is assumed that sulphide copper ores were processed in Italy in the late first half of the 4th millennium (Dolfini 2010, 718 ff. and Dolfini 2013, 34 ff.).

10.2.9.5 Type Pianetti[23]

This type includes a group of small daggers which, compared to the other types, do not have rivets. The shape of the rather slender daggers can be described as lancet-blade-shaped (Fig. 58). The cross-section is flat or rhombic. There are no true middle ribs. In the author's opinion, the piece with a middle rib from Vecciano, which provided the original name of the type, merely represents a fragment of a dagger of an unknown type. All in all, the compilation into one dagger type seems rather questionable due to the widely varying appearance of the pieces. The distribution of the type is so far limited to Latium in central Italy. Absolute dating is not available for this type. However, tomb 3 of Rinaldone is placed by Dolfini (2004, 238) in the earliest phase of the Italian Copper Age, dating between 3600-3300 BCE according to absolute dates (Dolfini 2013, 39). This agrees with the chronological placement of the tomb in the early half of the 4th millennium by Horn (2014, 85). A similar date can be assumed for the dagger from grave 4 from the eponymous site of Pianetti-Ortaccia, which was associated with a flat axe of the Pianetti-Kollmann type, which is also represented in grave 3 from Rinaldone (for more details cf. Horn 2014, 84 f.).

---

22 Italian chronology according to Dolfini (2013): Final Neolithic 3800-3600 BCE, Early Copper Age 3600-3300 BCE, Middle Copper Age 3300-2700 BCE, Late Copper Age 2700-2200 BCE.

23 Formerly Vecciano type according to Bianco Peroni (1994). However, as the piece from Vecciano was too damaged to be a diagnostic form, it was renamed accordingly (Horn 2014, 84).

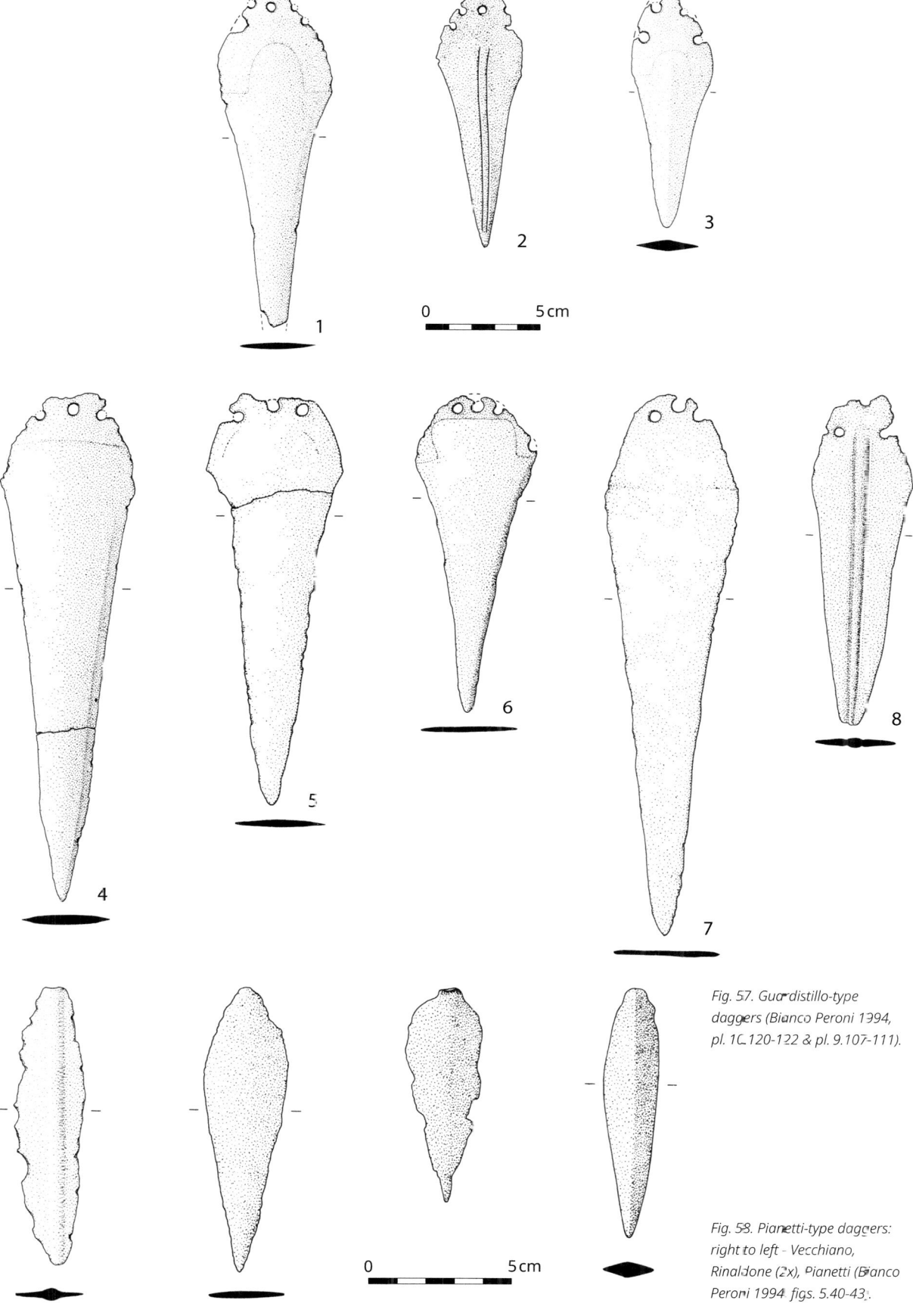

Fig. 57. Guardistillo-type daggers (Bianco Peroni 1994, pl. 10.120-122 & pl. 9.107-111).

Fig. 58. Pianetti-type daggers: right to left - Vecchiano, Rinaldone (2x), Pianetti (Bianco Peroni 1994 figs. 5.40-43).

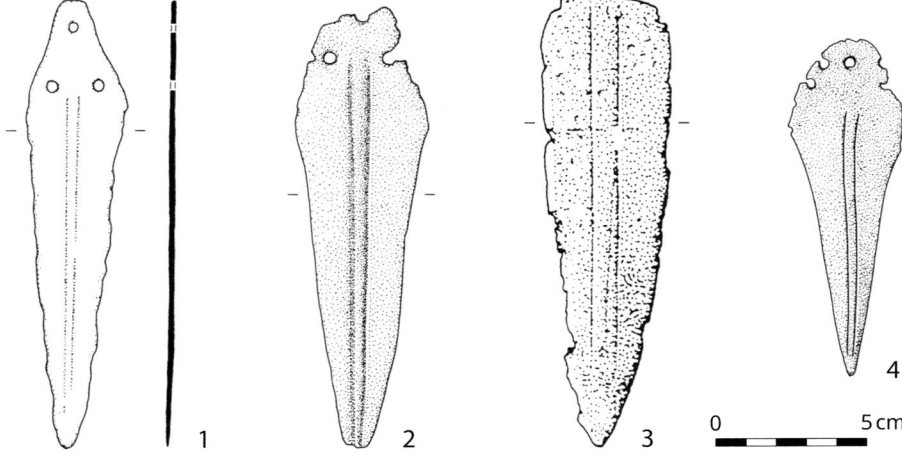

Fig. 59. Daggers with middle rib representation or imitation: 1. Bygholm; 2. Italy, location unknown; 3. Bygholm; 4. Chiusa d' Ermini (1. and 3., Matuschik 1998, 227, fig. 228.3 & 4; 2. and 4. Bianco Peroni 1994, pl. 9.111 & pl. 10.121).

10.2.9.6 Summary of the Italian daggers

While the Remedello, Buccino, and Gaudo types find no equivalents in the Chalcolithic dagger horizon of Europe and appear to be expressions of independent dagger development in the last third of the fourth millennium, the Guardistallo type shows a possible link to dagger development in the rest of Europe. As shown in the description of the aforementioned type, it exhibits a wide range of shapes. In the opinion of the author, this somewhat idiosyncratic compilation into one type by Bianco Peroni (1994) is not tenable. If one compares representatives of this type with the types defined by Matuschik (1998), some striking similarities with the variants Mondsee, Lovas A and B, and Vădastra of the type Cucuteni are noticeable. The formal similarities with the different variants indicate that a future revision of the typology of this group of daggers is necessary. At this point, only the similarity regarding the form, as well as the contemporaneity with the type Cucuteni, should be referred to for the time being. Apart from these similarities, three finds in particular point to a connection between the Italic region and the development of daggers in Central Europe. For example, the idea of the formation of central ribs could have reached present-day Italy with the dagger of the Malé Leváre type from San Francesco (cf. Fig. 51.6). The context — the piece comes from an Iron Age hoard — does not contradict this assumption. It is conceivable that the piece was found by chance in the prehistoric period and then deposited in the ground again in the Iron Age. The connection to the Alpine region is shown by a piece from Italy, without exact location, which shows great similarity to the dagger from Weyregg and can therefore be clearly attributed to the Lovas C variant of the Cucuteni type. On the one hand, they are similar in their outer form, and on the other hand, both have middle rib representations or imitations, as they are also known from the dagger from Bygholm (Fig. 59).

10.2.10 Greek daggers

Only a few daggers with a Neolithic/Chalcolithic date are available from the Greek area. In his overview of metal finds from Neolithic contexts, Zachos (2007) lists a total of nine daggers from five different sites (Alepotrypa, Aghios Dimitrios, Agia Marina, Corinth, and Chios). Alram-Stern (2014) shows further dagger finds from Strophilias, Tharrounia, Dimini, and Mikrothives on her distribution map of Chalcolithic copper finds (Fig. 60). As the primary literature referred to was not accessible and no further information or illustrations of these pieces are available, only the daggers listed by Zachos (2007) are considered here (Fig. 61).

Fig. 60. Overview of early Greek daggers according to Alram-Stern (2014): 1. Alepotrypa; 2. Aghios Dimitrios; 3. Mikrothives; 4. Dimini; 5. Tharrouria; 6. Strophilas; 7. Zas Cave (author's representation, map base NaturalEarthData).

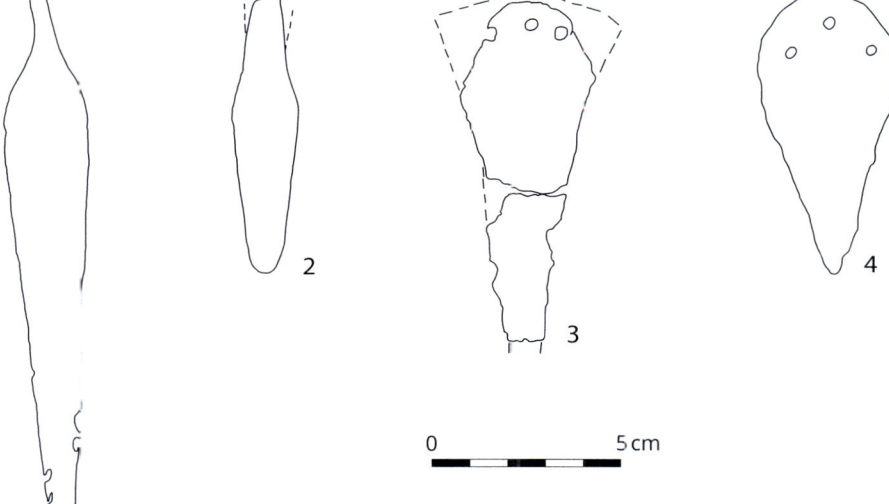

Fig. 61. Compilation of early Greek daggers: 1. Aghios Dimitrios; 2. Zas Cave; 3. Alepotrypa; 4. Aghia Marina (after Zachos 2007, fig. 11.6).

Due to the small number and sometimes poor preservation of the pieces, it is difficult to establish a type. Basically, however, two groups can be distinguished. The first group consists of small and stocky rivet daggers with triangular, flat blades. These can be further divided into specimens with rounded and straight hilt bases. The number of rivet holes varies between two and five. The second group, which consists of only three specimens, is characterised by a long, narrow shape. The specimen from Aghios Dimitrios has a tang hilt (*Griffangel*) and a unilateral middle rib, while the piece with a flange hilt from the Zeus cave on Naxos has a flat cross-section. It is not possible to decide on the type of hafting of the dagger from Corinth, which has at least a partial middle rib, as only one fragment is available. The dagger from Aghios Dimitrios dates to the late 5th millennium on the basis of a ^{14}C date. According to Alram-Stern (2014, 319), the Copper Age pottery from the Alepotrypa cave, where four of the daggers were also found, dates to a later period of the Chalcolithic. She places the younger Copper Age between c. 3600/3500 BCE and 3100/3000 BCE (*ibid.*, 306). According to Zachos (2007, 178), the daggers from

Agia Marina certainly belong to a Late Neolithic or Chalcolithic stratum, but cannot be more precisely dated. No further information is available on the pieces from Corinth and Chios, apart from the reference to their Neolithic date. Apart from a piece from Agia Marina, which is similar in shape to the Mondsee variant of the Cucuteni type, and the dagger from Aghios Dimitrios, which resembles the dagger from Neuenkirchen (see below), there are no striking typological similarities with the early daggers in the rest of Europe.

10.2.11 Daggers with tang hilt

While the daggers described so far, with the exception of the newly-introduced Lovas variant C of the Cucuteni type, represent for the most part a version of Matuschik's (1998) dagger typology, updated by new finds and new research results on absolute and relative chronology, supplemented by the Italian and Greek daggers, a new type must be introduced at this point due to the special nature of the new find from Neuenkirchen. Two other specimens from Baile Herculane (Romania) and Ayios Dhimitrios (Greece) (Figs. 62 and 63) can be added to the type of daggers with a tang hilt. As Matuschik (*ibid.*) points out, in the typological evaluation the hilt traditionally plays a particularly determining role in type formation, so that the tang hilt is the main feature of this type. In addition, this type has a long, narrow shape that gradually changes into a narrow, rectangular handle with varying degrees of shoulder formation. The asymmetry of the shoulders is conspicuous in all specimens, although this cannot be determined with absolute certainty in the case of the dagger from Neuenkirchen due to corrosion. The pieces have different cross-sections. The Neuenkirchen specimen has an almost semi-rhombic cross-section with a slight middle rib and signs of an attempt to carve out a middle rib on the opposing side. The piece from Ayios Dhimitrios has a flat cross-section, as shown in the illustration. A slight thickening on one side can only be assumed here at most. The drawing, however, shows shading on the blade, which at least indicates a one-sided, implied middle rib, which is also indicated in the published photograph. The cross-section of the dagger from Baile Herculane, on the other hand, is plano-convex with no discernible central ridge or midrib.

The dagger from Ayios Dhimitrios comes from a multi-period settlement site, and there from the uppermost part of a layer which Zachos (2007 and 2008) assigns to the early LN II (Greek Late Neolithic). Two radiometric dates are available from this layer: HD-10020, 5400 ±35 BP, 4341-4227 BCE (85.0%), 4203-4167 BCE (7.4%), 4128-4118 BCE (0.9%), 4096-4077 BCE (2.1%) and HD-10163, 5330 ±75 BP, 4331-4034 BCE (90.3%), 4025-3992 BCE (5.1%). Although Zachos (2008, 223) mentions from which trench both charcoal samples originate, he does not give any information about where they are located in the Late Neolithic layer, which is up to 1.30 m thick. With regard to the typo-chronological position of the dagger, Zachos (2007 and 2008) notes the dichotomy between the stratigraphically-unambiguous position in the Late Neolithic and the typological parallels from the Western Anatolian Early Bronze Age. In his 2007 article he notes: "The developed type of dagger would place it into the Early Bronze Age, as the Neolithic context was not that clear". The language suggests that the doubts about the Late Neolithic or Early Chalcolithic date are based more on typological than on stratigraphic considerations. Especially as he explicitly refers to the origin of the dagger and an awl from the 'Final Neolithic Stratum', and also refers to the piece from a secure Neolithic context later in the article (*ibid.*, 178). He finally confirms the affiliation to the Neolithic stratum in his following work, but does not want to exclude a later disturbance of the stratum (Zachos 2008, 27). However, he cannot prove such a disturbance on the basis of the findings. Rather, in three excavation sections the Neolithic stratum is clearly separated stratigraphically from the Bronze Age stratum by a sterile layer (*ibid.*, 14). In this context, it is

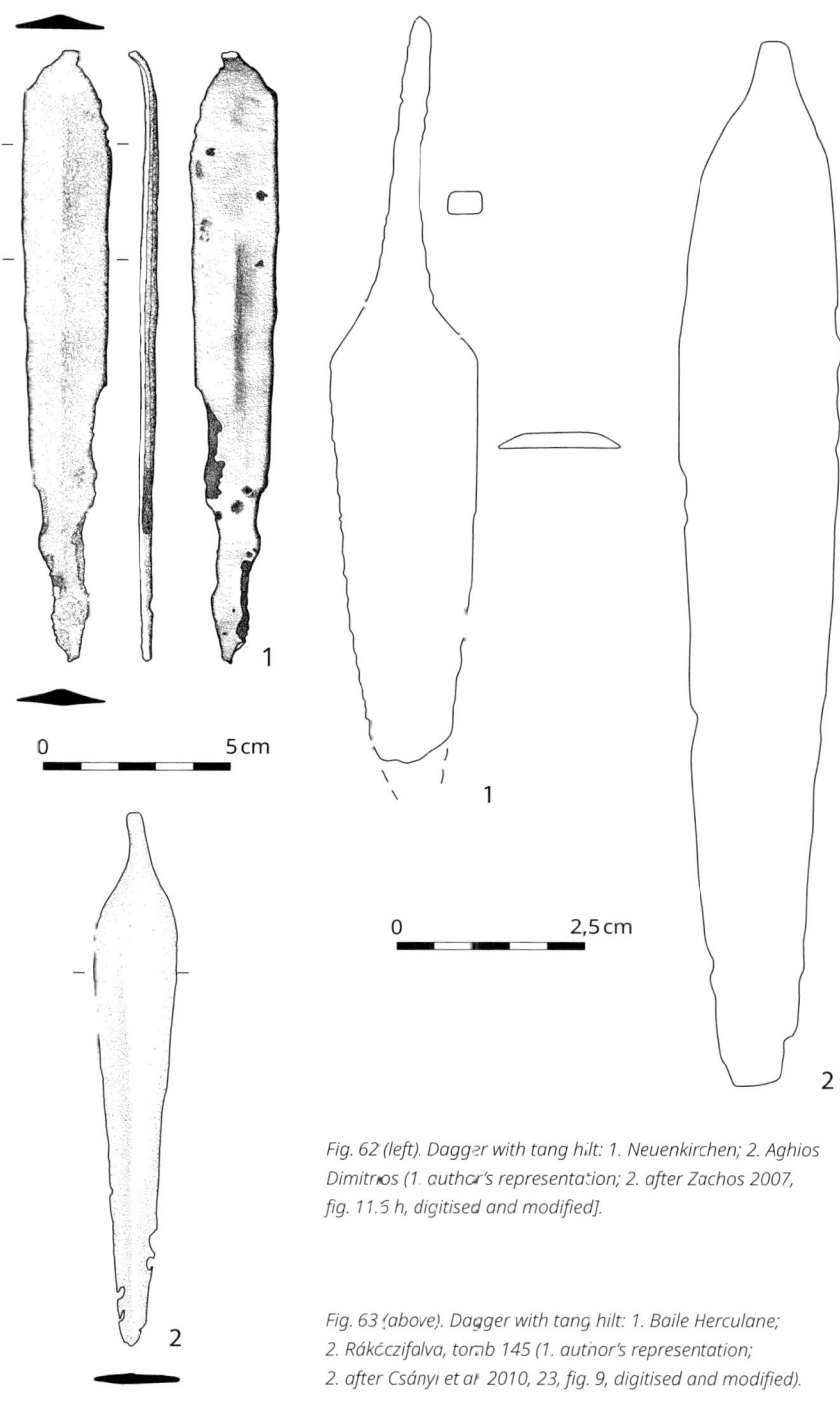

Fig. 62 (left). Dagger with tang hilt: 1. Neuenkirchen; 2. Aghios Dimitrios (1. author's representation; 2. after Zachos 2007, fig. 11.5 h, digitised and modified).

Fig. 63 (above). Dagger with tang hilt: 1. Baile Herculane; 2. Rákóczifalva, tomb 145 (1. author's representation; 2. after Csányi et al. 2010, 23, fig. 9, digitised and modified).

incomprehensible that the section from which the dagger originates is not stated. The quite understandable scepticism of Zachos (2007 and 2008) regarding an early date is based on the formal similarity of the dagger with a series of Early Bronze Age daggers with tang hilts from Western Anatolia. Such pieces from Chalcolithic contexts are unknown to him from the Balkans or from Western Anatolia. Typologically, he assigns the dagger to type Ia according to Stronach (1957, 90) and assumes the time horizon of Troy I (around 3000 BCE) for the earliest appearance of daggers with tang hilts (Zachos 2008, 27). The representatives of this type, however, have a transition to the tang that is clearly separated from the rest of the blade, whereas in the piece from Ayios Dhimitrios the transition from the blade to the tang is smooth. Other representatives of this type come from Cyprus, among other places, and date there to the middle of the 3rd millennium. Due to the lack of attribution to a cut and the location at the end of the Neolithic/Chalcolithic layer, it is not possible to make a definite assessment, so that the piece can be dated either from c. 4300/4000 cal BCE or from 3000 BCE.

The find from a cave near Baile Herculane, comes from a layer that is assigned to stage III of Coţofeni. Chronologically, Coţofeni is located between 3500 and 2500 BCE. As the radiometric results from Baile Herculane show, the stage classification is not secure, since the data from horizons II+III overlap not insignificantly. The following dates come from the horizon assigned to stage III:

- LJ 3534, 4360 ±100 BP, 3356-2859 BCE (91.4%), 2810-2753 BCE (3.1%), 2721-2702 BCE (0.9%);
- LJ-3535, 4350 ± 60 BP, 3322-3272 BCE, 3266-3236 BCE, (0.4%), 3116-2878 BCE (89.4%);
- LJ-3536, 4300 ± 60 BP, 3097-2856 BCE (86.6%), 2812-2748 BCE (6.9%), 2724-2698 BCE (1.8%);
- Stage II horizon: LJ-3533, 4460 ±80 BP, 3356-2922 BCE (95.4%)[24].

10.2.12 Summary of the dagger typochronology

The earliest known dagger form is the lancet-shaped daggers with a flat cross-section of the Pusztaistvánháza/Bodrogkeresztúr type. Following Brummack and Diaconescu (2014), Bodrogkeresztúr and thus the corresponding daggers date between 4300 and 4000 BCE. Three daggers from the Rákóczifalva cemetery possibly indicate other forms of hafting (tang hilt and rivets) for this type of dagger. Possibly a very early midrib is present. The dagger from the Greek Ayios Dhimitrios could also speak for such an early appearance of a tang hilt and a slight middle rib. Other lancet-shaped daggers of the Šebastovce type, some with a middle ridge on one side, exist from eastern Slovakia, dating to the turn of the 3rd-4th millennium and the first centuries of the 4th millennium. In the first half of the 4th millennium, a large number of types or variants appear, which regularly feature innovations such as middle ribs and ridges as well as rivets, without a more precise chronological sequence being possible to date. Thus, rivet daggers with a flat cross-section (type Frumuscia from 3900/3800 BCE) overlap chronologically with rivet daggers with central ridges (type Cucuteni, Var. Vădastra from 4000/3950-3800/3750 BCE) and rivet daggers with middle ribs (type Dolné Semerovce/Malé Leváre from 4000/3800 BCE). The daggers in the period between c. 4300 and 3800 BCE clearly represent the Balkano-Carpathian metallurgical province, with the Dolné Semerovce/Malé Leváre type marking a northern zone in the Polish-Slovak-Czech area (Matuschik 1998,245). Somewhat later, the rivet daggers of the Mondsee variant (from c. 3800/3700 BCE) as well as Lovas A and C (from c. 3740/3600) of the Cucuteni type begin to appear. The Mondsee variant also marks the emergence of the Northern Alpine metallurgical circle. This circle is characterised by independent copper processing and develops its own typological character, which, however, is initially derived from the Balkano-Carpathian metallurgical province both in terms of form and metallurgy (*ibid.*). While the Mondsee variant can be identified as a local product by its shape, an import is also possible for the northern Alpine evidence of the Lovas A variant, since arsenic copper is also known from forms of the Dinaric-Pannonian-Lower Danubian area (Matuschik, 1998, 234). Even more so, as the evidence is pointing more and

---

24 Further dates with a similarly high range come from the settlement site Ostrovul Corbului of the Coţofeni culture (3334-2984 cal. BCE) (Breuning 1987).

more in the direction of south-east Europe as the source of the Mondsee copper variety (see 8.6.6).

The influence of the Carpathian environment is particularly evident in a group of daggers with imitation middle ribs, which probably originated under the influence of daggers with middle ribs of the Dolné Semerovce/Malé Leváre type. The examples from Weyregg (Austria), Bygholm (Denmark), and an Italian dagger from an unknown site, which have a middle rib imitation, as well as the daggers with a single-sided middle rib (or mid ridge) from Kempfenhausen (Germany) and Bratislava (2x) (Slovakia), possibly define a horizon of imitation and experimentation that began at the latest in 3740 BCE, as shown by the dagger from Kempfenhausen. In addition to the production of new daggers — in the case of the piece from Weyregg, the imitation is said to have already been cast — existing pieces such as the dagger from Bygholm were reworked. At the end of the development from imitation without understanding the functional meaning to adaptation of technique and technology, one could see the dagger from Aspenstedt with a light middle rib on both sides, which according to the ^{14}C date of the tomb was produced before 3400/3300-3100 BCE. The fact that the pieces, in which the middle ridge, the middle rib or their imitation is already cast, are made of arsenic copper, which is typical for this area, also supports the idea of production within the Northern Alpine metallurgical circle. At about the same time as the beginning of the Northern Alpine metallurgy, the first daggers were also cast in Italy. As already pointed out in the description of the Guardistallo type, the Italian daggers seem to have been at least inspired by the Cucuteni type. The specimen from Italy with the imitation of a middle rib, which is very similar to the piece from Weyregg, and the fact that the Guardistallo type is roughly contemporaneous (from c. 3600 BCE) with the comparable variants of the Cucuteni type, underlines the connection to the Alpine or northern Alpine region. As a new typological element from about the second half of the 4th millennium onwards, facets along the cutting edges appear, among others, in the Lovas B variant of the Cucuteni type (c. 3600-3300 BCE), as well as in combination with middle ribs in the Balkány type (3300-2800/2700 BCE). In addition, a number of notched daggers occur in eastern Europe, some of which are already at the transition of the respective local Bronze Age. In Ukraine, these date to the same time as the lancet daggers, which also appear around 3300-3000 BCE, and in the area of present-day Bulgaria at the transition to the Early Bronze Age around c. 3200/3100 BCE. In the Usatovo group (3500-3100 BCE), located in the northern Black Sea area, notched daggers appear simultaneously with riveted daggers with middle rib of the Usatovo type, which has a contemporaneous distribution centre in present-day Poland. In Italy, an independent polymetallic metallurgy seems to have been established by the middle of the fourth millennium at the latest. This is supported, among other things, by the proven exploitation of a chalcopyrite source from Monte Loreto (Dolfini 2013, 40) and the dagger types Remedello, Gaudo, and Buccino, which are restricted to the Italian region. For Greece, a few triangular rivet daggers are also attested for the second half of the fourth millennium. Statements on the general development in this area are not possible due to the small number of finds and the difficult chronological positioning.

10.2.13 Typo-chronological classification of the dagger from Neuenkirchen

How can the Neuenkirchen specimen be placed chronologically in this early dagger horizon?

It has been shown above that this type of hilt/hafting was largely unknown in Neolithic and Chalcolithic Europe. As far as the author is aware, there are only two other examples besides Neuenkirchen that are equipped with a tang hilt and the chronological position of both is unclear. The piece from Ayios Dhimitrios in Greece dates to the end of the fifth millennium if it comes from the Chalcolithic layer as presented above. However, if it belongs to the following stratum, it can only be dated to around 3000 BCE. The cave find from Baile Herculane comes from a stratum assigned to Stage III of the long-lived Coţofeni group (3500-2500 BCE) (cf. above). Absolute dates from layers also attributed to Stage III suggest a chronological position in the last third of the fourth millennium at the earliest. That the idea of hafting by means of tangs was already known in the early fourth millennium is shown by numerous daggers from the Northwest Caucasian Maikop group (4000/3800-3000 BCE), whose contacts with Usatovo group are known. Far-reaching networks from the coast of the Black Sea to Poland are attested by daggers of the Usatovo type at this time, so that the concept of the tang hilt, or even individual daggers of this type, may well have reached Central Europe in a timely manner. In addition, the piece with a thorn-like extension from the Hungarian cemetery of Rákóczifalva (grave 145) suggests that this type of hilt may have been used in the last centuries of the fifth millennium.

A particularly eloquent sign of these connections between the Caucasus and Central Europe is shown by the striking iconographic similarities between the image programmes of painted or incised stone slabs taken from a stone chamber tomb of the Bernburg group from Göhlitzsch (Saale district), and those of a secondary burial in a tumulus of the Novosvobodnaya Group of Maikop (Rezepkin 2000, 27; Schunke 2013, 151). As outlined above, the technological innovation of the middle rib or middle ridges is certainly attested in Europe from c. 3900/3800 BCE at the latest. As a piece with at least one-sided, middle rib or ridge formation from the Hungarian cemetery of Rákóczifalva suggests (cf. above), the beginning of this development is already conceivable during the last third of the 5th millennium. A series of daggers with an asymmetrical blade cross-section, like the dagger from Neuenkirchen, is known from the early 4th millennium. In addition, one of these daggers from the Barca cemetery (grave 18) resembles the long, narrow piece from Neuenkirchen in its lancet shape. Absolute dates are also available for three of these daggers: Barca (3956-3798 and 3938-3703 BCE); Kempfenhausen (3720 BCE). The date from Barca provides a secure *terminus ante quem* for the manufacture of daggers with (asymmetrical) middle ribs or ridges. Based on the synthesis of typological considerations, absolute dating, and the results of trace element analysis, the author considers the dating of the manufacture of the dagger from Neuenkirchen around 4000 to 3700 BCE to be justified. The copper variety Nógrádmarcal supports this assumption, as it is used from the late 5th millennium onwards (Klassen 2000, 135, 222, Rosenstock et. al. 2016, 102). In addition, the related copper type indicates that the dagger does not originate from the northern Alpine metallurgical circle, but was probably made in the western Carpathian region. This makes the dagger from Neuenkirchen one of the oldest copper artefacts in Mecklenburg-Vorpommern, as well as in the northern group of the Funnel Beaker Societies.

10.3 The flat axe from Neuenkirchen

Flat axes represent one of the largest artefact groups in the copper inventory of the European Chalcolithic. While in the fifth millennium hammer axes and axe-adzes initially represent the predominant heavy tools, the ratio changes in the fourth millennium in favour of the flat axes, and from c. 3800 BCE they become the main — west of the Danube even the only —form of heavy tools (Rosenstock *et al.* 2016, 93). While the early flat axes mostly have a narrow and massive body — such a piece is found, for example, as an import in Bülow, Mecklenburg — less-thick axes develop at the turn of the fourth millennium. Thus, broad flat axes with slightly flared cutting edges, almost parallel edges, which are also less thick are known from Wallachia, as well as Transylvania (variants Ostrovul-Corbului and Petrești), the Balkan region, Bohemia, Moravia, and Slovakia, as well as from Austria (variants Vrádište and Vinča) and western Central Europe (type Altheim) (*ibid.*, 81). In the (northern) Alpine region, flat axes of this type are known from settlements of the Altheim, Mondsee, and Pfyner groups. In the northern group of the TRB there is also extensive evidence of trapezoidal axes, some of which are imports from the Northern Alpine area (Klassen 2000, 273).

Unfortunately, the flat axe from Neuenkirchen is incomplete, so that a type attribution can only be approximated. The typological characteristics of the fragment are: a thick butt with a straight, minimally-rounded end, a rectangular cross-section with a slightly convex shape and a narrow trapezoidal axe body. In addition, the piece appears relatively massive due to its approx. 3:1 ratio of width to thickness, with a still preserved length of 3.4 cm. As already described in section 8.2.2, the piece has minimal elevated ridges, which in the author's opinion, however, were not intentionally produced based on their small size. A further clue to the typological classification is provided by the metal analysis, which revealed an arsenic copper that can be assigned to the Mondsee variety. Based on the lead isotope ratios of the axe fragment, the most likely source for the copper was determined to be the deposit in Madjanpek in eastern Serbia, for which mining in the Chalcolithic period has been proven (Antonović 2018). Pernicka *et al.* (1993, 38) assume that the copper was already used at the beginning of the fourth millennium. As mentioned several times, this type of copper is heavily used by the Alpine metallurgical circle of Cortaillod, Pfyn, and Altheim, as well as the Pfyn-Altheim and Mondsee groups from about 3800 BCE onwards. In addition, a large percentage of the copper objects from the western Baltic region consists of this copper variety (Klassen 2000, 273)[25]. A look at the flat axe inventory of the northern group of the Funnel Beaker Group shows several specimens with thick, straight butts and slightly trapezoidal basic shapes, such as the three larger specimens from the Bygholm hoard, or the flat axes from Søby Hede or Hof Stenestad (Skudderup/Scania), the latter being the best typological parallel (Fig. 65.1). However, some of these pieces are considerably larger in size. Klassen (*ibid.*, 163) pointed out that some Scandinavian flat axe forms are regularly much larger and heavier than their typological counterparts from the northern Alpine region. Klassen (*ibid.*, 176) refers to the flat axe from Hof Stenestad (Skudderup/Scania) as a northern Alpine import that finds its best typological equivalent in the axe from the Goldberg in the Nördlinger Ries (cf. Fig. 64). On the basis of Altheim Group finds from the Goldberg and corresponding comparative finds of flat axes, especially the Bottighofen type in southern Germany (Fig. 65.2), the piece can be placed in the second half of Early Neolithic I (3750-3500 BCE) (*ibid.*). However, both the flat axe from Stenestad and the piece from the Goldberg, as well as the representatives of the Bottighofen type, have a broader butt than the Neuenkirchen specimen. Another possible typological parallel, which also corresponds well in size and width, is the flat axe from Kempfenhausen (Fig. 65.3). This axe is assigned to the Thayngen type, but can also be as assigned to the Altheim type due to the circumstances of the find (Turck 2010, 47; Driehaus 1960, 67). The pottery found in the settlement has similiarities with that associated with the Pfyn-Altheim group. The dendrochronological dating of the timbers of the settlement around 3720 BCE (cf. above) corresponds with this allusion (*ibid.*). Another typologically-related type

---

25   According to Klassen (2000, 293), the total weight of the copper finds in the western Baltic region is 28 kg, of which the Mondsee copper takes up 20 kg. If one follows Schmitz (2004) and considers the copper variety Riesebusch postulated by Klassen (2000) as Mondseekupfer, it is even 27 kg of 28 kg. (Klassen (*ibid.*) estimates the weight based on the measurements of approx. 80 % of the find material. For example, the chisel from Bülow, which weighs almost 700 g and is made of the purest copper, is missing, but there is a clear overabundance of the Mondsee copper variety).

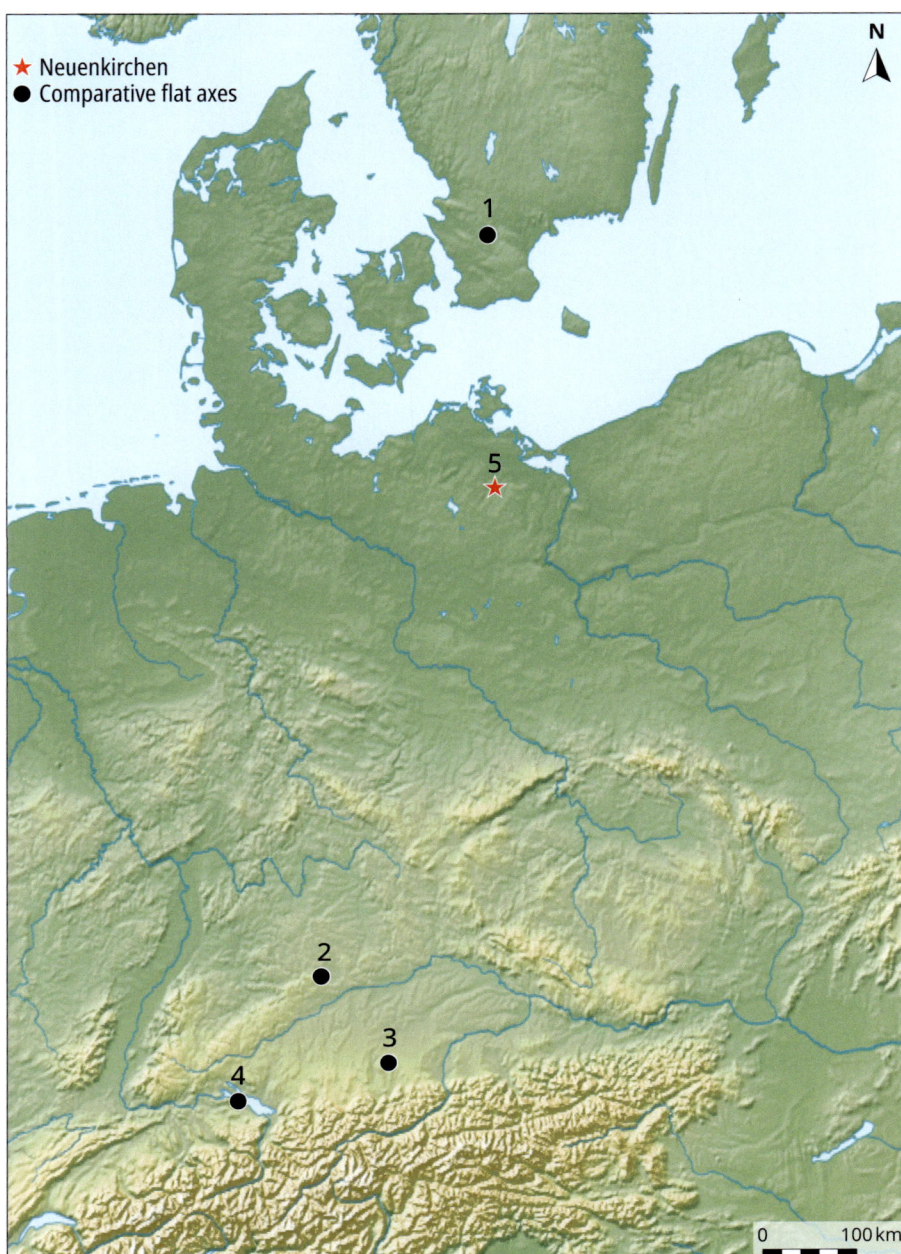

Fig. 64. Map of the flat axe
from Neuenkirchen and its
comparative finds: 1. Hof
Stenestad (Skudderup);
2. Goldberg; 3. Kempfenhausen;
4. Bottighofen; 5. Neuenkirchen
(map base NaturalEarthData).

is the flat axe from Slusegård in Denmark (see Klassen 2000, fig 56.), but the butt
of the flat axe from Neuenkirchen is thicker. Nevertheless, it shows a comparable
form of the upper part. Furthermore, an existing lead isotope analysis (Nørgaard
et al. 2021, 9 f.) show also similar values to the axe from Neuenkirchen, linking it
to roughly the same range of possible sources of the copper. Due to the possible
typological parallels described above, as well as the use of Mondsee copper for the
production, a dating of the flat axe from 3800/3700 BCE onwards is probable and
the piece is to be regarded as an import from the (northern) Alpine region. Such an
import into present-day Mecklenburg-Western Pomerania is already known with
the axe from Pantelitz (*ibid.*, 156). Nørgaard *et al.* (2021) However, trapezoidal flat
axes still occur in the northern Alpine regions, as well as Scandinavian regions, in
the second half of the fourth millennium 3500-3300 BCE, so that a later dating cannot
be completely ruled out (Klassen 2000, 236).

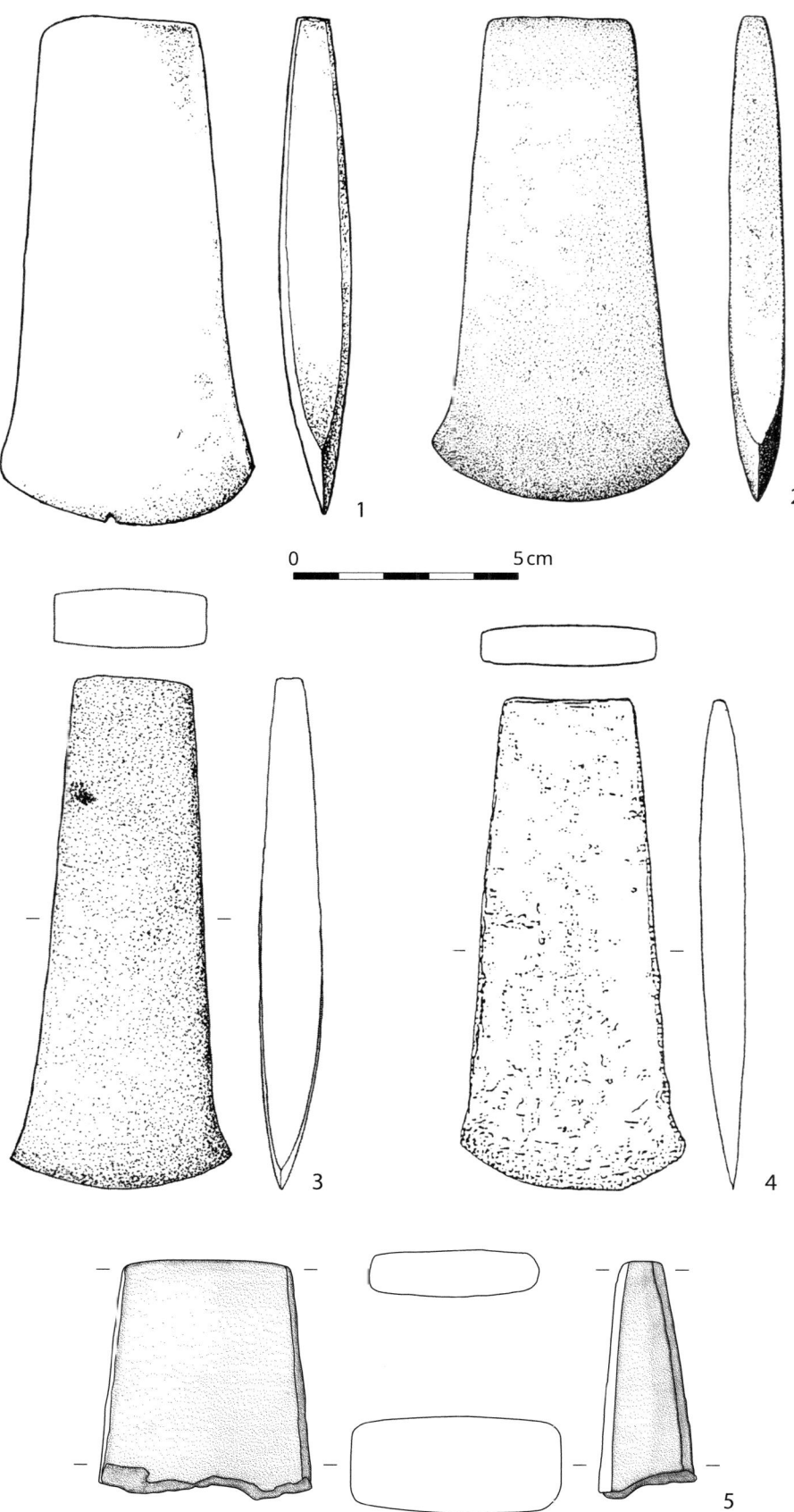

0   5 cm

Fig. 65. The flat axe from Neuenkirchen and its comparative finds: 1. Stenestad; 2. Goldberg; 3. Kempfenhausen; 4. Bottighofen; 5. Neuenkirchen (1., 2 & 4. Klassen 2000, 157, 177, figs. 67.2 & 78.1-2; 3. Pfederer et al. 2009, 130, fig. 7.1; 5. illustration by the author).

10.4 The arm spiral from Neuenkirchen

In the research, different names can be found for the spirals made of copper band or wire, sometimes also of sheet metal strips; for example, spiral arm ring, arm spiral, spiral band rings or wire spiral rings. Due to several Copper Age in situ finds from Southeast Europe, where the pieces were found still wrapped around the wrist or arm bones, they justify being referred to as arm jewellery. Although Klassen (2000, 53) rejects such an analogy, and the use of the term arm spiral for the large specimens from the western Baltic region, due to the lack of corresponding findings, this caution seems a bit excessive. Especially as the pieces from Velvary in the Czech Republic include spirals in his form of large spiral rings, which originate from such a find with a corresponding date in the 4th millennium. The group of objects, subsequently called spiral arm rings/arm spirals, shows a relatively similar spectrum of forms throughout the ages, due to its function. Without the context of the finds, the association of finds, and metal analyses, it is often difficult to date those pieces typo-chronologically which occur from the Early Copper Age to the Iron Age. Basically, research distinguishes between two groups according to the number of turns (Petrescu-Dîmbovița 1998, among others). The group with two to four turns is called spiral rings, and the group with five or more turns is called arm spirals. Terminologically, however, the designation 'small and large spiral arm rings' seem to make more sense here. The relatively arbitrary definition of the number of turns should also be viewed critically. Especially since in fragmented specimens it is usually impossible to decide which of the two groups they belong to. The cross-section of the copper band or wire is used as a further typological distinguishing feature. The spectrum ranges from round or u-shaped, to flattened triangular, to plano-convex, as well as lenticular. The overall shape is mainly cylindrical, in some cases also conical. The small and large spiral arm rings are widespread in south-eastern and eastern Europe, as well as in the area of the northern group of the TRB. Sporadically they are also known from the alpine and northern alpine area.

The specimen from Neuenkirchen belongs to the group of large arm spirals. A current compilation of this group of objects for the Copper Age is still pending; the last time this was done was by Zápotocký (1984) and Klassen (2000). For Bulgaria and Moldavia there are now overviews from the series 'Prehistoric Bronze Finds' (*Prähistorische Bronzefunde*), which also list the spiral arm rings for these areas (Dergačev 2002 and Todorova/Vajsov 2001). The following list is a summary from the above-mentioned authors, supplemented by two new finds from Hungary, and does not claim to be complete. Large arm spirals come from: Ariușd, Romania (1-5/6?), Cărbuna, Moldova (2), Giurgiulești, Moldova (2), Hăbășești, Romania (1), Čapli/Chapli, Ukraine (1), Izovare, Romania (1), Mindszent, Hungary (1), Hódmezővásárhelyi-Népkert, Hungary (1), Rákóczifalva, Hungary (2), Wyciąże, Poland (2), Skarbienice, Poland (4), Velvary, Czech Republic (2), Stollhof, Austria (2), Lödersdorf (1)[26], Austria (1), Hartberg, Austria (2)?[27], Hagenau, Germany (1)?[28], Neuenkirchen, Germany (1), Bygholm, Denmark (3), Handest, Denmark (1), Søby Hede, Denmark (1) (Figs. 66 and 67). In addition, there are numerous small arm spirals which, with four turns, just fall short of classification as large arm spirals. Often, as in the case of Cărbuna, these are associated with arm spirals classified as 'large', which have only one, sometimes even only half a turn more. It is unclear in the case of Ariușd how many large arm spirals the hoard contained, as records and finds

---

26   The find from Lödersdorf is similar to the other pieces in number of turns and diameter, but in length, band diameter and weight it only reaches half the minimum values of the southern Scandinavian pieces (Klassen 2000, 142).

27   Circumstances of discovery unclear, affiliation of the objects also uncertain (Neumann 2015, 98 & 357, A004).

28   There is no information about the piece (Klassen 2000, 142).

were partly lost in the chaos of war in 1945. Sztáncsuj (2005) lists six arm spirals in his reappraisal of the hoard, but only one of them, with five turns, corresponds to the definition of large arm spirals. Schroller (1933) deviates from this and shows a total of five spirals with 2x15, 2x5 and 1x4 turns. It is difficult to evaluate this, as Sztáncsuj (2005) describes the hoard and the circumstances of its documentation in detail, but does not refer to the work of Schroller (1933), and today only three fragments of the spirals remain. Large arm spirals with more than 5 turns, as listed by Schroller (*ibid.*), would be an exception in this area.

For the object group of large arm spirals, two areas seem to emerge for the Chalcolithic, which can be separated from each other temporally and spatially, as well as typologically and metallurgically. The first group is mainly distributed in South-Eastern Europe and isolated specimens come from Poland and Austria. Characteristic is a comparatively small size and the number of turns rarely exceeds five. Only the hoard finds at Stollhof, and possibly Ariuşd and Wyciąże, are evidence of significantly larger specimens, with about 15 and 10 turns respectively. The wire or band cross-section is often round and flat. However, there are also specimens with a plano-convex or lenticular cross-section. The group dates mainly to the 5th millennium, whereby the earliest securely-attested specimens can be dated as early as its first half. Thus, the two large arm spirals from Cărbuna are part of a hoard found in a vessel that can be assigned to Stage A of Trypillia (c. 4800-4600 BCE) (Sergeev 1963, 135; Müller *et al.* 2016, 1 ff.). Deviating from this, a later date is assumed, as the corresponding style of decoration only slowly spreads eastwards from the Romanian centre of innovation to the area of Trypillia. Since Cărbuna lies at the eastern border of the distribution area, there is a stylistic correspondence with the Precucuteni III level, but a chronological position in the early phase of Cucuteni level A (from c. 4600 BCE onwards) is postulated (cf. Klassen 2000, 192). Other pieces from Giurgiuleşti, Hăbăşeşti, Čapli, and Izovare come from contexts that date to Trypillia stages B1/B 1-2 or Cucuteni A (c. 4600-4100 BCE) (Dergačev 2002, 69 ff.). Large arm spirals from the Hungarian sites of Hódmezővásárhelyi-Népkert and Mindszent, both assigned to Tiszapolgár, as well as the specimens from the Rákóczifalva cemetery of Bodrogkeresztúr, can also be dated to the second half of the fifth millennium. For the latter cemetery, radiometric dating is available, proving an occupation between c. 4334-4075 BCE (Csányi *et al.* 2010, 263 f.). The specimen from Wyciąże comes from a cemetery that shows influences of Bodrogkeresztúr and the Lažňany-Hunyadihalom group, among others, in the ceramic material. The local Wyciąże-Złotniki group has a relatively long duration (Grabowska/Zastawny 2011, 153 ff.), so that a date from the middle of the fifth millennium to the middle of the fourth millennium is possible. An arm spiral from Wyciąże is associated with a vessel that shows influences from Bodrogkeresztúr (Kozłowski 1971, 80), suggesting a date before 4000 BCE. For the hoard find from Ariuşd, which possibly contains the largest arm spirals from the Southeast European region, the exact dating is still unclear. It is possible that it dates to stage A of Cucuteni (c. 4600-4200 BCE). However, since not all excavation results have been published, it is not clear whether the settlement continued after stage A2 (Sztáncsuj 2005, 99 f.). The depot find from Stollhof, which provides the only secure, large spiral arm rings with a two-digit number of turns[29], dates according to Klassen (2000) around 4000 BCE. He refers to the horizon of late Bodrogkeresztúr as *teminus ante quem* for the dating of the hoard. Since Bodrogkeresztúr, according to the new absolute data, ends earlier, the deposition must have happened before 4000 BCE and thus also the manufacture of the arm spirals. As far as analyses are available, the metal of the arm spirals is mostly pure copper. One specimen from the hoard

---

29 According to Wilk (2014, 221), another large spiral arm ring with 10 turns is supposed to come from either grave 6/33 or grave 4-5/32 at the site of Wyciąże. However, since it was not possible to access the primary literature and no illustration is available, this piece can only be considered with reservations.

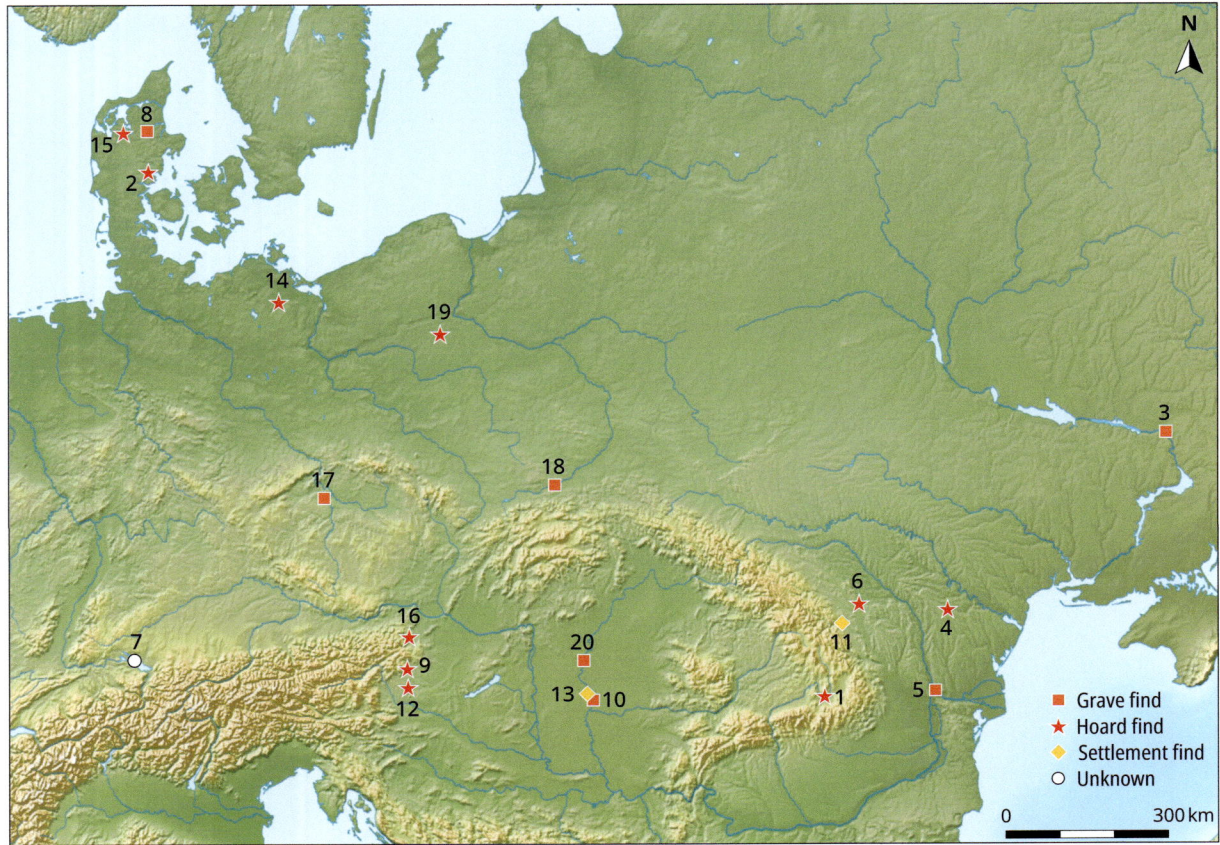

Fig. 66. Large arm spirals:
1. Ariușd; 2. Bygolm;
3. Čapli/Chapli;
4. Cărbuna; 5. Giurgiulești;
6. Hăbășești; 7. Hagenau;
8. Handest; 9. Hartberg;
10. Hódmezővásárhelyi- Népkert;
11. Izvoare; 12. Lödersdorf;
13. Mindzent; 14. Neuenkirchen;
15. Søby Hede; 16. Stollhof;
17. Velvary; 18. Wyciąże;
19. Skarbienice; 20. Rákóczifalva
(map base NaturalEarthdata).

of Cărbuna, as well as one specimen from Wyciąże, also show elevated levels of arsenic, antimony, and silver (Kozłowski 1971, 88; Dergačev 2002, 220). For parts of the hoard from Cărbuna, the use of copper from the Serbian mine Ai Bunar is suspected (Schmitz 2004, 501); the trace element composition of the piece from Wyciąże corresponds to the copper variety Handlova.

The second group comprises a group of large arm spirals that are exclusively distributed in Central Europe (Denmark, Poland, and the Czech Republic). It is distinguished from the first group by a higher number of turns (Bygholm 14, 9½, and 8; Søby Hede min. 7.5; Handest 5; Skarbienice 17, 17, 13, and 11½; Velvary 13). In addition, the cross-sections are clearly more profiled than in the south-eastern European representatives (Klassen 2000, 140). Another important distinguishing feature is the trace element composition, which shows arsenical copper for all pieces. Thus, all pieces are probably made of the Mondsee copper variety (*ibid.*, 142 ff.). Chronologically, this group is clearly younger. The Danish specimens are dated by Klassen (*ibid.*, 93) to the second half of the fourth millennium. In addition to the large arm spiral rings, the hoard find from Skarbienice contains fragments of band spirals, which, like the arm rings, are chronologically undiagnostic. Due to the composition of the hoard, it cannot be dated within Poland. However, since spiral rolls (*Spiralrollen*) and such arm rings are known from the northern group of the Funnel Beaker Societies, and the metal composition of the latter exactly matches one of the Bygholm pieces, Klassen (*ibid.*, 142) assumes a comparable date. The two specimens from Velvary come from a richly-furnished grave that is assigned to Proto-Rivnác and thus dates to the turn of the third millennium (*ibid.*, 142).

In summary, it can be said that arm spirals with double-digit numbers of turns from the fifth and early fourth millennium are a rarity in Europe so far. At present, only the specimens from Stollhof are securely attested; the representatives from

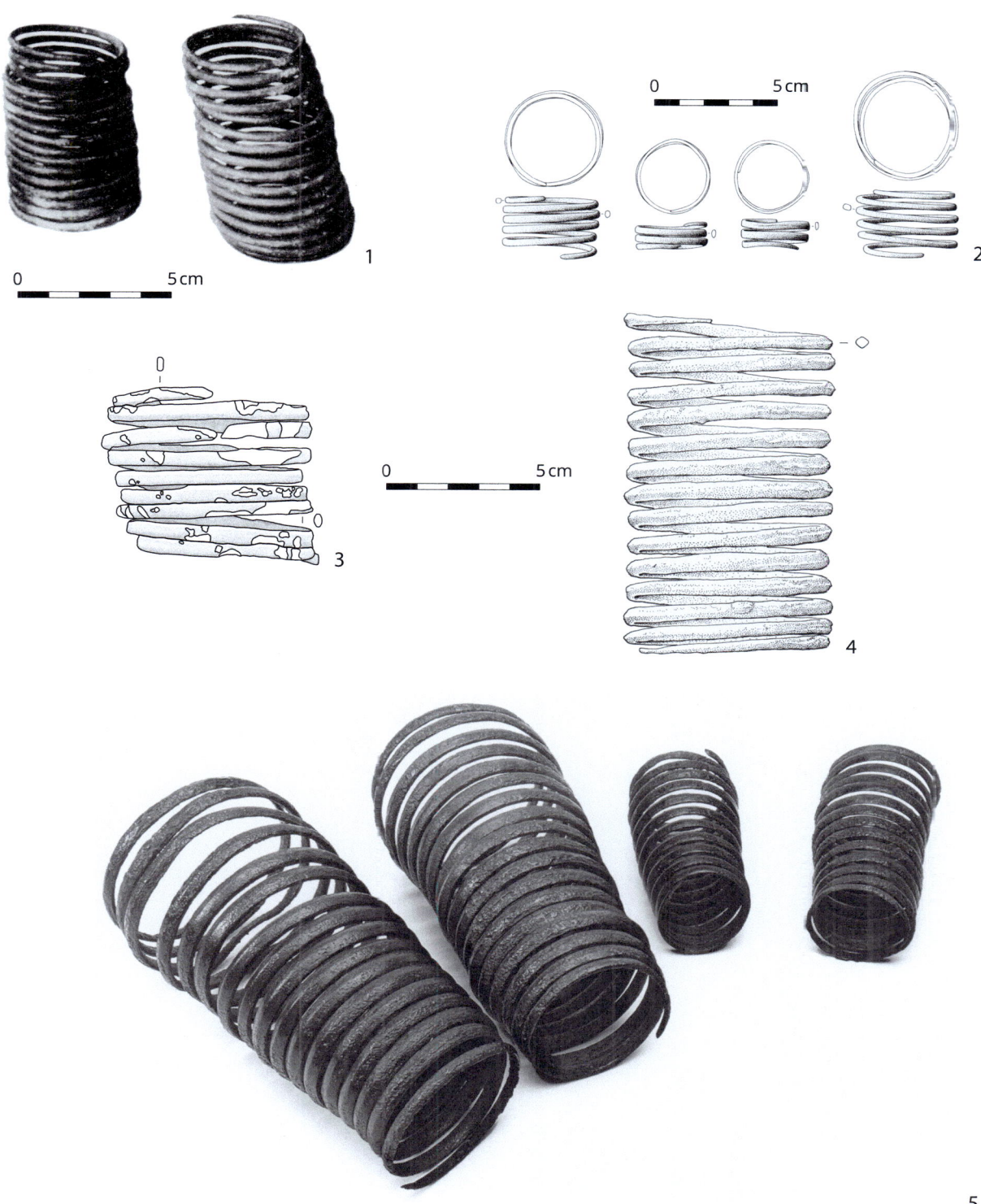

Fig. 67. Selection of large arm spirals of the European Chalcolithic: 1. Ariușd; 2. Cărbuna; 3. Neuenkirchen; 4. Bygholm; 5. Skarbiniec (1. Schroller 1933, pl. 4; 2. Dergačev 2002, pl. 3.53-54; 3. illustration by author; 4., Klassen 2000, pl. 23.94 G; 5. without scale, Lichter/Badisches Landesmuseum Karlsruhe 2010, 381, figs. 340-344; © Archaeological Museum in Poznań).

Wyciąże and Ariușd remain unclear. A group of large arm spirals with regularly higher numbers of turns made of arsenic copper stands out from these, which are restricted in their distribution to Denmark, Poland and Bohemia and can be dated from the middle of the 4th millennium onwards. If, like Klassen (2000, 142), the specimens from Velvary are distinguished from this group because of their much younger age, the latter remains restricted exclusively to northern Central Europe and around the middle of the fourth millennium. At first glance, the arm spiral from Neuenkirchen fits effortlessly into this group due to its geographical location and the higher number of turns (9¾). However, the metal composition of the piece clearly sets it apart from this group and it therefore probably belongs to the chronological region of the specimens from the hoard of Stollhof. Since the Neuenkirchen piece, unlike the Stollhof examples which are made of pure copper, was made of copper corresponding to the Nógrádmarcal copper type, it appears to have been manufactured a little later. The author considers the dating of the arm spiral to the end of the fifth millennium (around 4000 BCE) to be justified.

10.5 The band spiral from Neuenkirchen

Spiral rolls, band spirals, or band spiral rolls[30] are a long-lasting, or recurring, and geographically widespread form. Spiral rolls can basically be divided into the groups of sheet metal, wire, and band spiral rolls according to the material used. The spiral from Neuenkirchen belongs to the last group. Unfortunately, objects of this group are known in Europe from Copper Age, Bronze Age and Iron Age contexts, which makes a chronological classification difficult. Although this type varies in length, diameter, and width of the copper band, this also has no chronological value, as these different forms occur simultaneously in the different time periods. An example of this is the hoard find from Riesebusch, which dates to around 3500/3300 BCE and contained band spirals of different sizes and band widths. From the Mecklenburg Bronze Age, this is also shown by the pieces from Peckatel (Ludwigslust-Parchim district) and Rühlow (Mecklenburg Lake Plateau district) (Fig. 68). The latter hoard find, from the vicinity of Neuenkirchen, can be clearly dated to the Bronze Age on the basis of the axes, a spearhead, and a neck collar it contains, but the other objects it contains — a spectacle spiral (Brillenspirale), a large arm spiral, and the band spirals — demonstrate the difficulties of a typological approach if the latter are found without accompanying diagnostic finds. The arm and band spirals from Rühlow correspond in shape and size to the pieces from Neuenkirchen and the other Chalcolithic representatives. Likewise, the spectacle spirals are widespread in time, as well as geographically, and are known from the Copper Age hoards of Stollhof and Malé Leváre, among others. The Neuenkirchen band spiral, with its relatively wide band, finds very good equivalents in the specimens from Stollhof (Austria) and Årupgård (Denmark), between which, however, there is also a difference of about 500 years (for dating, cf. Klassen 2000, 81 ff. and 194 ff.). For such typo-chronologically insensitive objects, an analysis of the metal composition can provide clues to dating. In the case of the band spiral, it could be shown that it is copper of the variety Nógrádmarcal, which is in use around 4000 BCE (see above). Thus, at least a dating to the Early Copper Age, in which mainly pure copper is used, as well as to the Bronze Age or later, can most probably be excluded. A more precise dating is only possible indirectly through the finds associated with it and with comparable find complexes, such as Riesebusch, Årupgård or Stollhof.

---

30 In the literature, Klassen (2000) and Blajer (1990), among others, use the term "salta leona" or the type "salta leone" in connection with band spirals, but without describing what distinguishes this type. It is also not clear whether this is a type or a general term for band spirals, as both uses of the term exist. Due to this uncertainty, this term is not used.

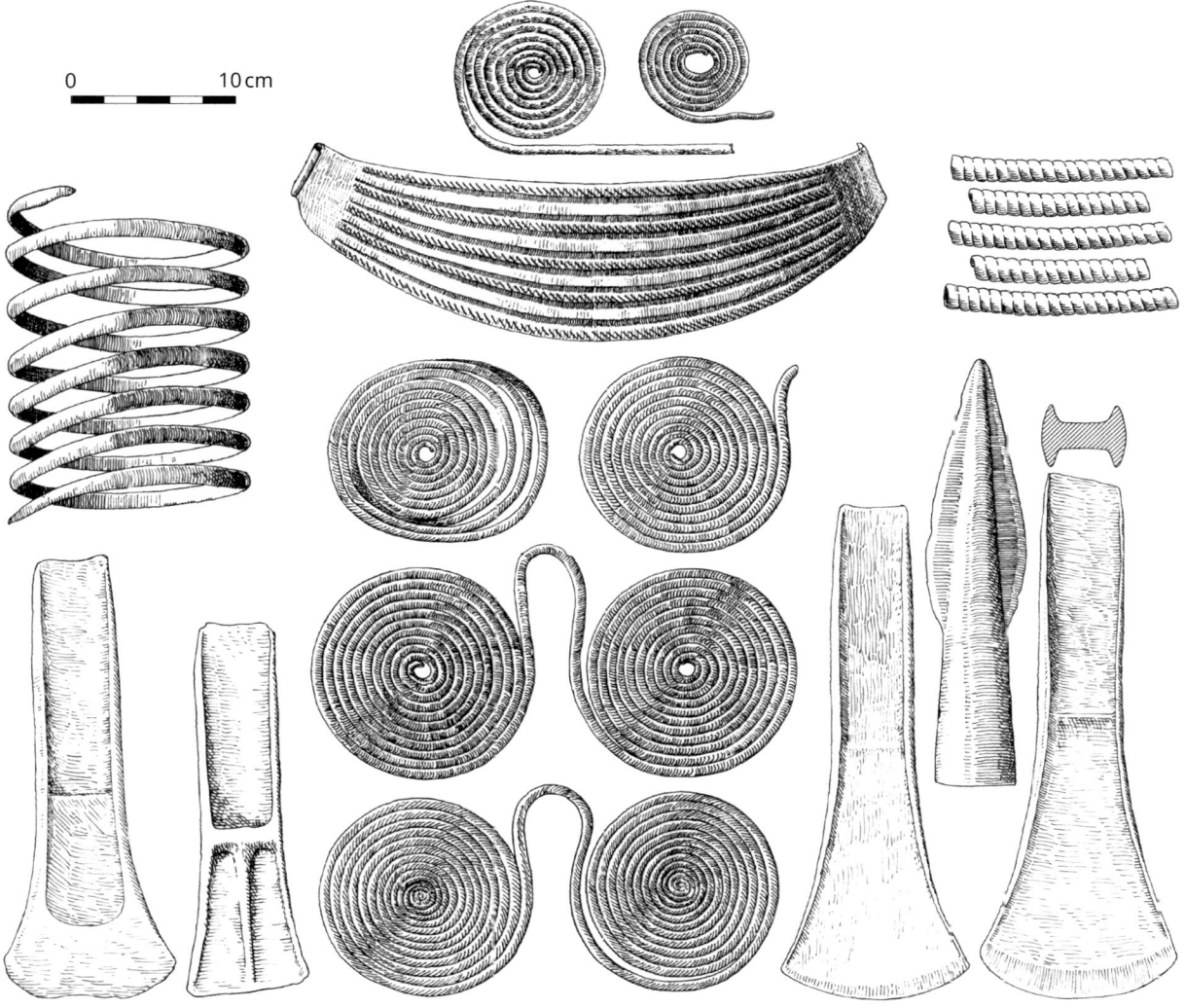

0   10 cm

10.6 The sheet metal fragment from Neuenkirchen

Fig. 68. Hoard find from Rühlow (Schubart 1972, pl. 59, modified).

The piece of sheet copper is so fragmented that it is impossible to decide on its original form. If we look at the range of forms of the European Chalcolithic, there is copper sheet jewellery in the form of pendants and small plates throughout. From Kosel in Schleswig-Holstein, in the district of Rendsburg-Eckernförde, there is also a wooden bowl that was covered with copper sheets. Another possibility would be that it belongs to the group of round metal discs known from southern Scandinavia, the eastern Carpathian region, the Carpathian Basin, and the Alpine region (Klassen 2000,191). A clue to the chronological position of the piece can only be given by the metal analysis, on the basis of which the related metal can be assigned to the copper variety Nógrádmarcal, and thus suggests a dating around 4000 BCE.

10.7 Excursus: *Pars pro toto* of a necklace of band spirals and pendants?

For the interpretation of the sheet metal fragment, it should be suggested at this point that it is considered as a (tongue-shaped) pendant which, together with the band spirals, possibly represents a necklace or part of one. Sheet copper jewellery in the form of tubes, beads, and pendants of various shapes, individually and combined into necklaces, appear increasingly in the first half of the fifth millennium. The first copper beads even appear, albeit very sporadically, in the first half of the sixth millennium (Rosenstock *et al.* 2016, 98). The combination of band spirals and copper-lead pendants is known from hoards such as Cărbuna (Moldavia), among others, without, however, providing in situ evidence of their belonging together in a necklace or chain. From Jordanów (Silesia, Bohemia, Moravia) and Brześć Kujawski (Poland), several of these necklaces are attested from graves. For example, from grave 23 from the eponymous site of Jordanów there comes a necklace made of tongue-shaped pendants and spiral rolls, which was found in the neck area of the c. 40-year-old male (Seger 1906, 120; Schlicht 1973, 23; Turck 2010, 53 ff.). Numerous inhumation graves (20) from the settlement site of Brześć Kujawski in Osłonki, województwo kujawsko-pomorskie (Kujawsko-Pomorskie Voivodeship) contained necklaces of copper beads or band spirals, several times combined with trapezoidal pendants (Grygiel 2008, fig. 761; Dirks/Stark 2016, 130 f.) (Fig. 69). Two necklaces are available from each of two graves in Třebestovice (Czech Republic), which are attributed to Jordanów. In grave 7, the remains of a necklace consisting of four trapezoidal pendants, a tongue-shaped pendant, copper beads, and shell rings were found at the head of the burial, which were presumably strung on a cord, as the preserved remains of a cord(!) indicate (Fig. 70). A similar combination, consisting of three tongue-shaped pendants, a small ribbon coil with two turns, and several copper sheet beads was found in the head area of the burial in grave 8 (Fig. 70). Two other graves (3 and 4) also contained — in the case of grave 3 in the head area of the burial — several copper sheet beads (Čtverák/Rulf 1989, 22). The examples from Osłonki, as well as Jordanów and Třebestovice, can be dated to the second half of the fifth millennium. The best-known example so far from present-day Germany is the necklace from a Baalberg child's grave (3800-3300 BCE) from Preußlitz near Bernburg, which also consists of spiral rolls and tongue-shaped pendants and was found in the neck area of the buried child (Preuß 1958, 202 f.; Preuß 1966, 31) (Fig. 69). From Baalberg (Middle Germany), Jordanów and Brześć-Kujawski (both Poland), as well as from the (North) Alpine region, further finds of tongue-shaped pendants and ribbon spiral scrolls are known, which can be interpreted as necklaces. For example, from the lakeside settlement near Tettnang-Langnau (Degersee I), which has an absolutely date of 3975 ± 10 BCE, come four elongated pendants (Fig. 71). A Baalberg grave at Büden (Jerichower Land district) contained four band spiral scrolls, and a Brześć Kujawski grave at Krusza Zamkowka (Poland) came six tongue-shaped pendants. Two necklaces made of copper beads and band spiral rolls come from Lödersdorf in Styria (Austria) (Böttcher 1982, 165 ff.; Jacobs 1986, K 20, no. 24; Czerniak 1980, 9 ff.; Müller 2001, 411 f.; Turck 2010, 39, Lichter/Badisches Landesmuseum Karlsruhe 2010).

A relatively new find from a burial site with megalithic and non-megalithic grave forms in Melzow, Brandenburg (Uckermark district) is particularly interesting due to its geographical proximity to the Neuenkirchen site. The small cemetery consists of two block chamber graves, four stone frame graves, two stone pavement graves, as well as a trapezoidal stone frame and at least four flat graves (Dirks/Stark 2016, 109 ff.). In a flat grave, which contained a double burial with an adult and a child, there were several copper finds. Among the skull and jaw remains of the child was a necklace of seven band spirals, two fragments of band spirals, and a tongue-shaped pendant. The X-ray of the remains (recovered as a block) showed that the elements were strung together in a chain. A larger band spiral had been pushed over a smaller chain segment (Fig. 71). Furthermore, a ring made of strips of sheet copper was found, in which a middle finger bone of an adult was still stuck, thus clearly indicating that it was a finger ring (ibid., 128 ff.). Other grave goods include two two-handled amphorae and a triangular flint flake with adhering pitch remains. The cemetery is assigned to the early to older Funnel Beaker Societies, whereby the amphorae indicate a clear influence of Middle German Baalberg (ibid.).

For the Neuenkirchen hoard find, the Melzow grave is significant in several respects. On the one hand, it becomes apparent that necklaces made of band spirals and pendants[31] are also represented in the area of the northern group of the TRB and thus the author's assumption that the band spirals and the sheet metal fragment from the Neuenkirchen hoard could well be part of such a necklace seems quite justified. Especially since another new find of a tongue-shaped pendant from the settlement site of the older Funnel Beaker Societies in Grünow (district of Uckermark) indicates the regular occurrence of such pendants also in north-eastern Germany. On the other hand, the absolute dates from the Melzow site show that pendants made of sheet copper were already present in this area in the first centuries of the fourth millennium. Radiometric analyses were carried out on a charcoal sample and a wood sample consisting of bark from the aforementioned grave, which resulted in the following dating: Poz-50743, 5165 ± 35 BP, 4045-3940 BCE (89.2%), 3857-3817 BCE (6.2%) and Poz-40742, 4910 ± 35 BP, 3766-3641 BCE. The discrepancy between the two dates is discussed in detail by Dirks and Stark (2016, 132) in their paper on the Melzow cemetery. They conclude that the younger charcoal sample is decisive for the dating of the grave. For the older date, the sample material was obtained from bark, where problems similar to the 'old wood effect' can occur. The bark of the tree is already laid down during the formation of the tree and components from the time of formation are still in the adult tree. Therefore, inaccuracies of several hundred years can occur with this sample material. On the basis of the date of the charcoal sample, the grave is therefore placed in the period around 3700 BCE and correlates well with the radiometric dates of Middle German Baalberg (3800/3700-3350 BCE), whose influence is also evident in the amphorae from the grave (ibid.).

The chronology of the grave becomes even more important against the background of the metal analyses carried out on the copper jewellery. First of all, an analysis of the trace element composition was carried out on six band spiral rolls, the pendant, and the aforementioned pendant from Melzow by means of a pXRF device, which revealed arsenic-containing copper other for all objects, although two groups with different arsenic contents emerged. Subsequently, two spirals and the finger ring were subjected to a laboratory-based elemental determination, and the lead isotope ratios were also analysed. The results confirmed the differentiation into two groups. While one group (finger ring and spiral) had high arsenic and low silver and antimony contents, the other group (another spiral) was characterised by lower arsenic contents but significantly increased silver and antimony values. However, the exact composition of the remaining band spirals, as well as the pendant, remains unclear. According to the metal composition, as well as the lead isotope ratios, the analysed objects match the Mondsee copper variety (ibid., 131). Unfortunately, the exact results of the investigation have not yet been published, so that a comparison of the metal analyses with the objects from Neuenkirchen is not possible. This is particularly regrettable for the band spiral, as it has a trace element combination that would correspond to the latter group, but is assigned to the Handlova copper

---

31 According to the author's knowledge, the necklace from Melzow is the most northerly representative of this combination of band spiral scrolls and pendants (not counting the possible band spiral and possible pendant from Neuenkirchen.

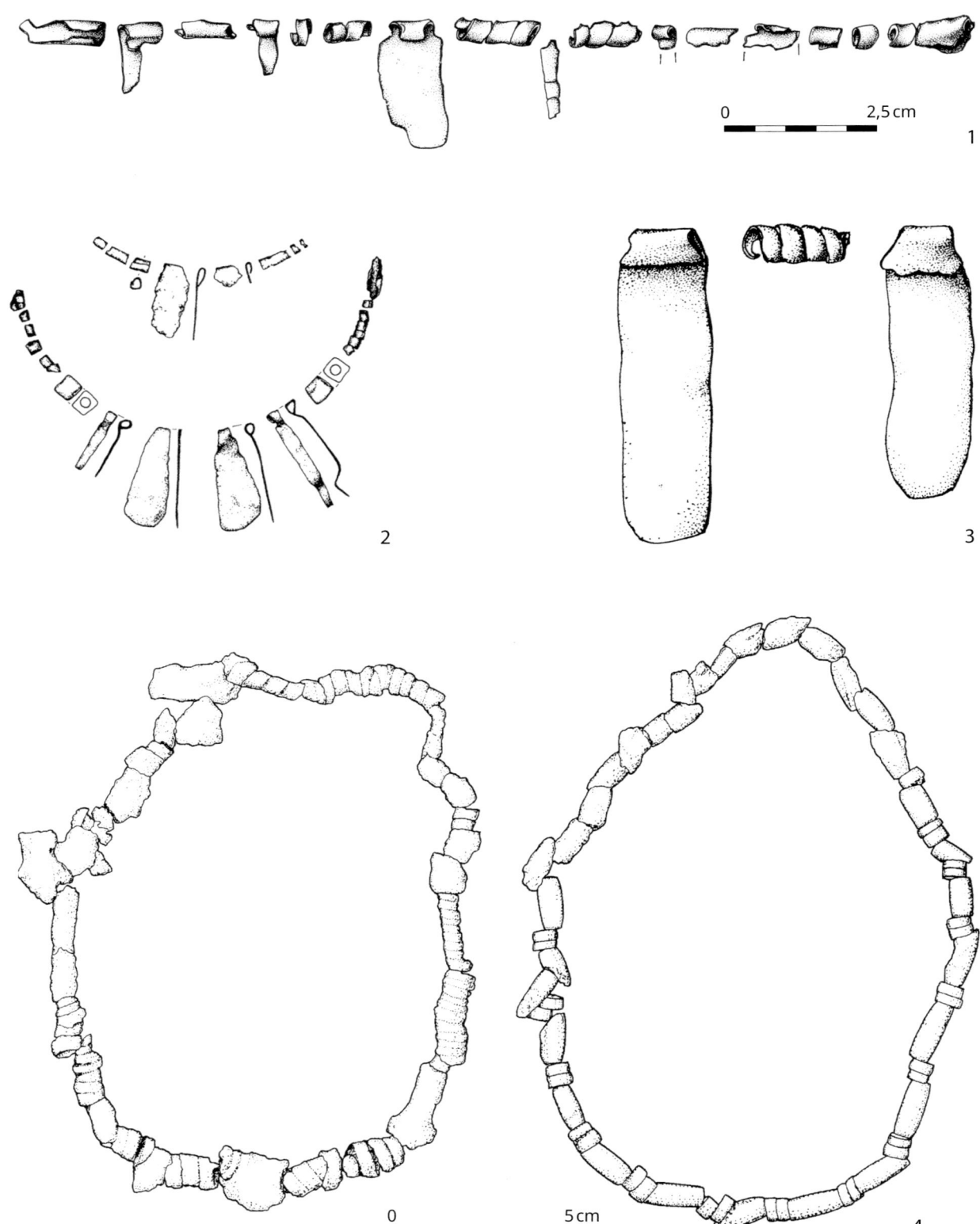

Fig. 69. Necklaces of copper jewellery: 1. Preußlitz; 2. Osłonki; 3. Jordanów; 4. Lödersdorf (Turck 2010, 56, fig. 66; 2. & 3., Dirks/Stark 2016, 136, fig. 26.8; 4., Turck 2010, 40, figs. 41 & 42).

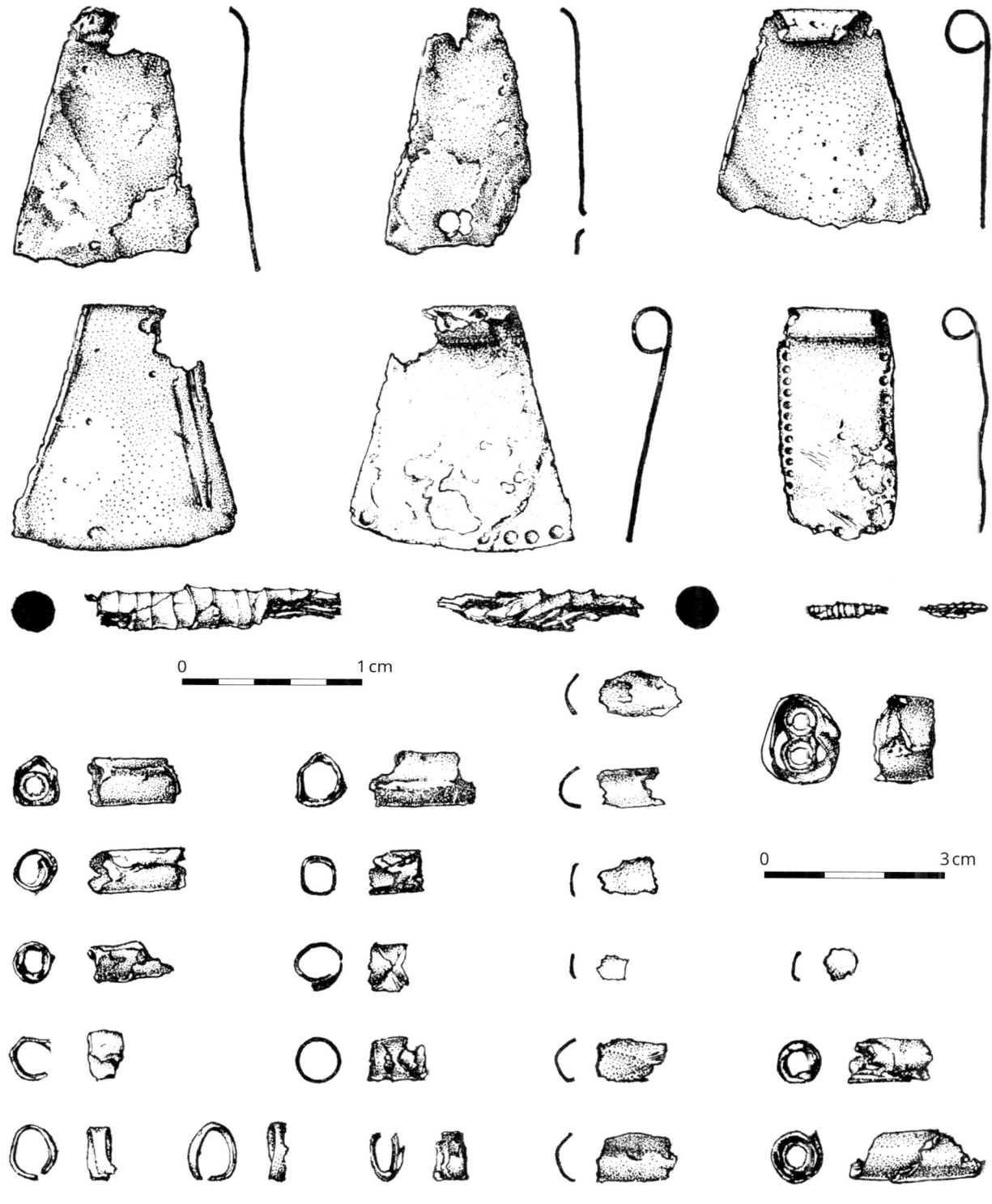

Fig. 70.1. Copper jewellery from Třebestovice: 1. grave 7; 2. grave 8 (Čtverák/Rulf 1989, 12 f., fig. 6).

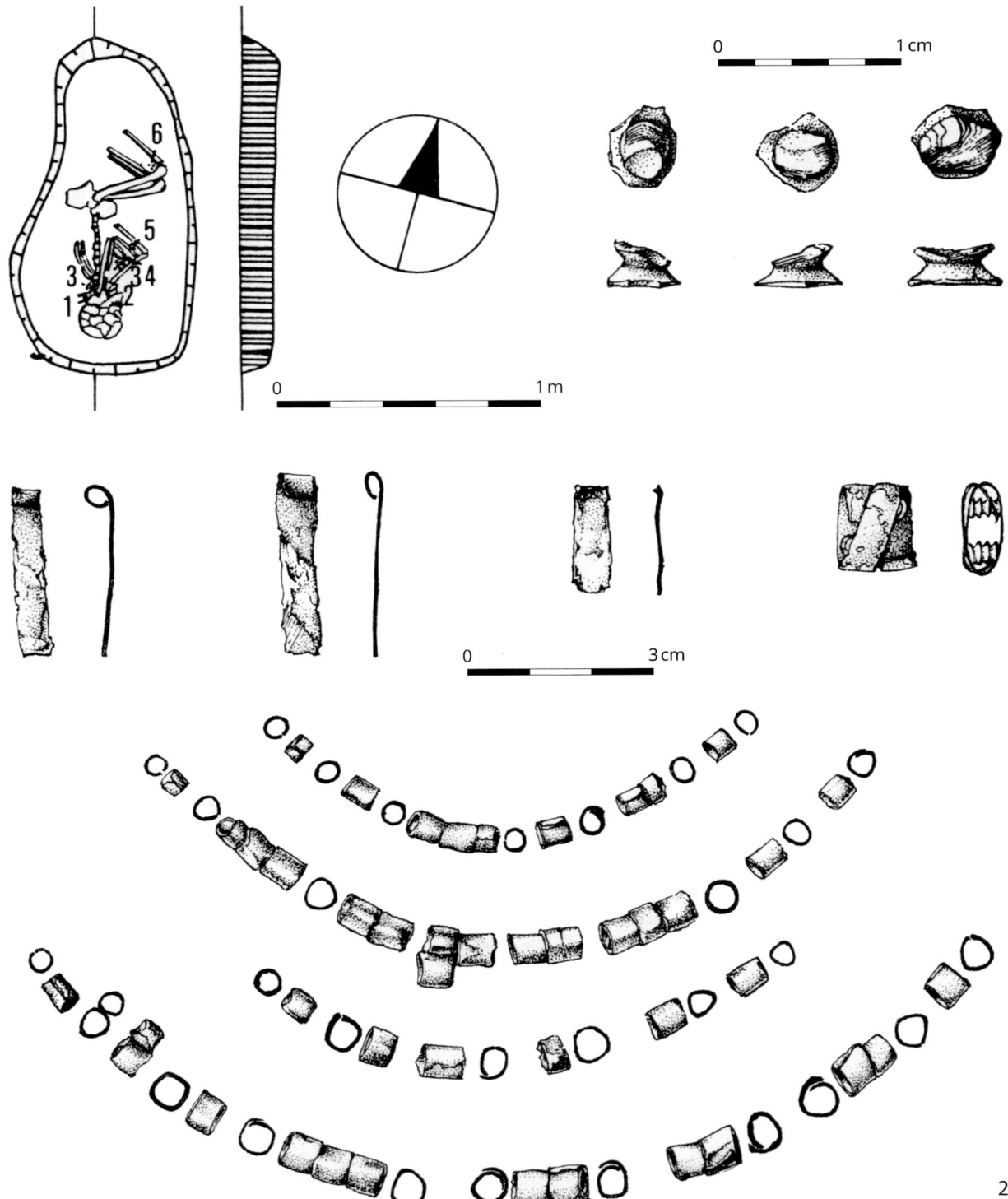

Fig. 70.2. Copper jewellery from Třebestovice (continued): 1. grave 7; 2. grave 8 (Čtverák/Rulf 1989, 12 f., fig. 7).

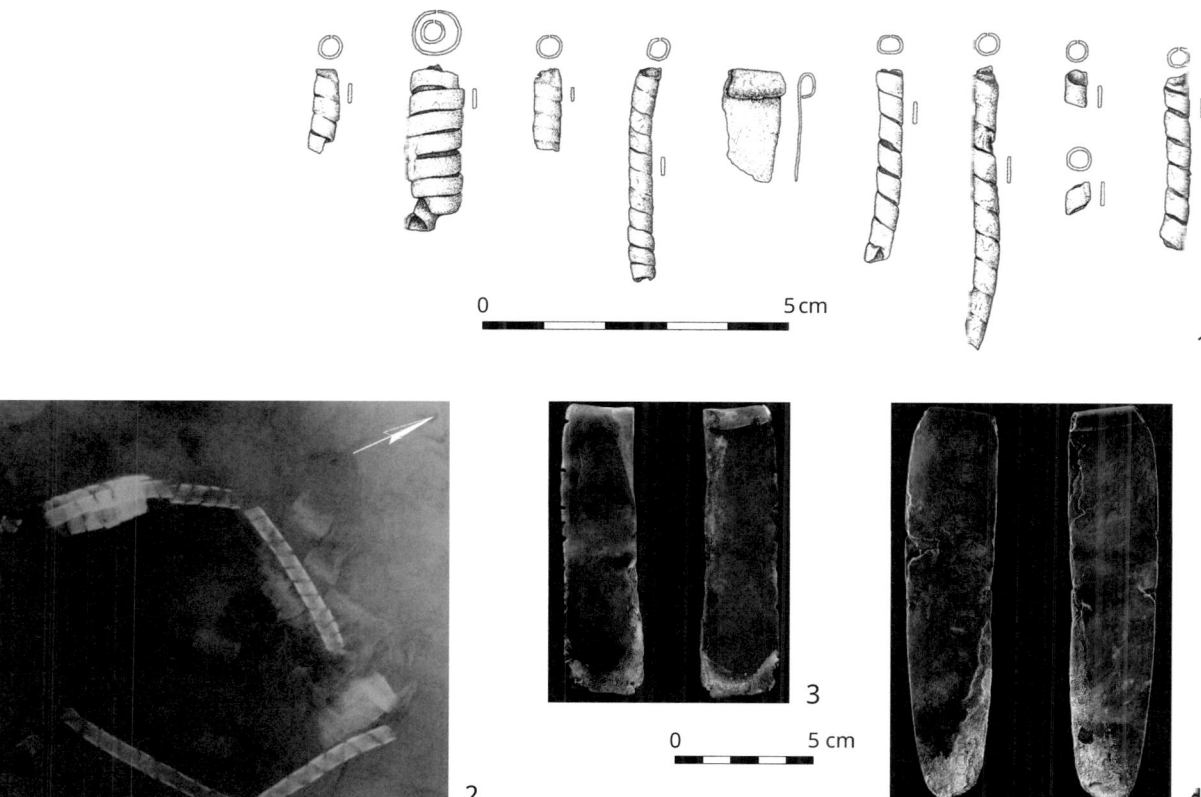

Fig. 71. 1. Copper necklace from Melzow; 2. X-ray of block recovery from Melzow; 3 and 4. Tongue-shaped pendants from Tettnang-Langnau (1. and 2. Dirks/Stark, 2016, 129, fig. 25 [1 © U. Dirks, BLDAM; 2. © St. Erather, BLDAM]; 3. and 4. Lichter/Badisches Landesmuseum Karlsruhe 2010, figs. 338-339; © Landesamt für Denkmalpflege im Regierungspräsidium Stuttgart/ Monika Erne).

variety due to its low arsenic content. Nevertheless, the ^{14}C data and the metal analyses provide certain evidence of objects made of Mondsee copper in the vicinity of Neuenkirchen and in the northern group of the TRB as early as the first centuries of the 4th millennium. This could be confirmed by the remains of arsenic copper from Plate, but trace element analyses and an exact dating of the finds are still pending. At least the amphora of the Baalberg type also found in this context points to the possibility of such an early dating.

As described above, necklaces of band spirals and pendants are a regularly-appearing form of sheet metal jewellery in the fifth and early fourth millennium, which also reaches the area of the northern group of the TRB from the Carpathian region. Based on this common combination of band spiral and pendant, such an approach also seems justified for the fragment from the hoard find of Neuenkirchen, even if other artefact forms, such as round thin discs, are possible.

10.8 Overall chronological assessment of the hoard from Neuenkirchen

As shown by the typological and metallurgical analyses, the dagger and the arm spiral can probably be dated to the end of the fifth and the beginning of the fourth millennium (around 4000 to 3800/3700 BCE). Based on the metal composition, this is also the case for the fragment and the band spirals. The youngest piece of the ensemble is the flat axe, which can be dated from 3800 to c. 3500/3300 BCE. The fact that objects made of the Mondsee copper variety already appear in the vicinity of Neuenkirchen in the course of the 38th century supports a dating of the hoard to the period in which the objects overlap in time, namely between 3800 and 3700 BCE. This period also marks the earliest possible time for the deposition of the objects. Due to the blurred chronological position of the axe, 3500/3300 BCE is also possible for the dating of the hoard and its deposition. While the focus so far has been mainly on the typological and chronological approach of the individual objects, the composition of the entire Neuenkirchen ensemble will be considered in the following, and compared with selected copper hoard finds in the corresponding period.

10.8.1 Selected hoard finds of the 4th millennium

10.8.1.1 The hoard find from Bygholm

The most important find of copper objects in the northern group of the Funnel Beaker Societies so far is the hoard from Bygholm, Denmark (Fig. 72), which has been a central point in the discussion about the early copper finds in this area since its discovery. The inventory includes four trapezoidal flat axes, three large arm spirals, and a dagger. All pieces are made of arsenic copper, which is referred to as Mondsee copper. The objects were placed on a sherd of decorated funnel beaker, on the basis of which three different dating approaches have been discussed in research. Klassen (2000, 79 ff.) discusses both the dating into the EN I by Menke (1989, 58 ff.) and Midgley (1992, 301), and into the EN II (Ebbesen 1979, 84 among others), or into the period between EN I to MN Ia (Hoika 1987, 123). Klassen (2000, 79 f.) categorically excludes the affiliation to the Volling group in EN I, since the rim and belly ornamentation of the beaker do not, or only very rarely, occur in this group. Only in the late Volling group do vessels appear that are decorated with ventral fringes (*Bauchfransen*), but these have a different vessel profile (*ibid.*, 80). He also does not want to follow the attribution to the Fuchsberg group of EN II. Although there are funnel beakers from this group with a similar profile and decoration, the differences in shape to the Bygholm beaker indicate that a contemporaneity cannot be postulated without further information (*ibid.*). The finds from the nearby settlement of Hanstedgard, which is assigned to MN Ia, also support a wider date range. Here, the material contains funnel beakers which, due to their profile and decoration, are comparable to the Bygholm beaker, but lack the characteristic edge engraving of the former. The rim decoration, in turn, is known from various vessels from the Fuchsberg period earthwork at Toftum. On the basis of this evidence, Klassen (*ibid.*) does not wish to date the Bygholm hoard more precisely than EN II to MN Ia. The ^{14}C-dates of the Fuchsberg group, the other earliest Middle Neolithic features, and the settlement of Hanstedgard are also found in this time range, so Klassen (*ibid.*) places the find between 3500-3300 cal. BCE. A dating before 3500 BCE would only be possible if the beaker is assigned to the Satrup Group (3800-3500 BCE), which is the only Early Neolithic group to show ventral fringe decoration. This local group has so far been found almost exclusively in Schleswig-Holstein, but some early-dated finds with ventral fringes from Jutland indicate the distribution of this group in this area. Thus, an earlier dating is also possible for the Bygholm beaker, but due to the low occurrence of finds from the Satrup group, it is not possible to make a definite statement (*ibid.*, 80 f.).

An interesting find for the chronology of the hoard comes from the immediate vicinity. A non-megalithic long mound was excavated in Rokær in 1998, about two kilometres from the site of Bygholm[32]. The original mound, which has been completely levelled by agricultural activities, originally measured 14 × 15 metres. The

---

32 A publication on Rokær is in preparation, so no illustration of the dagger is available at this time. All information is taken from the lecture "Rokær - an early Neolithic grave from Eastern Jutland, Denmark" by Anne Mette Kristiansen at the Archaeological Colloquium of the Institute for Pre- and Protohistory at Kiel University on 05.12.2016.

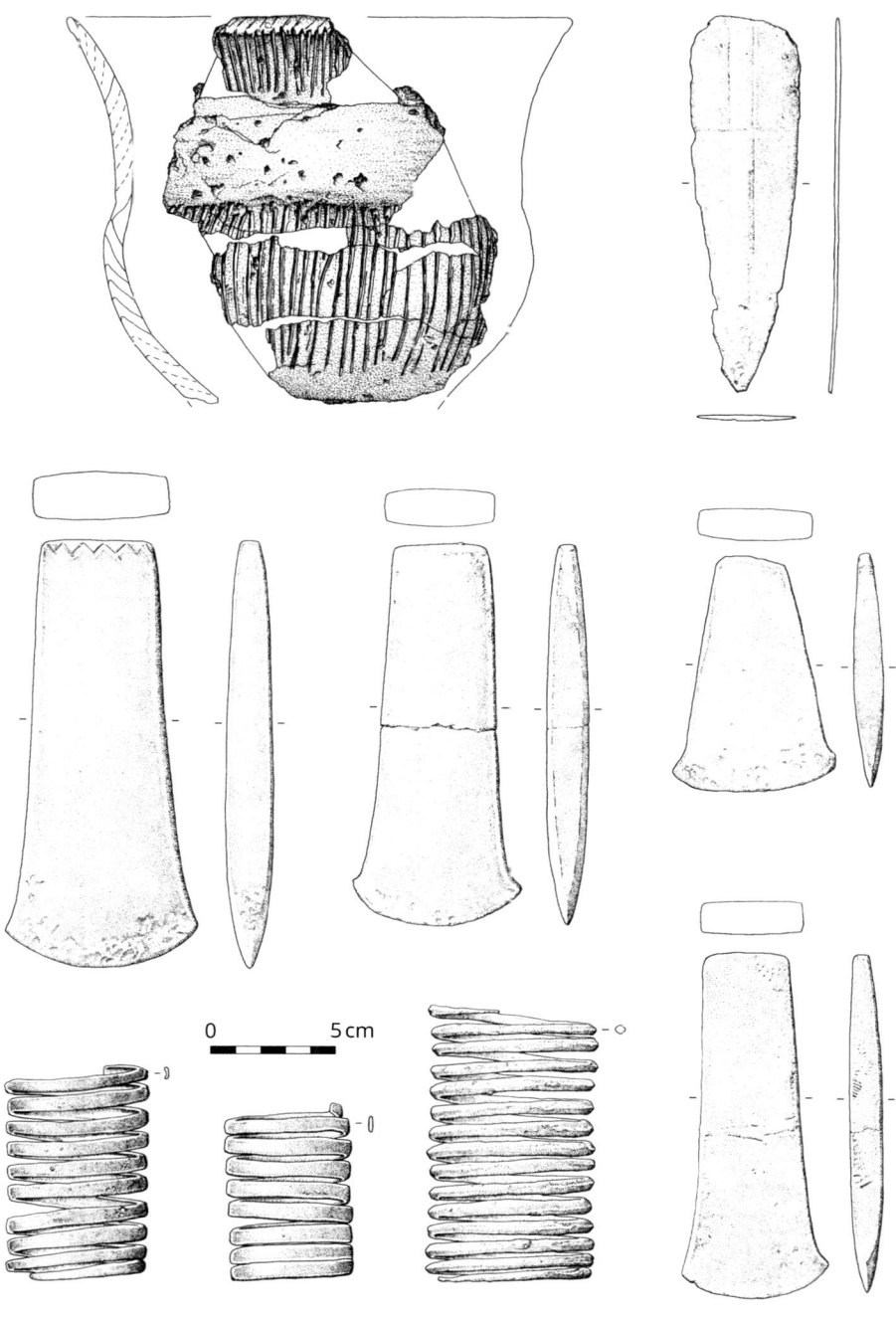

Fig. 72. Hoard find from Bygholm (Klassen 2000, 20, Fig. 2).

central and only grave of the mound was covered with a stone packing (3.5 × 1.5 m). No human remains have survived. On a black layer at the presumed head end of the burial lay two flint axes, as well as 206 amber beads of which five represent so-called amber suns. The flint dagger found in the middle of the grave, presumably at the waist level of the deceased, is exceptional. The 16.0 cm long, 3.0 cm wide and 0.8 cm thick specimen is made of one blade. Due to its manufacture, it has a central or median ridge on one side of the blade and thus an asymmetrical, plano-convex cross-section. The dagger is over-ground on the cutting edges and partly on the flat sides. As far as the author is aware, there is no typological parallel to the dagger found in the Nordic Early and beginning Middle Neolithic. The thick flint points occurring in the northern group of the TRB, which are addressed as halberd blades, differ significantly typologically. They are made of cores, are thicker on average, the cross-section is symmetrical (lenticular to rhombic) and, in contrast to the piece from Rokær, they are retouched over the entire surface and only rarely show traces of grinding (cf. Lübke 1999, 49 ff.). For dating purposes, a charcoal sample was obtained from the above-mentioned black layer which yielded the following date: K-7126, 4740 ±34 BP, 3636-3498 BCE (73.3%), 3435-3378 BCE (Rasmussen 2000, 332).

This grave find is interesting for the Bygholm hoard in several respects. On the one hand, the dagger from the grave at Rokær was probably made under the impression of the copper dagger from Bygholm. This is supported by the fact, as described above, that daggers are otherwise unknown in the area of the northern group of the TRB, and by the immediate proximity to Bygholm and the temporal overlap of the two finds. On the other hand, it is remarkable, if one assumes the simultaneity of burial and deposition, that the copper dagger and axes were not used as grave goods, but were deposited together with other copper objects. While flint axes and amber beads, as well as copper jewellery objects, are known from both deposits and graves, copper flat axes and daggers seem to be reserved for depots. The absolute date of the grave of Rokær also underlines a possible dating of the hoard of Bygholm before 3500 BCE. However, the second peak of the ^{14}C date falls within the period postulated by Klassen (2000) for the deposition, so that uncertainty about the dating remains.

10.8.1.2 The hoard find from Årupgård

Another hoard was found in the immediate vicinity of Bygholm, only one kilometre from the grave find at Rokær, in Årupgård. A flask with eyelets was buried with the mouth downwards, and contained two wire spiral rings, two band spirals, three copper sheet spirals, as well as a tube made from copper sheet, and 271 whole (as well as 177 fragmented) amber beads (Klassen 2000, 352 f.) (Fig. 73). One band spiral and one metal sheet spiral are made of an arsenic copper, which is considered to be Mondsee copper; the rest of the inventory of the hoard find was not analysed. While Sylvest and Sylvest (1960) do not want to consider the hoard more precisely as EN I/II because the form of the vessel is existing throughout the Early Neolithic, Klassen (2000, 81) places the hoard in EN II. His dating is based on the comparative find of a likewise undecorated flask from the nearby earthwork at Toftum, and the assumption that the deposition at Årupgård took place in an earthwork that had been destroyed during construction work and remained unidentified. The construction of such earthworks does not begin in the northern group of the TRB before EN II, so Klassen (*ibid.*) would like to rule out a dating to EN I.

10.8.1.3 The hoard find from Søby Hede

From Søby Hede in Denmark comes the hoard find of a flat axe and a large arm spiral (Fig. 74), for which no further information on the circumstances of the find is available, apart from the information that it came from a hill slope in a bog. Klassen (2000, 90) dates the deposit to EN II/MN A Ia because of the parallels to the large arm spirals from Bygholm.

10.8.1.4 The hoard find from Riesebusch

From Riesebusch in Schleswig-Holstein comes a hoard find of a copper flat axe, two rings made of wire or sheet metal strips, and several band spirals (Fig. 75). The number of turns can only be given as 13-16, as the hoard found during road construction work in 1912 never made it to the museum in its entirety and the remaining pieces are now lost. Klassen (2000, 90 f.) would also like to place the hoard find in EN II (MN A Ia). In his opinion, this is supported by the fact that the

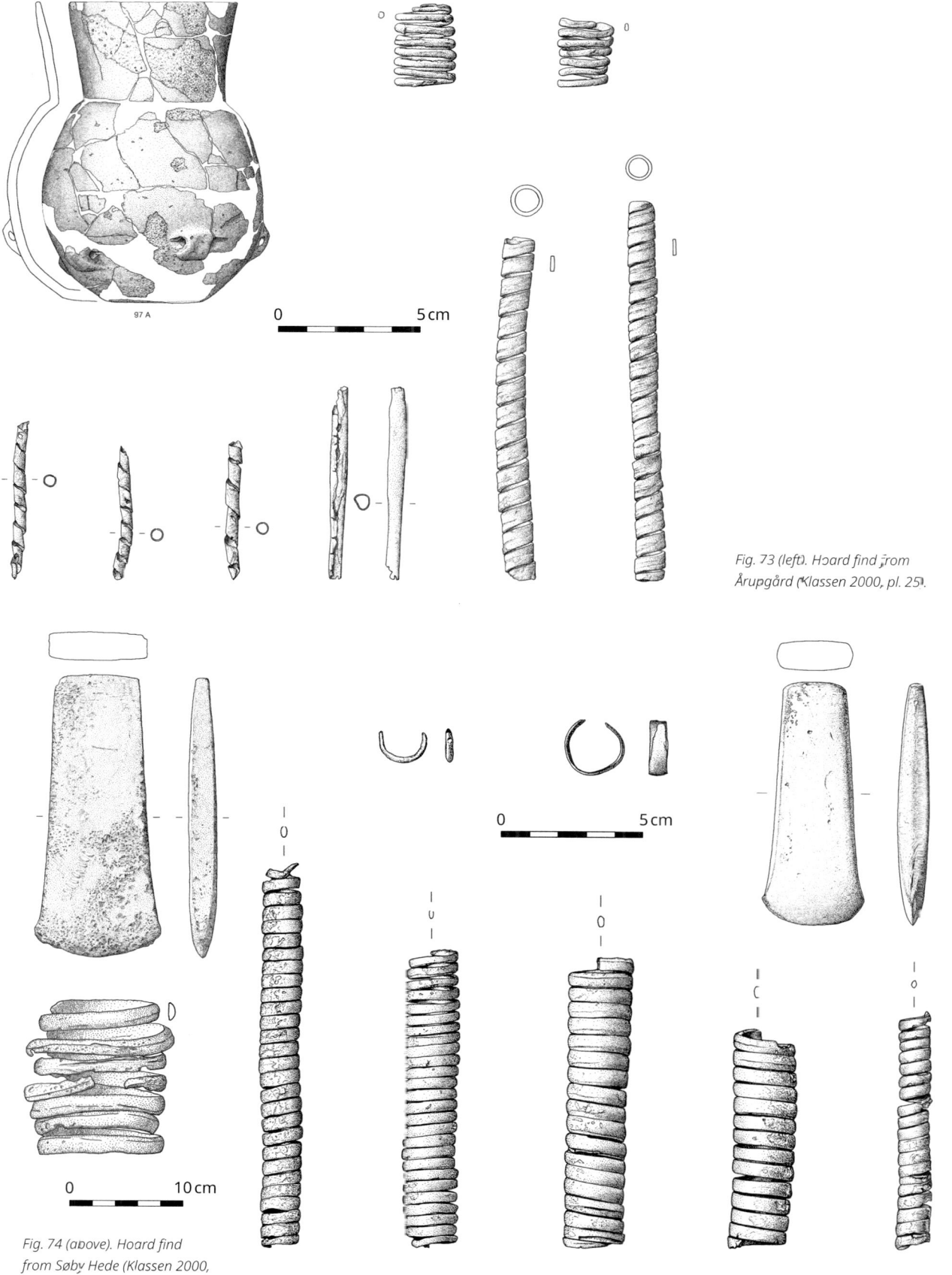

Fig. 73 (left). Hoard find from Årupgård (Klassen 2000, pl. 25).

Fig. 74 (above). Hoard find from Søby Hede (Klassen 2000, pl. 24.95).

Fig. 75. Hoard find from Riesebusch (Klassen 2000, pl. 26).

practice of depositing copper flat axes and jewellery together only occurred in southern Scandinavia in the period in question. He also dates two other depots with this combination of objects (Bygholm and Søby Hede) to EN II (MN A Ia), making such a dating of the Riesebusch hoard probable. On the other hand, he considers the chronological dating to be supported by the band spirals, since this type of artefact also occurs in the depot find from Årupgård, which also dates to EN II, and all band spirals show the same forging technique (*ibid.*).

10.8.1.5 The hoard find from Stollhof

From Stollhof, Austria, a hoard find containing two flat axes, nine band spirals, two large arm spirals, six spectacle spirals, a perforated plate, and two gold embossed discs is known (Fig. 76). Three band spirals and the two large arm spirals show great formal similarities with the corresponding specimens from the Neuenkirchen hoard. The unclear circumstances of the find, as well as doubts about the unity of the ensemble, were part of the research discussion for a long time, as was the chronology of the find. In the meantime, however, other hoard finds with a similar composition — for example from Hlinsko in the Czech Republic — have led to the assumption that the find complex is complete (Turck 2010, 28).

Klassen (2000,194) assigns the flat axes to type group I of Dobeš, which mainly occur in Tiszapolgár and Bodrogkeresztúr. However, there is no reliable evidence for these axes in the corresponding period. Therefore, Klassen (*ibid.*) assumes a *terminus ante quem* (=late Bodrogkeresztúr) for the pieces from Stollhof. Patay (1958, 45) has a different approach for one of the flat axes, assigning it to the Szákálhat type, which is regarded as typical for Bodrogkeresztúr. For the discs, good comparisons are available from the settlement and from the Brześć Kujawski cemetery, among others. The specimen from Hornstaad-Hörnle could be dated to the beginning of the 4th millennium (3913 to 3904 BCE) on the basis of its secure stratigraphic location and the available dendrochronological dating of the layer in which the disc was found (Klassen 2000, 197 and Turck 2010, 27). For grave 34 from Brześć Kujawski, where a comparable copper disc was found, Klassen (2000, 196) assumes a chronological position in an earlier phase of Brześć Kujawski. An intensive use of copper in this cultural group from 4250 BCE onwards is proven by a ^{14}C-dated grave find from Kruza Zamkova (*ibid.*). For the discs from Stollhof, a date from the late 5th millennium to the early 4th millennium is thus possible (*ibid.*). The same applies to spectacle spirals of the Malé Leváre type, variant Stollhof. There are equivalents in the specimens from a depot find from Jordanów in Rašovice, Czech Republic. Large arm spirals like the Stollhof specimens are attested from the middle of the 5th millennium at the latest. Klassen (*ibid.*, 195) assumes that the hoard dates to around 4000 BCE. If the more recent absolute dates for Bodrogkeresztúr are considered, a somewhat earlier date in the last centuries of the 5th millennium is to be expected, although with regard to the copper disc from Hornstad-Hörnle the possibility of a somewhat later date remains.

10.8.1.6 The hoard find from Lödersdorf

The exact context of an assemblage Lödersdorf, Austria is unclear; it consists of a flat axe, a flat axe fragment, an arm spiral, an animal sculpture, a necklace of beads and band spirals, a necklace of copper and bone beads, as well as flint blades (Fig. 77). As there are no known settlements in the immediate vicinity of the find, a burial or hoard context is assumed. The fact that all the examined objects are made of Mondsee copper speaks for the affiliation of the pieces (Neumann 2015, 357) to one hoard/burial. Turck (2010, 39 ff.) suggests, based on the arm spiral and the other copper jewellery, that the ensemble should be interpreted as burial objects. In

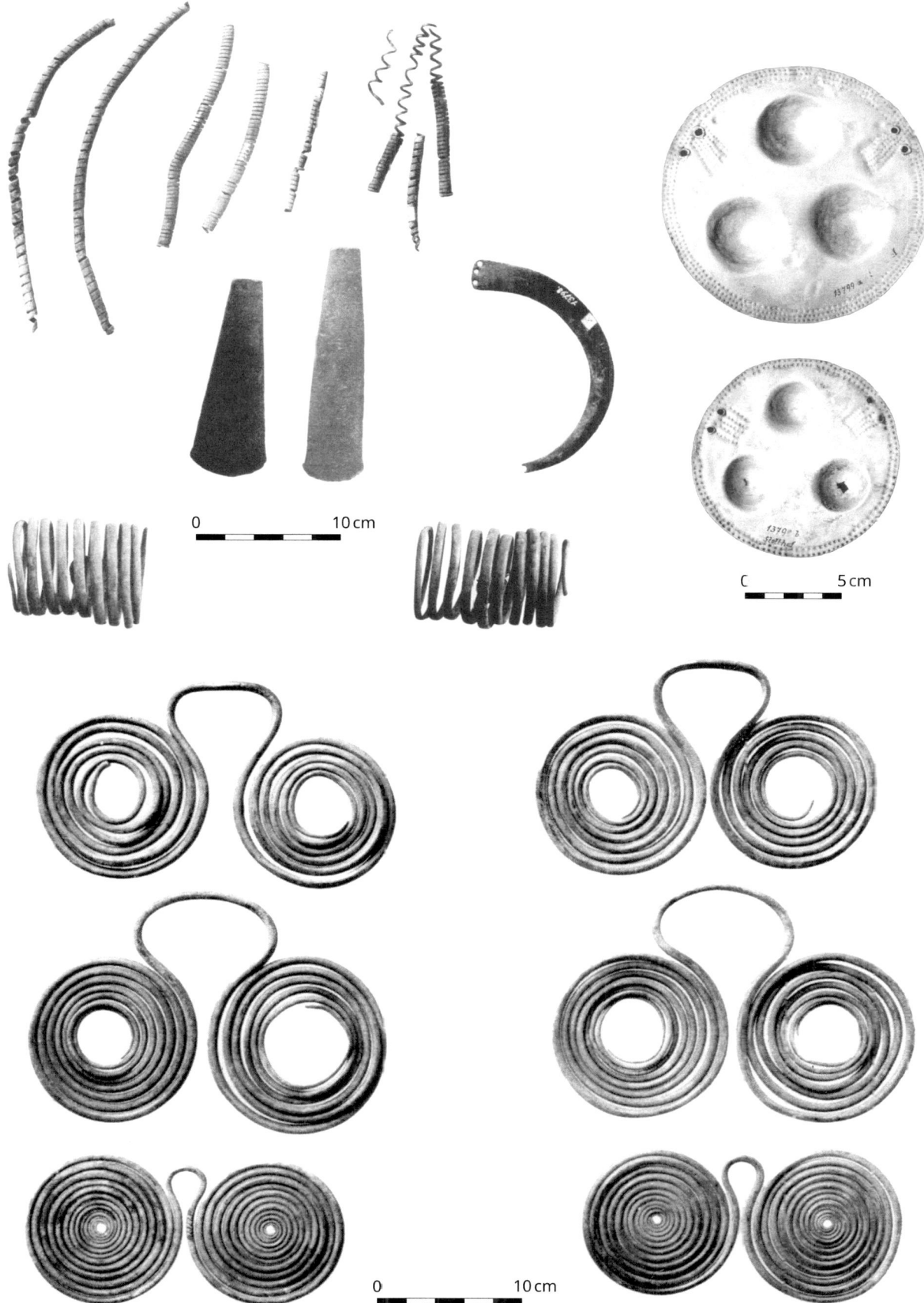

Fig. 76. Hoard find from Stollhof (Turck 2010, figs. 27-29).

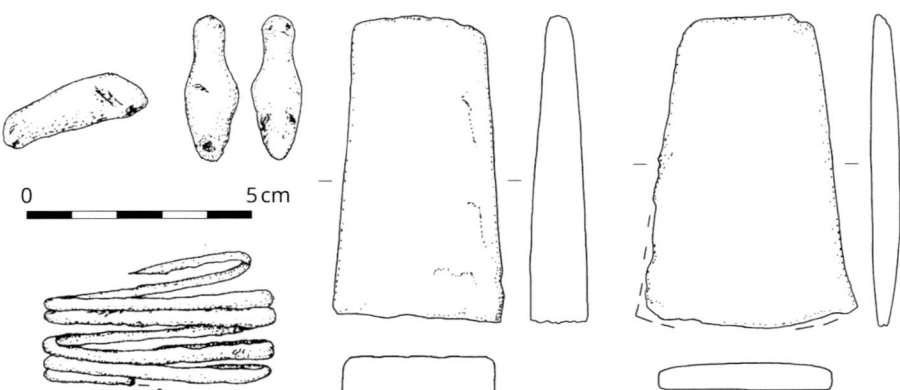

Fig. 77. Hoard find from Lödersdorf without necklaces (on this cf. Fig. 65.4) (Turck 2010, 39, Fig. 40).

doing so, he refers to corresponding grave finds of arm spirals and band spiral rolls (*Bandspiralrollen*) from Baalberg and Jordanów. On the basis of the connection to the Baalberg burials, the flat axe of the Altheim type, as well as the related Mondsee copper variety, he suggests a dating of the Lödersdorf ensemble to shortly before or around the middle of the 4th millennium. At this point, the interpretation as grave goods cannot be followed. Although it is certainly true that copper jewellery occurs as a component of Baalberg burials, as far as the author is aware there is no known case of the combination with copper flat axes. However, this circumstance does not necessarily contradict Turck's dating (*ibid.*). The related Mondsee copper, as well as the flat axe of the Altheim type, provide a solid dating basis, so that a date from 3800/3700 BCE onwards can be expected.

10.8.2 Neuenkirchen between Bygholm and Stollhof

Comparing the compositions of the hoard finds of the Funnel Beaker North Group with the composition of Neuenkirchen, similarities in the respective artefact groups represented are striking (cf. Figs. 17 and 72). The correspondence with the Bygholm deposit is particularly high, with daggers, arm spirals and flat axes, all components that are also represented in the Neuenkirchen hoard. The combination of band spirals and a copper flat axe is also known from the Riesebusch find. However, the ensemble from Neuenkirchen is unique, due to the addition of band spirals and probably a copper plate pendant. The association of flat axes, band spiral rolls, and arm spirals is also known in the Alpine region from the hoard find at Stollhof, which dates to the turn of the 4th millennium. A similar composition is found in the same area in the find from Lödersdorf, which is up to 500 years younger, but in which the arm spiral is much more delicate. The composition of the hoard from Neuenkirchen confirms the chronological position between the hoard finds from Stollhof and Bygholm, as there are similarities with both deposits.

At this point it should be noted that Klassen (2000, 138 ff.) does not see the large arm spirals of the northern group of the TRB in any connection with the specimens from Stollhof because of the chronological difference, and assumes a functionally-conditioned convergence phenomenon. In view of the hoard from Neuenkirchen, the presence of the Mondsee copper variety in the north from 3700 BCE at the latest (cf. 10.7, keyword Melzow and Plate), as well as the flint dagger from Rokær (cf. 10.8.1.1), an adjustment of the dating of the deposits from Bygholm and Årupgård is certainly within the realm of possibility. The pottery used for dating does not contradict this (cf. above). Since the other deposits with comparable artefacts are indirectly dated on the basis of the two hoard finds mentioned above, the entire depositional horizon of the Funnel Beaker North Group thus moves forward. A date of around 3600/3500 BCE (previously 3500-3300 BCE) is conceivable. If one accepts this assumption, the arm spirals of the northern group of the TRB may have been created under the influence of the specimen from Neuenkirchen, which itself was probably produced in the Carpathian region at the beginning of the 4th millennium and reached the North as an import. This hypothesis is supported by the fact that the phenomenon mentioned by Klassen (*ibid.*, 143) — namely that finds from the northern group of the TRB are significantly larger than typologically similar objects from the northern Alpine region — also applies to the Neuenkirchen arm spiral[33]. It is smaller than, for example, the examples from Bygholm or Skarbienice, which are also made of arsenic (Mondsee) copper. Since it is assumed that the older arm spirals from Stollhof also originate from the Balkan-Carpathian area (*e.g.* Turck 2010, 28 f.), this suggests that there is a connection between the early arm spirals of the south-eastern European area and those of the northern funnel beaker group, and that the arm spiral from Neuenkirchen is the link between the two find groups that Klassen (2000, 140) sought, indicating a connection between the two areas. The fact that larger arm spirals are found in the area of the northern group of the TRB could be explained by their use by different age groups. In the surroundings of Jordanow and Baalberg, arm spirals are often associated with child burials (Turck 2010, 41). This suggests that the arm spirals are adapted to the proportions of the wearers, and that in the northern group of the TRB they were possibly reserved for adults. Considering the small number of artefacts, and the fact that really large specimens are only attested with certainty from the hoard find at Bygholm, this remains for the time being only a working hypothesis.

---

33 Since the ends of the arm spiral from Neuenkirchen are not preserved, this circumstance cannot be definitively determined. In any case, the metal composition seems to be more decisive here.

11. Neuenkirchen in light of the Development of Early Metallurgy in Southeast Europe

The emergence of early metallurgy has been the subject of intensive research discussions over the last 100 years. As centres of innovation, Southeast Europe and the Near East have been particularly in focus, whereby the Near East has often been regarded as the source of impulses for the development in Southeast Europe. In their 2016 article, E. Rosenstock, S. Scharl and W. Schier compare the developments of copper use and metallurgy in both regions with the help of new research results, ^{14}C data, and lead isotope investigations. In doing so, they address the question of whether one of the regions mentioned represents the innovation centre of copper metallurgy or whether there are contemporary developments. They conclude that this question cannot yet be conclusively clarified, but show that around about 5000 BCE copper smelting metallurgy appears in both regions at the same time and that even south-eastern Europe is possible as a source of impulses for the Orient (*ibid.*, 106). In the following, the hoard find from Neuenkirchen will be fitted into the early horizon of copper metallurgy in south-eastern and central Europe as presented in detail by Rosenstock *et al.* (*ibid.*) and summarised here, taking into account the research results presented in this work (cf. Figs. 78 and 79 respectively).

The first copper objects made of malachite and azurite, but also of solid copper, appear in Southeast Europe in the course of secondary Neolithization in the late 7th and early 6th millennium. From this phase (6300-5400 BCE), which Rosenstock *et al.* (*ibid.*, 70) call "pre-metallurgical", copper finds are available from the Greek Nea Nikomedeia and the Serbian Lepenski Vir (III a and b), among others. The range of shapes includes beads, pins, and bent-over pins. In the late 6th and early 5th millennium, the number of copper objects and the diversity of artefact types increase significantly. From the northern Central Balkans, as well as the Carpathian Basin, neck and arm jewellery, but also the first heavy implements such as chisels, appear. Such objects are attested from settlement, hoard and grave contexts of the Neolithic groups Vinča, Sopot, Lengyel, Tisza, Herpály, Csöszhalom, Marica, Präcucuteni, and Petreşti. Around 5000 BCE, the mining (Rudna Glava) of copper ores and the smelting and casting of copper (Belovode and Ploćnik) are attested from the area of present-day Serbia. In the advancing 5th millennium, the number of heavy tools and other copper artefacts increases massively and reaches the relative and absolute maximum between 4200-4000 BCE. Until about the middle of the following 4th millennium, the number of objects decreases by more than two thirds (*ibid.*, 83 ff.). In their work, Rosenstock, Scharl and Schier (2016) were able to show that the spread of copper artefacts, and the knowledge of metallurgy associated with

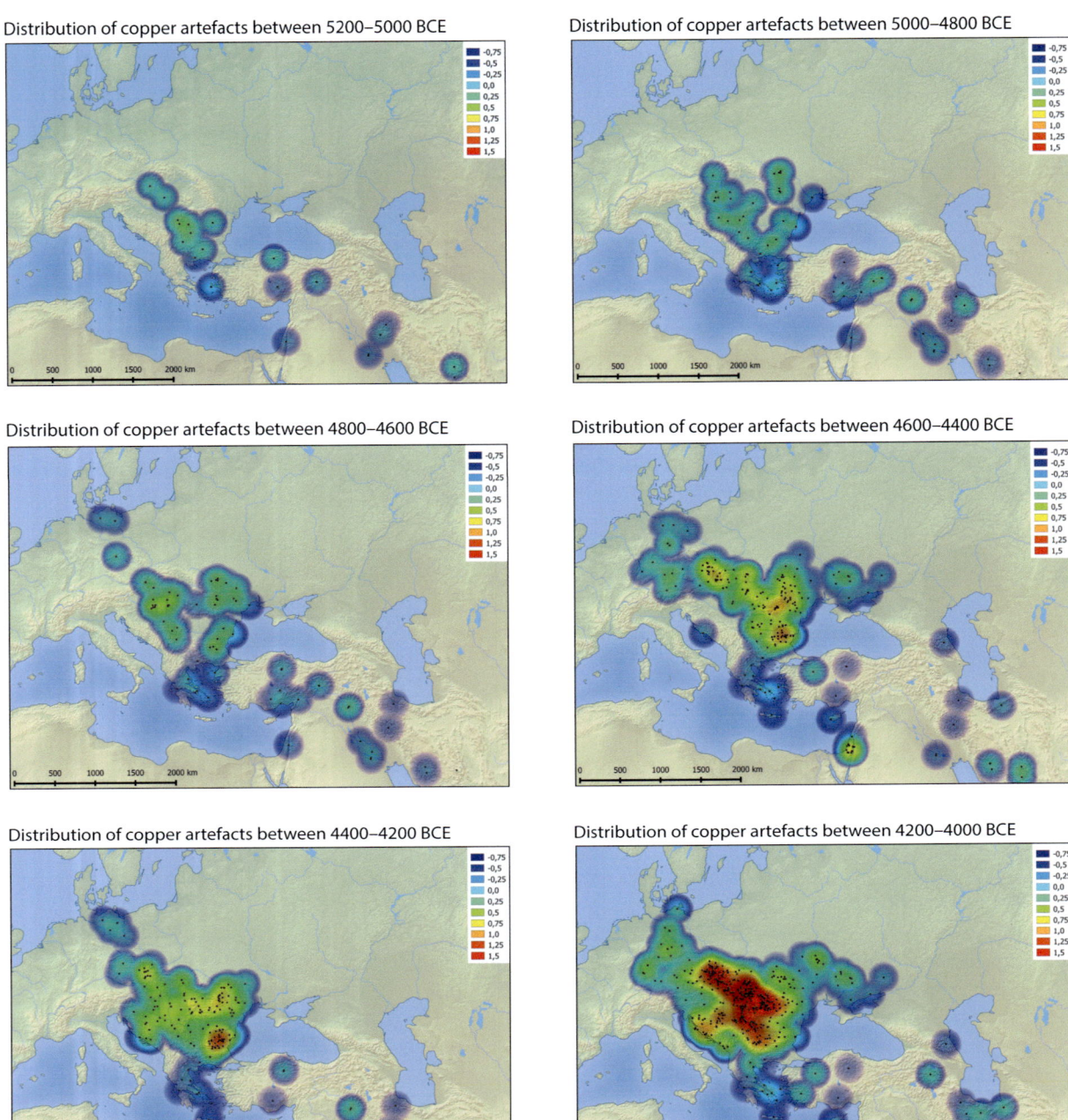

Fig. 78. Kernel density estimate of the distribution of copper artefacts in the time slices 5200-5000 BCE; 5000-4800 BCE; 4800-4600 BCE; 4600-4400 BCE; 4400-4200 BCE and 4200-4000 BCE, according to Rosenstock et al (2016, 85, fig 7-12). The calculation of the kernel density estimate was carried out with QGIS, and a search radius (kernel bandwidth) of 200 km and a biquadratic kernel; subsequently, all calculated grid values were logarithmised (with the programme SAGA) in order to obtain a comparably representable scale across all time slices. (Rosenstock et al. 2016, 86).

Distribution of copper artefacts between 4000–3800 BCE

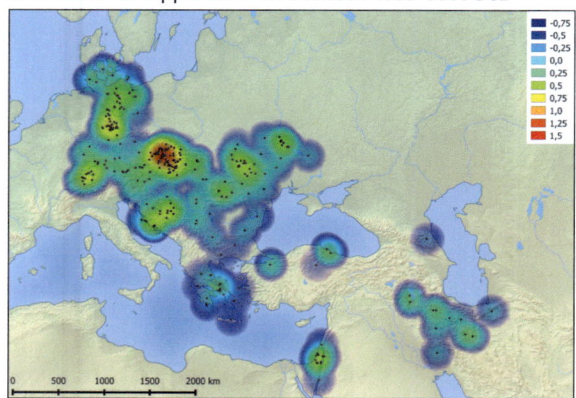

Distribution of copper artefacts between 3800–3600 BCE

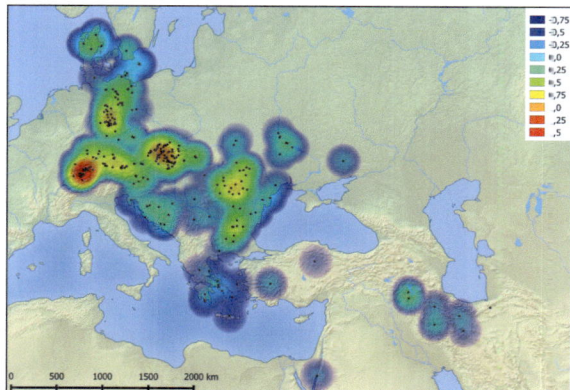

Distribution of copper artefacts between 3600–3400 BCE

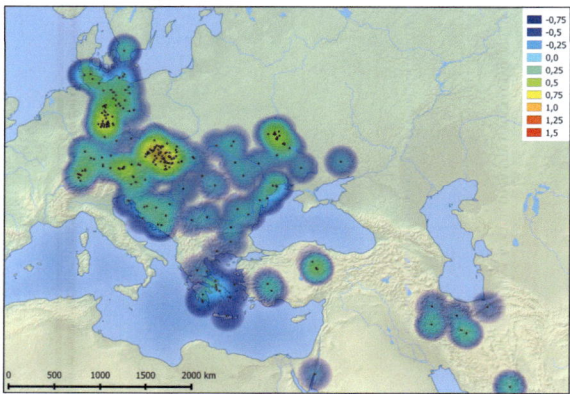

them, was not a linear diffusion process, but that centres of density replaced each other. In each case, the emergence of new centres of density is associated with a decline in a previously-existing centre (*ibid.*). For the time before 5200 BCE, the few finds indicate a centre of gravity in south-eastern Europe between Thessaly and Transylvania. Between 5200-5000 BCE, a concentration of artefacts is again recorded in the eastern Serbian and western Bulgarian mountain regions, while isolated finds are recorded in northern Hungary, western Bulgaria, and southern Romania. In the period between 5000 and 4800 BCE, three different centres of distribution stand out. One of the centres is the eastern Serbian mountain region mentioned above, where mining and processing (Rudna Glava/Belovode) already took place in the late 6th millennium. In addition, finds of small copper artefacts east of the Tisza and west of the Danube are represented in settlements and graves of Tisza and Lengyel (*ibid.*). The second region with a relative density of objects is in central and north-eastern Bulgaria, where isolated copper artefacts come from the contexts of Karanovo IV. Another distribution focus is in the area of the forest-steppe zone between Dnestr and Eastern Carpathians, from which isolated small artefacts from contexts of Pre-Cucuteni and early Trypillia are also known (*ibid.*).

In the following period between 4800 and 4600 BCE, when the first heavy tools in the form of chisels and hammer axes appear, the aforementioned three focal points remain. In addition, the distribution of copper artefacts within Pre-Cucuteni spreads to Moldavia, as can be seen from the hoard find from Cărbuna, which has already been mentioned several times. The first individual artefacts have already reached central and north-eastern Germany. Between 4600 and 4400 BCE, the finds in south-eastern Europe and in the Carpathian Basin became much more concentrated. The centres of distribution are north-eastern Bulgaria and Mutenia (Romania), as well as

Fig. 79. Kernel density estimate of the distribution of copper artefacts in the timeslices 4000-3800 BCE; 3800-3600 BCE and 3600-3400 BCE, according to Rosenstock et al. (2016, 85, fig. 13-15)

the north-western Pontic area between Dnestr and Eastern Carpathians (distribution area Cucuteni and Karanovo-Kodjadermen-Gumelnita). Numerous copper artefacts are also represented in the south-eastern Carpathian Basin and in Transylvania. For the first time, there is a concentration of finds in the area of western Slovakia. Also, in this time slice, isolated copper objects are represented in north-eastern Germany, as well as southern Germany (*ibid.*).

These centres of distribution remain essentially intact between 4400 and 4200 BCE. In the north-eastern Carpathian Basin (north-eastern Hungary, eastern Slovakia, Carpatho-Ukraine) an increasing density is shown, which is brought about with classical Tiszapolgár. The centre in western Slovakia and eastern Moravia, which was already present in the preceding time slice, is further concentrated. The copper artefacts increasingly spread westwards to the area around the Alps, as well as to the northern Alpine, central German, and north-eastern German regions (*ibid.*). In the late 5th millennium (4200-4000 BCE) the frequency of finds reaches its relative and absolute maximum. The distribution extends as a large contiguous area from north-western Bulgaria and eastern Serbia to northern Moravia. A core area, which is essentially associated with Bodrogkeresztúr, is located in Transylvania and the eastern half of the Carpathian Basin. Numerous Nógrádmarcal copper artefacts and the concentration of regionally well-defined forms also point to an independent copper metallurgy in the Western Carpathians (*ibid.*, 102). The southwestern section of the area extends from southwestern Hungary to Croatia. The western Pontic area, in contrast to the previous time slice, remains mostly free of finds (*ibid.*, 88). Again, the finds scatter westwards into the northern Alpine, central German, and north-eastern German areas, but without increasing significantly.

The picture changes significantly in the time slice between 4000 and 3800 BCE. The Western Slovak-Moravian area clearly emerges as a density centre, while in the area of the Tisza region and Transylvania only a few finds are now recorded (*ibid.*, 89). There is also a conspicuous centre of density in Central Germany, which radiates along the Elbe into present-day Brandenburg and Mecklenburg-Western Pomerania. In addition, a smaller concentration can be seen along the northern Oder. Smaller centres are evident in present-day Croatia and between the Dniester and Eastern Carpathians in the distribution area of Cucuteni (Stage AB), and in the area of Trypillia (Stage B2) on the middle Dnieper. In this time slice, copper finds also appear for the first time in the south-west German-Swiss area (*ibid.*).

Between 3800 and 3600 BCE, a centre of distribution develops between Lake Constance and the Swiss midlands, which extends eastwards into the distribution areas of Altheim and Mondsee. In this centre of density, there is much evidence of independent processing of copper, among other things in the form of casting crucibles and semi-finished products. The main centres of distribution in Central Germany and the Western Slovak-Moravian area continue to exist. The finds again spread to today's Mecklenburg-Western Pomerania and Brandenburg, and now also reach the northern Jutland and Swedish regions. In south-eastern Europe, there are indications of a concentration of finds in eastern Transylvania, which extends northwards into the distribution area of Cucuteni (Level B). To the south, the finds are scattered as far as Thrace.

In the period between 3600 and 3400 BC, the centres in central Germany, and western Slovakia and Moravia remain. The concentration of finds in the south-western German-Swiss area is hardly present any more. The southern European area, as well as the Carpathian Basin, are also free of finds except for isolated objects. Only on the middle Dnieper River, in the context of Trypillia (stage C1), a small concentration of finds is discernible. In the area of the Northern Funnel Beaker Group there are some finds in southern Jutland, Mecklenburg-Western Pomerania, as well as in northern Brandenburg.

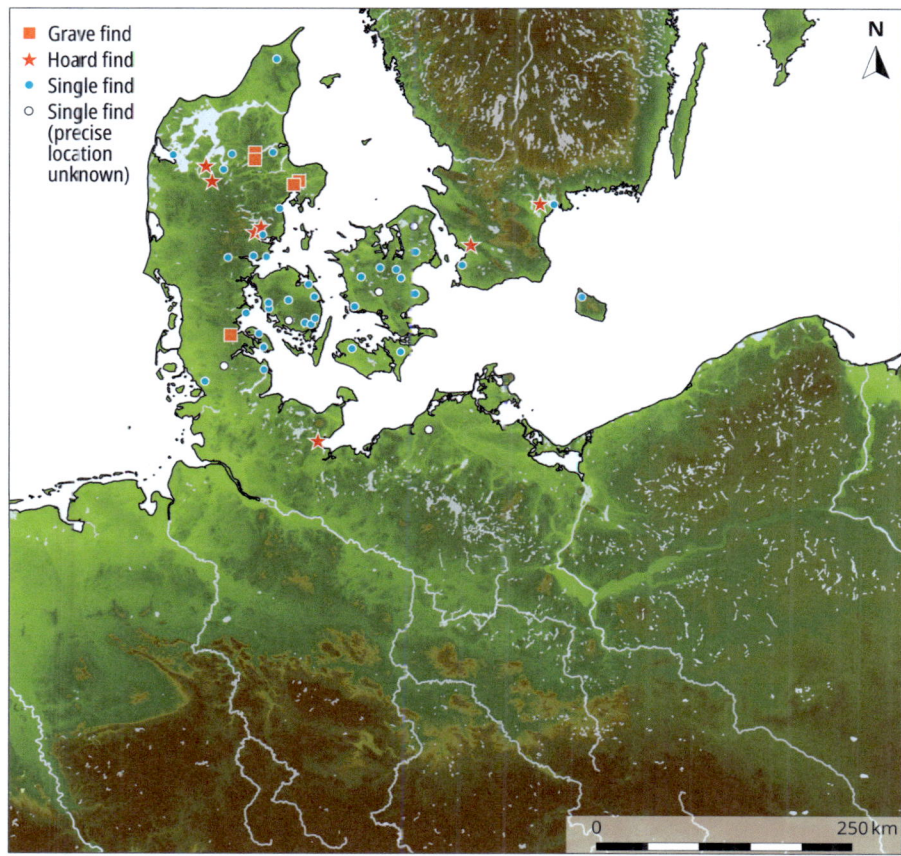

Fig. 80. Distribution of copper artefacts in the north between 3500 and 3300 BCE. 1. Single find; 2. Depot find; 3. Grave find according to Klassen (2000, 237, fig. 114).

The analysis by Rosenstock *et al.* (2016) ends with the time slice 3600-3400 BCE, although it seems that they only considered finds before 3500 BCE for southern Scandinavia and northern Germany. From this time onwards, according to Klassen (2000), the amount of metal in the area of the Funnel Beaker North Group increases rapidly, and a local metallurgy establishes itself, producing numerous independent forms from imported Mondsee copper (*ibid.*, 225). Around 3500 BCE, arsenic/antimony copper appears, which remains restricted to the area of the Funnel Beaker North Group (Fig. 80). Klassen (*ibid.*) assumes a separate copper variety here, with origins in central Sweden, which he calls "Riesebusch". This is contradicted by Schmitz (2004, 553 f.), who does not recognise a separate copper variety and shows, on the basis of the cluster analysis he carried out, that it is Mondsee copper. Around c. 3300 BCE, this metal-rich phase also ends in the area of northern group of the TRB (Klassen 2000, 238).

The development described above clearly shows that the north-eastern German region was already connected to the innovative region of south-eastern Europe at a very early stage, as shown, for example, by the chisel from Bülow and the axe-adze from Steinhagen. Around 4000 BCE, contacts between the West Slovak-Moravian centre of distribution, Central Germany, North-Eastern Germany, and Southern Scandinavia intensified. In the time slices 4200-4000 BCE and 4000-3800 BCE (according to Rosenstock *et al.* 2016), an independent production of copper artefacts from the Nógrádmarcal copper variety can be proven in the area of western Slovakia and Moravia. The synthesis with the considerations on typology, as well as the metal analyses of the objects from the Neuenkirchen hoard, confirms the interpretation that the dagger, the arm spiral, the band spirals, and the fragment may have arrived in present-day Mecklenburg-Western Pomerania as imports around 4000/3800 BCE from the western Slovak-Moravian region. The objects thus join the already-known flat axes from Raden and Kirch Jesar, as well as the axe-adze from Steinhagen, which are also made of the copper variety Nógrádmarcal. The interpretation of the axe as an early northern Alpine import, on the other hand, fits well with the subsequent time slice (3800-3600 BCE). In the (northern) Alpine region, the import of artefacts from the western Carpathian and south-eastern European regions is replaced by an independent, local production of objects made of the Mondsee copper variety in the course of the 39th century BCE. Nørgaard *et al.* (2021) argue for the origin of that copper variety from south-eastern Europe, so that at least material for the postulated independent production originated there. The flat axes from Pantelitz, Ruegen, and Neuenkirchen, imported from the northern Alpine region, probably via central Germany, thus stand at the beginning of the use of the Mondsee copper variety in the area of the northern group of the TRB, before independent production begins from c. 3500 BCE onwards. In light of the deliberate destruction of the flat axe from Neuenkirchen by hot-shorting metalwork (cf. 7.3.2.1), which represents clear knowledge about the material and metallurgy, an earlier start of independent metal production — including re-smelting and casting — seems possible, although any further archaeological evidence beyond this is missing.

12. Neuenkirchen – profane, ritual, and/or social practice?

The significance of hoard or depot finds has been the subject of intensive research for more than 150 years. The controversial discussion usually revolves around the question of whether these deposits are of a ritual or profane nature. The arguments used in this debate hardly changed between the mid-19th century and the end of the 20th century (Dietrich 2014, 468). Two major approaches can be summarised. The first approach looks at the circumstances of the depositions, particularly the environment in which the finds were deposited. Deposition in wet environments (such as bogs, ponds, lakes and rivers, among others) points to a ritual background, as these deposits are seen as final and irreversible. In contrast, hoards from dry environments are addressed as profane, as they are seen as reversibly deposited (*e.g.* Levy 1982). This view is problematic in several ways. On the one hand, Geißlinger (2004, 459 f.) points out that there are also types of bogs or areas that are not as inaccessible as is often assumed in archaeological research, which means that bog deposits do not necessarily have to be irreversibly deposited. On the other hand, the landscape has changed massively over the past millennia, so that objects once deposited in a wet environment have been found in today's dry surroundings, and vice versa. Furthermore, deposits in dry environments can also be considered irretrievably deposited if the deposit was based on criteria that have not been preserved in the archaeological context (Dietrich 2014, 468 ff.). A. Ballmer (2010, 125 ff.) shows such a scenario in the ethnographic example of the West Siberian Khanty, who also carry out depositions in dry areas. Such sacred areas are excluded from any profane use and may not be entered (*ibid.*). As a result, this deposition is also considered irreversible, but the underlying taboos leave no archaeologically tangible traces.

The second approach, pursued in the recent past, attempts to identify a structure in hoard finds. Numerous studies show that hoards in different regions and periods are subject to different rules concerning the composition, the selection of objects and the place of deposition. Moreover, different classes of objects seem to be reserved for certain contexts. Thus, objects are reserved for depositions and do not find their way into burials and vice versa (Dietrich 2014, 469 with extensive literature). How difficult it is to apply a uniform evaluation scheme regarding the distinction between ritual and profane depositions can be seen when applying Levy's (1982) frequently used subdivision scheme to the Neuenkirchen hoard. The deposition in a dry environment, the fragmented objects as well as the representative object group "tools" (flat axe) fall under the criteria Levy (*ibid.*, 24) gives for a profane deposition. In contrast, the weapon (dagger) contained in the hoard and the arrangement of the objects as well as (to a limited extent) the pottery, are characteristics of a ritual deposit. In addition to the already-mentioned subdivision criterion of wet/dry, the association of fragmented objects with a profane reason for deposition is also debatable. For example, Dietrich (2014, 469 ff.) suggests for the large Late Bronze Age hoards of the Carpathian Basin, which contain mostly broken pieces of objects, that these fragments (in this case specially-treated socketed axes) can represent symbols for whole objects. This can be seen as a group- and time-specific translation of a form of religious expression. The aforementioned discussion indicated, as Ballmer (2010, 121) also notes, that an exclusive distinction between 'profane' and 'sacred' does not exist.

The recent and latest research addresses deposition as a social practice that can sometimes be rooted in religious ideas but is not necessarily connected to them (ibid, 469). Mauss' (1990) ethnographic study of competitive gift exchange as a social practice played a major role. He describes a kind of festive competition in recent tribal societies on the Pacific coast of North America. In this process, the person who could raise the most valuable and extensive gifts in this gift exchange gains a significant social position or prestige. Moreover, not only the gift giver wins, but also other group members, because often debt relationships had to be entered into with other members of the group in order to be able to give away a sufficiently large gift. (Klassen 2000, 289). In the course of this practice, social structures and positions are not only negotiated and renegotiated within groups, but also between social associations. Moreover, it is not only the gift giver who gains, but also other group members, because often debt relationships had to be entered into with other members of the group in order to be able to give away a sufficiently large gift. (Klassen 2000, 289).

One of the manifestations of these social economies characterised by gift exchange is the 'potlatch' of the indigenous population groups on the Pacific Northwest coast of North America. There, for example, the group participating in the potlatch accepts the position of the hosts and the associated claims to a certain territory or resources by accepting the gifts (ibid.). The occasion for such a gift exchange could also be the honouring of a deceased chief and/or the installation of a successor. In the Pacific areas, this was often connected with the erection of dolmens or menhirs, which at the same time marked the claim to a certain territory (ibid.). However, the exchange of gifts took place not only between people, but also between people and supernatural powers (Mauss 1990, 39-49). The depositions of copper objects beyond the reach of humans can thus also be seen as gifts to the gods.

Klassen (2000) also refers to the 'potlatch' as a model of thought in his work on the copper finds of the northern group of the TRB. He shows the parallels with the very extreme forms of "potlatch" in indigenous groups of Northwest America. Since there was always an obligation to give something in return and this often had to be larger, this competition sometimes took on great proportions. However, wealth was not only distributed but also deliberately destroyed, which represented the greatest possible challenge to a competitor (ibid., 289). Before the arrival of the Europeans, slaves were sometimes killed for this purpose by means of a special stone device. This was later replaced by the destruction of sheet metal objects made of European copper (so-called 'coppers'), which was carried out with the same stone device. The fragments were then either distributed or thrown into the sea as a gesture of contempt for the 'enemy' (ibid.). In view of the depositions in bogs as well as the intentional destruction or damage of flat axes, as is known from some flat axes, he considers such a contest also possible for the northern group of the TRB, as this corresponds exactly to the treatment of the 'coppers'. He sees the special symbolic value of flat axes confirmed in the local manufacture as well as the decoration of a flat axe from Bygholm, with a pattern like that found on pottery. In this context, the numerous individual finds of flat axes can also be regarded as such deposits. Although the circumstances of the finds are often vague, the fact that not a single flat axe in the northern group of the TRB comes from a grave or settlement context speaks in favour of considering it as a single deposit. Since structural similarities in social organisation are assumed for the Funnel Beaker societies, which are partly connected with large-scale occurrences of certain phenomena such as megalithic construction, such a model of thought seems quite plausible (*ibid.*). Against this background, Klassen (*ibid.*) sees the deposit from Bygholm, which contained three intentionally damaged, one decorated and oversized flat axe and one dagger, as an expression of a Neolithic "potlatch". The hoard find from Neuenkirchen fits very well into this model of thought.

Another indicator is that all objects from Neuenkirchen were transformed before they were deposited. Not a single object is intact, all of them are in a fragmented or incomplete state. Traces of intentional destruction were found on the flat axe and the dagger. The same applies to the band spirals, which were presumably broken in two before being laid down. It is not possible to say whether the arm spiral was also destroyed due to the state of preservation and the fragile nature of the object. However, the fact that arm spirals from continental find complexes often occur in pairs (*ibid.*, 142) suggests that the single Neuenkirchen specimen may be a *pars pro toto*, as the author also suspects for the fragment and the band spirals. Such a transformation of the objects from Neuenkirchen would suggest that they could have entered the ground in the course of such a 'potlatch'. It should be noted at this point that the destruction of values is an extreme manifestation of 'potlatch' and that the core element of this social practice is, however, the circulation and redistribution of valuables. With their deposition (and destroying them beforehand), however, the objects are withdrawn from this circulation. This was probably not the rule in the funnel beaker societies, as the scarcity of large depositions indicate.

J. Müller (2017, 102), among others, is also convinced that the construction of the large number of megalithic graves, which took place in roughly the same period as the copper depositions, is integrated as a vital part of such a system of redistribution of wealth. In her dissertation, Wunderlich (2019) researched recent societies with a megalithic building tradition and the societies of the northern group of the TRB by means of a comparative, ethno-archaeological study. The results of her investigations on the Indonesian island of Sumba, as well as in Nagaland in the East Indian-West Burmese highlands, show that although there are, in part, considerable differences in size and decoration of the erected megaliths, they are not due to institutionalised social differences within or between villages. Rather, in both societies the erection festivals are decisive, which are organised by the donors of the stones, in the course of which they distribute their accumulated wealth and thereby gain prestige (*ibid.*). Another important result of the study in Nagaland is that the entire process of megalithic construction, in which each step and megalith is charged with its own significance, is strictly regulated and interspersed with religious ideas. For example, some of the stones represent deceased persons to whom a relationship must be established through dreams even during the selection of raw materials (*ibid.*). The actions of the participating persons are also marked by taboos and obligations. Interestingly, the number of participating persons is not determined by how many people are needed for the construction, but by how many people can be fed during the entire process of construction. The more participants, the higher the prestige gained (*ibid.*). J. Müller (2017, 102) also assumes similar processes in the Funnel Beaker societies of the North, where the principle of gift and counter-gift, as well as spirituality, structures everyday life.

The construction of causewayed enclosures can certainly also be seen in this light; starting around 3800 BCE, based on a tradition from the Paris Basin, they were also erected in the northern group of the TRB (*ibid.*, 81). In Mecklenburg-Western Pomerania, the newly discovered ditch structures in Plate, Ruthen, Zietlitz, and Gädebehn, which are attributed to influences from Middle German Baalberg (*ibid.*, 83), are currently the subject of scientific research. Interestingly, the two largest Funnel Beaker period copper depositions (Bygholm and Årupgård) can be associated with causewayed enclosures (Klassen 2000, 81 u. 291). During a fieldwalking survey of a causewayed enclosure of Michelsberg at Willebadesen-Peckelsheim (Westphalia), Dr. F. Jürgens, who is thanked here for the preliminary information, was able to report the discovery of a flat axe fragment (Jürgens/ Szillus 2019). At the aforementioned earthwork near Plate (Site 14), copper remains were found in one grave, along with a funnel beaker, a Baalberg-type amphora, and two arrowheads (cf. 10.7). Another grave was located in the entrance area of the earthwork between the two ditch terminals. Both graves were parallel and axially in the middle of a double row of pits leading perpendicularly towards the entrance area of the earthwork (Behrens *et al.* 2013, 325), so that a connection between the burial and the enclosure can be assumed. The extent to which the graves are regular burials or possibly associated with further ritual acts remains open for the time being, as the site is still being investigated.

In view of the early dating of Neuenkirchen proposed here and the fact that the deposition of destroyed objects was also carried out in the causewayed enclosures, it seems possible that the acquisition of prestige through redistribution of wealth described above first began with the construction of the causewayed enclosures and the activities that took place there. Later, this practice was supplemented, or partly replaced, by the construction of megalithic tombs and the deposition of objects there. Such a development can be traced, for example, for the site of Albersdorf-Dieksknöll in Schleswig-Holstein. Built in the 38th century BCE, the causewayed enclosure was the scene of at least 21 recutting and infilling events between 3880-3520 BCE (Dibbern 2016, 35 ff.). During this time, two fires also took place in the causewayed enclosure, the last of which, around 3520 BCE, is contemporaneous with the construction and occupation of the Albersdorf-Brutkamp megalithic tomb, about 1.5 km away. Although the burial continues to be visited, the intensity of use decreases considerably in the following centuries. At the same time, numerous activities take place at the aforementioned megalithic grave, such as the deposition and removal of objects, as well as other deposition processes (*ibid.*, 83 ff.; Müller 2017, 75 ff.). The fact that the deposition of copper objects does not necessarily have to be coupled with the construction of the megalithic graves is also shown by the copper hoard finds from the Polish sites of Kałdus and Skarbienice, among others, in the area of the Eastern Group of the Funnel Beaker Societies, where no megalithic graves are constructed. Thus, the Neuenkirchen deposit, which was deposited about 200-300 years before the first megalithic graves were erected in Mecklenburg-Western Pomerania (from about 3500 BCE), is likely to have been one of the earliest records of the social practice described above that structured society. The non-megalithic long mounds built in north-central Europe and in southern Scandinavia from c. 3800 BCE onwards seem to have played only a minor role in the area of present-day Mecklenburg-Western Pomerania. Although the longest known sites (220 m) come from Stralendorf in western Mecklenburg (Ludwigslust-Parchim district), most of them are found in the centres of distribution on the Cimbrian peninsula, in north-western Germany, in the Mittelelbe-Saale area and in northern and southern Poland. The few representatives in the extreme east of Western Pomerania seem to belong to the core area in north-western Poland in the area east of the Oder (cf. Müller 2017, p. 57).

Since copper finds such as axes and daggers are not known from megalithic graves and a connection between copper deposition and causewayed enclosure has also been demonstrated, another possible interpretation suggests itself. Possibly two religious/ritual/spiritual spaces are shown here, separated from each other. On the one hand, the megalithic tombs and the associated social practice of wealth distribution in society. On the other hand, the causewayed enclosure and copper depositions, which can be seen as a gift exchange between people and gods. In this context, the deposition of the objects would not mean that they are withdrawn from circulation, but rather brought into this exchange between the human and divine worlds. The transformation of the objects, as well as the careful arrangement of the deposition of Neuenkirchen, also favour this interpretation. Finally, it should be noted that there is still a considerable need for research into the relationship between the depositions of copper objects and the construction/ use of causewayed enclosures and that this assumption should initially only be understood as a working hypothesis.

13. Summary

The aim of this study was to address the hoard find from Neuenkirchen typo-chronologically and to clarify whether the depot find belongs to the horizon of early copper finds in the north, and if so, where it can be placed within it. After the introductory chapters on the history of research, the natural environment and the discussion on the chronology of the Funnel Beaker Societies, the settlements as well as the hoards and megalithic graves in the vicinity of the site were discussed. This was followed by a description of the circumstances of the discovery and a detailed description of the individual objects.

After an introductory excursus on use-wear analysis, the artefacts were analysed in this respect, and the conspicuous features were presented and interpreted. Signs of use and intentional destruction of objects were identified on the contents of the depot. This shows a dual transformation of the objects. First, through the extensive use and possible repairs of the objects, visible as, for example, the use-wear on the arm, spiral as well as on the dagger and flat axe fragment (cf. 7). Second, the intentional destruction of the objects before their deposition, which was proven for the dagger and the flat axe and is most likely true for the remaining objects (cf. *ibid.*).

Subsequently, the hoard inventory was subjected to an X-ray fluorescence analysis. The evaluation and interpretation were preceded by the basics of the possibilities and limitations of the method. In particular, the influence of patina on such measurements was explained and critically questioned. The pXRF analyses carried out by the author were complemented by ED-XRF measurements on samples drilled from the artefacts, which were performed by an external laboratory at a later time. It was found that the objects from the hoard were made of two types of copper known from the early metal horizon of the European Chalcolithic. Lead isotope analysis on the flat axe fragment from the hoard also revealed that the copper probably originated from the Madjanpek mine in eastern Serbia, although deposits in Ai Bunar, Bulgaria, cannot be excluded.

Following this, the finds from Mecklenburg-Western Pomerania from the corresponding period (c. 4100-2900/2800 BCE) were summarised and discussed in light of recent research. By far the largest section was then devoted to the typo-chronological positioning of the individual artefacts from the hoard find. The dagger was discussed particularly intensively, as the other objects have only limited significance due to their fragmentation or their chronologically unspecific character. For this purpose, the typo-chronological study by Matuschik (1998) was summarised as a basis, supplemented by new finds and updated based on new research results, especially absolute dating. In this context, it was possible to define the Neuenkirchen dagger as a representative of an independent type, the form of which can probably be traced back to models from the Black Sea region. In the synthesis of the typological analysis and the trace element composition, a chronological position around 4000-3800 BCE and an origin of the pieces from the western Carpathian region could be presented for the dagger, the arm spiral, the band spirals and the fragment. The difficult to classify flat axe fragment made from the Mondsee copper variety, with a date range between 3800-3500/3300 BCE, was considered to be an early northern Alpine import. The earliest possible date of deposition thus established is 3800/3700 BCE.

In the following chapter, with the help of comparative hoard finds of the 5th/4th millennium, it was discussed whether and how such an early date for the hoard in the northern group of the TRB could be explained. This confirmed a chronological position between the older find from Stollhof and the younger one from Bygholm, as there are similarities with both deposits. In the next chapter, the development of early metallurgy in south-eastern Europe was traced on the basis of the overview article by Rosenstock *et al.* (2016). Here it was shown that around 4000/3800 BCE imports from the western Slovak-Moravian area and around 3800/3600-3400 BCE from the northern Alpine area reached Mecklenburg-Western Pomerania, thus supporting the proposed dating of the hoard. This assumption is also supported by the reliable evidence for the Mondsee copper variety in the immediate vicinity of Neuenkirchen (at Melzow/Grünow), also around 3700 BCE. The other hoards of the northern group of the TRB, which can be dated somewhat younger, also consist exclusively of objects made of the Mondsee copper variety. An early dating is also supported by the fact that deposits in the corresponding area were also made as early as EN I, as shown by the examples of deposited axes pointed with pointed butts in Viervitz on the island of Ruegen (Kibbert 1980, 62), and Baalberg amphorae in Nustrow (Rostock district) and Louisenhof (Mecklenburg Lake Plateau district), among others (Staude 2013, 145 ff.). Another indication is the proven Early Funnel Beaker settlement in Warlin around 3700 BCE in the vicinity of the site.

The final chapter was devoted to the question of the context in which the hoard find from Neuenkirchen was deposited. First, a very abbreviated overview of the development of the research discussion on the significance of hoard finds was given. Subsequently, it could be shown that the Neuenkirchen hoard fits well into the interpretive model of redistribution of wealth based on ethno-archaeological studies, as proposed by Klassen (2000) and Müller (2017) for the northern group of the TRB. As shown, the hoard find from Neuenkirchen represents the oldest, multi-piece copper deposit in this area and indicates that this deposit practice was already part of the early Funnel Beaker societies before the construction of the megalithic graves. Whether the copper deposit was part of an extreme form of gift exchange between people or part of an exchange between the human and divine worlds could not be conclusively determined. However, the connection between causewayed enclosures and depositions, as well as the absence of axes and daggers in megalithic graves, points more to the latter.

The hoard find of Neuenkirchen shows the intensive relations between Chalcolithic societies which reached from the Baltic Coasts to the Carpathian Basin; from the latter came an influx of new technologies, materials, and subsistence strategies, the integration of which into the former started the transformation of local societies. This included not only economic aspects but also most likely changed beliefs and the perception of the after-life as well. The hoard from Neuenkirchen marks an earlier stage of a process which culminates in the erection of thousands of megalithic graves which, in addition to their cultural significance until the present day, transformed the landscape of the Neolithic world forever.

14. References

Adamczak *et al.* 2015
Adamczak, K., Kowalski, Ł., Bojarski, J., Weinkauf, M., Garbacz-Klempka, A., 2015. *Eneolithic metal objects hoard from Kałdus, Chełmno commune, Kujawsko-Pomorskie Voivodeship.* Sprawozdania Archeologiczne 67, 199- 219.

Alram-Stern 2014
Alram-Stern, E., 2014. Times of Change: Greece and the Aegean during the 4th Millennium BC. *In*: B. Horejs and M. Mehofer, eds. *Western Anatolia before Troy: proto-urbanisation in the 4th millenium BC?; proceedings of the International Symposium held at the Kunsthistorisches Museum Wien, Vienna, Austria, 21 - 24 November, 2012.* Oriental and European archaeology. Vienna: Verlag der Österreichischen Akademie der Wissenschaften, 305-327.

Aner/Kersten 1973
Aner, E. and Kersten, K., 1973. *Die Funde der älteren Bronzezeit des nordischen Kreises in Dänemark, Schleswig-Holstein und Niedersachsen 1, Fredriksborg und Kopenhagen Amt.* Neumünster: Wachholtz Verlag.

Aner/Kersten 1977
Aner, E. and Kersten, K., 1977. *Die Funde der Älteren Bronzezeit des Nordischen Kreises in Dänemark, Schleswig-Holstein und Niedersachsen. 3, Bornholms, Maribo, Odense und Svendborg Amter.* København/Neumünster: Wachholtz Verlag.

Aner/Kersten 1978
Aner, E. and Kersten, K., 1987. *Die Funde der Älteren Bronzezeit des Nordischen Kreises in Dänemark, Schleswig-Holstein und Niedersachsen. 4, Südschleswig-Ost: die Kreise Schleswig-Flensburg und Rendsburg-Eckernförde (nördlich des Nord-Ostsee-Kanals).* København/Neumünster: Wachholtz Verlag.

Aner/Kersten 1979
Aner, E. and Kersten, K., 1979. *Die Funde der älteren Bronzezeit des nordischen Kreises in Dänemark, Schleswig-Holstein und Niedersachsen 5 Südschleswig-West: Nordfriesland.* Neumünster: Wachholtz Verlag.

Aner/Kersten 1981
Aner, E. and Kersten, K., 1981. *Die Funde der Älteren Bronzezeit des Nordischen Kreises in Dänemark, Schleswig-Holstein und Niedersachsen. 6, Nordslesvig-Syd: Tønder, Åbenrå und Sønderborg Amter.* København/Neumünster: Wachholtz Verlag.

Aner/Kersten 1984
Aner, E. and Kersten, K., 1984. *Die Funde der Älteren Bronzezeit des Nordischen Kreises in Dänemark, Schleswig-Holstein und Niedersachsen. 7, Nordslesvig-Nord Haderslev Amt.* København/Neumünster: Wachholtz Verlag.

Aner/Kersten 1986

Aner, E. and Kersten, K., 1986. *Die Funde der Älteren Bronzezeit des Nordischen Kreises in Dänemark, Schleswig-Holstein und Niedersachsen. 8, Ribe Amt.* København/Neumünster: Wachholtz Verlag.

Aner *et al.* 1990

Aner, E., Kersten, K., Koch, E., 1990. *Die Funde der älteren Bronzezeit des nordischen Kreises in Dänemark, Schleswig-Holstein und Niedersachsen. 9, Vejle Amt.* Neumünster: Wachholtz Verlag.

Anthony 1996

Anthony, D.W., 1996. V. G. Childe's world system and the daggers of the Early Bronze Age. *In*: B. Wailes, ed. *Craft specialization and social evolution: in memory of V. Gordon Childe.* University Monographs 93. Philadelphia: University of Pennsylvania Press, Inc., 47-66.

Antonović 2018

Antonović, D., 2018. Eneolithic copper mines in the Balkans. *In*: J. Balen, I. Miloglav, D. Rajković, eds. *Back to the past: Copper Age in northern Croatia.* Zagreb: Archaeological Museum in Zagreb, 187–209.

Artursson *et al.* 2003

Artursson, M., Linderoth, T., Nilsson, M.-L., Svensson, M., 2003. Byggnadskultur i södra& mellersta Skandinavien. *In*: M. Svensson, ed. *I det neolitiska rummet. Skånska pår – Arkeologi längs Västkustbanan.* Lund: Riksantikvarieämbetet, 40-171.

Aspesi 2012

Aspesi, M., 2012. Le necropoli rinaldoniane del Palombaro e di Chiusa d'Ermini. Revisione degli scavi di Ferrante Rittatore Vonwiller. *In*: N. Negroni Catacchio, ed. *Preistoria e protostoria in Etruria: atti del decimo incontro di studi, Valentano (VT)-Pitigliano (GR), 10-12 settembre 2010: l' Etruria dal Paleolitico al Primo Ferro, lo stato delle ricerche.* Milano: Centro studi di preistoria e archeologia, 223-245.

Baales *et al.* 2010

Baales, M., Blank, R., Orschiedt, J., 2010. *Archäologie in Hagen: eine Geschichtslandschaft wird erforscht.* Essen: Klartext Verlag.

Bakker 1979

Bakker, J.A., 1979. *The TRB West group. Studies in the chronology and geography of the makers of hunebeds and Tiefstich pottery.* Cingula, Amsterdam: Sidestone Press.

Ballmer 2010

Ballmer, A., 2010. Zur Topologie des bronzezeitlichen Deponierens; Von der Handlungstheorie zur Raumanalyse. *Prähistorische Zeitschrift*, 85, 120–131.

Baron *et al.* 2011

Baron, S., Tămaş, C.G., Cauuet, B., Munoz, M., 2011. Lead isotope analyses of gold-silver ores from Roşia Montană (Romania): a first step of metal provenance study of Roman mining activity in Alburnus Maior (Roman Dacia). *Journal of Archaeological Science*, 38, 1090-1100.

Becker 1954

Becker, C.J., 1954. Die mittel-neolithischen Kulturen in Südskandinavien. *Acta archaeologica* 25, Copenhagen: Ejnar Munksgaard, 49-150.

Becker 1957

Becker, C.J., 1957. *Den tyknakkede flintøkse. Sudier over tragtbægerkulturens svære retøkser i mellem-neolitisk tid.* Aarbøger for nordisk oldkyndighed og historie, 1-37.

Behrens 1958

Behrens, H. 1958. Ein jungsteinzeitlicher Grabhügel von mehrschichtigem Aufbau in der Dölauer Heide bei Halle (Saale). *Jahreschrift für mitteldeutsche Vorgeschichte*, 41/42, 213- 242.

Behrens *et al.* 2013

Behrens, A., Fehr, I., Lüth, F., 2013. Kurze Fundberichte, Plate, Fpl. 14. *Bodendenkmalpflege in Mecklenburg-Vorpommern,* 2012, 324 f.

Behrens/Schröter 1980

Behrens, H. and Schröter, E., 1980. *Siedlungen und Gräber der Trichterbecherkultur und Schnurkeramik bei Halle (Saale): Ergebnisse von Ausgrabungen.* Landesmuseum für Vorgeschichte (Halle Saale): Veröffentlichungen. Berlin: Deutscher Verlag der Wissenschaften.

Beltz 1910

Beltz, R., 1910. *Die vorgeschichtlichen Altertümer des Grossherzogtums Mecklenburg-Schwerin: Vollständiges Verzeichnis der im Grossherzoglichen Museum zu Schwerin bewahrten Funde.* Berlin: Verlag von Reimer.

Beran 2015

Beran, J., 2015. Kupferzeit im Havelland. *Archäologie in Deutschland,* 1, 39.

Berlekamp 1956

Berlekamp, H., 1956. Eine Axthacke aus Steinhagen, Kr. Stralsund. Ausgrabungen und Funde. *Nachrichtenblatt der Landesarchäologie,* 1, 122-125.

Bianco Peroni 1994

Bianco Peroni, V., 1994. *I pugnali nell'Italia continentale.* Prähistorische Bronzefunde, Abteilung VI. Stuttgart: Franz Steiner Verlag.

Bicho *et al.* 2015

Bicho, N.F., Marreiros, J., Gibaja Bao, J.F., 2015. Use-Wear and Residue Analysis in Archaeology. *In*: J. Marreiros, J.F. Gibaja Bao, N.F. Bicho, eds. *Use-Wear and Residue Analysis in Archaeology.* Cham, Heidelberg, New York, Dordrecht, London: Springer International Publishing, 1-4.

Birkedahl 1990

Birkedahl, P., 1990. Handest. *In*: Kulturarvsstyrelsen (The Danish Cultural Heritage Agency), *Arkæologiske Udgravninger i Danmark 1989,* 168, Nr. 287.

Birkedahl 1994

Birkedahl, P., 1994. Kobberstenalder ved Handest. *In*: J. Hertz, S. Nielsen, H. Dam, C.J. Hansen, eds. *5000 år under motorvejen.* Copenhagen: Vejdirektoratet.

Blajer 1990

Blajer, W., 1990. *Skarby z wczesnej epoki brązu na ziemiach Polskich.* Prace Komisji Archeologicznej 28. Zakład Narodowy Imienia Ossolińskich Wydawnictwo Polskiej Akademii Nauk, Wrocław.

Blank 1989

Blank, R., 1989. Ein Kupferflachbeil aus dem Ruhrtal bei Schwerte-Villigst. *Hohenlimburger Heimatblätter für den Raum Hagen und Iserlohn,* 50 (168), 177-178.

Bohm 1935

Bohm, W., 1935. *Die aeltere Bronzezeit in der Mark Brandenburg.* Vorgeschichtliche Forschungen. Berlin/Leipzig: De Gruyter.

Bohm/Kreisausschuß des Kreises Westprignitz 1937

Bohm, W. and Kreisausschuß des Kreises Westprignitz, 1937. *Die Vorgeschichte des Kreises Westprignitz.* Leipzig: Kabitzsch Verlag.

Bottaini *et al.* 2015

Bottaini, C., Mirão, J., Figuereido, M., Candeias, A., Brunetti, A., Schiavon, N., 2015. Energy dispersive X-ray fluorescence spectroscopy/Monte Carlo simulation approach for the non-destructive analysis of corrosion patina-bearing alloys in archaeological bronzes: The case of the bowl from the Fareleira 3 site (Vidigueira, South Portugal). *Spectrochimica Acta Part B: Atomic Spectroscopy,* 103–104, 9-13.

Böttcher 1982

Böttcher, G., 1982. Ein Grab der Baalberger Gruppe mit Kupferschmuck von Büden, Kr. Burg, *Ausgrabungen und Funde Berlin* 27(4), 1982, 165–170.

Bourdieu *et al.* 2012
> Bourdieu, P., Pialoux, C., Schwibs, B., 2012. *Entwurf einer Theorie der Praxis auf der ethnologischen Grundlage der kabylischen Gesellschaft.* Suhrkamp-Taschenbuch Wissenschaft, 3. Aufl. Frankfurt am Main: Suhrkamp Verlag.

Bradley 1990
> Bradley, R., 1990. *The passage of arms an archaeological analysis of prehistoric hoards and votive deposits.* Cambridge: Cambridge University Press.

Brauer 1995
> Brauer, O., 1995. *Die frühneolithische Besiedlung des mecklenburgischen Binnenlandes bei Berücksichtigung der Ausgrabungen von Carpin, Kreis Mecklenburg-Strelitz. Ein Beitrag zur Neolithisierung des nördlichen Mitteleuropas.* Unpublizierte Masterarbeit, Universität Berlin.

Breunig 1987
> Breunig, P., 1987. *14C-Chronologie des vorderasiatischen, südost- und mitteleuropäischen Neolithikums.* Fundamenta Reihe A., Band 13. Köln: Böhlau.

Brindley 1986
> Brindley, A.L., 1986. The typochronology of the TRB West Group Pottery. *Palaeohistoria*, 28, 93-132.

Broholm 1938
> Broholm, H.C., 1938. Nye fund fra den ældste bronzealder. *Aarbøger for nordisk Oldkyndighed og Historie*, 65-85.

Broholm 1943
> Broholm, H.C., 1943. *Danmarks Bronzealder: 1. Samlede fund fra den aeldre Bronzealder.* København: Nyt Nordisk Forlag.

Broholm 1944
> Broholm, H.C., 1944. *Danmarks Bronzealder: 2. Kultur og folk i den aeldre Bronzealder.* København: Nyt Nordisk Forlag.

Brozio 2016
> Brozio, J., 2016. *Megalithanlagen und Siedlungsmuster im trichterbecherzeitlichen Ostholstein.* Frühe Monumentalität und soziale Differenzierung 9. Bonn: Habelt Verlag.

Brøndsted 1928
> Brøndsted, J., 1928. Vort Folks Oldtidsliv og forhistoriske Minder. *In*: A. Friis, A. Lindvad, M. Mackeprang, eds. *Det danske Folks Historie I.* København: Erichsen.

Brøndsted 1939
> Brøndsted, J., 1939. *Danmarks Oldtid*, Vol. I. Gyldendal: Copenhagen.

Brummack 2012
> Brummack, S., 2012. New Radiocarbon Dates from Eastern Slovakia. The Cases of Malé Raškovce and Barca Baloty. *In*: S. Hansen, P. Raczky, A. Anders, A. Reingruber, eds. *Neolithic and Copper Age between the Carpathians and the Aegean Sea: chronologies and technologies from the 6th to the 4th Millennium BCE; International Workshop Budapest 2012.* Bonn: Habelt Verlag, 1-19.

Brummack/Diaconescu 2014
> Brummack, S. and Diaconescu, D., 2014. A Bayesian approach to the AMS dates for the Copper Age in the Great Hungarian Plain. *Prähistorische Zeitschrift*, 89 (2), 242-260.

Buchwald/Leisner 1992
> Buchwald, V.F. and Leisner, P., 1992. A metallurgy study of 12 prehistoric bronze objects from Denmark. *Journal of Danish Archaeology*, 7, 64-102.

Buddenbohm 2010
> Buddenbohm, A., 2010. Der Geopark Mecklenburgische Eiszeitlandschaft – Eisrandlagen, jungquartäre Landschaftsgeschichte und Geotourismus. *In*: R. Lampe and S. Lorenz, eds. *Eiszeitlandschaften in Mecklenburg-Vorpommern.* Greifswald: Geozon, 72-76.

Burenholt 1991

Burenholt, G., 1991. *Arkeologi i Sverige. 1, Fångstfolk och herdar. 2a: omarbetade upplagan.* Högenas: Wiken.

Busch 1996

Busch, H., 1996. Zur Bewertung von Materialanalysen an patinierten Fundgegenständen. *Ausgrabungen und Funde im Freistaat Thüringen*, 1/1996, 2-9.

Chernykh 1978

Chernykh, E.N., 1978. *Gornoe Delo I Metallurgia v Drevneishei Boulgarii.* Sofia: Izdatelstvo bolgarskoi akademii nauk.

Chernykh 1992

Chernykh, E.N., 1992. *Ancient metallurgy in the USSR. The Early Metal Age.* New studies in archaeology 1. New York: Cambridge University Press.

Childe 1933

Childe, G., 1933. Scottish Megalithic Tombs And Their Affinities. *Transactions Of The Glasgow Archaeological Society.* New Series 8 (3). Edinburgh: Edinburgh University Press, 120- 30.

Constantinides *et al.* 2002

Constantinides, I., Adriaens, A., Adams, F., 2002. Surface characterization of artificial corrosion layers on copper alloy reference materials. *Applied Surface Science*, 189, 90-101.

Cronyn 1990

Cronyn, J. M., 1990. *The elements of archaeological conservation.* Routledge, London, New York.

Csányi *et al.* 2010

Csányi, M., Tárnoki, J., Raczky, P., 2010. Das kupferzeitliche Gräberfeld von Rákóczifalva - Bagiföld in Ungarn. *Das Altertum*, 55, Reading, Berkshire: Routledge, 241-270.

Čtverák/Rulf 1989

Čtverák, V. and Rulf, J., 1989. Funde des Jordanów-Kulturhorizontes aus Třebestovice, Bez. Nymburk. *Památky Archeologické LXXX*, 1, Prague: Vydavatel Archeologický ústav AV ČR, Praha, 5-29.

Cullberg 1968

Cullberg, C., 1968. *On artifact analysis a study in the systematics and classification of a Scandinavian Early Bronze Age; material with metal analysis and chronology as contributing factors.* Acta archaeologica Lundensia Series in 4. Bonn: Habelt Verlag.

Curry 2016

Curry, A., 2016. Slaughter at the bridge: Uncovering a colossal Bronze Age battle. *Science*, 351 (6280), 1384-1389.

Czerniak 1980

Czerniak, L., 1980. *Rozwój społeczeństw kultury późnej ceramiki wstęgowej na Kujawach.* Seria Archaeologia 16, Poznan: Wydawnictwo Naukowe UAM.

Dani 2013

Dani, J., 2013. The Significance of Metallurgy at the Beginning of the Third Millennium BCE in the Carpathian Basin. *In*: V. Heyd, G. Kulcsár, V. Szeverényi, eds. *Transitions to the Bronze Age interregional interaction and socio-cultural change in the third millennium BCE Carpathian basin and neighbouring regions.* Budapest: Archaeolingua, 203-232.

de Marinis 2006

de Marinis, R.C., 2006. Aspetti della metallurgia dell'et`a del Rame e dell'antica et`a del Bronzo in Toscana. *Rivista di Scienze Preistoriche*, 56, 211-272.

Dergačev 2002

Dergačev, V.A., 2002. *Die äneolithischen und bronzezeitlichen Metallfunde aus Moldavien.* Prähistorische Bronzefunde, Abteilung XX. Stuttgart: Franz Steiner Verlag.

Diachenko/Harper 2016

Diachenko, A. and Harper, T.K., 2016. The absolute chronology of Late Trypillia sites: a regional approach. *Sprawozdania Archeologiczne*, 68, 81-105.

Diaconescu 2014

Diaconescu, D., 2014. New remarks about the typology and the chronology of the Pločnik and čoka copper hammeraxes. *In*: W. Schier and F. Draşovean, eds. *The Neolithic and Eneolithic in Southeast Europe: new approaches to dating and cultural Dynamics in the 6th to 4th Millennium BC.* Prähistorische Archäologie in Südosteuropa. Rahden/Westf.: Verlag Marie Leidorf GmbH, 221-242.

Dibbern 2016

Dibbern, H. 2016. *Das trichterbecherzeitliche Westholstein eine Studie zur neolithischen Entwicklung von Landschaft und Gesellschaft.* Frühe Monumentalität und soziale Differenzierung 8. Bonn: Habelt Verlag.

Dietrich 2014

Dietrich, O., 2014. Learning from 'Scrap' about Late Bronze Age Hoarding Practices: A Biographical Approach to Individual Acts of Dedication in Large Metal Hoards of the Carpathian Basin. *European Journal of Archaeology*, 17 (3), 468-486.

Dirks/Stark 2016

Dirks, U. and Stark, J., 2016. Ein Bestattungsplatz der frühen bis älteren Trichterbecherkultur bei Melzow, Lkr. Uckermark. *Veröffentlichungen zur brandenburgischen Landesarchäologie*, 47, 109-138.

Dobeš 1989

Dobeš, M., 1989. Zu den äneolithischen Kupferflachbeilen in Mähren, Böhmen, Polen und in der DDR. Das Äneolithikum und die früheste Bronzezeit (C14 3000-2000 b.c.) in Mitteleuropa: kulturelle und chronologische Beziehungen Acta des XIV. *Internationalen Symposiums Prag - Liblice 20.-24.10.1986*, 15, 39-48.

Dolfini 2004

Dolfini, A., 2004. La necropoli di Rinaldone (Montefiascone, Viterbo): rituale funerario e dinamiche sociali di una comunità eneolithica in Italia centrale. *Bullettino di Paletnologia Italiana*, 95 (2004), 127-277.

Dolfini 2010

Dolfini, A., 2010. The origins of metallurgy in central Italy: new radiometric evidence. *Antiquity*, 84 (325), 707-723.

Dolfini 2013

Dolfini, A., 2013. The Emergence of Metallurgy in the Central Mediterranean Region: A New Model. *European Journal of Archaeology*, 16, 21–62.

Dolfini/Crellin 2016

Dolfini, A. and Crellin, R.J., 2016. Metalwork wear analysis: The loss of innocence. *Journal of Archaeological Science*, 66, 78–87.

Dombrowsky 2011

Dombrowsky, A., 2011. Kurze Fundberichte, Weltzin, Fpl. 24. *Bodendenkmalpflege in Mecklenburg-Vorpommern 2010*, 58, 316.

Driehaus 1960

Driehaus, H.-J., 1960, *Die Altheimer Gruppe und das Jungneolithikum in Mitteleuropa.* Mainz: Verlag des römisch-germanischen Zentralmuseums.

Ebbesen 1975

Ebbesen, K., 1975. Die jüngere Trichterbecherkultur auf den dänischen Inseln. *Arkaeologiske Studier*, 2, København: Akademisk Forlag.

Ebbesen 1978

Ebbesen, K., 1978. Tragtbaegerkultur i Nordjylland: Studier over Jaettestuetiden. *Nordiske Fortidsminder*, Serie B, København: Kgl. Nordiske Oldskriftselskab.

Ebbesen 1979

Ebbesen, K., 1979. Stordyssen i Vedsted: Studier over tragtboegerkulturen i Sønderjylland. *Arkaeologiske Studier*, 6, København: Akademisk Forlag.

Ebbesen 1994a

Ebbesen, K., 1994a. Simple, tidligneolitiske grave. *Aarbøger for nordisk oldkyndighed og historie,* 1992 (1994), 47-102.

Ebbesen 1994b

Ebbesen, K., 1994b. Tragtbaegerkulturens dolkstave. *Aarbørger for nordisk oldkyndighed og historie* 1992, (1994), 103-136.

Eckert 1985

Eckert, J., 1985. Stichwort „Rheine". *Ausgrabung und Funde Westfalen-Lippe,* 3, 402-405.

Eckert 1999

Eckert, J., 1999. Das Großsteingrab von Rheine. *Rheine gestern - heute – morgen,* 43 (2), 96-105.

Eggert 2001

Eggert, M.K.H., 2001. *Prähistorische Archäologie: Konzepte und Methoden.* UTB für Wissenschaft. Tübingen und Basel: A. Francke Verlag.

Ekkholm 1927

Ekkholm, G., 1927. Stichwort „Nordischer Kreis". *In*: M. Ebert, ed. *Reallexikon der Vorgeschichte.* Berlin: Walter de Gruyter, 6-109.

Endtmann 1998

Endtmann E., 1998. Untersuchungen zur spät- und nacheiszeitlichen Vegetationsentwicklung des Leckerpfuhls (Mönchsheider Sander, NE Brandenburg). *Verhandlungen des Botanischen Vereins von Berlin und Brandenburg, 131,* 137–166.

Endtmann 2004

Endtmann, E., 2004. *Die spätglaziale und holozäne Vegetations- und Siedlungsgeschichte des östlichen Mecklenburg-Vorpommerns – Eine paläoökologische Studie.* Unpubl. Dissertation, Universität Greifswald.

Eurenius 1888

Eurenius, M., 1888. *Katalog öfver den kulturhistorisk-etnografiska afdelningen af Malmö Museum upprättad år 1888: med fyra planscher.* Malmö.

Feeser *et al.* 2016

Feeser, I., Dörfler, W., Czymzik, M., Dreibrodt, S., 2016. A mid-Holocene annually laminated sediment sequence from Lake Woserin: The role of climate and environmental change for cultural development during the Neolithic in Northern Germany. *The Holocene,* 26 (6), 1-17.

Feeser/Dörfler 2015

Feeser, I. and Dörfler, W. 2015. The Early Neolithic in pollen diagrams from eastern Schleswig-Holstein and western Mecklenburg – evidence for a 1000 years cultural adaptive cycle? *In*: J. Kabaciński, S. Hartz, D. Raemaekers, T. Terberger, eds. *The Dąbki Site in Pomerania and the Neolithisation of the North European Lowlands (c. 5000–3000 calBC).* Archäologie und Geschichte im Ostseeraum 8. Rahden/Westf.: Verlag Marie Leidorf, 291-306.

Fischer 1956

Fischer, U., 1956. *Die Gräber der Steinzeit im Saalegebiet: Studien über neolithische und frühbronzezeitliche Grab- und Bestattungsformen in Sachsen-Thüringen.* Vorgeschichtliche Forschungen 15. Berlin: Walter de Gruyter.

Firbas 1948

Firbas, F., 1948. *Spät- und nacheiszeitliche Vegetationsgeschichte Mitteleuropas nördlich der Alpen.* Allgemeine Waldgeschichte 1. Jena: Fischer.

Forssander 1936

Forssander, J.E., 1936. *Der ostskandinavische Norden während der ältesten Metallzeit Europas.* Skrifter utgivna av. Kungl. Humanistiska Vetenskapssamfundet i Lund 22. Lund: Gleerup.

Frank/Pernicka 2012

Frank, C. and Pernicka, E., 2012. Copper Artefacts of their Mondsee Group and their possible sources. *In*: M.S. Midgley and J. Sanders, eds. *Lake Dwellings after*

Robert Munro Proceedings from the Munro International Seminar: The Lake Dwellings of Europe 22nd and 23rd October 2010, University of Edinburgh. Leiden: Sidestone Press, 113-138.

Furholt 2017

Furholt, M., 2017. *Das ägäische Neolithikum und Chalkolithikum. Transformationen sozialer Handlungsmuster in Anatolien und Griechenland zwischen 6500 und 4000 v. Chr.* Neolithikum und Chalkolithikum in Südosteuropa 3. Bonn: In Kommission bei Habelt Verlag.

Gale *et al.* 2000

Gale, N.H., Stos-Gale, Z.A., Radouncheva, A., Ivanov, I., Lilov, P., Todorov, T., Panayotov, I., 2000. Early metallurgy in Bulgaria. Годищник иа Департамеит Археология – НБУ/АИМ, IV-V, *Annuary of Department of Archaeology - NBU/IAM,* IV-V, 102-168.

Gale *et al.* 2003

Gale, N.H., Stos-Gale, Z.A., Radouncheva, A., Ivanov, I., Lilov, P., Todorov, T., Panayotov, I., 2003. Early Metallurgy in Bulgari. *In*: P. Craddock and J. Lang, eds. *Mining and Metal Production Through the Ages.* London: British Museum Press, 122-173.

Gauss *et al.* 2013

Gauss, R.K., Bátora, J., Nowaczinski, E., Rassmann, K., Schukraft, G., 2013. The Early Bronze Age settlement of Fidvár, Vráble (Slovakia): reconstructing prehistoric settlement patterns using portable XRF. *Journal of Archaeological Science,* 40 (7), 2942-2960.

Geißlinger 2004

Geißlinger, H., 2004. Nichtsakrale Moordepots - dänische Beispiele aus der frühen Neuzeit. *Germania* 82.2, 459–489.

Gergova *et al.* 2010

Gergova, D., Ivanov, Y., Dermendzhiyev, N., Radoslavova, G., Tankova, V., Khristova, R., 2010. Спасителни разкопки на Обект 36, АМ "Тракия", Лот 4, при с. Драганци, община Карнобат. *Археологически открития и разкопки през 2009,* 119-123.

Gleser 2015

Gleser, R., 2015. Ein Technologiesprung - Frühes Metall. Wissen, Funktion, Symbol. *In*: T. Otten, J. Kunow, M.M. Rind, M.C. Trier, eds. *Revolution jungSteinzeit: Archäologische Landesausstellung Nordrhein-Westfalen.* Schriften zur Bodendenkmalpflege in Nordrhein-Westfalen 11 (1). Darmstadt: Theiss-Verlag, 250-259.

Glob 1975

Glob, P.V., 1975. De dødes lange huse. *Skalk,* 6, 10-14.

Glob 1980

Glob, P.V., 1980. *Danefae: Til Hendes Majestaet Dronning Margarethe II.* København: Nationalmuseet.

Götze 1907

Götze, A., 1907. *Die vor- und frühgeschichtlichen Denkmäler des Kreises Ostprignitz.* Berlin: Voss.

Govedarica/Hauptmann 2004

Govedarica, B. and Hauptmann, H., 2004. *Zepterträger - Herrscher der Steppen: die frühen Ockergräber des älteren Äneolithikums im karpatenbalkanischen Gebiet und im Steppenraum Südost- und Osteuropas = Les Porteurs de sceptres - les seigneurs des steppes: les premières tombes à ocre de l'ancien Enéolithique dans la région carpato-balkanique et dans les steppes du Sud- Est et de l'Est de l'Europe.* Heidelberger Akademie der Wissenschaften, Internationale Interakademische Kommission für die Erforschung der Vorgeschichte des Balkans, Monographien 6. Mainz am Rhein: Philipp von Zabern.

Govedarica/Manzura 2015

Govedarica, B. and Manzura, I., 2015. The Copper Age Settlement of Karlstal on Orlovka (Southwest Ukraine). *In*: S. Hansen, P. Raczky, A. Anders, A. Reingruber, eds. *Neolithic and Copper Age between the Carpathians and the Aegean Sea: chronologies and technologies from the 6th to the 4th Millennium BCE. International Workshop Budapest 2012.* Archäologie in Eurasien 31. Bonn: Habelt Verlag, 437-456.

Grabowska/Zastawny 2011

Grabowska, B. and Zastawny, A., 2011. Materiały kręgu lendzielsko-polgarskiego ze st. 5 w Modlnicy, pow. krakowski. *In:* J. Kruk and A. Zastawny, eds. *Modlnica, st. 5. Od neolitu środkowego do wczesnej epoki brązu. Via Archaeologica. Źródła z badań wykopaliskowych na trasie autostrady A4 w Małopolsce.* Kraków: Krakowski Zespół do Badań Autostrad, 95-172.

Grygiel 2008

Grygiel, R., 2008. *Neolit i początki epoki brązu w rejonie Brześcia Kujawskiego i Osłonek; 2. Środkowy neolit grupa Brzesko-Kujawska kultury lendzielskiej.* Łódź: Fundacja Badań Archeologicznych Imienia Profesora Konrada Jażdżewskiego.

Günther/Viets 1992

Günther, K. and Viets, M., 1992. *Die Megalithgräber Henglarn I und Wewelsburg im Paderborner Land.* Bodenaltertümer Westfalens 28. Münster: Aschendorffsche Verlagsbuchhandlung.

Hahn-Weinheimer et al. 1995

Hahn-Weinheimer P., Hirner A., Weber-Diefenbach K., 1995. *Röntgenfluoreszenzanalytische Methoden; Grundlagen und praktische Anwendung in den Geo-, Material- und Umweltwissenschaften.* Wiesbaden: Vieweg.

Hafner 2005

Hafner, A., 2005. Sutz-Lattrigen, Hauptstation. Rettungsgrabungen 1988-2003: neolithische Ufersiedlungen. *Archäologie in Kanton Bern*, 6A, 41-48.

Hafner *et al.* 2010

Hafner, A., Fischer, J., Francuz, J., 2010. Sutz-Lattrigen. Abschluss der Rettungsgrabungen Neue Station und kommende Aufgaben. *Archäologie Bern - Jahrbuch des Archäologischen Dienstes des Kantons Bern 2010*, 132-135.

Hage 2016

Hage, F., 2016. *Büdelsdorf/Borgstedt. Eine trichterbecherzeitliche Kleinregion.* Frühe Monumentalität und soziale Differenzierung 11. Bonn: Habelt Verlag.

Hall 1961

Hall, E. T., 1961. Surface-enrichment of buried metals. *Archaeometry* 4, 62–66.

Hallström 1934

Hallström, G., 1934. Segersta och Hanebo socknars fornhistoria. *In:* N.C. Humble, ed. *Två hälsingesocknar: några anteckningar till Segersta och Hanebo socknars historia.* Bollnäs: Segersta Hembygdsförenings Förlag.

Hansen 2013

Hansen, S., 2013. Innovative Metals: Copper, Gold and Silver in the Black Sea Region and the Carpathian Basin During the 5th and 4th Millennium BC. *In:* S. Burmeister, S. Hansen, M. Kunst, N. Müller-Scheessel, eds. *Metal matters: innovative technologies and social change in prehistory and antiquity.* Rahden/Westf.: Verlag Marie Leidorf, 137-167.

Hansen *et al.* 2015

Hansen, S., Toderaş, M., Reingruber, A., Wunderlich, J., Benecke, N., Gatsov, I., Marinova, E., Müller, M., Nachev, C., Nedelcheva, P., Nowacki, D., Röpke, A., Wahl, J., Zäuner, S., 2015. Pietrele an der Unteren Donau: Bericht über die Ausgrabungen und geomorphologischen Untersuchungen im Sommer 2011. *Eurasia antiqua*, 18 (2012), 1-68.

Hartz/Lübke 2005

Hartz, S. and Lübke, H. 2005. Zur chronostratigraphischen Gliederung der Ertebølle-Kultur und frühesten Trichterbecher-Kultur in der südlichen Mecklenburger Bucht. *Bodendenkmalpflege in Mecklenburg-Vorpommern*, 52 (2004), 119-143.

Helfert 2013

Helfert, M., 2013. Die portable energiedispersive Röntgenfluoreszenzanalyse (P-ED-RFA) –Studie zu methodischen und analytischen Grundlagen ihrer Anwendung in der archäologischen Keramikforschung. *In*: B. Ramminger, O. Stilborg, M. Helfert, eds. *Naturwissenschaftliche Analysen vor- und frühgeschichtlicher Keramik III.* Habelt, Bonn, 14–47.

Helfert/Böhme 2010

Helfert M. and Boehme D., 2010. Herkunftsbestimmung von römischer Keramik mittels portabler energiedispersiver Röntgenfluoreszenzanalyse (-P-ED-RFA). Erste Ergebnisse einer anwendungsbezogenen Teststudie. *In*: B. Ramminger and O. Stilborg, eds. *Naturwissenschaftliche Analysen vor- und frühgeschichtlicher Keramik: Methoden, Anwendungsbereiche I, Auswertungsmöglichkeiten.* Habelt, Bonn, 11-30.

Hellmundt 1964

Hellmundt, A., 1964. *Die vor- und frühgeschichtlichen Denkmäler und Funde des Kreises Ueckermünde.* Die Vor- und Frühgeschichtlichen Denkmäler und Funde im Gebiet der DDR 3. Schwerin: Petermänken Verlag.

Herbich/Tunia 2009

Herbich, T. and Tunia, K., 2009. Geofizyczne badania duzych konstrukcji neolitycznych na terenach lessowych. Casus Slonowice. *Archeologia Polski*, 54, 13-35.

Hingst 1985

Hingst, H., 1985. Großsteingräber in Schleswig-Holstein. *Offa. Berichte und Mitteilungen zur Urgeschichte, Frühgeschichte und Mittelalterarchäologie*, 42, 57-112: Ill.

Hinz/Dittmer 1954

Hinz, H. and Dittmer, E., 1954. *Vorgeschichte des nordfriesischen Festlandes.* Die vor- und frühgeschichtlichen Denkmäler und Funde in Schleswig-Holstein 3. Neumünster: Wachholtz.

Hinz *et al.* 2012

Hinz, M., Furholt, M., Raetzel-Fabian, D., Müller, J., Rinne, C., Sjögren, K.G., Wotzka, H.P., 2012. RADON - Radiocarbon dates online 2012. Central European database of 14C dates for the Neolithic and Early Bronze Age. *Journal of Neolithic Archaeology* 2012, 1-4. doi: 10.12766/jna.2012.65.

Hoika 1987

Hoika, J., 1987. *Das Mittelneolithikum zur Zeit der Trichterbecherkultur in Nordostholstein: Untersuchungen zu Archäologie und Landschaftsgeschichte. Mit einem Exkurs zu den Ausgrabungen am Flintholm im Bundsø auf Alsen.* Offa Bücher: Untersuchungen aus dem Institut für Ur- und Frühgeschichte der Christian-Albrechts-Universität Kiel 61. Neumünster: Wachholtz Verlag.

Hoika 1990a

Hoika, J., 1990a. Megalithic Graves In The Funnel Beaker Societies of Schleswig-Holstein. *Przglad Archeologiczny*, 37, 53-119.

Hoika 1990b

Hoika, J., 1990b. Zum Übergang vom Früh- zum Mittelneolithikum in der Trichterbecherkultur. *In*: D. Jankowska, ed. *Die Trichterbecherkultur. Neue Forschungen und Hypothesen.* Material des Internationalen Symposiums, Dymaczewo, 20.-24. Sept. 1988, 1. Poznań: Adam Mickiewicz University Press, 197-217.

Hoika 1994

Hoika, J., 1994. Zur Gliederung der frühneolithischen Trichterbecherkultur in Holstein *In*: J. Hoika, and J. Meurers-Balke, eds. *Beiträge zur frühneolithischen Trichterbecherkultur im westlichen Ostseegebiet 1.*, Neumünster: Wachholtz, 85-132.

Hollnagel 1962

Hollnagel, A., 1962. *Die vor- und frühgeschichtlichen Denkmäler und Funde des Kreises Neubrandenburg.* Vor- und Frühgeschichtlichen Denkmäler und

Funde im Gebiet der Deutschen Demokratischen Republik 2. Schwerin: Peter-mänken Verlag.

Hollnagel/Schulz 1973

Hollnagel, A. and Schulz, W., 1973. *Die ur- und frühgeschichtlichen Denkmäler und Funde des Kreises Strasburg.* Beiträge zur Ur- und Frühgeschichte der Bezirke Rostock, Schwerin und Neubrandenburg. Berlin: Deutscher Wissenschafts-Verlag.

Horn 2013

Horn, C., 2013. Weapons, fighters and combat: spears and swords in Early Bronze Age Scandinavia. *Danish Journal of Archaeology*, 2 (1), 20- 44.

Horn 2014

Horn, C., 2014. *Studien zu den europäischen Stabdolchen.* Universitätsforschungen zur prähistorischen Archäologie 246. Bonn: Habelt Verlag.

Horn/Holstein 2017

Horn, C. and Holstein, I.V., 2017. Dents in our confidence: The interaction of damage and material properties in interpreting use-wear on copper-alloy weaponry. *Journal of Archaeological Science*, 81, 90–100.

Hülle 1938

Hülle, W., 1938. Auswertung der Ergebnisse für die Vorgeschichte (Unter bes. Berücksichtigung Mitteldeutschlands). *In:* W. Witter, ed. *Die Ausbeutung der mitteldeutschen Erzlagerstätten in den frühen Metallzeiten.* Die älteste Erzgewinnung im nordischen-germanischen Lebenskreis 1. Leipzig: Curt Kabitzsch, 174-224.

Hurtig *et al.* 1957

Hurtig, T., Fukarek, F., Stübs, J., 1957. *Physische Geographie von Mecklenburg.* Berlin: Deutscher Verlag der Wissenschaften.

Hutloff 1940

Hutloff, H., 1940. Ein kupferzeitliche Axtfund aus Frankfurt (Oder). *Prähistorische Zeitschrift*, 30/31 (1939/40), 392-395.

Ivanova 2013

Ivanova, M., 2013. *The Black Sea and the early civilizations of Europe, the Near East and Asia.* New York: Cambridge University Press.

Jacobs 1986

Jacobs, J., 1986. *Jungsteinzeitliche Metallfunde auf dem Gebiet der DDR.* Unpublizierte Diplomarbeit, Halle.

Jacobs 1989

Jacobs, J., 1989. Jungsteinzeitliche Metallfunde auf dem Gebiet der DDR. *Zeitschrift für Archäologie*, 23, 1-17.

Jacobs 1994

Jacobs, J., 1994. Ein „wiedergefundenes" Flachbeil aus Kupfer von Hagenow in Mecklenburg. *In:* C. Ahrens, ed. *Hammaburg. Neue Folge 10. Vor- und Frühgeschichte aus dem niederelbischen Raum.* Neumünster: Wachholtz Verlag, 99-103.

Jacobson/Bradshaw 1981

Jacobson, G. and Bradshaw, R., 1981. The selection of sites for paleovegetational studies. *Quaternary Research*, 16, 80–96.

Jahns 2000

Jahns, S., 2000. Late-glacial and Holocene woodland dynamics and land-use history of tthe Lower Oder valley, north-eastern Germany, based on two, AMS ^{14}C-dated, pollen profiles. *Vegetation History and Archaeobotany*, 9, 111-123.

Jahns 2001

Jahns, S., 2001. On the Late Pleistocene and Holocene history of vegetation and human impact in the Ücker valley, north-eastern Germany. *Vegetation History and Archaeobotany*, 10, 97-104.

Janssen 1935

Janssen, H.L., 1935. *Die Germanen in Mecklenburg im 2. Jahrtausend v. Chr.* Mannus-Bücherei 54. Leipzig: Curt Rabitsch.

Jantzen *et al.* 2014
Jantzen, D., Saalow, L., Schmidt, J.P., 2014. *Pipeline: Archäologie Ausgrabungen auf den großen Ferngastrassen in Mecklenburg-Vorpommern.* Schwerin: Mecklenburg-Vorpommern Landesamt für Kultur und Denkmalpflege.

Jarovoj 1990
Jarovoj, E.V., 1990. *Kurgany ėneolita - ėpochi bronzy Nižnego Podnestrov'ja.* Kišinev: Shtiintsa.

Jażdżewski 1936
Jażdżewski, K., 1936. *Kultura Pucharów Lejkowatych w Polsce Zachodniej i Środkowej.* Poznań: Polskie Towarzystwo Prehistoryczne.

Jensen 1979
Jensen, J., 1979. *Danmarkshistorien: Bronzealderen.* Skovlandets folk 1. København: Sesam.

Jürgens/Szillus 2019
Jürgens, F. and Szillus, C., 2019. Das älteste Metall in Ostwestfalen – ein neues Kupferbeil aus Willebadessen-Peckelsheim. *Archäologie in Westfalen-Lippe 2018,* 55-58.

Kalčev 2002
Kalčev, P., 2002. *Das frühbronzezeitliche Gräberfeld von Stara Zagora - „Bereketska mogila" (Bulgarien).* Saarbrücker Studien und Materialien zur Altertumskunde 8. Bonn: Habelt Verlag.

Kalicz 1968
Kalicz, N., 1968. Die Frühbronzezeit in Nordost-Ungarn: Abriss der Geschichte des 19.-16. Jahrhunderts v.u.Z. Archaeologia Hungarica 45. Budapest: Akadémiai Kiadó.

Kalicz 1982
Kalicz, N., 1982. Die terminologischen und chronologischen Probleme der Kupfer- und Bronzezeit in Ungarn. *In:* A. Aspes, and B. Bagolini, eds. *Il passaggio dal neolitico all'età del bronzo nell'Europa centrale e nella regione Alpina. Problemi cronologici e terminologici: atti del X Simposio internazionale sulla fine del Neolitico e gli inizi dell'età del Bronzo in Europa, Lazise - Verona 8-12 aprile 1980.* Verona: Museo Civico di Storia Naturale, 117-137.

Kanter 2000
Kanter, L., 2000. Das Tollense-Becken – ein ehemaliges Tunneltal. *Neubrandenburger Geologische Beiträge,* 1, 11-23.

Karsten 1994
Karsten, P., 1994. *Att kasta yxan sjön: En studie över rituell tradition och förändring utifrån skånska neolitiska offerfynd.* Acta Archaeologica Lundensia 8. Lund: Almqvist & Wiksell.

Keiling 1971
Keiling, H., 1971. Älterbronzezeitliche Flachgräber von Raden, Kreis Güstrow. *Jahrbuch für Bodendenkmalpflege in Mecklenburg 1970,* 193-224.

Keiling 1987
Keiling, H., 1987. *Die Kulturen der mecklenburgischen Bronzezeit.* Archäologische Funde und Denkmale aus dem Norden der DDR: Museumskatalog. Schwerin: Landesarchäologie Mecklenbug-Vorpommern.

Kersten 1936
Kersten, K., 1936. *Zur älteren nordischen Bronzezeit.* Veröffentlichungen der Schleswig-Holsteinischen Universitätsgesellschaft Reihe 2, Forschungen zur Vor- und Frühgeschichte aus dem Museum vorgeschichtlicher Altertümer in Kiel. Neumünster: Wachholtz Verlag.

Kersten 1958
Kersten, K., 1958. *Die Funde der älteren Bronzezeit in Pommern.* Beiheft zum Atlas der Urgeschichte 7. Hamburg: Hamburgisches Museum für Völkerkunde und Vorgeschichte.

Kibbert 1980

Kibbert, K., 1980. *Die Äxte und Beile im mittleren Westdeutschland I.* Prähistorische Bronzefunde, Abt. 9 (10). München: C.H. Beck'sche Verlagsbuchhandlung.

Kienlin/Ottaway 1998

Kienlin, T.L. and Ottaway, B.S., 1998. Flanged axes of the northalpine region:
an assessment of the possibilities of use wear analysis on metal artifacts. *In*: C.
Mordant, M. Perno, V. Rychner, eds. *L'Atelier du bronzier en Europe du XX au VIII
siècle avant notre ère.* Du mineral au métal, du métal à l'objet 2. Paris: Comité des
Travaux Historiques et Scientifiques, 271-286.

Kirsch 1993

Kirsch, E., 1993. *Funde des Mittelneolithikums im Land Brandenburg.* Forschungen zur Archäologie im Land Brandenburg. Potsdam: Brandenburgisches
Landesamt für Denkmalpflege.

Kirsch/Brandenburgisches Landesmuseum für Ur- und Frühgeschichte 1994

Kirsch, E. and Brandenburgisches Landesmuseum für Ur- und Frühgeschichte,
1994. *Beiträge zur älteren Trichterbecherkultur in Brandenburg.* Forschungen zur
Archäologie im Land Brandenburg. Potsdam: Brandenburgisches Landesamt für
Denkmalpflege.

Klassen 1998

Klassen, L., 1998. Fremmede Fugle. *Skalk*, 2, 30-32.

Klassen 2000

Klassen, L., 2000. *Frühes Kupfer im Norden Untersuchungen zu Chronologie,
Herkunft und Bedeutung der Kupferfunde der Nordgruppe der Trichterbecherkultur.* Jutland Archaeological Society 36. Åarhus: Aarhus University Press.

Klassen *et al.* 2011

Klassen, L., Dobeš, M., Pétrequin, P., 2011. Dreieckige Kupferflachbeile in Mitteldeutschland und Böhmen. Zum kulturgeschichtlichen Hintergrund einer be-
merkenswerten Fundgruppe. *Alt-Thüringen*, 41, 7-36.

Klassen/Pernicka 1998

Klassen, L. and Pernicka, E., 1998. Eine kreuzschneidige Axthacke aus Südskandinavien? Ein Beispiel für die Anwendungsmöglichkeiten der Stuttgarter Analyse-
datenbank. *Archäologisches Korrespondenzblatt*, 28 (1), 35-45.

Klassen/Stürup 2001

Klassen, L. and Stürüp, S., 2001. Decoding the Riesebusch-copper: Lead-isotope
analysis applied to early neolithic copper finds from south Scandinavia. *Prähistorische Zeitschrift*, 76/1, 55–73.

Klatt 2009

Klatt, S., 2009. Die neolithischen Einhegungen im westlichen Ostseeraum,
Forschungsstand und Forschungsperspektiven. *In*: T. Terberger, ed. *Neue
Forschungen zum Neolithikum im Ostseeraum. Archäologie und Geschichte im
Ostseeraum 5.* Rahden/Westf.: Verlag Marie Leidorf, 7-134.

Klimscha 2010

Klimscha, F., 2010. Kupferne Flachbeile und Meißel mit angedeuteten Randle-
isten: Ihre Bedeutung für die Entstehung und Verbreitung technischer Inno-
vationen in Europa und Vorderasien im 4.-3. Jahrtausend v. Chr. *Germania*,
88, 101–144.

Klimscha 2016

Klimscha, F., 2016. *Pietrele 1: Beile und Äxte aus Stein Distinktion und Kommunikation
während der Kupferzeit im östlichen Balkangebiet.* Archäologie in Eurasien 34.
Bonn: Habelt Verlag.

Klinger *et al.* 2012

Klinger, S., Schierhold, K., Baales, M Gleser, R., Schultz, M., 2012. Die Toten in den
Galeriegräbern von Erwitte- Schmerlecke – erste Erkenntnisse. *Archäologie in
Westfalen-Lippe*, 2011, 50-52.

Knight 2017
  Knight, M.G., 2017. The deliberate destruction of Late Bronze Age socketed axeheads in Cornwall. *Cornish Archaeology*, 56, 203–224.

Knight 2019
  Knight, M.G., 2019. Going to Pieces: Investigating the Deliberate Destruction of Late Bronze Age Swords and Spearheads. *Proceedings of the Prehistoric Society*, 85, 251–272.

Knight 2021
  Knight, M.G., 2021. There's Method in the Fragments: A Damage Ranking System for Bronze Age Metalwork. *European Journal* of *Archaeology*, 24 (1), 48–67.

Knight 2022
  Knight, M.G., 2022. *Fragments of the Bronze Age. The destruction and deposition of metalwork in South-West Britain and its wider context.* Prehistoric Society Research Papers 13. Oxford, Philadelphia: Oxbow Books.

Knöll 1959
  Knöll, H., 1959. *Die nordwestdeutsche Tiefstichkeramik und ihre Stellung im nord- und mitteleuropäischen Neolithikum.* Veröffentlichungen der Altertumskommission im Provinzialinstitut für Westfälische Landes- und Volkskunde 3. Münster: Aschendorff.

Knöll 1970
  Knöll, H., 1970. Zur Keramik aus dem westfälischen Steinkistengrab von Dalmer, Kreis Beckum. *Germania*, 48, 112-115.

Knöll 1983
  Knöll, H., 1983. *Die Megalithgräber von Lengerich-Wechte (Kreis Steinfurt).* Bodenaltertümer Westfalens 21. Münster: Aschendorff.

Koch 1998
  Koch, E., 1998. *Neolithic bog pots from Zealand, Møn, Lolland and Falster.* Nordiske Fortidsminder B 16. Kopenhagen: Det Kongelige Nordiske Oldskriftselskab.

Kozłowski 1971
  Kozłowski, j.K., 1971. Eneolityczne groby szkieletowe z Nowej Huty-Wyciąża. *In:* Państwowe Muzeum Archeologiczne, ed. *Materiały Starożytne i Wczesnośredniowieczne 1.* Breslau: Zakład Narodowy im. Ossolińskich, 65-97.

Kristiansen 1978
  Kristiansen, K., 1978. The consumption of wealth in Bronze Age Denmark. A study in the dynamics of economic processes in tribal societies. *In:* K. Kristiansen and C. Paludan-Müller, eds. *New directions in Scandinavian archaeology.* Studies in Scandinavian prehistory and early history 1. Odense: National Museum of Denmark, 158–190.

Kristiansen 1984
  Kristiansen, K., 1984. Krieger und Häuptlinge in der Bronzezeit Dänemarks. Ein Beitrag zur Geschichte des bronzezeitlichen Schwertes. *Jahrbuch des Römisch-Germanischen Zentralmuseums Mainz*, 31, 187–208.

Kristiansen 2002
  Kristiansen, K., 2002. The tale of the sword - swords and swordfighters in Bronze Age Europe. *Oxford Journal of Archaeology*, 21 (4), 319–332.

Kröhnke 1900
  Kröhnke, O., 1900. *Untersuchungen vorgeschichtlicher Bronzen Schleswig-Holsteins.* Hamburg: O. Meissner.

Kuijpers 2019
  Kuijpers, M.H.G., 2019. *An Archaeology of Skill: Metalworking Skill and Material Specialization in Early Bronze Age Central Europe.* Routledge Studies in Archaeology. Oxford, New York: Routledge.

Kunkel 1926
  Kunkel, O., 1926. *Aus Pommerns Urgeschichte.* Berlin: Emil Hartmann.

Kunkel 1931
Kunkel, O., 1931. *Pommersche Urgeschichte in Bildern.* Stettin: Leon Sauniers Buchhandlung.

Kunkel 1939
Kunkel, O., 1939. Urgeschichte. *Baltische Studien*, Neue Folge 41, 259-316.

Kunze 2001
Kunze, E., 2001. *Korrosion und Korrosionsschutz: Band 1 Einführung und wissenschaftliche Grundlagen.* Berlin: Wiley-VCH.

Kupka 1937
Kupka, P., 1937. Besprechung zu E. Sprockhoffs Zur Megalithkultur Nordwestdeutschlands. Nachrichten zur Niedersachsens Urgeschichte 4, 1930, 1-55. *In: Beiträge zur Geschichte, Landes- und Volkskunde der Altmark VI*, Stendal: Trommler, 63-72.

Kuzmanov *et al.* 2005
Kuzmanov, K., Ivaacanu, P., Connor, G.O., 2005. Porphyry Cu-Au and epithermal Au-Ag deposits in the southern Apuseni Mountains, Romania. *In*: D. Blundell, N. Arndt, P.R. Cobbold, C. Heinrich, eds. *Geodynamics and ore deposit evolution in Europe*. Amsterdam: Elsevier, 46-47.

Lange 2012
Lange, J., 2012. *Geochemische Multi-Element Analyse im Bereich eines Hausgrundrisses der frühbronzezeitlichen Siedlung Fidvár bei Vráble (SW-Slowakei) mit Hilfe von Röntgenfluoreszensanalytik.* Unpublizierte Bachelorarbeit, Heidelberg 2012.

Langenheim 1935
Langenheim, K., 1935. *Die Tonware der Riesensteingräber in Schleswig-Holstein.* Veröffentlichungen der Schleswig-Holsteinischen Universitätsgesellschaft 2, Forschungen zur Vor- und Frühgeschichte aus dem Museum vorgeschichtlicher Altertümer in Kiel. Neumünster: Wachholtz.

Laux 2000
Laux, F., 2000. *Die Äxte und Beile in Niedersachsen I: (Flach-, Randleisten- und Absatzbeile).* Prähistorische Bronzefunde Abteilung IX, Stuttgart: Franz Steiner Verlag.

Lazarovici *et al.* 2015
Lazarovici, G., Lazarovici, C.-M., Constantinescu, B., 2015. New Data and Analyses on Gold Metallurgy during the Romanian Copper Age. *In*: S. Hansen, P. Raczky, A. Anders, A. Reingruber, eds. *Neolithic and Copper Age between the Carpathians and the Aegean Sea.* Bonn: Habelt Verlag, 325-352.

Levy 1982
Levy, J.E., 1982. *Social and religious organization in Bronze Age Denmark: An analysis of ritual hoard finds.* British Archaeological Reports International Series 124. Oxford: British Archaeological Reports.

Lichter/Badisches Landesmuseum Karlsruhe 2010
Lichter, C. and Badisches Landesmuseum Karlsruhe, 2010. *Jungsteinzeit im Umbruch: Die „Michelsberger Kultur" und Mitteleuropa vor 6000 Jahren.* Katalog zur Ausstellung im Badischen Landesmuseum Karlsruhe 20.11.2010 - 15.5.2011. Darmstadt: Primus Verlag.

Lies 1966
Lies, H., 1966. Spätneolithische und älterbronzezeitliche Gräber von Barleben. *Jahreschrift für mitteldeutsche Vorgeschichte*, 50, 61-102.

Lindqvist 1912
Lindqvist, S., 1912. Från Nerikes sten- och bronsålder. *Meddelanden Från Föreningen Örebro Läns Museum*, Örebro.

Lisch 1865
Lisch, G.C.F., 1865. Kupferner Keil von Kirch-Jesar. *In*: G.C.F. Lisch, ed. *Jahrbücher des Vereins für Mecklenburgische Geschichte und Alterthumskunde, aus den Arbeiten des Vereins 30.* Schwerin: Stiller, 136-139.

Lissauer 1904

Lissauer, A., 1904. Erster Bericht über die Tätigkeit der von der Deutschen Anthropologischen Gesellschaft gewählten Kommission für prähistorische Typenkarten: Erstattet auf der 35. Allgemeinen Versammlung in Greifswald am 4. August 1904. *Zeitschrift für Ethnologie,* 36, 537-607.

Liversage 1992

Liversage, D., 1992. *Barkaer: Long barrows and settlements.* Arkaeologiske Studier 9. København: Akademisk Forlag.

Löffler/Bode 2013

Löffler, I. and Bode, M., 2013. Zwei neolitische Kupferfunde aus Isernloh und der Bilsteinhöhle. *Archäologie in Westfalen-Lippe 2012*, 201- 204.

Lomborg 1962

Lomborg, E., 1962. Zur Frage der bandkeramischen Einflüsse in Skandinavien. *Acta archaeologica,* 33, 1-38.

Lorenz 2012

Lorenz, L., 2012. Keramiklaufzeiten und die Nutzungsdauer nordostdeutscher Megalithgräber, *In*: M. Hinz and J. Müller, eds. *Siedlung, Grabenwerk, Großsteingrab. Studien zu Gesellschaft, Wirtschaft und Umwelt der Trichterbechergruppen im nördlichen Mitteleuropa.* Frühe Monumentalität und soziale Differenzierung 2. Bonn: Habelt Verlag, 61-86.

Lorenz 2018

Lorenz, L., 2018. *Kommunikationsräume neolithischer Gesellschaften in der nordmitteleuropäischen Tiefebene.* Frühe Monumentalität und soziale Differenzierung 14. Bonn: Habelt Verlag.

Lorenzen 2014

Lorenzen, S., 2014. Das Tollensetal - Naturraum und Landschaftsgeschichte. *In*: D. Jantzen, J. Orschiedt, J. Piek, T. Terberger, eds. *Tod im Tollensetal: Forschungen zu den Hinterlassenschaften eines bronzezeitlichen Gewaltkonfliktes in Mecklenburg-Vorpommern. Teil 1 Die Forschungen bis 2011.* Beiträge zur Ur- und Frühgeschichte Mecklenburg-Vorpommerns 50. Schwerin: Landesamt für Kultur und Denkmalpflege Mecklenburg-Vorpommern, 15-28.

Lorenzen 1967

Lorenzen, W., 1967. *Untersuchungen einer Kupferspirale aus dem Hortfund von Riesebusch, Kr. Eutin.* Offa. Berichte und Mitteilungen zur Urgeschichte, Frühgeschichte und Mittelalterarchäologie 24. 106-107.

Lübke 1999

Lübke, H., 1999. Die dicken Flintspitzen aus Schleswig-Holstein. Ein Beitrag zur Typologie und Chronologie eines Großgerätetyps der Trichterbecherkultur. *Offa* 54/55, 1997/1998, 49-95.

Lüth 2005

Lüth, F., 2005. Das erste Metall im Norden - Ein 6000 Jahre alter Kupferschatz aus Neuenkirchen, Lkr. Mecklenburg-Strelitz. *In*: F. Lüth and H. Jöns, eds. *Die Autobahn A20 - Norddeutschlands längste Ausgrabung. Archäologische Forschungen auf der Trasse zwischen Lübeck und Stettin.* Schwerin: Landesamt für Kultur und Denkmalpflege, 43-46.

Lutz *et al.* 1998

Lutz, J., Pernicka, E., Matuschik, I., Rassmann, K., 1998. Die frühesten Metallfunde in Mecklenburg-Vorpommern im Lichte neuer Metallanalysen. Vom Endmesolithikum bis zur frühen Bronzezeit. *Bodendenkmalpflege in Mecklenburg-Vorpommern,* 45 (1997), 41-67.

Madsen 1978

Madsen, T., 1978. Et yngre stenalders koppersmykke fra en dysse ved Soed. *Nordslesvigske museer: årbog for museerne i Sønderjyllands amt,* 5, 15-20.

Madsen 1980a
Madsen, T., 1980. Earthern Long Barrows and Timber Structures: Aspects of the Early Neolithic Mortuary Practice in Denmark. *Proceedings of the Prehistoric Society.* 45 (1979), 301- 320.

Madsen 1980b
Madsen, T., 1980. En tidiligneolitisk langhøj ved Rude i Østjylland. *Kuml,* 28 (1979), 79- 108.

Madsen 1982
Madsen, T., 1982. Settlement Systems of Early Agricultural Societies in East Jutland, Denmark: A Study of Change. *Journal of Anthropological Archaeology,* 1, 229-239.

Madsen 1988
Madsen, T., 1988. Causedwayed enclosures in South Scandinavia. *In:* C. Burgess, P. Topping, C. Mordant, M. Maddison, eds. *Enclosures and Defences in the Neolithic of Western Europe.* British Archaeological Reports International Series 403. 2, Oxford: British Archaeological Reports, 301-336.

Madsen 1998
Madsen, T., 1998. Die Jungsteinzeit in Südskandinavien. *In:* J. Preuss and M. Rothe, eds. *Das Neolithikum in Mitteleuropa: Kulturen - Wirtschaft - Umwelt vom 6. bis 3. Jahrtausend v.u.Z.: Übersichten zum Stand der Forschung.* Weissbach: Beier & Beran, 423-450.

Madsen/Petersen 1984
Madsen, T. and Petersen, J.E., 1984. Tidligneolitiske anlæg ved Mosegården. Regionale og kronologiske forskelle i tidligneolitikum. *Kuml,* 31 (1982/83), 61-120.

Manfredini *et al.* 2009
Manfredini, A., Fugazzola, D., Sarti, L., Silvestrini, M., Martini, F., Conati, B.C., Muntoni, I.M., Pizziolo, G., Volante, N., 2009. Adriatico e Tirreno a confronto. *Rivista di Scienze Preisoriche,* 59, 115-180.

Manso *et al.* 2015
Manso, M., Schiavon, N., Queralt, I., Arruda, A.M., Sampaio, J.M., Brunetti, A., 2015. Alloy characterization of a 7th Century BC archeological bronze vase — Overcoming patina constraints using Monte Carlo simulations. *Spectrochimica Acta Part B: Atomic Spectroscopy,* 107, 93-96.

Marcoux *et al.* 2002
Marcoux, E., Grancea, L., Lupulescu, M., Milesi, J.-P., 2002. Lead isotope signatures of epithermal and porphyry-type ore deposits from Romanian Carpathian Mountains. *Mineralium Deposita,* 37, 173-184.

Mareş 2002
Mareş, I., 2002. *Metalurgia aramei în neo-eneoliticul României = The metallurgy of copper in the Romanian Neo-eneolithic.* Seria arheologie. Suceava: Editura Bucovina Istorică.

Matuschik 1998
Matuschik, I., 1998. Kupferfunde und Metallurgie-Belege, zugleich ein Beitrag zur Geschichte der kupferzeitlichen Dolche Mittel-, Ost- und Südosteuropas. *In:* M. Mainberger, ed. *Das Moordorf von Reute: archäologische Untersuchungen in der jungneolithischen Siedlung Reute-Schorrenried.* Staufen i. Br: Teraqua CAP, 207-261.

Maurer 2014
Maurer, J., 2014. Die Mondsee-Gruppe: Gibt es Neuigkeiten? Ein allgemeiner Überblick zum Stand der Forschung. *In:* L. Husty and K. Schmotz, eds. *Vorträge des 32. Niederbayrischen Archäologentages.* Rahden-Westf.: VML, 145-190.

Maus 1990
Mauss, M., 1990. *The gift. The form and reason for exchange in archaic societies.* Norton, New York.

Mende 1985
Mende, J., 1985. Die ur- und frühgeschichtliche Fundplätze der Gemarkung Neu-enkirchen, Kreis Neubrandenburg. *Mitteilungen des Bezirkfachausschusses für Ur- und Frühgeschichte*, 32, 39-60.

Mende 2001
Mende, J., 2001. Siedlungsreste der Trichterbecherkultur unter einem zerstörten Hügelgrab bei Warlin, Lkrs. Mecklenburg-Strelitz. *Archäologische Berichte aus Mecklenburg-Vorpommern*, 8, 21-39.

Menka 1989
Menke 1988
Menke, M., 1988. Zu den frühen Kupferfunden des Nordens, *Acta Archaeologica* 59, 1988, 15–66.

Mennenga 2017
Mennenga, M., 2017. Zwischen Elbe und Ems; Die Siedlungen der Trichter-becherkultur in Nordwestdeutschland. *Frühe Monumentalität und soziale Differenzierung 13*. Bonn: Habelt Verlag.

Midgley 1985
Midgley, M.S., 1985. *The origin and function of the earthen long barrows of Northern Europe*. British Archaeological Reports International Series 259. Oxford: British Archaeological Reports.

Midgley 1992
Midgley, M., 1992. *TRB culture; The first farmers of the North European Plain*. Edinburgh: Edinburgh University Press.

Mödlinger/Piccardo 2013
Mödlinger, M. and Piccardo, P., 2013. Corrosion on prehistoric Cu–Sn-alloys: the influence of artificial environment and storage. *Applied Physics A*, 113 (4), 1069-1080.

Molloy 2007
Molloy, B., 2007. What's the bloody point? Fighting with Irish Bronze Age weapons. *In*: B. Molloy, ed. *The cutting edge: Studies in ancient and medieval combat*. Stroud: Tempus Publishing Ltd., 90-11.

Molloy 2008
Molloy, B., 2008. Martial arts and materiality: a combat archaeology perspective on Aegean swords of the fifteenth and fourteenth centuries BC. *World Archaeology*, 40 (1), 116–134.

Molloy 2009
Molloy, B., 2009. For Gods or Men? A Reappraisal of the Function of European Bronze Age Shields. *Antiquity*, 83, 1052-1064.

Molloy 2010
Molloy, B., 2010. Swords and Swordsmanship in the Aegean Bronze Age. *American Journal of Archaeology*, 114 (3), 403-428.

Molloy 2011
Molloy, B., 2011. Use-wear analysis and use-patterns of Bronze Age swords. *In*: M. Uckelmann and M. Mödlinger, eds. *Bronze age warfare. Manufacture and use of weaponry*. British Archaeological Reports International Series 2255. Oxford: Archaeopress, 67-84.

Montelius 1893
Montelius, O., 1893. Finnas i Sverige minnen från en kopperålder. *Svenska Form-innesförenigens Tidskrift*, 8 (1891/93), 203-238.

Montelius 1895
Montelius, O., 1895. *Les temps préhistoriques en Suède et dans les autres pays scandinaves*. Paris: Leroux.

Montelius 1898
Montelius, O., 1898. *Die Chronologie der ältesten Bronzezeit in Norddeutschland und Skandinavien*. Archiv für Anthropologie 25. Braunschweig: Vieweg.

Montelius 1900a
  Montelius, O., 1900. *Die Chronologie der ältesten Bronzezeit in Nord-Deutschland und Skandinavien.* Archiv für Anthrolopolgie 25-26. Braunschweig: Vieweg.

Montelius 1900b
  O. Montelius, Die Chronologie der ältesten Bronzezeit in Norddeutschland und Skandinavien. Sonderabdruck aus Archiv für Anthropologie XXV und XXVI (Braunschweig 1900).

Montelius 1903
  Montelius, O., 1903. *Die älteren Kulturperioden in Orient und Europa. 1. Die Methode.* Stockholm: K.L. Beckmans Buchdruckerei.

Montelius 1917
  Montelius, O., 1917. Minnen från vår forntid. Stockholm: P.A. Norstedt & Söners Förlag.

Müller 1988
  Müller, D.W., 1988. Grabkammer vom mitteldeutschen Typ mit Menhir von Langeneichstädt, Kr. Querfurt. Ausgrabung und Funde. *Archäologische Berichte und Informationen*, 33, 192-199.

Müller 1914
  Müller, S., 1914. Sønderjyllands Bronzealder. *Aarbøger for nordisk Oldkyndighed og Historie*, 1914, 195-384.

Müller 2001
  Müller, J., 2001. *Soziochronologische Studien zum Jung- und Spätneolithikum im Mittelelbe-Saale-Gebiet (4100-2700 v. Chr.): eine sozialhistorische Interpretation prähistorischer Quellen.* Vorgeschichtliche Forschungen 21. Rahden/Westf.: Leidorf.

Müller 2011
  Müller, J., 2011. Vom Aufräumen der Landschaft. Jungsteinzeit in Nordmitteleuropa. *Archäologie in Deutschland*, 2 (2011), 18- 21.

Müller 2012
  Müller, J., 2012. Aspenstedt-Großer Berg: Ein spätneolithisches Grab mit kupfernem Nietdolch – Hinweis auf eine „verpasste" Innovation. *Prähistorische Zeitung*, 87 (1), 44-57.

Müller 2017
  Müller, J., 2017. *Großsteingräber - Grabenwerke - Langhügel frühe Monumentalbauten Mitteleuropas.* Archäologie in Deutschland. Darmstadt: Theiss.

Müller *et al.* 2012
  Müller, J., Brozio, J.-P., Demnick, D., Fritsch, B., Furholt, M., Hage, F., Hinz, M., Lorenz, L., Mischka, D., Rinne, C., 2012. Periodisierung der Trichterbecher-Gesellschaften. Ein Arbeitsentwurf. *In*: M. Hinz and J. Müller, eds. *Siedlung, Grabenwerk, Großsteingrab Studien zu Gesellschaft, Wirtschaft und Umwelt der Trichterbechergruppen im nördlichen Mitteleuropa.* Frühe Monumentalität und soziale Differenzierung 2. Bonn: Habelt Verlag, 29-33.

Müller *et al.* 2016
  Müller, J., Hofmann, R., Brandstetter, L., Ohlrau, R., Videjko, M.J., 2016. Chronology and Demography: How Many People Lived in a Mega-Site? *In*: J. Müller, K. Rassmann, M.J. Videjko, eds. *Trypillia Mega-Sites and European prehistory 4100-3400 BCE.* Themes in contemporary archaeology 2. London, New York: Routledge, 134-170.

Müller/Kohl 1966
  Müller, H.M. and Kohl, G., 1966. Radiocarbondatierungen zur jüngeren Vegetationsentwicklung Südostmecklenburgs. *Flora oder Allgemeine botanische Zeitung*, 156 (4), 408-418.

Müller/Lohrke 2012
  Müller, J. and Lohrke, B., 2012. Aspenstedt-Großer Berg: Ein spätneolithisches Grab mit kupfernem Nietdolch – Hinweis auf eine „verpasste" Innovation. *Prähistorische Zeitschrift*, 87 (1), 44-57.

Müller/Mestorf 1878
Müller, S. and Mestorf, J., 1878. *Die nordische Bronzezeit und deren Periodenthei-lung.* Jena: H. Costenoble.

Müller/Staude 2012
Müller, J. and Staude, K., 2012. Typologien, Vertikalstratigraphien und absolutch-ronologische Daten: Zur Chronologie des nordwestmecklenburgischen Trichter-becherfundplatzes Triwalk, *In*: M. Hinz and J. Müller, eds. *Siedlung, Grabenwerk, Großsteingrab. Studien zu Gesellschaft, Wirtschaft und Umwelt der Trichterbech-ergruppen im nördlichen Mitteleuropa.* Frühe Monumentalität und soziale Differ-enzierung 2. Bonn: Habelt Verlag, 35-59.

Müller/Rassmann 2016
Müller, J. and Rassmann, K., 2016. Introduction. *In*: J. Müller, K. Rassmann, M. J. Videjko, eds. *Trypillia Mega-Sites and European prehistory 4100-3400 BCE.* Themes in contemporary archaeology 2. London, New York: Routledge, 1-6.

Nagel 1985
Nagel, E., 1985. *Die Erscheinungen der Kugelamphorenkultur im Norden der DDR.* Berlin: VEB Deutscher Verlag der Wissenschaften.

Nagel 1991
Nagel, E., 1991. Zur Chronologie der Mecklenburgischen Trichterbecherkultur, *In*: D. Jankowska, ed. *Die Trichterbecherkultur. Neue Forschungen und Hypothe-sen II.* Poznań: Instytut Prahistorii Uniwersytetu im. Adama Mickiewicza.

Nagel/Welcher 1992
Nagel, E. and Welcher, K.-P., 1992. Eine Siedlung der Trichterbecherkultur bei Gristow, Kreis Greifswald. *Bodendenkmalpflege in Mecklenburg-Vorpommern* 39, 7-72.

Němejcová-Pavúková 1970
Němejcová-Pavúková, V., 1970. Kultúra s kanelovanou keramikou. *In*: A. Točík, ed. *Slovensko v mladšej dobe kamennej.* Bratislava: Vydavateľstvo SAV, 182-206.

Neumann 2015
Neumann, D., 2015. *Landschaften der Ritualisierung: die Fundplätze kupfer- und bronzezeitlicher Metalldeponierungen zwischen Donau und Po.* Berlin, Boston: De Gruyter.

Neumann 1996
Neumann, H., 1996. Oldtidsbebyggelsen på Haderslev næs. *Haderslev Amts Museum*, 12, 13-24.

Nielsen 1982
Nielsen, J.N., 1982. Iron Age Settlement and Cemetry at Sejflod in Himmerland, North Jütland. Excavations 1973-1980. *Journal of Danish Archaeology*, 1982 (1), 105-117 & 169, Nr. 16.

Nielsen/Rassmussen 1986
Nielsen, J.N. and Rassmussen, M., 1986. *Sejlflod – en jernalderlandsby ved Lim-fjorden.* Ålborg: Ålborg Historiske Museum.

Niklasson 1925
Niklasson, N.H., 1925. Studien über die Walternienburg-Bernburger Kultur. *Jahresschrift für die Vorgeschichte der sächsisch-thüringischen Länder*, 13, 1-183.

Nilius 1971
Nilius, I., 1971. *Das Neolithikum in Mecklenburg zur Zeit und unter besonderer Berücksichtigung der Trichterbecherkultur.* Schwerin: Volksdruckerei Ludwigslust.

Nilius 1973
Nilius, I., 1973. Die Siedlung der Trichterbecherkultur bei Gristow, Kr. Greifswald. Ein Beitrag zum neolithischen Siedlungswesen in Mecklenburg. *Zeitschrift für Archäologie* 7, 239-270.

Nilius 1975
Nilius, I., 1975. Bemerkungen zu einigen auffälligen Keramikfunden in der Trich-terbechersiedlung von Gristow, Kreis Greifswald. *In*: J. Preuß, F. Schlette, eds.

Symbolae Praehistoricae. Festschrift zum 50. Geburtstag von Friedrich Schlette.
Berlin, Boston: De Gruyter.

Nørgaard 2017

Nørgaard, H.W., 2017. Portable XRF on Prehistoric Bronze Artefacts: Limitations and Use for the Detection of Bronze Age Metal Workshops. *Open Archaeology*, 3 (1).

Nørgaard *et al.* 2021

Nørgaard, H.W., Pernicka, E., Vandkilde, H., 2021. Shifting networks and mixing metals: Changing metal trade routes to Scandinavia correlate with Neolithic and Bronze Age transformations, *PLoS ONE*, 16 (6), e0252376.

Nordmann 1927

Nordmann, C.A., 1927. Den Yngre Stenåldern i Mellan-Väst och Nordeuropa. *In*: K. Friis-Johansen, ed. *De Forhistoriske Tider i Europa II*. Kopenhagen: Koppel, 1-168.

Nordmann 1935

Nordmann, C.A., 1935. The megalithic culture of northern Europe. *Finska Forn-minnesföreningens Tidsskrift*, 39.

Northover 1996a

Northover, J.P., 1996. Comparison of Metal Analyses by Different Laboratories and Methods. *In*: H. Vandkilde, ed. *From Stone to Bronze. The Metalwork of the Late Neolithic and Earliest Bronze Age in Denmark.* Jutland Archaeology Society Publikations 32. Aarhus: Aarhus University Press, 359-367.

Northover 1996b

Northover, J.P., 1996. Metal Analysis and Metallography of Early Metal Objects from Denmark. *In*: H. Vandkilde, ed. *From Stone to Bronze. The Metalwork of the Late Neolithic and Earliest Bronze Age in Denmark.* Jutland Archaeology Society Publikations 32. Aarhus: Aarhus University Press, 321-358.

Novotná 1982

Novotná, B., 1982. Zur Stellung einiger Kupferdolche an der mittleren Donau. *Thracia praehistorica*, Pulpudeva 3, 311-319.

Oldeberg 1942

Oldeberg, A., 1942. *Metallteknik under Förhistorisk Tid.* Metallteknik under Förhistorisk Tid 1. Lund: O. Harrassowitz.

Oldeberg 1974

Oldeberg, A., 1974. *Die ältere Metallzeit in Schweden 1.* Stockholm: Kungl. Vitterhets Historie och Antikvitets Akademien.

Oldeberg 1976

Oldeberg, A., 1967. *Die ältere Metallzeit in Schweden 2.* Stockholm: Kungl. Vitterhets Historie och Antikvitets Akademien.

Orfanou/Rehren 2015

Orfanou, V. and Rehren, T., 2015. A (not so) dangerous method: pXRF vs. EPMA-WDS analyses of copper-based artefacts. *Archaeological and Anthropological Sciences*, 7 (3), 387-397.

O'Flaherty 2007a

O'Flaherty, R., 2007. The Irish Early Bronze Age halberd: practical experiment and combat possibilities. *In*: B. Molloy, ed. *The cutting edge: Studies in ancient and medieval combat.* Stroud: History Press Ltd. 77-89.

O'Flaherty 2007b

O'Flaherty, R., 2007. *A weapon of choice – experiments with a replica Irish Early Bronze Age halberd. Antiquity*, 81 (312), 423–434.

O'Kelly 1989

O'Kelly, M.J., 1989. *Early Ireland: An introduction to Irish prehistory.* Cambridge: Cambridge University Press.

Ó Ríordáin 1937

Ó Ríordáin, S.P., 1937. The Halberd in Bronze Age Europe. A study in prehistoric origins, evolution, distribution, and chronology. *Archaeologia*, 86, 195-321.

Ottaway 1973a

Ottaway, B., 1973. An analysis of cultural relations in neolithic north - central Europe based on copper ornaments. *In*: C. Renfrew, ed. *The explanation of cultural change - models in archaeology.* London: Duckworth, 609-616.

Ottaway 1973b

Ottaway, B., 1973. The earliest copper ornaments in Northern Europe. *Proceedings of the Prehistoric Society*, 39, 294-331.

Otto/Witter 1952

Otto, H. and Witter, W., 1952. *Handbuch der ältesten vorgeschichtlichen Metallurgie in Mitteleuropa.* Leipzig: Johann Ambrosius Barth.

Passariello *et al.* 2010

Passariello, I., Talamo, P., D'Onofrio, A., Barta, P., Lubritto, C., Terrasi, F., 2010. Contribution of Radiocarbon Dating to the Chronology of Eneolithic in Campania (Italy). *Geochronometria*, 35 (1), 25-33.

Patay 1958

Patay, P., 1958. Kupferzeitliche Goldfunde. *Archaeologiai Értesítő*, 85, 37-46.

Patay 2005

Patay, P., 2005. *Kupferzeitliche Siedlung Tiszaluc.* Inventaria Praehistorica Hungariae IPH XI. Budapest: Magyar Nemzeti Múzeum.

Pavúk 2010

Pavúk, J., 2010. Neuere äneolithische Kupferfunde aus der Westslowakei. *Slovenská archeológia LVIII*, 2, 229-242.

Pernicka 1990

Pernicka, E., 1990. Gewinnung und Verbreitung der Metalle in prähistorischer Zeit. *Jahrbuch des Römisch-Germanischen Zentralmuseums Mainz*, 37, 21-129.

Pernicka 1999

Pernicka, E., 1999. Trace element fingerprinting of ancient copper: a guide to technology or provenance? *In*: S.M.M. Young, M.A. Pollard, P. Budd, R.A. Ixer, eds. *Metals in Antiquity. International symposium at Harvard University from 10 to 13 September 1997.* Oxford: Archaeopress, 163-172.

Pernicka *et al.* 1993

Pernicka, E., Begemann, F., Schmitt-Strecker, S., Wagner, G.A., 1993. Eneolithic and Early Bronze Age copper artefacts from the Balkans and their relation to Serbian copper ores. *Praehistorische Zeitschrift*, 68, 1-54.

Petrescu-Dîmbovița 1998

Petrescu-Dîmbovița, M., 1998. *Der Arm- und Beinschmuck in Rumänien.* Prähistorische Bronzefunde, Abteilung X. Stuttgart: Franz Steiner Verlag.

Petzsch 1926

Petzsch, W., 1926. Wertvolle Neuerwerbungen des Stralsunder Museums von der Insel Ruegen. *Prähistorische Zeitschrift*, 17, 233-241.

Petzsch 1933

Petzsch, W., 1933. Zum Depotfund von Bygholm. *Mannus*, 25,137-145.

Pflederer *et al.* 2009

Pflederer, T., Mainberger, M., Beer, H., 2009. Außenposten am Rand der Alpen: Die jungneolithische Seeufersiedlung Berg-Kempfenhausen. *Bericht der bayrischen Bodendenkmalpflege*, 50, 125-136.

Pittioni 1957

Pittioni, R., 1957. *Urzeitlicher Bergbau auf Kupfererz und Spurenanalyse: Beiträge zum Problem der Relation Lagerstätte-Fertigobjekt.* Archaeologia Austriaca. Wien: Deuticke.

Pollmann 2015

Pollmann, H.-O., 2015. Die Galeriegräber von Warburg. Die Skelette aus der Galeriegrabnekropole von Warburg und aufgehende Steimauern in der Siedlung Warburg-Menne. *In*: T. Otten, J. Kunow, M.M. Rind, M. C. Trier, eds. *Revolution jungSteinzeit: Archäologische Landesausstellung Nordrhein-Westfalen.* Schriften zur Bodendenkmalpflege in Nordrhein-Westfalen. Darmstadt: Theiss, 395-398.

Preuß 1958

Preuß, J., 1958. Ein Grabhügel der Baalberger Gruppe von Preußlitz, Kr. Bernburg. *Jahresschrift für mitteldeutsche Vorgeschichte,* 41/42, 197-212.

Preuß 1966

Preuß, J., 1966. *Die Baalberger Gruppe in Mitteldeutschland.* Berlin: Deutscher Verlag der Wissenschaften.

Priebe 1938

Priebe, H., 1938. *Die Westgruppe der Kugelamphoren.* Jahresschrift für die Vorgeschichte der sächsisch-thüringischen Länder 28, Beiträge zur Steinzeitforschung. Saale: Gebauer-Schwetschke 1-114.

Primas 1996

Primas, M., 1996. *Velika Gruda 1 Hügelgräber des frühen 3. Jahrtausends v. Chr. im Adriagebiet - Velika Gruda, Mala Gruda und ihr Kontext.* Universitätsforschungen zur prähistorischen Archäologie. Bonn: Habelt Verlag.

Przybyla/Tunia 2013

Przybyla, M. and Tunia, K., 2013. Investigations in 2012 of the southern part of the Funnel Beaker culture temenos at Słonowice near the Małoszówka river. *In:* P. Włodarczak and S. Kadrow, eds. *Environment and subsistence: forty years after Janusz Kruk's „Settlement studies".* Studien zur Archäologie in Ostmitteleuropa 11. Rzeszów: Institute of Archaeology Rzeszów University, 139-160.

R Core Team 2016

R Core Team, R: A Language and Environment for Statistical Computing. Vienna, Austria. Online verfügbar unter https://www.R-project.org/ (State: 2016).

Raczky/Siklósi 2013

Raczky, P. and Siklósi, Z., 2013. Reconsideration of the Copper Age chornology of the eastern Carpathian Basin: a Bayesian approach. *Antiquity,* 87, 555-573.

Radivojević *et al.* 2010

Radivojević, M., Rehren, T., Pernicka, E., Šljivar, D., Brauns, M., Borić, D., 2010. On the origins of extractive metallurgy: new evidence from Europe. *Journal of Archaeological Science,* 37, 2775-2787.

Raetzel-Fabian 2000

Raetzel-Fabian, D., 2000. *Calden: Erdwerk und Bestattungsplätze des Jungneolithikums; Architektur, Ritual, Chronologie.* Universitätsforschungen zur prähistorischen Archäologie. Bonn. Habelt Verlag.

Randsborg 1970

Randsborg, K., 1970. Eine kupferne Schmuckscheibe aus einem Dolmen in Jütland. *Acta archaeologica,* 41, 181-190.

Randsborg 1980a

Randsborg, K., 1980. Kobberalder. *Skalk,* 1980-5, 9-11.

Randsborg 1980b

Randsborg, K., 1980. Omkring to kobberøkser fra stenalderen. Årbog for Svendborg & Omegns Museum, 1979, 7-11.

Randsborg 1988

Randsborg, K., 1988. The neolithic copper discs from Rude, Jutland and Hřivice. *Acta archaeologica,* 58 (1987), 234-236.

Rasmussen 2000

Rasmussen, K.L., 2000. ¹⁴C-dateringer, København 2000. *Arkæologiske Udgravninger i Danmark - Archaeological excavations in Denmark 2000,* 2000, 332.

Rassmann/Schafferer 2012

Rassmann, K. and Schafferer, G., 2012. Demography, Social Identities, and the Architecture of Megalithic Graves in the South-Western Baltic Area. *In:* J. Müller and M. Hinz, eds. *Siedlung, Graberwerk, Großsteingrab: Studien zu Ge-*

sellschaft, Wirtschaft und Umwelt der Trichterbechergruppen im nördlichen Mitteleuropa. Frühe Monumentalität und soziale Differenzierung 2. Bonn: Habelt Verlag, 107-120.

Rech *et al.* 1979

Rech, M., Struve, K.W., Hinz, H., 1979. *Studien zu Depotfunden der Trichterbecher- und Einzelgrabkultur des Nordens.* Offa-Bücher 39. Neumünster: Wachholtz Verlag.

Rehren *et al.* 2012

Rehren, T., Boscher, L., Pernicka, E., 2012. Large scale smelting of speiss and arsenical copper at Early Bronze Age Arisman, Iran. *Journal of Archaeological Science,* 39 (6), 1717–27.

Rehren/Prange 1998

Rehren T. and Prange, M., 1998. Lead metal and patina - a comparison. *In*: T, Rehren, A. Hauptmann, J.D. Muhly, eds. *Metallurgica antiqua: in honour of Hans-Gert Bachmann and Robert Maddin.* Bochum: Deutsches Bergbaumuseum, 183-196.

Reimer *et al.* 2013

Reimer, P., Bard, E., Bayliss, A., Beck, W.J., Blackwell, P.G., Bronk Ramsey, C., Buck, C.E., Edwards, L., Friedrich, M., Grootes, P.M., Guilderson, T.P., Haflidason, H., Hajdas, I., Hatté, C., Heaton, T.J., Hoffmann, D.L., Hogg, A.G., Hughen, K.A., Kaiser, F., Kromer, B., Manning, S.W., Niu, M., Reimer, R.W., Richards, D.A., Scott, M., Southon, J.R., Staff, J.R., Turney, C.S.M., Plicht, J.v.d., 2013. IntCal13 and Marine13 Radiocarbon Age Calibration Curves 0–50,000 Years cal BP. *Radiocarbon,* 55 (4), 1869- 1887.

Reinecke 1930

Reinecke, P., 1930. Ein Kupferfund aus der Dolmenzeit. *Mainzer Zeitschrift,* 1929/1930, 58- 67.

Reyman 1936

Reyman, T., 1936. *Groby z wczesnej epoki bronzowej w Goszycach, w pow. miechowskim.* Przegląd Archeologiczny Tom 5, Roczniki 15-18. Poznań: Polskie Towarzystwo Prehistoryczne, 101-103.

Rezepkin 2000

Rezepkin, A. D., 2000. *Das frühbronzezeitliche Gräberfeld von Klady und die Majkop-Kultur in Nordwestkaukasien.* Archäologie in Eurasien 10. Rahden/Westfalen: Verlag Marie Leidorf.

Richardson *et al.* 2010

Richardson, T., Graham, M., Lindsay, R., Lyon, S., Scantlebury, D., Stott, H., Cottis, B., eds., 2010. *Shreir's Corrosion.* Oxford: Elsevier.

Robbiola et al. 1998

Robbiola, L., Blengino, J-M., Fiaud C., 1998. Morphology and mechanisms of formation of natural patinas on archaeological Cu–Sn alloys. *Corrosion Science* 40, 2083-2111.

Robbiola/Portier 2006

Robbiola, L. and Portier, R., 2006. A global approach to the authentication of ancient bronzes based on the characterization of the alloy–patina–environment system. *Journal of Cultural Heritage* 7, 1-12.

Röschmann 1963

Röschmann, J., 1963. *Vorgeschichte des Kreises Flensburg.* Die Vor- und Frühgeschichtlichen Denkmäler und Funde in Schleswig- Holstein 6. Neumünster: Wachholtz Verlag.

Rosenstock *et al.* 2016

Rosenstock, E., Scharl, S., Schier, W., 2016. Ex oriente lux? - Ein Diskussionsbeitrag zur Stellung der frühen Kupfermetallurgie Südosteuropas. *In*: M. Bartelheim, B. Horejs, R. Krauß, E. Pernicka, eds. *Von Baden bis Troia Ressourcennutzung, Metal-*

lurgie und Wissenstransfer: eine Jubiläumsschrift für Ernst Pernicka. Oriental and European archaeology. Rahden, Westf.: Verlag Marie Leidorf, 59-122.

Rydbeck 1926

Rydbeck, O., 1926. Nyare förvärv från koppar- och bronsåldern i Lunds universitets historiska museum. *Fornvännen,* 21-22, 281-306.

Rydbeck 1928

Rydbeck, O., 1928. Stenåldershavets nivåförändringar och nordens äldsta bebyggelse. *Kungliga Humanistiska Vetenskapssamfundet i Lund,* 1927/1928, 35-130.

Rydbeck 1939

Rydbeck, O., 1939. Forminnen i Villands häräd. *Skånes Hembygdsförbunds Årsbok,* 1939, 3ff.

Saalow 2010

Saalow, L., 2010. Kurze Fundberichte. *Bodendenkmalpflege in Mecklenburg-Vorpommern,* 57 (2009), 412.

Sáez/Lerma 2015

Sáez, C. and Lerma, I.M., 2015. Traceology On Metal. Use-Wear Marks on Copper-Based Tools and Weapons. *In*: J. Marreiros, J. F. Gibaja Bao, N. F. Bicho, eds. *Use-Wear and Residue Analysis in Archaeology.* Cham, Heidelberg, New York, Dordrecht, London: Springer Verlag, 171-188.

Sangmeister *et al.* 1968

Sangmeister, E., Junghans, S., Schröder, M., 1968. *Kupfer und Bronze in der frühen Metallzeit Europas: Katalog der Analysen Nr. 985 - 10040.* Studien zu den Anfängen der Metallurgie 2. Berlin: Gebr. Mann Verlag.

Sangmeister *et al.* 1974

Sangmeister, E., Junghans, S., Schröder, M. 1974. *Mainz. Römisch-Germanisches Zentral-Museum., Kupfer und Bronze in der frühen Metallzeit Europas: Katalog der Analysen Nr. 10041 - 22000.* Studien zu den Anfängen der Metallurgie 2. Berlin: Gebr. Mann Verlag.

Schanz 2014

Schanz, E., 2014. Siedlungsgeschichte im Tollensegebiet - Ein Überblick. *In*: D. Jantzen, J. Orschiedt, J. Piek, T. Terberger, eds. *Tod im Tollensetal: Forschungen zu den Hinterlassenschaften eines bronzezeitlichen Gewaltkonfliktes in Mecklenburg-Vorpommern. Teil 1 Die Forschungen bis 2011.* Beiträge Ur- Frühgeschichte Rostock, Schwerin, Neubrandenburg. Schwerin: Landesarchäologie MV, 21-27.

Schauer 1979

Schauer, P., 1979. Eine urnenfelderzeitliche Kampfweise. *Archäologisches Korrespondenzblatt,* 9 (1), 65-87.

Schierhold 2019

Schierhold, K., 2019. Case-Study of Erwitte-Schmerlecke, Westphalia. An archaeological contribution to Hessian Westphalian Megaliths and their role in early monumentality of the Northern European Plain. *In*: J. Müller, M. Hinz, M. Wunderlich, eds. *Megaliths – Societies – Landscapes. Early Monumentality and Social Differentiation in Neolithic Europe. Proceedings of the international conference »Megaliths – Societies – Landscapes.* Frühe Monumentalität und soziale Differenzierung 18 (Proceedings of the international conference »Megaliths – Societies – Landscapes. Early Monumentality and Social Differentiation in Neolithic Europe« (16th–20th June 2015) in Kiel). Bonn: Habelt Verlag, 289-318.

Schierhold/Hiß 2012

Schierhold, K. and Hiß, M., 2012. *Studien zur hessisch-westfälischen Megalithik: Forschungsstand und -perspektiven im europäischen Kontext.* Münstersche Beiträge zur ur- und frühgeschichtlichen Archäologie 6 Rahden/Westf.: Verlag Marie Leidorf.

Schirren 2004

Schirren, M., 2004. Kurze Fundberichte. Stichwort Nustrow, Lkr. Bad Doberan. *Bodendenkmalpflege in Mecklenburg,* 52, 622

Schirren 2008
> Schirren, M., 2008. Kurze Fundberichte. Stichwort Nadrensee, Lkr. Uecker-Randow. *Bodendenkmalpflege in Mecklenburg-Vorpommern*, 55, 265.

Schirren 2015
> Schirren, M., 2015. Kurze Fundberichte. Stichwort Niepars, Lkr. Vorpommern-Ruegen. *Bodendenkmalpflege in Mecklenburg-Vorpommern*, 61, 243.

Schlicht 1954
> Schlicht, E., 1954. 2. Urgeschichtliche Denkmalpflege. Fundbericht für das Jahr 1953. Stichwort Emmeln. *Jahrbuch des Emsländischen Heimatvereins*, 1954, 197 f.

Schlicht 1957
> Schlicht, E., 1957. Die Untersuchung eines zerstörten Steingrabes bei Uelsen. *Jahrbuch des des Heimatvereins der Grafschaft Bentheim*, 4, 15 ff.

Schlicht 1973
> Schlicht, E., 1973. *Kupferschmuck aus Megalithgräbern Nordwestdeutschlands*. Aus Niedersachsens Frühzeit 42. Hildesheim: Wachholtz Verlag.

Schmidt/Sterum 1987
> Schmidt, O.A. and Sterum, N.T., 1987. Kongenshøjvej. *Journal of Danish Archaeology*, 5 (261), Nr. 12.

Schmitz 2004
> Schmitz, A., 2004. *Typologische, chronologische und paläometallurgische Untersuchungen zu den frühkupferzeitlichen Kupferflachbeilen und Kupfermeißeln in Alteuropa*. Saarbücken: Saarländische Universitäts- und Landesbibliothek.

Schneeweiß 2000
> Schneeweiß, J. 2000. *Der Werder. Mecklenburg und seine Besiedlung in frühgeschichtlicher Zeit*. Weissbach: Beier & Beran.

Schoknecht 1991
> Schoknecht, U. ed. 1991. *Zislow – Ergebnisse archäologischer Untersuchungen*. Beiträge zur Archäologie Mecklenburg-Vorpommerns 25. Lübstorf: Archäologisches Landesmuseum Mecklenburg-Vorpommern.

Schoknecht 1996
> Schoknecht, T., 1996. *Pollenanalytische Untersuchungen zur Vegetations-, Siedlungs- und Landschaftsgeschichte in Mittelmecklenburg*. Beiträge zur Ur- und Frühgeschichte Mecklenburg-Vorpommerns 29. Lübstorf: Archäologisches Landesmuseum für Mecklenburg-Vorpommern.

Schreiner 2007
> Schreiner, M., 2007. *Erzlagerstätten im Hrontal, Slowakei. Genese und Prähistorische Nutzung*. Rahden/Westf.: Verlag Marie Leidorf.

Schrickel 1966
> Schrickel, W., 1966. *Westeuropäische Elemente im neolithischen Grabbau Mitteldeutschlands und die Galeriegräber Westdeutschlands und ihre Inventare*. Beiträge zur ur- und frühgeschichtlichen Archäologie des Mittelmeer-Kulturraumes 4/5. Bonn: Habelt Verlag.

Schroller 1933
> Schroller, H., 1933. *Die Stein- und Kupferzeit Siebenbürgens*. Vorgeschichtliche Forschungen 8. Berlin: De Gruyter.

Schubart 1972
> Schubart, H., 1972. *Die Funde der älteren Bronzezeit in Mecklenburg*. Offa-Bücher 26. Neumünster: Wachholtz Verlag.

Schuldt 1953
> E. Schuldt, Kurze Fundberichte. Jahrbuch für Bodendenkmalpflege in Mecklenburg 1953, 1953, 165.

Schuldt 1966
> Schuldt, E., 1966. Der Grossdolmen von Liepen, Kreis Rostock. *Bodendenkmalpflege in Mecklenburg*, 1966, 46-70.

Schuldt 1970
Schuldt, E., 1970. Tätigkeitsbericht des Museums für Ur- und Frühgeschichte Schwerin für die Zeit vom 1.4.1969 bis 31.3.1970. *Ausgrabungen und Funde Berlin* 15.

Schuldt 1972a
Schuldt, E., 1972. *Die mecklenburgischen Megalithgräber; Untersuchungen zu ihrer Architektur und Funktion.* Berlin: Deutscher Verlag d. Wiss.

Schuldt 1972b
Schuldt, E., 1972. *Steinzeitliche Keramik aus Mecklenburg.* Schwerin: Museum für Ur- und Frühgeschichte.

Schuldt 1974
Schuldt, E., 1974. Die steinzeitliche Inselsiedlung im Malchiner See bei Basedow, Kreis Malchin. *Bodendenkmalpflege in Mecklenburg-Vorpommern* 1973, 7-65.

Schulz 1983
Schulz, H.D., 1983. Zuordnung von Kupfer-Metall zum Ausgangserz. Möglichkeiten und Grenzen der Methode. *Prähistorische Zeitschrift,* 58 (1), 1-14.

Schüßler 1939
Schüßler, H., 1939. Die Feldmark Hornshagen und ihr Reichtum an vorgeschichtlichen Funden. *Mecklenburg: Zeitschrift des Heimatbundes Mecklenburg,* 34 (2), 97-101.

Schunke 2013
Schunke, T., 2013. Klady - Göhlitzsch. Vom Kaukasus nach Mitteldeutschland oder umgekehrt? *In*: H. Meller, ed. *3300 BC: mysteriöse Steinzeittote und ihre Welt.* Mainz a. Rhein: Nünnerich-Asmus, 151-155.

Schwabedissen 1979
Schwabedissen, H., 1979. Zum Alter der Großsteingräber in Norddeutschland. *In*: H. Schirnig, ed. *Großsteingräber in Niedersachsen 24.* Hildesheim: Verlagsbuchhandlung, 143-160.

Scott 2002
Scott, D.A., 2002. *Copper and Bronze in Art: Corrosion, Colorants, Conservation.* Los Angeles: Getty Conservation Institute.

Seger 1906
Seger, H., 1906. Die Steinzeit in Schlesien. *Archiv für Anthropologie* Neue Folge V, 1/2, 1906, 118-141.

Sehested 1878
Sehested, F., 1878. *Fortidsminder og Oldsager fra Egnen om Broholm.* Kjøbenhavn: Reitzel.

Selent 2014
Selent, A., 2014. Hochinteressant! Jungesteinzeitliche Kulturschicht und rätselhafte Kreisgräben bei Jatznick, Lkr. Vorpommern-Greifswald. *In*: D. Jantzen, L. Saalow, J.-P. Schmidt, eds. *Pipeline Archäologie. Ausgrabungen auf den großen Ferngastrassen in Mecklenburg-Vorpommern.* Schwerin: Landesamt für Kultur und Denkmalpflege Mecklenburg-Vorpommern, 67-76.

Semenov 1964
Semenov, S.A., 1964. *Prehistoric technology: An experimental study of the oldest tools and artefacts from traces of manufacture and wear.* London: Adams & Dart.

Sergeev 1963
Sergeev, G.P., 1963. Tré du Tripolje antérieur près du village Karboune. *Sowjetskaja Archeologija,* 193 (1), 135-155.

Sprockhoff 1930
Sprockhoff, E., 1930. Zur Megalithkultur Nordwestdeutschlands. *Nachrichten aus Niedersachsens Urgeschichte,* 4, 1-56.

Sprockhoff 1938
Sprockhoff, E., 1938. *Die nordische Megalithkultur.* Handbuch der Urgeschichte Deutschlands. Berlin/Leipzig: De Gruyter.

Stadler 1995

Stadler, P., 1995. Ein Beitrag zur Absolutchronologie des Neolithikums in Ostösterreich aufgrund der ¹⁴C-Daten. *In*: E. Lenneis, C. Neugebauer-Maresch, E. Ruttkay, eds. *Jungsteinzeit im Osten Österreichs*. Wissenschaftliche Schriftenreihe Niederösterreich 102/105. St. Pölten-Wien: Niederösterreichisches Pressehaus.

Stapel 2008

Stapel, B., 2008. Stichwort „Beckum-Dalmer". *Neujahrsgruß. Jahresbericht der LWL-Archäologie für Westfalen und der Altertumskommission für Westfalen*, 2008, 64.

Stapel 2015

Stapel, B., 2015. Begrabene Böden, Gräber, Häuser. Der spätneolithische Fundplatz Heek-Ammerter Mark, Kr. Borken (Münsterland). *In*: T. Otten, J. Kunow, M.M. Rind, M.C. Trier, eds. *Revolution jungSteinzeit: Archäologische Landesausstellung Nordrhein-Westfalen*. Schriften zur Bodendenkmalpflege in Nordrhein-Westfalen. Darmstadt: Theiss, 376-379.

Stapfer *et al.* 2018

Stapfer, R.B., Heitz, C., Hinz, M., Hafner, A., 2018. Portable Röntgenfluoreszenzanalytik (pXRF): Mit dem „Labor in der Hand" der Vergangenheit auf der Spur. *In*: T. Burri and R.B. Stapfer, eds. *Naturwissenschaftliche Methoden in der Archäologie*. Mitteilungen der Naturforschenden Gesellschaft in Bern 75. Bern: Seline Aldrige, rubmedia.

Staude 2013

Staude, K., 2013. *Lineares Grubenwerk und Siedlungsplatz Triwalk, Landkreis Nordwestmecklenburg zur Chronologie der Trichterbecherkultur in Mecklenburg-Vorpommern*. Dissertation, Christian-Albrechts-Universität zu Kiel.

Steffens 2009

Steffens, J., 2009. *Die neolithischen Fundplätze von Rastorf, Kreis Plön. Eine Fallstudie zur Trichterbecherkultur im nördlichen Mitteleuropa am Beispiel eines Siedlungsraums*. Universitätsforschungen zur prähistorischen Archäologie 170. Bonn: Habelt Verlag.

Sterum 1986

Sterum, N.T., 1986. Kongenshøjvej. *Arkæologiske Udgravninger i Danmark 1985*, 109 (254).

Stieren 1929

Stieren, A., 1929. *Ein Bericht über die Grabungen und Funde für die Jahre 1925 bis 1928*. Bodenaltertümer Westfalens 1. Münster i.W.: Westfälische Vereinsdruckerei A.-G.

Stronach 1957

Stronach, D.B., 1957. The development and diffusion of metal types in early Bronze Age Anatolia. *Anatolian Studies*, 7 (1957), 89-125.

Stos-Gale *et al.* 1998

Stos-Gale, Z.A., Gale, N.H., Annetts Lilov, N., Todorov, T., Lilov, P., Raduncheva, A., Panayotov, I., 1998. Lead isotope data from the Isotrace Laboratory, Oxford: Archaeometry Database 5, Ores from Bulgaria. *Archaeometry*, 40 (1), 217-226.

Stos-Gale/Bajenaru 2020

Stos-Gale, Z.A. and Bajenaru, R., 2020. The Aegean and the Black Sea connecting southeast Europe and Anatolia during the Early bronze Age: evidence from metal finds in Bulgaria, Greece and western Turkey. *In*: J. Maran, R. Bajenaru, S.-C. Ailincai, A.D. Popescu, S. Hansen, eds. *Objects, ideas and travellers. Contacts between the Balkans, the Aegean and Western Anatolia during the Bronze and Early iron Age*. Universitätsforschungen zur Prähistorischen Archäologie 350, Institut für Ur- und Frühgeschichte der Universität Heidelberg. Bonn: Habelt Verlag, 265-285.

Stos-Gale/Gale 2009

Stos-Gale, Z.A., and Gale, N.H., 2009. Metal provenancing using isotopes and the Oxford archaeological lead isotope database (OXALID). *Archaeological and Anthropological Sciences*, 1(3), 195-213.

Stubenrauch 1904

Stubenrauch, A., 1904. *Die Maaßsche prähistorische Sammlung im Museum der Gesellschaft für Pommersche Geschichte und Altertumskunde.* Baltische Studien, Neue Folge 8. Stettin: Herrcke & Lebeling, 96-129.

Sylvest/Sylvest 1959

Sylvest, B. and Sylvest, I., 1959. En skovlfuld rav og lidt metal. *Skalk: nyt om gammelt,* 1, 17-18.

Sylvest/Sylvest 1960

Sylvest, B. and Sylvest, I., 1960. Arupgardfunde. *Kuml,* 1960, 9-25.

Szpunar 1987

Szpunar, A., 1987. *Die Beile in Polen I: (Flachbeile, Randleistenbeile, Randleistenmeißel).* Prähistorische Bronzefunde 16, Abteilung IX. München: C.H. Beck.

Sztáncsuj 2005

Sztáncsuj, S.J., 2005. The Early Copper Age hoard from Ariușd (Erösd). *In:* G. Dumitroaia, J. Chapman, O. Weller, C. Preoteasa, R. Munteanu, D. Nicolae, D. Monah, eds. *Cucuteni. 120 years of research time to sum up.* Piatra-Neamț: Constantin Matasă, 85-105.

Terberger 1997

Terberger, T., 1997. Zur ältesten Besiedlungsgeschichte Mecklenburg-Vorpommerns. *Archäologische Berichte aus Mecklenburg-Vorpommern,* 4, 6-22.

Terberger/Piek 1998

Terberger, T. and Piek, J., 1998. Zur absoluten Chronologie der Steinzeit in Mecklenburg-Vorpommern. *Bodendenkmalpflege in Mecklenburg-Vorpommern* 1997, 7-40.

Thornton 2009

Thornton, C.P., 2009. The Emerge of Complex Metallurgy on the Iranian Plateau: Escaping the Levantine Paradigm. *Journal of World Prehistory,* 22, 301–327.

Todorova/Vajsov 2001

Todorova, C. and Vajsov, I., 2001. *Der kupferzeitliche Schmuck Bulgariens.* Prähistorische Bronzefunde 6, Abteilung XX. Stuttgart: Franz Steiner Verlag.

Tostmann 2001

Tostmann, K.-H., 2001. *Korrosion Ursachen und Vermeidung.* Weinheim: Wiley-VCH Verlag.

Tuck *et al.* 2010

Tuck, C.D.S., Powell, C.A., Nuttall, J., 2010. 3.07 - Corrosion of Copper and its Alloys. *In:* T. Richardson, M. Graham, R. Lindsay, S. Lyon, D. Scantlebury, H. Stott, eds. *Shreir's Corrosion.* Oxford: Elsevier, 1937-1973.

Turck 2010

Turck, R., 2010. *Die Metalle zur Zeit des Jungneolithikums in Mitteleuropa: Eine sozialarchäologische Untersuchung.* Universitätsforschungen zur Prähistorischen Archäologie 185. Bonn: Habelt Verlag.

Vajsov 1993

Vajsov, I., 1993. Die frühesten Metalldolche Südost- und Mitteleuropas. *Prähistorische Zeitschrift,* 68, 103–145.

Vajsov 2002

Vajsov, I., 2002. Das Grab 982 und die Protobronzezeit in Bulgarien. *In:* H. Todorova, ed. *Durankulak II - Die prähistorischen Gräberfelder.* Sofia: Publishing House Anubis, 159-176.

Vandkilde 1996

Vandkilde, H., 1996. *From stone to bronze: the metalwork of the Late Neolithic and Earliest Bronze Age in Denmark.* Jutland Archaeological Society publications 32. Højbjerg: Jutland Archaeological Society.

Vang-Petersen 1992

Vang-Petersen, P., 1992. Danefæ 1991. *Arkæologiske Udgravninger i Danmark,* 1991, 212.

Vang-Petersen 1995
Vang-Petersen, P., 1995. Danefæ. *Arkæologiske Udgravninger i Danmark, 1994*, 231-253.

Vergély *et al.* 2006
Vergély, H., Vaquer, J., Remicourt, M., 2006. Les poignards métalliques et lithiques du Chalcolithique pré-campaniforme des petits et Grands Causses dans le Midi de la France. *In*: J. Gascó, F. Leyge, P. Gruat, eds. *Hommes et passé des Causses. Hommage à Georges Costantini*. Toulouse: Centre d'Anthropologie, 155-179.

Viets 1993
Viets, M., 1993. *Das Megalithgrab Espel I, Gemeinde Recke, Kreis Steinfurt: mit einem Anhang der Funde aus Megalithgrab II*. Bodenaltertümer Westfalens 29. Münster: Aschendorff.

Vogt 2009
Vogt, J., 2009. Der Fundplatz Brunn 17 im Landkreis Mecklenburg-Strelitz, Ergebnisse einer Grabung unter besonderer Berücksichtigung der trichterbecherzeitlichen Funde und Befunde. *In*: T. Terberger, ed. *Neue Forschungen zum Neolithikum im Ostseeraum*. Archäologie und Geschichte im Ostseeraum 5. Rahden/Westf.: Verlag Marie Leidorf, 135-236.

Voss 1880
Voss, A., ed. 1880. *Katalog der Ausstellung prähistorischer und anthropologischer Funde Deutschlands*. Berlin: Berg & v. Holten.

Voß *et al.* 1998
Voß, H.-U., Hammer, P., Lutz, J., Bachmann, H.-G., 1998. *Römische und germanische Bunt- und Edelmetallfunde im Vergleich. Archäometallurgische Untersuchungen ausgehend von elbgermanischen Körpergräbern*. Mainz am Rhein: Philipp von Zabern.

Vulpe 1975
Vulpe, A., 1975. *Die Äxte und Beile in Rumänien*. Prähistorische Bronzefunde 2, Abteilung IX. München:

Wagenbreth/Steiner 2015
Wagenbreth, O. and Steiner, W., 2015. *Geologische Streifzüge: Landschaft und Erdgeschichte zwischen Kap Arkona und Fichtelberg*. Berlin [u.a.]: Deutscher Vlg. für Grundstoffindustrie.

Walter 1898
Walter, E., 1898. Die steinzeitlichen Gefäße des Museums Stettin. *In*: Gesellschaft für Pommersche Geschichte und Altertumskunde, ed. *Festschrift zum fünfundzwanzigjährigen Jubiläum des Herrn Gymnasialdirektor Professor H. Lemcke als Vorsitzenden der Gesellschaft für Pommersche Geschichte und Alterthumskunde*. Beiträge zur Geschichte und Alterthumskunde Pommerns. Stettin: Herrcke & Lebeling, 1-20.

Walter 1901
Walter, E., 1901. *Ueber Alterthümer und Ausgrabungen in Pommern im Jahre 1900*. Baltische Studien: Neue Folge 5. Stettin: Herrcke & Lebeling, 245-250.

Walter 1904
Walter, E., 1904. *Ueber Alterthümer und Ausgrabungen in Pommern in 1902-03*. Baltische Studien: Neue Folge 8. Stettin: Herrcke & Lebeling, 152-163.

Walter 1910
Walter, E., 1910. *Ueber Altertümer und Ausgrabungen in Pommern im Jahre 1909*. Baltische Studien: Neue Folge14. Stettin: Herrcke & Lebeling, 174-189.

Walter 1913
Walter, E., 1913. *Ueber Altertümer und Ausgrabungen in Pommern im Jahre 1912*. Baltische Studien Neue Folge 17. Stettin: Herrcke & Lebeling, 324-337.

Watt 1993
Watt, M., 1993. Det antikvariske arbejde 1991-1993. *In*: A.V. Knudsen, ed. *Fra Bornholms Museum 1991-1993*. Rønne: Bornholms Museum, 65-88.

Weiss 2014

Weiss, U., 2014. Aus den Anfängen des Hausbaus. *In*: D. Jantzen, L. Saalow, J.-P. Schmidt, eds. *Pipeline: Archäologie. Ausgrabungen auf den großen Ferngastrassen in Mecklenburg-Vorpommern*. Schwerin: Landesamt für Kultur und Denkmalpflege Mecklenburg-Vorpommern, 67-76.

Wetzel 1969

Wetzel, G., 1969. Ein Dünenwohnplatz bei Lanz, Kreis Ludwigslust. *Bodendenkmalpflege in Mecklenburg* 1967, 129-169.

Wilk 2014

Wilk, S., 2014. An elite burial from the Copper Age: Grave 8 at the cemetery of the Lublin Volhynian culture at Site 2 in Książnice, Świętokrzyskie Province. *Analecta Archaeologica Ressoviensia*, 9, 209-258.

Witter 1940

Witter, W., 1940. Die Glockenbecherkultur, Remedello und Bygholm. *Mitteilungen der Anthropologischen Gesellschaft Wien*, 70, 1-101.

Wollf 1991

Wollf, C., 1991. Zislow und das Früh- bis ältere Mittelneolithikum im ehemaligen Bezirk Neubrandenburg. *In*: U. Schoknecht, ed. *Zislow - Ergebnisse archäologischer Untersuchungen*. Beiträge zur Ur- und Frühgeschichte Mecklenburg-Vorpommerns 25. Schwerin: Landesarchäologie MV, 17-54.

Wunderlich 2019

Wunderlich, M., 2019. *Megalithic monuments and social structures. Comparative studies on recent and funnel beaker societies*. Scales of transformation 5. Leiden: Sidestone Press.

Zachos 2007

Zachos, K.L., 2007. The Neolithic Background: A Reassesment. *In*: P.M. Day and R.C.P. Doonan, eds. *Metallurgy in the Early Bronze Age Aegean*. Oxford: Oxbow Books, 168-206.

Zachos 2008

Zachos, K.L., 2008. *Ayios Dhimitrios, a prehistoric settlement in the Southwestern Peloponnese: the Neolithic and Early Helladic periods*. British Archaeological Reports British Series 1770. Oxford: British Archaeological Reports Oxford Ltd.

Zalai-Gaál 2016

Zalai-Gaál, I., 2016. Tiszapolgár-Bodrogkeresztúr-Hunyadihalom: Wirkungen und Gegenwirkungen am Ende der Hochkupferzeit im Ostkarpatenbecken. *In*: K.E. Bǎčvarov and R. Gleser, eds. *Southeast Europe and Anatolia in prehistory: essays in honor of Vassil Nikolov on his 65th anniversary*. Universitätsforschungen zur prähistorischen Archäologie 293. Bonn: Habelt Verlag.

Zapaśnik 1997

Zapaśnik, B., 1997. Neolityczny sztylet. *Wiedza i Życie 4*, http://archiwum.wiz.pl/1997/97040400.asp.

Zápotocký 1984

Zápotocký, M., 1984. Armringe aus Marmor und anderen Rohstoffen im jüngeren Neolithikum Böhmens und Mitteleuropas – Náramky z mramoru a jiných surovin v mladším neolitu Čech a střední Evropy – Braslety iz marmora i drugich materialov v neolite Čechii i Central'noj Jevropy. *Památky archeologické*, 75, 50- 130.

Zápotocký 1992

Zápotocký, M., 1992. *Streitäxte des mitteleuropäischen Äneolithikums*. Quellen und Forschungen zur Prähistorischen und Provinzialrömischen Archäologie 6. Weinheim: Verlag VCH Acta humaniora.

Zepezauer 2000

Zepezauer, M.-A., 2000. *Fundchronik Kreis Steinfurt*. Ausgrabungen und Funde in Westfalen-Lippe, Beiheft 4. Münster: Westfälisches Museum für Bodendenkmalpflege, Museum für Archäologie.

Zimmermann 2007

Zimmermann, T., 2007. Ein kupferzeitlicher Dolch im eisenzeitlichen Italien - die notwendige Revision einer „sardischen" Stichwaffe aus dem Depotfund von San Francesco, Bologna. *Archäologisches Korrespondenzblatt*, 37 (1), 51-56.

Zinkovskij/Petrenko 1987

Zinkovskij, K.V. and Petrenko, V.G., 1987. Burials with traces of ochre in Usatovo burial grounds. *Sowjetskaja Archeologija 1987*, 4, 24-39.

Zwicker 1979

Zwicker, U., 1979. Distribution of metallic elements in patina layers. *Mikrochimica Acta Supplementa*, 8, 393-419.

Plates

Plate 1. Dagger from the hoard find from Neuenkirchen, find site 45, Mecklenburg Lake Plateau district. Photo: Agnes Heitmanr. (University of Kiel).

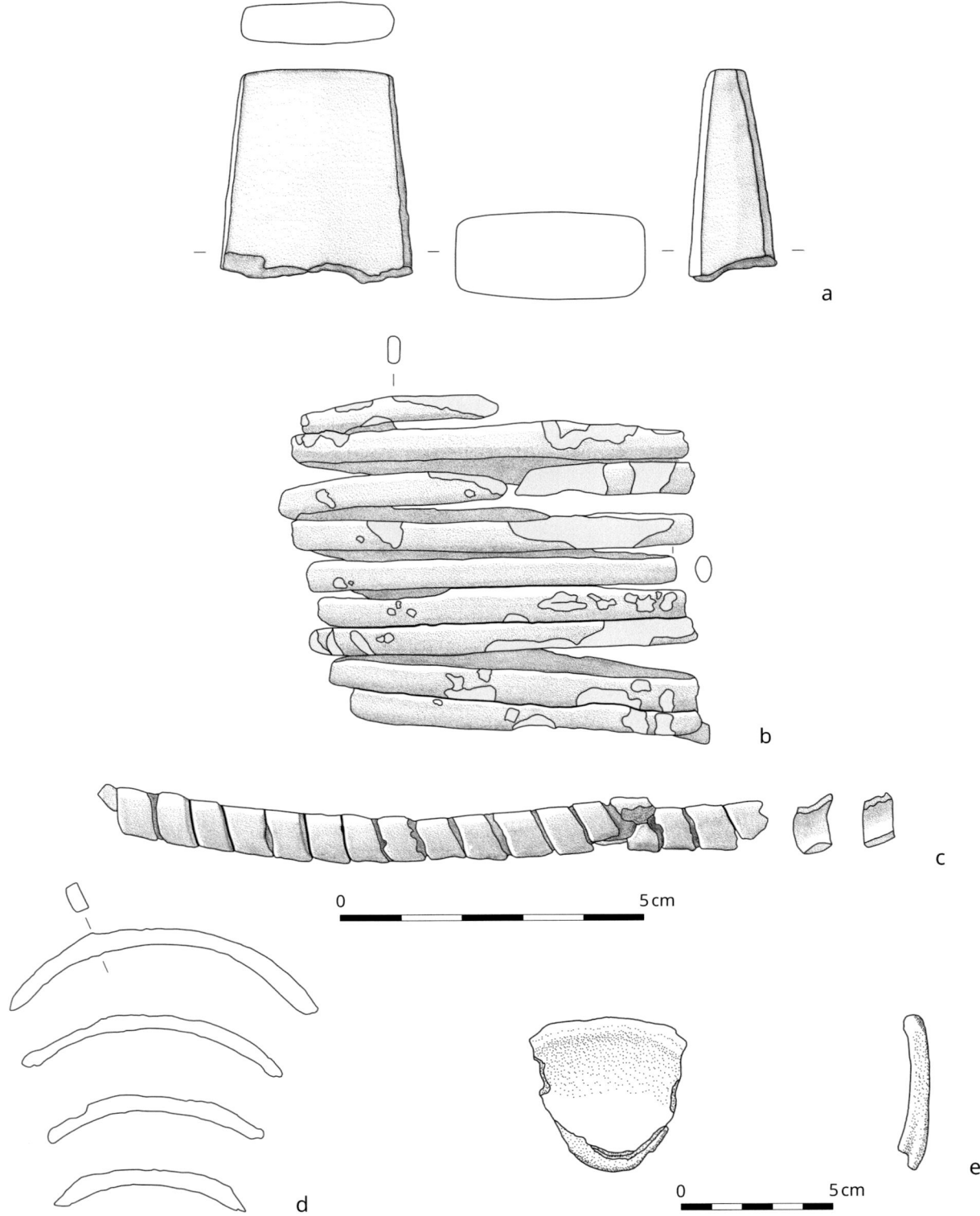

Plate 2. Hoard find from Neuenkirchen, find site 45, Mecklenburg Lake Plateau district. a) Flat axe fragment; b) Spiral arm ring; c) Band spiral; d) Fragments of spiral arm ring; e) Sheet metal fragment.

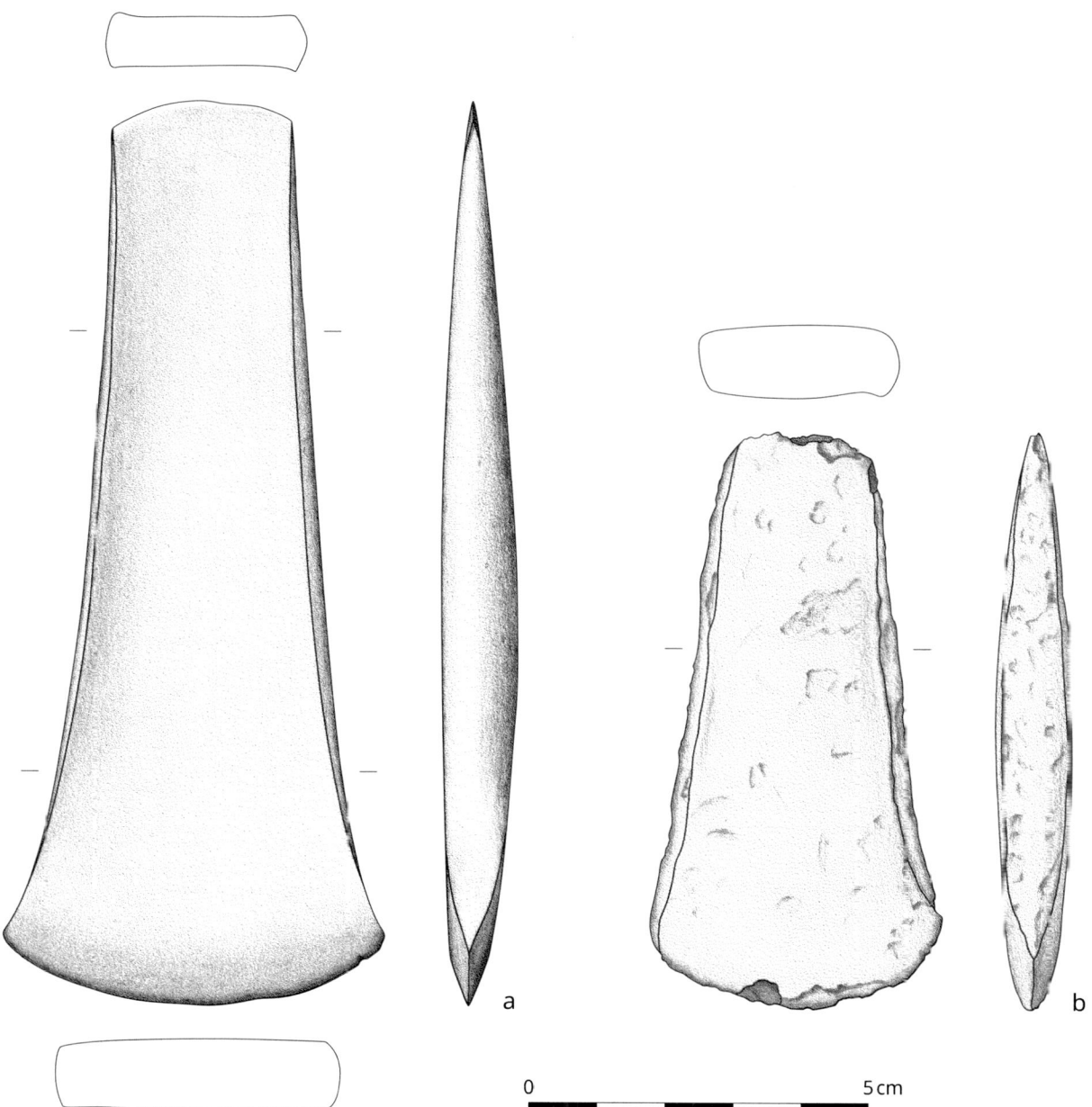

Plate 3. a) Flat axe from Weltzin, Mecklenburg Lake Plateau district; b) Flat axe from Greifswald, Western Pomerania-Greifswald district.

Plate 4. Hoard find from Neuenkirchen, site 45, Mecklenburg Lake Plateau district. a) Spiral arm ring with fragments; b) Band spiral and fragments; c) Flat axe fragment; d) Sheet metal fragment. Photo: A. Heitmann & S. Jagiolla (University of Kiel).

STPAS: Scales of Transformation in Prehistoric and Archaic Societies

The book series 'Scales of Transformation in Prehistoric and Archaic Societies' (STPAS) is an international scientific series that covers major results deriving from or being associated with the research conducted in the Collaborative Research Centre 'Scales of Transformation: Human-Environmental Interaction in Prehistoric and Archaic Societies' (CRC 1266). Primarily located at Kiel University, Germany, the CRC 1266 is a large interdisciplinary project investigating multiple aspects of socio-environmental transformations in ancient societies between 15,000 and 1 BCE across Europe.

Volume 1
Das Jungneolithikum in Schleswig-Holstein
Sebastian Schultrich | 2018
ISBN: 9789088907425
Format: 210x280mm | 506 pp. | Language: German | 43 illus. (bw) | 103 illus. (fc)
Keywords: Late Neolithic, Single Grave Culture, Corded Ware Culture, transformation, solid stone axe, battle axe, fragments of axes | Jungneolithikum, Einzelgrabkultur, Schnurkeramische Kultur, Transformation, Felsgesteinäxte, Streitäxte, Axtfragmente

Volume 2
Embracing Bell Beaker
Adopting new ideas and objects across Europe during the later 3rd millennium BC (c. 2600-2000 BC)
Jos Kleijne | 2019
ISBN: 9789088907555
Format: 210x280mm | 300 pp. | Language: English | 91 illus. (fc)
Keywords: archaeology; Late Neolithic; Bell Beaker phenomenon; settlement archaeology; innovation; network analysis; mobility; prehistoric potter

Volume 3
Habitus?
The Social Dimension of Technology and Transformation
Edited by Sławomir Kadrow & Johannes Müller | 2019
ISBN: 9789088907838
Format: 210x280mm | 232 pp. | Language: English | 15 illus. (bw) | 65 illus. (fc)
Keywords: European prehistory; archaeology; habitus; technology; transformation; social dimension; ethnoarchaeology

Volume 4
How's Life?
Living Conditions in the 2nd and 1st Millennia BCE
Edited by Marta Dal Corso, Wiebke Kirleis, Jutta Kneisel, Nicole Taylor, Magdalena
Wieckowska-Lüth, Marco Zanon | 2019
ISBN: 9789088908019
Format: 210x280mm | 220 pp. | Language: English | 29 illus. (bw) | 43 illus. (fc)
Keywords: Bronze Age, domestic archaeology, household archaeology, daily life,
routine activities, diet, waste, violence, health, natural resources, food production

Volume 5
Megalithic monuments and social structures
Comparative studies on recent and Funnel Beaker societies
Maria Wunderlich | 2019
ISBN: 9789088907869
Format: 210x280mm | 382 pp. | Language: English | 114 illus. (bw) | 246 illus. (fc)
Keywords: Megalithic graves, monumentality, Funnel Beaker Complex, ethnoar-
chaeology, Sumba, Nagaland, social organisation, cooperation

Volume 6
Gender Transformations in Prehistoric and Archaic Societies
Edited by Julia Katharina Koch & Wiebke Kirleis | 2019
ISBN: 9789088908217
Format: 210x280mm | 502 pp. | Language: English | 114 illus. (bw) | 58 illus. (fc)
Keywords: academic fieldwork; gender archaeology; social archaeology; environ-
mental archaeology; history of archaeology; Mesolithic; Neolithic; Bronze Age; Iron
Age; Europe; South-west Asia; Central Asia

Volume 7
Maidanets'ke
Development and decline of a Trypillia mega-site in Central Ukraine
René Ohlrau | 2020
ISBN: 9789088908484
Format: 210x280mm | 326 pp. | Language: English | 141 illus. (bw) | 93 illus. (fc)
Keywords: settlement archaeology; prehistoric archaeology; early urbanism;
geophysical survey; paleodemography; Trypillia; mega-site

Volume 8
Detecting and explaining technological innovation in prehistory
Edited by Michela Spataro & Martin Furholt | 2020
ISBN: 9789088908248
Format: 210x280mm | 248 pp. | Language: English | 22 illus. (bw) | 37 illus. (fc)
Keywords: archaeology; prehistory; technology; innovation; invention; tradition;
chaîne opératoire; knowledge acquisition; knowledge transfer; Neolithic; Bronze
Age; Iron Age; ethnography; ceramic; metal; bone

Volume 9
Archaeology in the Žitava Valley I
The LBK and Želiezovce settlement site of Vráble
Edited by Martin Furholt, Ivan Cheben, Johannes Müller, Alena Bistáková,
Maria Wunderlich & Nils Müller-Scheeßel | 2020
ISBN: 9789088908972

Format: 210x280 | 546 pp. | Language: English | 50 illus. (bw) | 157 illus. (fc)
Keywords: European Early Neolithic; LBK, settlement patterns; social organization; social conflict; village and neighbourhood structures; burial rites; enclosure; excavation report

Volume 10
Hellenistic Architecture and Human Action
A Case of Reciprocal Influence
Edited by Annette Haug & Asja Müller | 2020
ISBN: 9789088909092
Format: 210x280mm | 208 pp. | Language: English | 38 illus. (bw) | 29 illus. (fc)
Keywords: Classical archaeology; Hellenistic architecture; agency; perception

Volume 11
Interdisciplinary analysis of the cemetery Kudachurt 14
Evaluating indicators of social inequality, demography, oral health and diet during the Bronze Age key period 2200-1650 BCE in the Northern Caucasus
Katharina Fuchs | 2020
ISBN: 9789088909030
Format: 210x280mm | 406 pp. | Language: English | 25 illus. (bw) | 137 illus. (fc)
Keywords: North Caucasian archaeology; Bronze Age; burial practice; social inequality; human remains; palaeopathology; oral health; C and N stable isotopes

Volume 12
Tripolye Typo-chronology
Mega and Smaller Sites in the Sinyukha River Basin
Liudmyla Shatilo | 2021
ISBN: 9789038909511
Format: 210x280mm | 422 pp. | Language: English | 100 illus. (bw) | 90 illus. (fc)
Keywords: Prehistoric archaeology; Tripolye; chronology; mega-sites; Sinyukha River Basin; pottery; carbon dating; typochronology; Eastern Europe

Volume 13
Vom Kollektiv zum Individuum
Transformationsprozesse am Übergang vom 4. zum 3. Jahrtausend v. Chr. in der Deutschen Mittelgebirgszone
Clara Drummer | 2022
ISBN: 9789464270129
Format: 210x280mm | 343 pp. | Language: German | 53 illus. (bw) | 95 illus. (fc)
Keywords: Neolithic; Germany; Lower Mountain Range; migrations; identities; social transformations; Corded Ware; Bell Beaker; funerary archaeology; ancient DNA

Volume 14
Millet and What Else?
The Wider Context of the Adoption of Millet Cultivation in Europe
Edited by Wiebke Kirleis, Marta Dal Corso & Dragana Filipović | 2022
ISBN: 9789464270150
Format: 210x280mm | 328 pp. | Scales of Transformation 14 | Series: Scales of Transformation | Language: English | 61 illus. (bw) | 13 illus. (fc) | Keywords: archaeology; millet; Europe prehistory; Bronze Age; archaeobotany; zooarchaeology; miliacin; prehistoric agriculture

Volume 15

The Life and Journey of Neolithic Copper Objects

Transformations of the Neuenkirchen Hoard, North-East Germany (3800 BCE)

Henry Skorna | 2022

ISBN: 9789464270303

Format: 210x280mm | 198 pp. | Scales of Transformation 15 | Series: Scales of Transformation | Language: English | 50 illus. (bw) | 37 illus. (fc) | Keywords: neolithic; copper; metallurgy; hoard; isotopes; archaeometry; dagger; transformation